S0-BDL-495

Testimonies to Ministers

and Gospel Workers

Testimonies to Ministers

and Gospel Workers

Selected from "Special Testimonies to Ministers and Workers," Numbers One to Eleven; and Series B, Numbers One to Eighteen; with numerous selections from other booklets and from periodicals.

by Ellen G. White

Pacific Press® Publishing Association
Nampa, Idaho
Oshawa, Ontario, Canada

ISBN 0-8163-2003-9

Printed in U.S.A.

Contents

16. ELEVATE THE STANDARD

17. APPEAL AND WARNING

18. VITAL PRINCIPLES OF RELATIONSHIP

Preface to Third Edition

Among the materials once available but out of print at the time of Mrs. White's death in 1915 were a number of Special Testimony pamphlets, including a series published in the 1890's which bore the title, *Special Testimonies to Ministers and Workers.* This series of eleven is often referred to as *Special Testimonies,* Series A. In response to the request that the instruction found in these special testimonies be again made available, *Testimonies to Ministers and Gospel Workers* was published in 1923. This was one of the first E. G. White books of posthumous issuance.

Testimonies to Ministers first appeared in a *Testimony*-size volume. A second edition with larger typeface and page size was published in 1944. Several printings of both editions have supplied the field for four decades. For greater ease in handling and reference this third edition has been issued in the convenient *Testimony*-size page, but with no change in page content.

During the decade which followed the 1888 General Conference session held in Minneapolis, Minnesota, vital messages came from the messenger of the Lord to the central church at Battle Creek, to the General Conference Committee, and to other responsible men at the heart of the work. These messages rang with calls for regeneration and reformation of life, urging the reader to live by the vital principles of the word of God and to experience a personal relationship with our Lord and Saviour Jesus Christ.

After they had been received and read in Battle Creek, many of these messages were printed in tract form as *Special Testimonies to the Battle Creek Church* and *Special Testimonies to Ministers and*

Workers. Copies were furnished by the General Conference Committee to leading ministers and workers throughout the field. These messages were heart-probing, soul-stirring, faithful in warning against evil, yet encouraging, as they continually pointed to the great love of God and the fullness of Christ's power to save to the uttermost.

As to the selection of material for this volume, drawn as it was from the pamphlet testimonies, the publisher's Preface to the first edition issued in 1923 informs us that:

"The committee having it in charge have been limited by the size of the volume decided upon, and by the large number of these tracts of small circulation. Therefore not all that was contained in the eleven specials has been placed in this volume. The reasons are that (1) some portions have been reprinted in volumes issued since the specials were printed; (2) other portions pertained to matters that were purely local, or that are past and gone; (3) still other things are more fully and strongly covered in other documents reprinted in this volume."

The source of each article, with date of first publication, is indicated in footnote references. Some "fillers" are credited at the close. In this third edition the lists of items "for further study" have been somewhat expanded to include references to related material appearing in E. G. White compilations published subsequent to 1923.

Certain of the counsels and reproofs from the pen of Ellen G. White can be better understood if the reader is in possession of a knowledge of the circumstances which prevailed at the time the messages were written. Certain details of denominational history which were familiar to the readers of the testimony pamphlets and the first edition of this book are unknown to most readers of today.

A Historical Foreword, which follows immediately, has therefore been added to this third edition, to present those high points of denominational development which furnish the background leading up to the crucial 1890's. The relevant historical events of that period have been concisely recounted. Appendix notes have also been supplied, keyed to the mention of certain places, situations, or events. These notes will aid the reader in ascertaining correctly the intent of the author in the messages here presented.

A survey of the materials comprising this volume will reveal that in the main the content of a given section was drawn from a single pamphlet. With these pamphlet materials there were placed a few related items drawn from the *Review and Herald* articles and other E. G. White sources of a general character. There are two articles from *Special Testimonies,* Series B.

Special Testimonies, Series B, consisted of 19 pamphlets published by Mrs. White or by denominational organizations between the years 1903 and 1913. The subject matter was varied, and most of it was of local application. This can be seen from the titles.

1. Letters to Physicians and Ministers (1903)
2. Letters to Physicians and Ministers (Late 1904 or 1905)
3. Letters to Sanitarium Workers in Southern California (1905)
4. The Spirit of Unity (1905)
5. An Earnest Appeal in Behalf of the Boulder, Colorado, Sanitarium (1905)
6. Youth Going to Battle Creek to Obtain an Education (1905)

7. Messages of Warning and Instruction to Seventh-day Adventists Regarding Dangers Connected With the Medical Missionary Work (1906)
8. The Strengthening of Our Institutions and Training Centers and a Plea for Medical Missionary Evangelists (1907)
9. Individual Responsibility and Christian Unity (1907)
10. Jehovah Is Our King (1908)
11. The Madison School (1908)
12. The Oakwood Manual Training School (Cir. 1908)

12x. The Huntsville School (Cir. 1908)

13. The New England Sanitarium (1908)
14. The Paradise Valley Sanitarium (1909)
15. Sanitarium Workers (1911)
16. Selections From the Testimonies for Students and Workers of Our Sanitariums (1911)
17. The Unwise Use of Money and the Spirit of Speculation (1911)
18. The Nashville Sanitarium (1912)
19. The Spirit of Sacrifice (1913)

To this list are sometimes added two items which did not carry the "Series B" identification:

20. Appeals for Unity (1912)
21. Recreation (Cir. 1913)

With objectives quite different from the envelope-size *Special Testimony* pamphlets of the 1890's, and appearing in a larger page size, these were from the outset designated as *Special Testimonies,* Series B. Their predecessors of the 1890's, with messages for ministers and workers, became known as "Series A," although not so designated at the time of publication.

General matter of lasting usefulness to the church, as first published in "Series B" articles, was subsequently embodied in volumes 8 and 9 of *Testimonies for the Church,* and in *Counsels on Health, Counsels on Stewardship, Medical Ministry,* and *Selected Messages.* Two articles from the "Series B" collection appear in this volume. They are: "Jehovah Is Our King," pages 477-484 and "Individual Responsibility and Christian Unity," pages 485-505.

Working over a period of many years, Mrs. White often repeated certain lines of counsel. To reprint all that had appeared in the earlier pamphlets and writings would burden the reader with a repetition of subject matter and also with the details of local or personal matters not now of general significance. Concerning the material selected for this volume, the Preface to the first edition stated:

"The committee have earnestly and prayerfully sought to present in the one modest volume the best and strongest of the tract-printed matter, and believe that the portions omitted are more than covered by that which has been gathered from other tracts of limited circulation."

Those responsible for this third edition of *Testimonies to Ministers* say with the publishers in 1923 that this convenient volume is sent forth with the earnest prayer that it may be, to all to whom it may come, a source of instruction in the deep things of God; that it may revive the hopes and energies of God's people; that it may help to bring reformation of life where needed, and in all of us the Christian graces that will reveal Christ to the world; and that it may bring us all nearer together by bringing us all closer to the heart of our blessed Lord.

THE BOARD OF TRUSTEES OF THE
ELLEN G. WHITE ESTATE.

Washington, D.C.
May 10, 1962.

Historical Foreword

As noted in the Preface to this third edition, *Testimonies to Ministers* consists of materials drawn from several sources, primarily Ellen G. White articles which have appeared in the *Review and Herald* and pamphlets bearing testimonies to the Battle Creek church and to the leading workers of the cause. The larger part of the content of this volume was written in the years 1890-1898, with some earlier and later materials drawn in to augment certain areas of counsel. Section 1, "The Church of Christ," gives assurance of the tender regard in which God holds His church, and contains clear-cut promises of the church's triumph. This is followed by warnings and counsels to ministers and administrators.

The decade of the 1890's was an interesting, yet in some ways distressing, period in the experience of Seventh-day Adventists. The church was growing, more than doubling its membership in the ten-year period. With rapidity its workers were entering new countries. Institutions at home and abroad were brought into being. The original provisions for organization devised at the first General Conference session in 1863 were being rapidly outgrown. Older established institutions were expanding and entering upon a period of popularity with both Seventh-day Adventists and the world. This growth was fraught with many perils, from liberalism on one hand to consolidation and centralization on the other hand. Then, in and through the experience of this period, there were elements reflecting the aftermath of the 1888 General Conference session held in Minneapolis, Minnesota, where certain doctrinal issues were discussed heatedly and at length. A number of men identified themselves with one camp or the other, with their decisions influenced not alone by the doctrinal arguments presented, but also molded by attitudes toward the Spirit of Prophecy counsels. In some cases these attitudes were not wholesome. Through most of this period, Ellen White was in Australia, laboring to build up the work in that newly entered land and leading out in the establishment of a college and a sanitarium in that continent.

This volume bears the title of *Testimonies to Ministers and Gospel Workers.* It is not devoted essentially to instruction as to how the work of the minister should be conducted, as is *Gospel Workers.* This volume contains messages given to admonish, warn, reprove, and counsel the ministers of the church, with special attention given to perils peculiar to men who stand in positions of responsibility. Some of the reproofs are severe, but the assurance is given that God in His chastening, "wounds only that He may heal, not cause to perish."—*Testimonies to Ministers,* page 23.

The reproofs and counsels directed to ministers and especially administrators were not published initially by Ellen G. White, but rather by the president of the General Conference, and later the General Conference Committee. For the most part they were messages directed originally to the president of the General Conference, O. A. Olsen, and his associates in administrative work, particularly in Battle Creek. He and his committee placed them in print that their fellow ministers and fellow administrators might have the benefit of the reproofs which pointed out wrongs, and the counsels and encouragement associated with the reproof.

A REVIEW OF SIGNIFICANT HISTORY

As we review certain situations in our church history which form the background for the messages of the 1890's, we uncover clues which enable us better to understand these messages. Let us turn back the pages of history and look at some important developments.

From the very outset, Sabbath-keeping Adventists were characterized by their eagerness to understand God's will and to walk in His way. In their advent experience of the mid-1840's they had witnessed the stable Protestant churches, with their creedal stakes firmly driven, turn from great truths taught in the word of God. Many of these Adventists had been cast out of these churches because of their advent hope, a hope which sprang from the Scriptures. They had seen their former brethren enter into active opposition to those who held and expounded Bible truths. This led them to be fearful of formality and church organization. But as the way began to open for the heralding of the third angel's message, the need for organization developed, and in January, 1850, Ellen White was shown that the Sabbath-keeping Adventists should bring their work into order, for "everything in heaven was in perfect order."—Ms. 11, 1850.

Earnest efforts to bring about church organization spanned the decade of the 1850's. They culminated in 1860 in the choice of the name "Seventh-day Adventists," and, in 1861, in plans for the organization of local churches and state conferences. Then in 1863, the state conferences were bound together in the General Conference. Painstaking care was exercised to avoid the first step in forming a creed, for it was apparent that the church could not have creedal stakes firmly driven, and at the same time be free to follow God's opening providences as revealed through a study of the word of God and the revelations of the Spirit of Prophecy. An excellent statement reviewing God's providence in instituting church order appears on pages 24-32.

At the time of the organization of the General Conference in 1863, a General Conference Committee of three men was chosen. The major interests of the church consisted of the several state conferences and a publishing house located at Battle Creek, Michigan. In the evangelistic field, increasing success came to Seventh-day Adventist ministers. Their work consisted mainly in preaching the distinctive truths of the gospel message, including the Sabbath, the state of the dead, the second advent, and the sanctuary. Many of the men were drawn into discussions and debates involving the law of God and other vital Bible truths. Imperceptibly, not a few of those who engaged in such discussions became self-reliant, and there developed in their hearts a spirit of sureness, self-dependence, and argumentativeness. In time this bore unwholesome fruit.

INSTITUTIONAL DEVELOPMENT

Institutional development followed quickly on the heels of the organization of the General Conference. In the vision given to Ellen White in December, 1865, a medical institution was called for, and in response the leaders opened a small health institute in Battle Creek in September, 1866. Less than a decade later, in the messages which came from the pen of Ellen White, a school was called for. In 1874, Battle Creek College was built. Thus three major institutional developments forged ahead in Battle Creek, drawing an ever-enlarging number of Seventh-day Adventists into a rapidly growing denominational center. Men of business experience were called in to care for the business interests of the institutions. As the business interests expanded and developed and prospered, some of these men came to trust more in their business acumen than in God's messages of guidance. To them, business was business.

Before a decade had passed the denomination was confronted with a struggle between the interests of an educational program founded on Spirit of Prophecy principles and the educational program of the world, guided by men steeped in worldly policies and methods.

The pioneers of the Seventh-day Adventist Church were largely self-made men. They were men of consecration, ability, and skill. One has but to read their writings to discern this. But, knowing the limitations of their scholastic backgrounds, they were inclined to feel very humble. When there came into their midst in the early 1880's an educator bearing his degrees, it is not surprising that he should be pushed ahead into the position of leadership in the educational work. Elevated quickly to a position of high trust at a time when he knew but little of the doctrines and history of Seventh-day Adventists, he was found to be unprepared for the responsibilities placed upon him.

The issues became painfully acute, with leaders and laymen in Battle Creek taking sides. Some were swept off their feet by the leadership of an educator with his degrees, while others endeavored to stand with those things set forth in the Spirit of Prophecy counsels. The outcome was disastrous to the college and to the experience of those involved. Battle Creek College was closed for a year. Things said and positions taken left their marks on the experience of not a few leaders and church members.

It was in this period that the articles comprising *Testimonies for the Church,* volume 5, pages 9-98, were published, first in a pamphlet entitled *Testimony for the Battle Creek Church.* This pamphlet included not only that which was later republished in volume 5, but also more personal references dealing with individuals and situations in Battle Creek. One needs but to read the titles to sense the atmosphere of the times. The second chapter, "Our College," carries subheadings, "The Bible as a Textbook," "Object of the College," and "Teachers in the College." Following chapters are entitled: "Parental Training," "Important Testimony," "The Testimonies Slighted," "Workers in Our College," "Jealousy and Faultfinding Condemned."

These were difficult days, and as Ellen White went the following year into the 1883 General Conference session at Battle Creek, she was divinely led to give a series of morning addresses to Seventh-day Adventist ministers, presenting practical lines of counsel. Significantly, among these was one devoted to "Christ Our Righteousness." (See *Selected Messages,* b. 1, pp. 350-354.) These historic circumstances form part of the background for the E. G. White counsels found in this volume.

THE 1880'S A PERIOD OF NOTABLE ADVANCE

Although the church had sent J. N. Andrews to Europe in 1874, while it was engaged in building the college, not until the decade of the 1880's did the church move into a period of notable missions advance and institutional development. In 1882 two new schools were started, one at Healdsburg, California, and the other at South Lancaster, Massachusetts. In 1885 the publishing work was established in Basel,

Switzerland, in the newly built Central Publishing House. The same year workers were sent to Australia, and soon the Echo Publishing Company was established in Melbourne. The personal presence of Ellen G. White in Europe in the years 1885-1887 brought strength and encouragement to the work in the countries she visited.

As one reviews certain points in the development of denominational history, there grows upon him an awareness of the reality of the conflict between the forces of righteousness and the forces of evil. The church which had emerged was the remnant church of prophecy, with God's message for the times. The great adversary did all within his power to bring the work to naught.

THE SETTING OF THE 1888 MINNEAPOLIS CONFERENCE

One of the enemy's most effective measures was to lead good men to take positions which ultimately brought hindrance to the work they loved. This was seen in the spirit which developed in the hearts of men who engaged in discussions and debates. It was seen in the experience of businessmen connected with the cause. It was seen in the experience of missionaries going out to new countries, who, with narrow concepts of the work, found it difficult to move forward in the way God would have them take. It was seen in the tendency shown by some to depend upon the leaders at Battle Creek for guidance in the minute affairs of a far-flung mission work. It was seen in the way leading men at Battle Creek, heavily burdened with institutional work, attempted to give detailed direction to the work in distant lands of which they knew little.

As the Seventh-day Adventist Church came to the

close of the year 1887, it had a total world membership of 25,841, with twenty-six local conferences and one mission in North America and four local conferences and six missions overseas. The General Conference Committee consisted of seven men, the committee having been cautiously enlarged in 1882 from three members to five and in 1886 from five to seven. To take care of the legal business of the cause, the General Conference Association had been formed with a Board of five trustees. Various branches of the work had developed into somewhat autonomous organizations, such as the "International Sabbath School Association," the "Health and Temperance Association," and the "International Tract and Missionary Association." As has been noted, for two years, mid-1885 to 1887, Ellen White had been in Europe. Now she was back in the United States, residing at her Healdsburg, California, home. There were two publishing houses in operation in the United States: the Review and Herald in Battle Creek, Michigan, and the Pacific Press in Oakland, California. Each of these publishing houses did considerable commercial work to keep its equipment and personnel fully employed, and thus to maintain facilities needed for denominational printing. At each of these offices a leading journal was published, *The Review and Herald* in Battle Creek and *Signs of the Times* in Oakland.

During the preceding year or two some differences of opinion had been expressed in articles appearing in these journals, concerning the law in Galatians. In each case the editors of the journals championed opposing positions. Ellen White, while still in Switzerland, wrote to the editors of *Signs of the Times* counseling against publishing articles with conflicting views. This message is to be found in *Counsels to Writers and Editors*, pages 75-82.

THE GENERAL CONFERENCE OF 1888

The General Conference session of 1888 was called for Minneapolis, Minnesota, October 17 to November 4. This was preceded by a week-long Biblical Institute, at which there were discussions as to whether the Huns or the Alemanni should constitute one of the ten kingdoms of Daniel 2 and 7, and Revelation 13. Uriah Smith, editor of the *Review and Herald,* took a certain position and A. T. Jones, editor of *Signs of the Times,* took another. E. J. Waggoner, also from the Pacific Press, conducted studies on the atonement and the law of God, and Elder Jones presented justification by faith. These discussions continued into the session itself, and occasionally there was bitter disputation. Some of the ministers had come to the Conference to debate certain questions, rather than to study truth. Ellen White was present, and she called for all to approach these presentations with open hearts and open minds. She urged a careful, prayerful study of the topics under discussion.

Somehow the issues came to be identified with certain men. To many, the message of righteousness by faith struck home, and there was a response of heart and soul which led to victorious experience in personal Christian living. There were others who identified themselves with certain cautious and conservative leaders from Battle Creek who saw what they thought were perils in some of the teachings presented. When the Conference came to a close, these men had failed to gain the blessing God had in store for them.

There is no record of the discourses which were presented at the Conference by others than Ellen G. White, for it was not the custom of that time to publish the addresses. A *General Conference Bulletin* was issued, but it was a simple sheet carrying news about the events of the Conference and presenting the business proceedings. No action was taken on the Biblical questions discussed.

At that meeting Elder O. A. Olsen was elected president of the General Conference, but he was in Europe during the Conference. On November 27, 1888, William C. White, a member of the General Conference Committee, wrote Elder Olsen that "the delegates at the close of the meeting carried away very different impressions. Many felt that it was one of the most profitable meetings that they ever attended; others that it was the most unfortunate Conference ever held."

DIFFERING ATTITUDES TOWARD RIGHTEOUSNESS BY FAITH

Ellen White was much in the field during the next two years, endeavoring to lead the churches and conferences to a deeper, fuller understanding of the important message of righteousness by faith. She spoke of this Bible truth as one which, though "new to many minds," was in reality "old truth in new framework."—Ellen G. White, *Review and Herald,* July 23, 1889, reprinted in *Selected Messages,* b. 1, p. 355.

She was able to report during the following General Conference session, held in Battle Creek from October 18 to November 5, 1889, that "the spirit that was in the meeting at Minneapolis is not here. All moves off in harmony. There is a large attendance of delegates. Our five o'clock morning meeting is well attended, and the meetings good. All the testimonies to which I have listened have been of an elevating character. They say that the past year has been the best of their life; the light shining forth from the word of God has been clear and distinct—justification by faith, Christ our righteousness. The experiences have been very interesting.

"I have attended all but two morning meetings. At eight o'clock Brother Jones speaks upon the subject of justification by faith, and great interest is manifested. There is a growth in faith and in the knowledge of our Lord and Saviour Jesus Christ."—Ellen G. White Manuscript 10, 1889, published in *Selected Messages,* b. 1, p. 361.

Unfortunately, several among the leaders of our work connected with the General Conference and our institutions at Battle Creek ranked themselves on the negative side and established in the very heart of the work of the church a hard core of resistance. Within the next few years, many of those who had placed themselves in this camp saw their mistake and made heartfelt confessions. But there were some who stubbornly resisted. Some of these, connected with the business interests of the church and our institutions, made their influence felt well through the 1890's. It was of such that Ellen White in 1895 wrote as recorded on page 363: "The righteousness of Christ by faith has been ignored by some; for it is contrary to their spirit, and their whole life experience."

In this volume, from page 76 and onward, frequent reference will be found to Minneapolis and its aftermath, and to the experience of some who were involved.

At the session of 1888, the General Conference Committee was materially changed. O. A. Olsen was called from Europe to take the presidency of the General Conference, replacing George I. Butler. Elder Butler was ill, and, although not present at the Minneapolis Conference session, had placed himself with those on the negative side of the issue. He went into a period of retirement and cared for his invalid wife for ten years or more, then made a good comeback and again occupied positions of responsibility in the denomination.

Elder Olsen, a man in full sympathy with the emphasis placed on the truth of righteousness by faith, and one who was ever loyal to the Spirit of Prophecy counsels, found it difficult to meet certain of the problems at Battle Creek. Particularly hard were problems arising from the rapid development of institutions and the enlargement of the work in Battle Creek to the detriment of the work elsewhere.

CONSOLIDATION AND ITS ATTENDANT PROBLEMS

At the General Conference session of 1889, consideration was given to problems arising from the operation of two large publishing houses, one in Battle Creek and the other on the Pacific Coast. A committee of twenty-one was appointed to give study to the consolidation of the denomination's publishing interests. The action also called for consideration of a similar organization "for the purpose of controlling all our educational interests and owning the property, thus bringing them under one general management; also, another to control our health institutions."—*General Conference Bulletin,* Nov. 6, 1889, p. 149. This committee brought its report to the session of 1891. The proposal made was that the General Conference Association, as the corporation formed to represent the legal interests of the church, should take over all the publishing interests and operate the publishing houses from one headquarters. It was recognized that with the larger interests to be placed in the hands of this legal association, the membership should be enlarged to twenty-one. These proposals were adopted by the Conference.

Subsequent records indicate that steps were taken to consolidate the church's worldwide activities, which had been under the management of various committees, and place them under the control of the General Conference Association with its committee of twenty-one.

The leading officers of the General Conference Committee were also leading officers of the General Conference Association. However, with the members of both committees usually scattered throughout the world, the routine business fell largely into the hands of a few men in Battle Creek, some of whom were deeply involved in the business interests of the institutions there.

Not all that was contemplated in the action calling for consolidation came about, but sufficient did materialize to start a train of movement toward consolidation and to load the General Conference Association with the financial obligations of the publishing houses, tract societies, educational institutions, and sanitariums throughout the world. With a full meeting of the committee held only rarely, it was inevitable that routine decisions affecting the interests of the cause throughout the world were made by a handful of men in Battle-Creek—often no more than four, five, or six men. In her communications Ellen G. White protested the moves toward consolidation, and other moves which did not bear God's endorsement. (See *Life Sketches,* pages 319-330, chapter, "Danger in Adopting Worldly Policy in the Work of God.")

The situation at Battle Creek, involving both institutions and the General Conference, seems to be well summed up in the article, "Thou Shalt Have No Other Gods Before Me," written in September, 1895, and appearing on pages 359-364. The reader would do well to peruse this carefully.

The E. G. White communications to Elder Olsen, president of the General Conference and of the General Conference Association, contained many messages of reproof to those who would take upon themselves the responsibility of making decisions touching so intimately the work of the denomination around the world. Much of this instruction sent to Elder Olsen is to be found in *Testimonies to Ministers.* As noted above, he put the messages into print, that the instruction and warning might be sent to others.

FAR-REACHING PUBLISHING-HOUSE PROBLEMS

Unfortunately the step of expediency taken in our publishing work in early years, which led the publishing houses to take in commercial work, deeply involved these institutions in the mere business of printing. It reached the point at times when approximately 70 percent of the printing was commercial work and 30 percent denominational printing. Those responsible for the financial interests of the publishing houses envisioned the work in their hands as that of printers, and this led them to accept for publication manuscripts of a character which should never have been printed on the presses of the church. (See *Testimonies,* vol. 7, pp. 161-168, chapter "Commercial Work," and *Selected Messages,* b. 2, pp. 350, 351, "The Perils of Hypnosis.")

At the same time, some men in responsible positions in the publishing work turned from important basic principles which had governed our institutions in the remuneration of its personnel. It was reasoned that the work had reached its state of prosperity because of the special skills and talents of those who served in managerial lines; therefore these men should be favored by special remuneration more in keeping with their positions in management. As a result, certain men in key positions received remuneration double that of a skilled factory worker.

The same spirit led the management of the publishing house at Battle Creek to take every step within its power to gain control of the literary products it handled, and this resulted in cutting off a fair royalty income to authors of the books published by the house. In this way the income of the publishing house was enhanced. It was argued that those in positions of management in the publishing house were in a better position to understand the needs of the cause, and know how to use profits which came from literature, than were the individual authors. The authors, they felt, might fall short in proper stewardship of royalty incomes. In several communications, Ellen White, writing to those in positions of management, pointed out that selfishness motivated such plans. Counsel in this area is found in *Testimonies,* volume 7, pages 176-180.

GENERAL CONFERENCE PRESIDENT PUBLISHES TESTIMONIES

The influence of selfish, grasping methods and the exercise of "kingly power," as Ellen G. White termed it, were contagious. Elder Olsen, president of the General Conference, in his hope that he could stay the evil work of such influences, made available to the ministers of the church many of the messages of counsel which came to him and other leaders in Battle Creek during this critical period. These messages, published in pamphlet form, were sent out as special instruction to ministers and workers. They were often prefaced by an earnest statement signed by the president of the General Conference or by the Committee. In Elder Olsen's introduction to the second of these numbered pamphlets, written about 1892, he states:

"We feel it our duty again to send you some selections from recent writings from Sister E. G. White that have not as yet been in print, and also to call attention to some very important extracts from writings which have already been published. We do this to bring the truths contained therein fresh to your minds. They are worthy of most careful consideration. . . .

"For three years the Spirit of God has been especially appealing to our ministry and people to cast aside their cloak of self-righteousness and to seek the righteousness which is of God by faith in Christ Jesus. But, oh, how slow and hesitating we have been. . . . The testimony and earnest entreaties of the Spirit of God have not found a response in our hearts that God designed they should. In some instances, we have felt free even to criticize the testimony and warnings sent by God for our good. This is a serious matter. What is the result?—It is a coldness of heart, a barrenness of soul, that is truly alarming.

"Is it not time to raise a voice of warning? Is it not time for each individual to take these things home to himself and ask, 'Is it I?' . . .

"In the following testimony, our dangers are again pointed out to us in a way that we cannot misunderstand them. The question is, will we take heed to the counsel of God and seek Him with all the heart, or will we treat these warnings with the neglect and indifference that we have many times in the past? God is in earnest with us and we must not be slow to respond."

To the sixth of these pamphlets, Elder Olsen wrote on November 22, 1896, these introductory words:

"During the past few months, I have received a number of communications from Sister E. G. White, which contain most valuable instruction to myself and to all our laborers; and knowing that all the workers connected with the cause of present truth would be benefited personally and helped in their work by having this instruction, I have collected this matter, and had it printed in this little tract for their benefit. It is not necessary that I ask for it a careful and prayerful study, for I know it will receive this."

It was not an easy task for Ellen White to pen such stirring messages of rebuke and reproof, nor was it easy for the recipients to accept these messages as applying in the personal experience and then set about to make the corrections which were called for. They were published in the 1890's by the president of the General Conference and by the General Conference Committee as pamphlets, that all ministers might be warned. Then materials were republished in the body of *Testimonies to Ministers* in 1923, to keep before every Seventh-day Adventist minister and administrator perils which could seriously militate against the interests of the work of God.

Ellen White did not implicate each minister and administrator by the message of rebuke. "How my heart goes out in rejoicing," she wrote, "for those who walk in humility of mind, who love and fear God. They possess a power far more valuable than learning or eloquence."—Page 161. Here and there through the articles in this volume she speaks of "some" who have taken the wrong course, "some" who have been unresponsive to the messages which God has sent.

The counsels warning against the exercise of "kingly

power" and authority, the counsels that man should not look to his fellowmen for guidance in every detail of the work, are carefully balanced with counsels concerning independence of spirit and action, as recorded on pages 314-316. It is urged that conference presidents should be trusted and sustained, as recorded on pages 327, 328.

These are the backgrounds of the 1890's and of the messages in *Testimonies to Ministers.* This is the picture of the conditions which were worsening from month to month, from year to year, as the Seventh-day Adventist Church, pushing forward in an ever-widening evangelistic, institutional, and missions program, approached the turn of the century.

THE GENERAL CONFERENCE OF 1901

Ellen G. White, just back in the United States after a nine-year sojourn in Australia, was invited to attend the General Conference session of 1901, held in Battle Creek. It was the first session she had attended in a ten-year period. The president of the General Conference, G. A. Irwin, made his opening address. Then Ellen White pressed to the front of the assembly, desirous of speaking. Earnestly she addressed the conference, pointing out the manner in which the work of God had been circumscribed as a few men in Battle Creek carried the responsibility of a work far beyond their grasp. She testified that these men and the cause were injured as they encouraged others to look to them for guidance in every phase of the work. She pointed out that there were some men in responsible places who had lost the spirit of consecration so essential to their work. At that meeting she cried out, "What we want now is a reorganization. We want to begin at the foundation and build on a different principle."—*General Conference Bulletin,* April 3, 1901.

What took place in the ensuing three weeks is a thrilling story. The message was heeded. Carefully the brethren went to work. Union conferences were formed, binding local conferences together in smaller units, with the responsibilities carried by men in the field. The several associations which represented the branches of general church activity, such as the Sabbath school work and the home-missionary work, took steps to become departments of the General Conference. The General Conference Committee, consisting of thirteen men, was enlarged to twenty-five. In 1903 the committee was further enlarged to include those connected with the newly organized departments of the General Conference. Within a few years' time, five hundred men were carrying the responsibilities that prior to the General Conference of 1901 had been carried by a handful of men.

Through this reorganization, provision was made for those who were in local fields to make decisions relating to the work in hand. So sound were the foundations laid, that when continued growth made it advisable, the denomination was able to move without any great problems into the development of divisions of the General Conference. In this plan, great areas of the world field were knit together, union conferences becoming units in the division organization.

BATTLE CREEK INSTITUTIONS SUFFER GOD'S JUDGMENTS

Unfortunately, not all of the counsels sounded by Ellen White at that General Conference session of 1901 were heeded. Changes which should have been made in two of the institutions at Battle Creek were not made. Before twelve months rolled around, during the night of February 18, 1902, the sanitarium burned.

Before 1902 passed, the publishing house was also in ashes. This great loss of denominational property was recognized as a judgment from God, inflicted because men failed to heed and follow the counsel given. Warnings had been sounded, but they had gone unheeded. Now God spoke in a way that none could misunderstand.

The church headquarters was moved away from Battle Creek with its attendant problems and, in the providence of God, established in Washington, D.C. The publishing house was reestablished in the capital of the nation, and the leaders resolved that the time of the employees and equipment should be devoted 100 percent to the publication of the message of the church. The sanitarium was rebuilt in Battle Creek, but unfortunately its great interests were soon wrested from the church. Battle Creek ceased to be the denominational center, as the world headquarters was transferred to Takoma Park.

"EXCEPT AS WE SHALL FORGET"

The closing section of this volume is drawn essentially from communications written in 1907 and 1914. Ellen White had occasion to review "Vital Principles of Relationship," particularly in the article "Jehovah Is Our King," a message she read at the Southern California camp meeting in August, 1907; and the article, "Individual Responsibility and Christian Unity," read by her at the 1907 session of the California Conference held in January. These articles recapitulate the points comprising the main themes of the volume. These counsels, restated, reminded all that to lose sight of these principles would imperil the church.

History can repeat itself, and human beings can be guilty of forgetting. Earnest endeavors have been made to avoid a repetition of the mistakes made at Battle Creek. Wrote Mrs. White, "We have nothing to fear for the future except as we shall forget the way the Lord has led us."—Page 31. The administrators and ministerial laborers of the church have ever before them these messages of warning and admonition, to help them avoid making the mistakes of former years. And, closely associated with these more specific warnings, are general warnings relating to the high moral and spiritual plane of the work of the minister.

The messages in this volume, dealing so intimately with the hearts and souls of those who stood as shepherds of the flock and of those who carried administrative responsibilities, would apply today only if the conditions described existed again. None should err in applying the reproofs to all ministers at any and all times. Nor should the intimate knowledge of some of the problems and crises met through the years ever dim our confidence in the glorious triumph of the cause of God.

Ellen White, to whom God had revealed the secrets of the hearts of men and the weaknesses and deficiencies of humanity, did not lose confidence in God's chosen workmen. To her, the fact that God sent messages of reproof to those who erred, was not an indication that they were forsaken, but rather an evidence of God's love, "for whom the Lord loveth He chasteneth." Nor did the setbacks which came to the cause as the battle raged between the forces of evil and the forces of righteousness leave her with despondency of heart, for she discerned that "we have as Bible Christians ever been on gaining ground" (*Selected Messages,* b. 2, p. 397), and that "the God of Israel is still guiding His people, and that He will continue to be with them, even to the end" (*Life Sketches,* pages 437, 438).

This foreword is designed to inform the reader as to the historical setting of the contents of this volume. There are a number of references to specific experiences, movements, and institutions, that may seem somewhat obscure to us who live so many decades away from the events. To give information which will guide to a better understanding of such references, appendix notes have been supplied.

It is not the work of the custodians of the Ellen G. White writings to explain or interpret the counsels which have been given. It is their privilege and at times their responsibility to present the historical setting of certain situations, and to present in their context other counsels which may help the reader to understand better and thus rightly to interpret the writings. That this may be accomplished, and that the church under God-fearing leaders may go forward in triumph for the finishing of the precious work of God, is the sincere wish of the

THE BOARD OF TRUSTEES OF THE
ELLEN G. WHITE ESTATE.

Washington, D.C.
May 10, 1962.

"Every scribe which is instructed unto the kingdom of heaven is like unto a man that is an householder, which bringeth forth out of his treasure things new and old."

Matthew 13:52.

[Introductory pages 1-14 of the previous edition have been replaced by pages i-xxxviii in this edition.]

The Church of Christ 1

The Object of His Supreme Regard

Melbourne, Australia, December 23, 1892.

Dear Brethren of the General Conference:

I testify to my brethren and sisters that the church of Christ, enfeebled and defective as it may be, is the only object on earth on which He bestows His supreme regard. While He extends to all the world His invitation to come to Him and be saved, He commissions His angels to render divine help to every soul that cometh to Him in repentance and contrition, and He comes personally by His Holy Spirit into the midst of His church. "If Thou, Lord, shouldest mark iniquities, O Lord, who shall stand? But there is forgiveness with Thee, that Thou mayest be feared. I wait for the Lord, my soul doth wait, and in His word do I hope. My soul waiteth for the Lord more than they that watch for the morning. . . . Let Israel hope in the Lord: for with the Lord there is mercy, and with Him is plenteous redemption. And He shall redeem Israel from all his iniquities."

Ministers and all the church, let this be our language, from hearts that respond to the great goodness and love of God to us as a people and to us individually, "Let Israel hope in the Lord from henceforth and forever." "Ye that stand in the house of the Lord, in the courts of the house of our God, praise the Lord; for the Lord is good: sing praises unto His name; for it is pleasant. For the Lord hath chosen Jacob unto Himself, and Israel for His peculiar treasure. For I know that the

General Conference Bulletin, 1893, pages 408, 409. Read before the General Conference in session, February 26, 1899.

Lord is great, and that our Lord is above all gods." Consider, my brethren and sisters, that the Lord has a people, a chosen people, His church, to be His own, His own fortress, which He holds in a sin-stricken, revolted world; and He intended that no authority should be known in it, no laws be acknowledged by it, but His own.

Satan has a large confederacy, his church. Christ calls them the synagogue of Satan because the members are the children of sin. The members of Satan's church have been constantly working to cast off the divine law, and confuse the distinction between good and evil. Satan is working with great power in and through the children of disobedience to exalt treason and apostasy as truth and loyalty. And at this time the power of his satanic inspiration is moving the living agencies to carry out the great rebellion against God that commenced in heaven.

CLEAR, DECIDED DISTINCTIONS

At this time the church is to put on her beautiful garments—"Christ our righteousness." There are clear, decided distinctions to be restored and exemplified to the world in holding aloft the commandments of God and the faith of Jesus. The beauty of holiness is to appear in its native luster in contrast with the deformity and darkness of the disloyal, those who have revolted from the law of God. Thus we acknowledge God and recognize His law, the foundation of His government in heaven and throughout His earthly dominions. His authority should be kept distinct and plain before the world, and no laws are to be acknowledged that come in collision with the laws of Jehovah. If in defiance of God's arrangements the world be allowed to influence our decisions or our actions, the purpose of God is defeated. However specious the pretext, if the church waver here, there is written against her in the books of heaven a betrayal of the most sacred trusts, and treachery to the kingdom of Christ. The church is firmly and decidedly to hold her principles before the whole heavenly universe and the kingdoms of the world; steadfast fidelity in maintaining the honor and sacredness of the law of God will attract the notice and admiration of even the world, and many will, by the good works which they shall behold, be led to glorify our Father in heaven. The loyal and true bear the credentials of heaven, not of earthly potentates. All men shall know who are the disciples of Christ, chosen and faithful, and shall know them when crowned and glorified as those who honored God and whom He has honored, bringing them into possession of an eternal weight of glory. . . .

The Lord has provided His church with capabilities and blessings, that they may present to the world an image of His own sufficiency, and that His church may be complete in Him, a continual representation of another, even the eternal world, of laws that are higher than earthly laws. His church is to be a temple built after the divine similitude, and the angelic architect has brought his golden measuring rod from heaven, that every stone may be hewed and squared by the divine measurement and polished to shine as an emblem of heaven, radiating in all directions the bright, clear beams of the Sun of Righteousness. The church is to be fed with manna from heaven and to be kept under the sole guardianship of His grace. Clad in complete armor of light and righteousness, she enters upon her final conflict. The dross, the worthless material, will be consumed, and the influence of the truth testifies to the world of its sanctifying, ennobling character. . . .

DIVINE EXPERIMENTS

The Lord Jesus is making experiments on human hearts through the exhibition of His mercy and abundant grace. He is effecting transformations so amazing that Satan, with all his triumphant boasting, with all his confederacy of evil united against God and the laws of His government, stands viewing them as a fortress impregnable to his sophistries and delusions. They are to him an incomprehensible mystery. The angels of God, seraphim and cherubim, the powers commissioned to cooperate with human agencies, look on with astonishment and joy, that fallen men, once children of wrath, are through the training of Christ developing characters after the divine similitude, to be sons and daughters of God, to act an important part in the occupations and pleasures of heaven.

To His church, Christ has given ample facilities, that He may receive a large revenue of glory from His redeemed, purchased possession. The church, being endowed with the righteousness of Christ, is His depository, in which the wealth of His mercy, His love, His grace, is to appear in full and final display. The declaration in His intercessory prayer, that the Father's love is as great toward us as toward Himself, the only-begotten Son, and that we shall be with Him where He is, forever one with Christ and the Father, is a marvel to the heavenly host, and it is their great joy. The gift of His Holy Spirit, rich, full, and abundant, is to be to His church as an encompassing wall of fire, which the powers of hell shall not prevail against. In their untainted purity and spotless perfection, Christ looks upon His people as the reward of all His suffering, His humiliation, and His love, and the supplement of His glory—Christ, the great center from which radiates all glory. "Blessed are they which are called unto the marriage supper of the Lamb."

For further study: *Gospel Workers,* pages 200, 331, 501, 502; *The Desire of Ages,* pages 441, 680.

The Church the Property of God

The church is the property of God, and God constantly remembers her as she stands in the world, subject to the temptations of Satan. Christ has never forgotten the days of His humiliation. In passing from the scenes of His humiliation, Jesus has lost none of His humanity. He has the same tender, pitying love, and is ever touched with human woe. He ever bears in mind that He was a Man of Sorrows and acquainted with grief. He forgets not His representative people who are striving to uphold His downtrodden law. He knows that the world that hated Him, hates them. Although Jesus Christ has passed into the heavens, there is still a living chain binding His believing ones to His own heart of infinite love. The most lowly and weak are bound by a chain of sympathy closely to His heart. He never forgets that He is our representative, that He bears our nature.

Jesus sees His true church on the earth, whose greatest ambition is to cooperate with Him in the grand work of saving souls. He hears their prayers, presented in contrition and power, and Omnipotence cannot resist their plea for the salvation of any tried, tempted member of Christ's body. "Seeing then that

---

Review and Herald, October 17, 1893.

we have a great High Priest, that is passed into the heavens, Jesus the Son of God, let us hold fast our profession. For we have not an high priest which cannot be touched with the feeling of our infirmities; but was in all points tempted like as we are, yet without sin. Let us therefore come boldly unto the throne of grace, that we may obtain mercy, and find grace to help in time of need." Jesus ever liveth to make intercession for us. Through our Redeemer what blessings may not the true believer receive? The church, soon to enter upon her most severe conflict, will be the object most dear to God upon earth. The confederacy of evil will be stirred with power from beneath, and Satan will cast all the reproach possible upon the chosen ones whom he cannot deceive and delude with his satanic inventions and falsehoods. But exalted "to be a Prince and a Saviour, to give repentance to Israel, and remission of sins," will Christ, our representative and head, close His heart, or withdraw His hand, or falsify His promise? No; never, never.

IDENTIFIED WITH HIS CHURCH

God has a church, a chosen people; and could all see as I have seen how closely Christ identifies Himself with His people, no such message would be heard as the one that denounces the church as Babylon. God has a people who are laborers together with Him, and they have gone straight forward, having His glory in view. Listen to the prayer of our Representative in heaven: "Father, I will that they also, whom Thou hast given Me, be with Me where I am; that they may behold My glory." Oh, how the divine Head longed to have His church with Him! They had fellowship with Him in His suffering and humiliation, and it is His highest joy to have them with Him to be partakers of His glory. Christ claims the privilege of having His church with Him. "I will that they also, whom Thou hast given Me, be with Me where I am." To have them with Him is according to covenant promise and agreement with His Father. He reverently presents at the mercy seat His finished redemption for His people. The bow of promise encircles our Substitute and Surety as He pours out His petition of love, "Father, I will that they also, whom Thou hast given Me, be with Me where I am; that they may behold My glory." We shall behold the King in His beauty, and the church will be glorified.

Like David, we may now pray, "It is time for Thee, Lord, to work: for they have made void Thy law." Men have gone on in disobedience to God's law until they have reached a point of insolence that is unparalleled. Men are training in disobedience, and are fast approaching the limit of God's forbearance and love; and God will surely interfere. He will surely vindicate His honor and repress the prevailing iniquity. Will God's commandment-keeping people be carried away with the prevailing iniquity? Will they be tempted, because universal scorn is placed upon the law of God, to think less of that law which is the foundation of His government both in heaven and in earth? No. To His church His law becomes more precious, holy, honorable, as men cast upon it scorn and contempt. Like David they can say, "They have made void Thy law. Therefore I love Thy commandments above gold; yea, above fine gold. Therefore I esteem all Thy precepts concerning all things to be right; and I hate every false way."

The church militant is not now the church triumphant; but God loves His church and describes through the prophet how He opposes and resists Satan, who is clothing the children of God in the blackest and most defiled garments, and pleading for the privilege of destroying them. The angels of God were protecting them from the assaults of the enemy. The prophet says:

"And he showed me Joshua the high priest standing before the Angel of the Lord, and Satan standing at his right hand to resist him. And the Lord said unto Satan, The Lord rebuke thee, O Satan; even the Lord that hath chosen Jerusalem rebuke thee: is not this a brand plucked out of the fire? Now Joshua was clothed with filthy garments, and stood before the Angel. And He answered and spake unto those that stood before Him, saying, Take away the filthy garments from him. And unto him He said, Behold, I have caused thine iniquity to pass from thee, and I will clothe thee with change of raiment. And I said, Let them set a fair miter upon his head. So they set a fair miter upon his head, and clothed him with garments. And the Angel of the Lord stood by. And the Angel of the Lord protested unto Joshua, saying, Thus saith the Lord of hosts; If thou wilt walk in My ways, and if thou wilt keep My charge, then thou shalt also judge My house, and shalt also keep My courts, and I will give thee places to walk among these that stand by."

FALSE TEACHERS TO BE SHUNNED

When men arise, claiming to have a message from God, but instead of warring against principalities and powers, and the rulers of the darkness of this world, they form a hollow square, and turn the weapons of warfare against the church militant, be afraid of them. They do not bear the divine credentials. God has not given them any such burden of labor. They would tear down that which God would restore by the Laodicean message. He wounds only that He may heal, not cause to perish. The Lord lays upon no man a message that will discourage and dishearten the church. He reproves, He rebukes, He chastens; but it is only that He may restore and approve at last. How glad my heart was made by the report from the General Conference that many hearts were softened and subdued, that many made humble confessions, and cleared away from the door of the heart the rubbish that was keeping the Saviour out. How glad I was to know that many welcomed Jesus in as an abiding guest. How is it that these pamphlets denouncing the Seventh-day Adventist Church as Babylon* were scattered abroad everywhere, at the very time when that church was receiving the outpouring of the Spirit of God? How is it that men can be so deceived as to imagine that the loud cry consists in calling the people of God out from the fellowship of a church that is enjoying a season of refreshing? Oh, may these deceived souls come into the current, and receive the blessing, and be endued with power from on high.

For further study: *Early Writings,* pages 97-104; *Testimonies,* vol. 5, pp. 394, 484, 582.

Every teacher must be a learner, that his eyes may be anointed to see the evidences of the advancing truth of God. The beams of the Sun of Righteousness must shine into his own heart if he would impart light to others.—*Review and Herald,* February 18, 1890.

*See Appendix.

Organization and Development

It is nearly forty years since organization was introduced among us as a people.* I was one of the number who had an experience in establishing it from the first. I know the difficulties that had to be met, the evils which it was designed to correct, and I have watched its influence in connection with the growth of the cause. At an early stage in the work, God gave us special light upon this point, and this light, together with the lessons that experience has taught us, should be carefully considered.

From the first our work was aggressive. Our numbers were few, and mostly from the poorer class. Our views were almost unknown to the world. We had no houses of worship, but few publications, and very limited facilities for carrying forward our work. The sheep were scattered in the highways and byways, in cities, in towns, in forests. The commandments of God and the faith of Jesus was our message.

UNITY IN FAITH AND DOCTRINE

My husband, with Elders Joseph Bates, Stephen Pierce, Hiram Edson, and others who were keen, noble, and true, was among those who, after the passing of the time in 1844, searched for the truth as for hidden treasure.

We would come together burdened in soul, praying that we might be one in faith and doctrine; for we knew that Christ is not divided. One point at a time was made the subject of investigation. The Scriptures were opened with a sense of awe. Often we fasted, that we might be better fitted to understand the truth.

Christian Experience and Teachings of Ellen G. White, pages 192-205. *Written in 1901.

After earnest prayer, if any point was not understood it was discussed, and each one expressed his opinion freely; then we would again bow in prayer, and earnest supplications went up to heaven that God would help us to see eye to eye, that we might be one as Christ and the Father are one. Many tears were shed.

We spent many hours in this way. Sometimes the entire night was spent in solemn investigation of the Scriptures, that we might understand the truth for our time. On some occasions the Spirit of God would come upon me, and difficult portions were made clear through God's appointed way, and then there was perfect harmony. We were all of one mind and one spirit.

We sought most earnestly that the Scriptures should not be wrested to suit any man's opinions. We tried to make our differences as slight as possible by not dwelling on points that were of minor importance, upon which there were varying opinions. But the burden of every soul was to bring about a condition among the brethren which would answer the prayer of Christ that His disciples might be one as He and the Father are one.

Sometimes one or two of the brethren would stubbornly set themselves against the view presented, and would act out the natural feelings of the heart; but when this disposition appeared, we suspended our investigations and adjourned our meeting, that each one might have an opportunity to go to God in prayer and, without conversation with others, study the point of difference, asking light from heaven. With expressions of friendliness we parted, to meet again as soon as possible for further investigation. At times the power of God came upon us in a marked manner, and when clear light revealed the points of truth, we would weep and rejoice together. We loved Jesus; we loved one another.

Our numbers gradually increased. The seed that was sown was watered of God, and He gave the increase. At first we assembled for worship, and presented the truth to those who would come to hear, in private houses, in large kitchens, in barns, in groves, and in schoolhouses; but it was not long before we were able to build humble houses of worship.

THE INTRODUCTION OF CHURCH ORDER

As our numbers increased, it was evident that without some form of organization there would be great confusion, and the work would not be carried forward successfully. To provide for the support of the ministry, for carrying the work in new fields, for protecting both the churches and the ministry from unworthy members, for holding church property, for the publication of the truth through the press, and for many other objects, organization was indispensable.

Yet there was strong feeling against it among our people. The first-day Adventists* were opposed to organization, and most of the Seventh-day Adventists entertained the same ideas. We sought the Lord with earnest prayer that we might understand His will, and light was given by His Spirit that there must be order and thorough discipline in the church—that organization was essential. System and order are manifest in all the works of God throughout the universe. Order is the law of heaven, and it should be the law of God's people on the earth.

We had a hard struggle in establishing organization. Notwithstanding that the Lord gave testimony after testimony upon this point, the opposition was strong, and it had to be met again and again. But we knew

*See Appendix.

that the Lord God of Israel was leading us, and guiding by His providence. We engaged in the work of organization, and marked prosperity attended this advance movement.

As the development of the work called upon us to engage in new enterprises, we were prepared to enter upon them. The Lord directed our minds to the importance of the educational work. We saw the need of schools, that our children might receive instruction free from the errors of false philosophy, that their training might be in harmony with the principles of the word of God. The need of a health institution had been urged upon us, both for the help and instruction of our own people and as a means of blessing and enlightenment to others. This enterprise also was carried forward. All this was missionary work of the highest order.

RESULTS OF UNITED EFFORT

Our work was not sustained by large gifts or legacies; for we have few wealthy men among us. What is the secret of our prosperity? We have moved under the orders of the Captain of our salvation. God has blessed our united efforts. The truth has spread and flourished. Institutions have multiplied. The mustard seed has grown to a great tree. The system of organization has proved a grand success. Systematic benevolence* was entered into according to the Bible plan. The body has been "compacted by that which every joint supplieth." As we have advanced, our system of organization has still proved effectual.

Let none entertain the thought that we can dispense with organization. It has cost us much study and many prayers for wisdom, that we know God has answered, to erect this structure. It has been built up by His

*See Appendix.

direction, through much sacrifice and conflict. Let none of our brethren be so deceived as to attempt to tear it down, for you will thus bring in a condition of things that you do not dream of. In the name of the Lord I declare to you that it is to stand, strengthened, established, and settled. At God's command, "Go forward," we advanced when the difficulties to be surmounted made the advance seem impossible. We know how much it has cost to work out God's plans in the past, which have made us as a people what we are. Then let everyone be exceedingly careful not to unsettle minds in regard to those things that God has ordained for our prosperity and success in advancing His cause.

Angels work harmoniously. Perfect order characterizes all their movements. The more closely we imitate the harmony and order of the angelic host, the more successful will be the efforts of these heavenly agents in our behalf. If we see no necessity for harmonious action, and are disorderly, undisciplined, and disorganized in our course of action, angels, who are thoroughly organized and move in perfect order, cannot work for us successfully. They turn away in grief, for they are not authorized to bless confusion, distraction, and disorganization. All who desire the cooperation of the heavenly messengers must work in unison with them. Those who have the unction from on high will in all their efforts encourage order, discipline, and union of action, and then the angels of God can cooperate with them. But never, never will these heavenly messengers place their endorsement upon irregularity, disorganization, and disorder. All these evils are the result of Satan's efforts to weaken our forces, to destroy our courage, and prevent successful action.

Satan well knows that success can only attend order and harmonious action. He well knows that everything connected with heaven is in perfect order, that subjection and perfect discipline mark the movements of the angelic host. It is his studied effort to lead professed Christians just as far from heaven's arrangement as he can; therefore he deceives even the professed people of God and makes them believe that order and discipline are enemies to spirituality, that the only safety for them is to let each pursue his own course, and to remain especially distinct from bodies of Christians who are united and are laboring to establish discipline and harmony of action. All the efforts made to establish order are considered dangerous, a restriction of rightful liberty, and hence are feared as popery. These devoted souls consider it a virtue to boast of their freedom to think and act independently. They will not take any man's say-so. They are amenable to no man. I was shown that it is Satan's special work to lead men to feel that it is God's order for them to strike out for themselves and choose their own course independent of their brethren.

INDIVIDUAL RESPONSIBILITY AND CHRISTIAN UNITY

God is leading a people out from the world upon the exalted platform of eternal truth, the commandments of God and the faith of Jesus. He will discipline and fit up His people. They will not be at variance, one believing one thing and another having faith and views entirely opposite, each moving independently of the body. Through the diversity of the gifts and governments that He has placed in the church, they will all come to the unity of the faith. If one man takes his views of Bible truth without regard to the opinion of his brethren, and justifies his course, alleging that he has a right to his own peculiar views, and then presses them upon others, how can he be fulfilling the prayer of Christ? And if another and still another arises, each asserting his right to believe and talk what he pleases without reference to the faith of the body, where will be that harmony which existed between Christ and His Father, and which Christ prayed might exist among His brethren?

Though we have an individual work and an individual responsibility before God, we are not to follow our own independent judgment, regardless of the opinions and feelings of our brethren; for this course would lead to disorder in the church. It is the duty of ministers to respect the judgment of their brethren; but their relations to one another, as well as the doctrines they teach, should be brought to the test of the law and the testimony; then, if hearts are teachable, there will be no divisions among us. Some are inclined to be disorderly, and are drifting away from the great landmarks of the faith; but God is moving upon His ministers to be one in doctrine and in spirit.

It is necessary that our unity today be of a character that will bear the test of trial. . . . We have many lessons to learn, and many, many to unlearn. God and heaven alone are infallible. Those who think that they will never have to give up a cherished view, never have occasion to change an opinion, will be disappointed. As long as we hold to our own ideas and opinions with determined persistency, we cannot have the unity for which Christ prayed.

When a brother receives new light upon the Scriptures, he should frankly explain his position, and every minister should search the Scriptures with the spirit of candor to see if the points presented can be substantiated by the Inspired Word. "The servant of the Lord must not strive; but be gentle unto all men, apt to teach, patient, in meekness instructing those that oppose themselves; if God peradventure will give them repentance to the acknowledging of the truth." 2 Timothy 2:24, 25.

WHAT HATH GOD WROUGHT!

In reviewing our past history, having traveled over every step of advance to our present standing, I can say, Praise God! As I see what God has wrought, I am filled with astonishment, and with confidence in Christ as leader. We have nothing to fear for the future except as we shall forget the way the Lord has led us.

We are now a strong people, if we will put our trust in the Lord; for we are handling the mighty truths of the word of God. We have everything to be thankful for. If we walk in the light as it shines upon us from the living oracles of God, we shall have large responsibilities, corresponding to the great light given us of God. We have many duties to perform because we have been made the depositaries of sacred truth to be given to the world in all its beauty and glory. We are debtors to God to use every advantage He has entrusted to us to beautify the truth by holiness of character, and to send the messages of warning, and of comfort, of hope and love, to those who are in the darkness of error and sin.

Thank God for what has already been done in providing for our youth facilities for religious and intellectual training. Many have been educated to act a part in the various branches of the work, not only in America, but in foreign fields. The press has furnished literature that has spread far and wide the knowledge of truth. Let all the gifts that like rivulets have swelled the stream of benevolence be recognized as a cause of thanksgiving to God.

We have an army of youth today who can do much if they are properly directed and encouraged. We want our children to believe the truth. We want them to be blessed of God. We want them to act a part in well-organized plans for helping other youth. Let all be so trained that they may rightly represent the truth, giving the reason of the hope that is within them, and honoring God in any branch of the work where they are qualified to labor. . . .

As the disciples of Christ it is our duty to diffuse light which we know the world has not. Let the people of God "be rich in good works, ready to distribute, willing to communicate; laying up in store for themselves a good foundation against the time to come, that they may lay hold on eternal life." 1 Timothy 6:18, 19.

For further study: *Early Writings,* pages 97-107; *Testimonies,* vol. 4, pp. 16-20; vol. 5, pp. 617-621; *Selected Messages,* b. 1, pp. 206-208.

The Remnant Church Not Babylon

I have been made very sad in reading the pamphlet that has been issued by Brother S.* and by those associated with him in the work he has been doing. Without my consent, they have made selections from the *Testimonies,* and have inserted them in the pamphlet they have published, to make it appear that my writings sustain and approve the position they advocate. In doing this they have done that which is not justice or righ-

---

Review and Herald, August 22 to September 12, 1893.
*See Appendix.

teousness. Through taking unwarrantable liberties they have presented to the people a theory that is of a character to deceive and destroy. In times past many others have done this same thing, and have made it appear that the *Testimonies* sustained positions that were untenable and false.

I have had light to the effect that the position taken by Brother S. and his sympathizers is not true, but one of the "lo, heres" and "lo, theres" that will characterize the days in which we are living. As a sample of the way in which Brother S. has compiled this pamphlet, I will give the following incident: I wrote a private letter to one of our ministers, and in kindness, thinking that it might be a help to Brother S., this brother sent a copy of it to him; but instead of regarding it as a matter for his personal help, he prints portions of it in the pamphlet as an unpublished testimony, to sustain the position he had taken. Is this honorable? There was nothing in the testimony to sustain the position Brother S. holds; but he misapplied it, as many do the Scriptures, to the injury of his own soul and the souls of others. God will judge those who take unwarrantable liberties and make use of dishonorable means in order to give character and influence to what they regard as truth. In the use of a private letter sent to another, Brother S. has abused the kindly efforts of one who desired to help him. The parties publishing the pamphlet on the *Loud Cry,* and the fall of all the churches, give evidence that the Holy Spirit of God is not working with them. "By their fruits ye shall know them."

Those who receive the pamphlets advocating these false positions, will receive the impression that I sustain these positions, and am united with these workers in proclaiming what they term the "new light." I know that their message is mingled with truth, but the truth is misapplied and wrested by its connection with error. I would say to the brother who sent to these men a copy of a letter I had written him, that I have not one thought of censuring you, and no one should cast the least blame upon you concerning the matter. If I should misjudge and censure you, when your motives and intentions were good, I should incur the displeasure of God. If the brother you desired to help has taken liberties, and has betrayed your confidence, do not blame yourself and grieve over the results of his unfaithfulness.

INSTRUCTION TO THE DISCIPLES

There are matters in the *Testimonies* that are written, not for the world at large, but for the believing children of God, and it is not appropriate to make instruction, warning, reproof, or counsel of this character public to the world. The world's Redeemer, the Sent of God, the greatest Teacher the children of men ever knew, presented some matters of instruction, not to the world, but to His disciples alone. While He had communications designed for the multitudes that thronged His steps, He also had some special light and instruction to impart to His followers which He did not impart to the great congregation, as it would neither be understood nor appreciated by them. He sent His disciples forth to preach, and when they returned from their first missionary labor and had various experiences to relate concerning their success in preaching the gospel of the kingdom of God, He said unto them, "Come ye yourselves apart into a desert place, and rest awhile." In a place of seclusion Jesus imparted to His followers such instruction, counsel, cautions, and corrections as He saw were needed in their manner of work; but the instruction He then gave them was not to be thrown broadcast to the promiscuous company, for His words were designed for His disciples only.

On several occasions when the Lord had wrought works of healing, He charged those whom He had blessed to tell His deed to no one. They ought to have heeded His injunctions and realized that Christ had not lightly required silence on their part, but had a reason for His command, and they should in no wise have disregarded His expressed desire. It ought to have been sufficient for them to know that He desired them to keep their own counsel, and had good reasons for His urgent request. The Lord knew that in healing the sick, in working miracles for the restoring of sight to the blind, and for the cleansing of the leper, He was endangering His own life; for if the priests and rulers would not receive the evidences He gave them of His divine mission, they would misconstrue, falsify, and make charges against Him. It is true that He did many miracles openly, yet in some instances He requested that those whom He had blessed should tell no man what He had done for them. When prejudice was aroused, envy and jealousy cherished, and His way hedged up, He left the cities, and went in search of those who would listen to and appreciate the truth He came to impart.

The Lord Jesus thought it necessary to make many things clear to His disciples which He did not open to the multitudes. He plainly revealed to them the reason of the hatred manifested toward Him by the scribes, Pharisees, and priests, and told them of His suffering, betrayal, and death; but to the world He did not make these matters so plain. He had warnings to give to His followers, and He unfolded to them the sorrowful developments that would take place, and what they were to expect. He gave to His followers precious instruction that even they did not comprehend until after His death, resurrection, and ascension. When the Holy Spirit was poured out upon them, all things were brought to their remembrance, whatsoever He had said unto them.

A BETRAYAL OF CONFIDENCE

It was a betrayal of sacred trust to take that which Jesus designed should be kept secret, and publish it to others, and bring upon the cause of truth reproach and injury. The Lord has given to His people appropriate messages of warning, reproof, counsel, and instruction, but it is not appropriate to take these messages out of their connection and place them where they will seem to give force to messages of error. In the pamphlet published by Brother S. and his associates, he accuses the church of God of being Babylon, and would urge a separation from the church. This is a work that is neither honorable nor righteous. In compiling this work, they have used my name and writings for the support of that which I disapprove and denounce as error. The people to whom this pamphlet will come will charge the responsibility of this false position upon me, when it is utterly contrary to the teachings of my writings and the light which God has given me. I have no hesitancy in saying that those who are urging on this work are greatly deceived.

A FALSE MESSAGE

For years I have borne my testimony to the effect that when any arise claiming to have great light, and yet advocating the tearing down of that which the Lord through His human agents has been building up, they are greatly deceived, and are not working along the lines where Christ is working. Those who assert that the Seventh-day Adventist churches constitute Babylon, or any part of Babylon, might better stay at home. Let them stop and consider what is the message to be proclaimed at this time. In place of working with divine agencies to prepare a people to stand in the day of the Lord, they have taken their stand with him who is an accuser of the brethren, who accuses them before God day and night. Satanic agencies have been moved from beneath, and they have inspired men to unite in a confederacy of evil, that they may perplex, harass, and cause the people of God great distress. The whole world is to be stirred with enmity against Seventh-day Adventists, because they will not yield homage to the papacy, by honoring Sunday, the institution of this antichristian power. It is the purpose of Satan to cause them to be blotted from the earth, in order that his supremacy of the world may not be disputed.

SATAN'S ACCUSATIONS

The scene of Satan's accusation was presented before the prophet. He says, "He showed me Joshua the high priest standing before the Angel of the Lord, and Satan standing at his right hand to resist him." Jesus is our great High Priest in heaven. And what is He doing? He is making intercession and atonement for His people who believe in Him. Through His imputed righteousness, they are accepted of God as those who are manifesting to the world that they acknowledge allegiance to God, keeping all His commandments. Satan is full of malignant hatred against them, and manifests to them the same spirit that he manifested to Jesus Christ when He was upon earth. When Jesus was before Pilate, the Roman ruler sought to release Him, and desired that the people should choose to release Jesus from the ordeal through which He was about to pass. He presented before the clamoring multitude the Son of God and the criminal Barabbas, and inquired, "Whom will ye that I release unto you? Barabbas, or Jesus which is called Christ?" "They said, Barabbas. Pilate saith unto them, What shall I do then with Jesus which is called Christ? They all say unto him, Let Him be crucified."

The world was stirred by the enmity of Satan, and when asked to choose between the Son of God and the criminal Barabbas, they chose a robber rather than Jesus. The ignorant multitudes were led, by the deceptive reasonings of those in high position, to reject the Son of God, and choose a robber and murderer in His stead. Let us all remember that we are still in a world where Jesus, the Son of God, was rejected and crucified, where the guilt of despising Christ and preferring a robber rather than the spotless Lamb of God still rests. Unless we individually repent toward God because of transgression of His law, and exercise faith toward our Lord Jesus Christ, whom the world has rejected, we shall lie under the full condemnation that the action of choosing Barabbas instead of Christ merited. The whole world stands charged today with the deliberate rejection and murder of the Son of God. The word bears record that Jews and Gentiles, kings, governors, ministers, priests, and people—all classes and sects who reveal the same spirit of envy, hatred, prejudice, and unbelief manifested by those who put to death the Son of God—would act the same part, were the opportunity granted, as did the Jews and people of the time of Christ. They would be partakers of the same spirit that demanded the death of the Son of God.

In the scene representing the work of Christ for us, and the determined accusation of Satan against us,

Joshua stands as the high priest, and makes request in behalf of God's commandment-keeping people. At the same time Satan represents the people of God as great sinners, and presents before God the list of sins he has tempted them to commit through their lifetime, and urges that because of their transgressions, they be given into his hands to destroy. He urges that they should not be protected by ministering angels against the confederacy of evil. He is full of anger because he cannot bind the people of God into bundles with the world, to render to him complete allegiance. Kings and rulers and governors have placed upon themselves the brand of antichrist, and are represented as the dragon who goes to make war with the saints—with those who keep the commandments of God and who have the faith of Jesus. In their enmity against the people of God, they show themselves guilty also of the choice of Barabbas instead of Christ.

THE WORLD CALLED TO ACCOUNT

God has a controversy with the world. When the judgment shall sit, and the books shall be opened, He has an awful account to settle, which would now make the world fear and tremble were men not blinded and bewitched by satanic delusions and deceptions. God will call the world to account for the death of His only-begotten Son, whom to all intents and purposes the world has crucified afresh, and put to open shame in the persecution of His people. The world has rejected Christ in the person of His saints, has refused His messages in the refusal of the messages of prophets, apostles, and messengers. They have rejected those who have been colaborers with Christ, and for this they will have to render an account.

Satan stands at the head of all the accusers of the

brethren; but when he presents the sins of the people of God, what does the Lord answer? He says, "The Lord rebuke [not Joshua, who is a representative of the tried and chosen people of God, but] thee, O Satan; even the Lord that hath chosen Jerusalem rebuke thee: is not this a brand plucked out of the fire? Now Joshua was clothed with filthy garments, and stood before the Angel." Satan had represented the chosen and loyal people of God as being full of defilement and sin. He could depict the particular sins of which they had been guilty. Had he not set the whole confederacy of evil at work to lead them, through his seductive arts, into these very sins? But they had repented, they had accepted the righteousness of Christ. They were therefore standing before God clothed with the garments of Christ's righteousness, and "He answered and spake unto those that stood before Him, saying, Take away the filthy garments from him. And unto him He said, Behold, I have caused thine iniquity to pass from thee, and I will clothe thee with change of raiment." Every sin of which they had been guilty was forgiven, and they stood before God as chosen and true, as innocent, as perfect, as though they had never sinned.

THE ENCOURAGING WORD

"And I said, Let them set a fair miter upon his head. So they [the angels of God] set a fair miter upon his head, and clothed him with garments. And the Angel of the Lord stood by [Jesus their Redeemer]. And the Angel of the Lord protested unto Joshua, saying, Thus saith the Lord of hosts; If thou wilt walk in My ways, and if thou wilt keep My charge, then thou shalt also judge My house, and shalt also keep My courts, and I will give thee places to walk among these that stand by." I wish that all who claim to believe present truth would think seriously of the wonderful things presented in this chapter. However weak and compassed with infirmity the people of God may be, those who turn from disloyalty to God in this wicked and perverse generation, and come back to their allegiance, standing to vindicate the holy law of God, making up the breach made by the man of sin under the direction of Satan, will be accounted the children of God, and through the righteousness of Christ will stand perfect before God. Truth will not always lie in the dust to be trampled underfoot of men. It will be magnified and made honorable; it will yet arise and shine forth in all its natural luster, and will stand fast forever and ever.

WORDS OF ACCUSATION NOT OF GOD

God has a people in which all heaven is interested, and they are the one object on earth dear to the heart of God.* Let everyone who reads these words give them thorough consideration, for in the name of Jesus I would press them home upon every soul. When anyone arises, either among us or outside of us, who is burdened with a message which declares that the people of God are numbered with Babylon, and claims that the loud cry is a call to come out of her, you may know that he is not bearing the message of truth. Receive him not, nor bid him Godspeed; for God has not spoken by him, neither has He given a message to him, but he has run before he was sent. The message contained in the pamphlet called the *Loud Cry,* is a deception. Such messages will come, and it will be claimed for them that they are sent of God, but the claim will be false; for they are not filled with light, but with dark-

*See Appendix.

ness. There will be messages of accusation against the people of God, similar to the work done by Satan in accusing God's people, and these messages will be sounding at the very time when God is saying to His people, "Arise, shine; for thy light is come, and the glory of the Lord is risen upon thee. For, behold, the darkness shall cover the earth, and gross darkness the people: but the Lord shall arise upon thee, and His glory shall be seen upon thee."

A WORK OF DECEPTION

It will be found that those who bear false messages will not have a high sense of honor and integrity. They will deceive the people, and mix up with their error the *Testimonies* of Sister White, and use her name to give influence to their work. They make such selections from the *Testimonies* as they think they can twist to support their positions, and place them in a setting of falsehood, so that their error may have weight and be accepted by the people. They misinterpret and misapply that which God has given to the church to warn, counsel, reprove, comfort, and encourage those who shall make up the remnant people of God. Those who receive the *Testimonies* as the message of God will be helped and blessed thereby; but those who take them in parts, simply to support some theory or idea of their own, to vindicate themselves in a course of error, will not be blessed and benefited by what they teach. To claim that the Seventh-day Adventist Church is Babylon, is to make the same claim as does Satan, who is an accuser of the brethren, who accuses them before God night and day. By this misusing of the *Testimonies,* souls are placed in perplexity, because they cannot understand the relation of the

Testimonies to such a position as is taken by those in error; for God intended that the *Testimonies* should always have a setting in the framework of truth.

Those who advocate error will say, "The Lord saith," "when the Lord hath not spoken." They testify to falsehood, and not to truth. If those who have been proclaiming the message that the church is Babylon had used the money expended in publishing and circulating this error, in building up, instead of tearing down, they would have made it evident that they were the people whom God is leading.

There is a great work to be done in the world, a great work to be done in foreign lands. Schools must be established in order that youth, children, and those of more mature age may be educated as rapidly as possible to enter the missionary field. There is need not only of ministers for foreign fields, but of wise, judicious laborers of all kinds. The Macedonian cry is sounding from all parts of the world, "Come over, . . . and help us." With all the responsibility upon us to go and preach the gospel to every creature, there is great need of men and means, and Satan is at work in every conceivable way to tie up means, and to hinder men from engaging in the very work that they should be doing. The money that should be used in doing the good work of building houses of worship, of establishing schools for the purpose of educating laborers for the missionary field, of drilling young men and women so that they may go forth and labor patiently, intelligently, and with all perseverance that they may be agents through whom a people may be prepared to stand in the great day of God, is diverted from a channel of usefulness and blessing into a channel of evil and cursing.

The great day of God is upon us, and hasteth greatly, and there is a great work to be done, and it must be done speedily. But we find that amid the work that is to be done, there are those professing to believe the present truth who know not how to expend the means entrusted to them, and because of a lack of meekness and lowliness of heart they do not see how great is the work to be done. All those who learn of Jesus will be laborers together with God. But those who go forth to proclaim error, expending time and money in a vain work, lay upon the true workers in new fields increased burden; for instead of devoting their time to advocating truth, they are obliged to counteract the work of those who are proclaiming falsehood and claiming that they have the message from heaven.

If those who have done this kind of work had felt the necessity of answering the prayer of Christ that He offered to His Father just previous to His crucifixion,—that the disciples of Christ might be one as He was one with the Father,—they would not be wasting the means entrusted to them and so greatly needed to advance the truth. They would not be wasting precious time and ability in disseminating error, and thus necessitate the devoting of the laborer's time to counteracting and quenching its influence. A work of this character is inspired, not from above, but from beneath.

"Who is among you that feareth the Lord, that obeyeth the voice of His servant, that walketh in darkness, and hath no light? let him trust in the name of the Lord, and stay upon his God. Behold, all ye that kindle a fire, that compass yourselves about with sparks: walk in the light of your fire, and in the sparks that ye have kindled. This shall ye have of Mine hand; ye shall lie down in sorrow." The message that has been borne by those who have proclaimed the church to be Babylon has made the impression that God has no church upon earth.

A LIVING CHURCH

Has God no living church? He has a church, but it is the church militant, not the church triumphant. We are sorry that there are defective members, that there are tares amid the wheat. Jesus said: "The kingdom of heaven is likened unto a man which sowed good seed in his field: but while men slept, his enemy came and sowed tares among the wheat, and went his way. . . . So the servants of the householder came and said unto him, Sir, didst not thou sow good seed in thy field? from whence then hath it tares? He said unto them, An enemy hath done this. The servants said unto him, Wilt thou then that we go and gather them up? But he said, Nay; lest while ye gather up the tares, ye root up also the wheat with them. Let both grow together until the harvest: and in the time of harvest I will say to the reapers, Gather ye together first the tares, and bind them in bundles to burn them: but gather the wheat into my barn."

In the parable of the wheat and the tares, we see the reason why the tares were not to be plucked up; it was lest the wheat be rooted up with the tares. Human opinion and judgment would make grave mistakes. But rather than have a mistake made, and one single blade of wheat rooted up, the Master says, "Let both grow together until the harvest;" then the angels will gather out the tares, which will be appointed to destruction. Although in our churches, that claim to believe advanced truth, there are those who are faulty and erring, as tares among the wheat, God is long-suffering and patient. He reproves and warns the erring, but He does not destroy those who are long in learning the lesson He would teach them; He does not uproot the tares from the wheat. Tares and wheat are to grow together till the harvest; when the wheat comes to its full growth and development, and because of its character when ripened, it will be fully distinguished from the tares.

The church of Christ on earth will be imperfect, but God does not destroy His church because of its imperfection. There have been and will be those who are filled with zeal not according to knowledge, who would purify the church, and uproot the tares from the midst of the wheat. But Christ has given special light as to how to deal with those who are erring, and with those who are unconverted in the church. There is to be no spasmodic, zealous, hasty action taken by church members in cutting off those they may think defective in character. Tares will appear among the wheat; but it would do more harm to weed out the tares, unless in God's appointed way, than to leave them alone. While the Lord brings into the church those who are truly converted, Satan at the same time brings persons who are not converted into its fellowship. While Christ is sowing the good seed, Satan is sowing the tares. There are two opposing influences continually exerted on the members of the church. One influence is working for the purification of the church, and the other for the corrupting of the people of God.

JUDAS GIVEN OPPORTUNITIES

Jesus knew that Judas was defective in character, but notwithstanding this, He accepted him as one of the disciples, and gave him the same opportunities and privileges that He gave to the others whom He had chosen. Judas was left without excuse in the evil course he afterward pursued. Judas might have become a doer of the word, as were eventually Peter and James and John and the other disciples. Jesus gave precious lessons of instruction, so that those who were associated with Him might have been converted, and have no need of clinging to the defects that marred their characters.

THE CHURCH NOT PERFECT

Some people seem to think that upon entering the church they will have their expectations fulfilled, and meet only with those who are pure and perfect. They are zealous in their faith, and when they see faults in church members, they say, "We left the world in order to have no association with evil characters, but the evil is here also;" and they ask, as did the servants in the parable, "From whence then hath it tares?" But we need not be thus disappointed, for the Lord has not warranted us in coming to the conclusion that the church is perfect; and all our zeal will not be successful in making the church militant as pure as the church triumphant. The Lord forbids us to proceed in any violent way against those whom we think erring, and we are not to deal out excommunications and denunciations to those who are faulty.

Finite man is likely to misjudge character, but God does not leave the work of judgment and pronouncing upon character to those who are not fitted for it. We are not to say what constitutes the wheat, and what the tares. The time of the harvest will fully determine the character of the two classes specified under the figure of the tares and the wheat. The work of separation is given to the angels of God, and not committed into the hands of any man.

False doctrine is one of the satanic influences that

work in the church, and brings into it those who are unconverted in heart. Men do not obey the words of Jesus Christ, and thus seek for unity in faith, spirit, and doctrine. They do not labor for the unity of spirit for which Christ prayed, which would make the testimony of Christ's disciples effective in convincing the world that God had sent His Son into the world, "that whosoever believeth in Him should not perish, but have everlasting life." If the unity for which Christ prayed existed among the people of God, they would bear living testimony, would send forth a bright light to shine amid the moral darkness of the world.

SATAN PERMITTED TO TEMPT

Instead of the unity which should exist among believers, there is disunion; for Satan is permitted to come in, and through his specious deceptions and delusions he leads those who are not learning of Christ meekness and lowliness of heart, to take a different line from the church, and break up, if possible, the unity of the church. Men arise speaking perverse things to draw away disciples after themselves. They claim that God has given them great light; but how do they act under its influence? Do they pursue the course that the two disciples pursued on their journey to Emmaus? When they received light, they returned and found those whom God had led and was still leading, and told them how they had seen Jesus and had talked with Him.

Have the men who have claimed to have light concerning the church pursued this course? Have they gone to those who are chosen of God to bear a living testimony, and given them evidence that this light would better qualify them to prepare a people to stand in the great day of God? Have they sought counsel of those who have been and are still bearing the truth, and giving to the world the last message of warning? Have they counseled with those who have had a deep experience in the things of God? Why were these men, so full of zeal for the cause, not present at the General Conference held at Battle Creek, as were the devout men at Jerusalem at the time of the outpouring of the Holy Spirit? At the great heart of the work, men opened their treasures of light; and while the Lord was pouring out His Spirit upon the people, did these men receive of the heavenly anointing? While the deep movings of the Spirit of God were made manifest among the people, and souls were being converted, and hard hearts broken, there were those who were listening to the suggestions of Satan, and they were inspired with zeal from beneath to go forth and proclaim that the very people receiving of the Holy Spirit, who are to receive the latter rain and the glory that is to lighten the whole earth, were Babylon. Did the Lord give these messengers their message? No, for it was not a message of truth.

THE CHURCH THE LIGHT OF THE WORLD

Although there are evils existing in the church, and will be until the end of the world, the church in these last days is to be the light of the world that is polluted and demoralized by sin. The church, enfeebled and defective, needing to be reproved, warned, and counseled, is the only object upon earth upon which Christ bestows His supreme regard. The world is a workshop in which, through the cooperation of human and divine agencies, Jesus is making experiments by His grace and divine mercy upon human hearts. Angels are amazed as they behold the transformation of character brought about in those who yield themselves to God, and they express their joy in songs of rapturous praise to God and to the Lamb. They see those who are by nature the children of wrath, converted and becoming laborers together with Christ in drawing souls to God. They see those who were in darkness becoming lights to shine amid the moral night of this wicked and perverse generation. They see them becoming prepared by a Christlike experience to suffer with their Lord, and afterward to be partakers with Him in His glory in heaven above.

God has a church on earth who are lifting up the downtrodden law, and presenting to the world the Lamb of God that taketh away the sins of the world. The church is the depositary of the wealth of the riches of the grace of Christ, and through the church eventually will be made manifest the final and full display of the love of God to the world that is to be lightened with its glory. The prayer of Christ that His church may be one as He was one with His Father will finally be answered. The rich dowry of the Holy Spirit will be given, and through its constant supply to the people of God they will become witnesses in the world of the power of God unto salvation.

There is but one church in the world who are at the present time standing in the breach, and making up the hedge, building up the old waste places; and for any man to call the attention of the world and other churches to this church, denouncing her as Babylon, is to do a work in harmony with him who is the accuser of the brethren. Is it possible that men will arise from among us, who speak perverse things, and give voice to the very sentiments that Satan would have disseminated in the world in regard to those who keep the commandments of God, and have the faith of Jesus? Is there not work enough to satisfy your zeal in presenting the truth to those who are in the darkness of error? As those who have been made stewards of means and ability, you have been misapplying your Lord's goods in disseminating error. The whole world is filled with hatred of those who proclaim the binding claims of the law of God, and the church who are loyal to Jehovah must engage in no ordinary conflict. "We wrestle not against flesh and blood, but against principalities, against powers, against the rulers of the darkness of this world, against spiritual wickedness in high places." Those who have any realization of what this warfare means will not turn their weapons against the church militant, but with all their powers will wrestle with the people of God against the confederacy of evil.

Those who start up to proclaim a message on their own individual responsibility, who, while claiming to be taught and led of God, still make it their special work to tear down that which God has been for years building up, are not doing the will of God. Be it known that these men are on the side of the great deceiver. Believe them not. They are allying themselves with the enemies of God and the truth. They will deride the order of the ministry as a system of priestcraft. From such turn away, have no fellowship with their message, however much they may quote the *Testimonies* and seek to entrench themselves behind them. Receive them not, for God has not given them this work to do. The result of such work will be unbelief in the *Testimonies,* and, as far as possible, they will make of none effect the work that I have for years been doing.

Almost my whole lifetime has been devoted to this

work, but my burden has often been made heavier by the arising of men who went forth to proclaim a message that God had not given them. This class of evil workers have selected portions of the *Testimonies,* and have placed them in the framework of error, in order by this setting to give influence to their false testimonies. When it is made manifest that their message is error, then the *Testimonies,* brought into the companionship of error, share the same condemnation; and people of the world, who do not know that the testimonies quoted are extracts from private letters used without my consent, present these matters as evidence that my work is not of God or of truth, but falsehood. Those who thus bring the work of God into disrepute will have to answer before God for the work they are doing.

A DIVINELY APPOINTED MINISTRY

God has a church, and she has a divinely appointed ministry. "And He gave some, apostles; and some, prophets; and some, evangelists; and some, pastors and teachers; for the perfecting of the saints, for the work of the ministry, for the edifying of the body of Christ: till we all come in the unity of the faith, and of the knowledge of the Son of God, unto a perfect man, unto the measure of the stature of the fullness of Christ: that we henceforth be no more children, tossed to and fro, and carried about with every wind of doctrine, by the sleight of men, and cunning craftiness, whereby they lie in wait to deceive; but speaking the truth in love, may grow up into Him in all things, which is the head, even Christ."

The Lord has His appointed agencies, and a church that has lived through persecution, conflict, and darkness. Jesus loved the church, and gave Himself for it, and He will replenish, refine, ennoble, and elevate it, so that it shall stand fast amid the corrupting influences of this world. Men appointed of God have been chosen to watch with jealous care, with vigilant perseverance, that the church may not be overthrown by the evil devices of Satan, but that she shall stand in the world to promote the glory of God among men. There will ever be fierce conflict between the church and the world. Mind will come into contact with mind, principle with principle, truth with error; but in the crisis soon to culminate, which has already begun, the men of experience are to do their God-appointed work, and watch for souls as they that must give an account.

Those who are carrying this message of error, denouncing the church as Babylon, are neglecting their God-appointed work, are in opposition to organization, in opposition to the plain command of God spoken by Malachi in regard to bringing all the tithes into the treasury of God's house, and imagine that they have a work to do in warning those whom God has chosen to forward His message of truth. These workers are not bringing greater efficiency to the cause and kingdom of God, but are engaged in a work similar to that in which the enemy of all righteousness is engaged. Let these men who are rising up against the ways and means ordained of God to forward His work in these days of peril divest themselves of all unscriptural views concerning the nature, office, and power of God's appointed agencies.

Let all understand the words that I now write. Those who are laborers together with God are but His instruments, and they in themselves possess no essential grace or holiness. It is only when they are cooperating with heavenly intelligences that they are successful. They are but earthen vessels, the depositaries in which God places the treasure of His truth. Paul may plant, and Apollos water, but it is God alone that gives the increase.

God speaks through His appointed agencies, and let no man, or confederacy of men, insult the Spirit of God by refusing to hear the message of God's word from the lips of His chosen messengers. By refusing to hear the message of God, men close themselves in a chamber of darkness. They shut their own souls away from vast blessings and rob Christ of the glory that should come to Him, by showing disrespect to His appointed agencies.

BEWARE OF FALSE TEACHERS

God is not the author of confusion, but of peace. But Satan is a vigilant, unsleeping foe, ever at work upon human minds, seeking a soil in which he can sow his tares. If he finds any whom he can press into his service, he will suggest ideas and false theories, and make them zealous in advocating error. The truth not only converts, but works the purification of its receiver. Jesus has warned us to beware of false teachers. From the beginning of our work, men have arisen from time to time, advocating theories that were new and startling. But if those who claim to believe the truth would go to those who have had experience, would go to the word of God in a teachable, humble spirit, and examine their theories in the light of truth and with the aid of the brethren who have been diligent Bible students, and at the same time make supplication unto God, asking, Is this the way of the Lord, or is it a false path in which Satan would lead me? they would receive light, and would escape out of the net of the fowler.

Let all our brethren and sisters beware of anyone who would set a time for the Lord to fulfill His word in regard to His coming, or in regard to any other promise He has made of special significance. "It is not for you to know the times or the seasons, which the Father hath put in His own power." False teachers may appear to be very zealous for the work of God, and may expend means to bring their theories before the world and the church; but as they mingle error with truth, their message is one of deception, and will lead souls into false paths. They are to be met and opposed, not because they are bad men, but because they are teachers of falsehood and are endeavoring to put upon falsehood the stamp of truth.

What a pity it is that men will go to such pains to discover some theory of error when there is a whole storehouse of precious gems of truth by which the people might be enriched in the most holy faith. Instead of teaching truth they let their imagination dwell upon that which is new and strange, and throw themselves out of harmony with those whom God is using to bring the people up upon the platform of truth. They cast aside all that has been said in regard to unity of sentiment and feeling, and trample upon the prayer of Christ as though the unity for which He prayed were unessential, and there were no necessity for His followers to be one, even as He is one with the Father. They go off on a tangent, and, Jehulike, call to their brethren to follow their example of zeal for the Lord.

If their zeal led them to work in the same lines in which their brethren who have carried the heat and burden of the day are working, if they were as persevering to overcome discouragements and obstacles as their brethren have been, they might well be imitated, and God would accept them. But men are to be condemned who start out with a proclamation of wonderful light, and yet draw away from the agents whom God is leading. This was the way in which Korah, Dathan, and Abiram did, and their action is recorded as a warning to all others. We are not to do as they have done—accuse and condemn those upon whom God has laid the burden of the work.

Those who have proclaimed the Seventh-day Adventist Church as Babylon, have made use of the *Testimonies* in giving their position a seeming support; but why is it that they did not present that which for years has been the burden of my message—the unity of the church? Why did they not quote the words of the angel, "Press together, press together, press together"? Why did they not repeat the admonition and state the principle, that "in union there is strength, in division there is weakness"? It is such messages as these men have borne that divide the church, and put us to shame before the enemies of truth; and in such messages is plainly revealed the specious working of the great deceiver, who would hinder the church from attaining unto perfection in unity. These teachers follow the sparks of their own kindling, move according to their own independent judgment, and cumber the truth with false notions and theories. They refuse the counsel of their brethren, and press on in their own way until they become just what Satan would desire to have them—unbalanced in mind.

I warn my brethren to guard against the working of Satan in every form. The great adversary of God and man is exulting today that he has succeeded in deceiving souls, and in diverting their means and ability into harmful channels. Their money might have been used to advance present truth, but instead of this it has been expended in presenting notions that have no foundation in truth.

ANOTHER EXAMPLE

In 1845 a man by the name of Curtis* did a similar work in the State of Massachusetts. He presented a false doctrine, and wove into his theories sentences and selections from the testimonies, and published his theories in the *Day Star,* and in sheet form. For years these productions bore their baleful fruit, and brought reproach upon the testimonies that, as a whole, in no way supported his work. My husband wrote to him, and asked him what he meant by presenting the testimonies interwoven with his own words, in support of that which we were opposed to, and requested him to correct the impression that his work had given. He flatly refused to do so, saying that his theories were truth, and that the visions ought to have corroborated his views, and that they virtually did support them, but that I had forgotten to write out the matters that made his theories plain.

Ever since the beginning of the work, one after another has risen up to do this kind of work, and I have had to go to the trouble and incur the expense of contradicting these falsehoods. They have published their theories and have deceived many souls, but may God guard the sheep of His pasture.

I urge those who claim to believe the truth, to walk in unity with their brethren. Do not seek to give to the world occasion to say that we are extremists, that we are disunited, that one teaches one thing, and one another. Avoid dissension. Let everyone be on guard, and be careful to be found standing in the gap to make up the breach, in place of standing at the wall seeking

---

*See Appendix.

to make a breach. Let all be careful not to make an outcry against the only people who are fulfilling the description given of the remnant people who keep the commandments of God and have faith in Jesus, who are exalting the standard of righteousness in these last days.

God has a distinct people, a church on earth, second to none, but superior to all in their facilities to teach the truth, to vindicate the law of God. God has divinely appointed agencies—men whom He is leading, who have borne the heat and burden of the day, who are cooperating with heavenly instrumentalities to advance the kingdom of Christ in our world. Let all unite with these chosen agents, and be found at last among those who have the patience of the saints, who keep the commandments of God, and have the faith of Jesus.

THE LETTER

The following is the letter sent to Brother S.*:

"Napier, New Zealand, March 23, 1893.

"Dear Brother S.:

"I address to you a few lines. I am not in harmony with the position that you have taken, for I have been shown by the Lord that just such positions will be taken by those who are in error. Paul has given us warning to this effect: 'Now the Spirit speaketh expressly, that in the latter times some shall depart from the faith, giving heed to seducing spirits, and doctrines of devils.'

"My brother, I learn that you are taking the position that the Seventh-day Adventist Church is Babylon, and that all that would be saved must come out of her. You are not the only man the devil has deceived in this matter. For the last forty years, one man after

*See Appendix.

another has arisen, claiming that the Lord has sent him with the same message; but let me tell you, as I have told them, that this message you are proclaiming is one of the satanic delusions designed to create confusion among the churches.

"My brother, you are certainly off the track. The second angel's message was to go to Babylon [the churches] proclaiming her downfall, and calling the people to come out of her. This same message is to be proclaimed the second time. 'And after these things I saw another angel come down from heaven, having great power; and the earth was lightened with his glory. And he cried mightily with a strong voice, saying, Babylon the great is fallen, is fallen, and is become the habitation of devils, and the hold of every foul spirit, and a cage of every unclean and hateful bird. For all nations have drunk of the wine of the wrath of her fornication, and the kings of the earth have committed fornication with her, and the merchants of the earth are waxed rich through the abundance of her delicacies. And I heard another voice from heaven, saying, Come out of her, My people, that ye be not partakers of her sins, and that ye receive not of her plagues. For her sins have reached unto heaven, and God hath remembered her iniquities.'

"My brother, if you are teaching that the Seventh-day Adventist Church is Babylon, you are wrong. God has not given you any such message to bear. Satan will use every mind to which he can attain access, inspiring men to originate false theories or go off on some wrong tangent, that he may create a false excitement, and thus divert souls from the true issue for this time. I presume that some may be deceived by your message, because they are full of curiosity and desire for some new thing.

"It makes me feel sad indeed that you should be deceived in any way by the suggestions of the enemy; for I know the theory that you are advocating is not truth. In advancing the ideas you do, you will do great injury to yourself and to others. Do not seek to misinterpret, and twist, and pervert the *Testimonies* to substantiate any such message of error. Many have passed over this ground, and have done great harm. As others have started up full of zeal to proclaim this message, again and again, I have been shown that it was not truth.

"I understand that you are also proclaiming that we should not pay tithe. My brother, take 'off thy shoes from off thy feet;' for the place whereon you are standing is holy ground. The Lord has spoken in regard to paying tithes. He has said, 'Bring ye all the tithes into the storehouse, that there may be meat in Mine house, and prove Me now herewith, saith the Lord of hosts, if I will not open you the windows of heaven, and pour you out a blessing, that there shall not be room enough to receive it.' But while He pronounces a blessing upon those who bring in their tithes, He pronounces a curse upon those who withhold them. Very recently I have had direct light from the Lord upon this question, that many Seventh-day Adventists were robbing God in tithes and offerings, and it was plainly revealed to me that Malachi has stated the case as it really is. Then how dare any man even think in his heart that a suggestion to withhold tithes and offerings is from the Lord? Where, my brother, have you stepped out of the path? Oh, get your feet back in the straight path again.

"We are near the end, but if you or any other man shall be seduced by the enemy, and led on to set the time for Christ's coming, he will be doing the same evil work which has wrought the ruin of the souls of those who have done it in the past.

"If you are wearing the yoke of Christ, if you are lifting His burden, you will see that there is plenty to do in the same lines wherein the servants of God are laboring—in preaching Christ and Him crucified. But anyone who shall start up to proclaim a message to announce the hour, day, or year of Christ's appearing has taken up a yoke and is proclaiming a message that the Lord has never given him.

"God has a church upon the earth who are His chosen people, who keep His commandments. He is leading, not stray offshoots, not one here and one there, but a people. The truth is a sanctifying power; but the church militant is not the church triumphant. There are tares among the wheat. 'Wilt thou then that we . . . gather them up?' was the question of the servant; but the master answered, 'Nay; lest while ye gather up the tares, ye root up also the wheat with them.' The gospel net draws not only good fish, but bad ones as well, and the Lord only knows who are His.

"It is our individual duty to walk humbly with God. We are not to seek any strange, new message. We are not to think that the chosen ones of God who are trying to walk in the light compose Babylon. The fallen denominational churches are Babylon. Babylon has been fostering poisonous doctrines, the wine of error. This wine of error is made up of false doctrines, such as the natural immortality of the soul, the eternal torment of the wicked, the denial of the pre-existence of Christ prior to His birth in Bethlehem, and advocating and exalting the first day of the week above God's holy and sanctified day. These and kindred errors are presented to the world by the various churches, and thus the Scriptures are fulfilled that say, 'For all nations have drunk of the wine of the wrath of her fornication.' It is a wrath which is created by false doctrines, and when kings and presidents drink this wine of the wrath of her fornication, they are stirred with anger against those who will not come into harmony with the false and satanic heresies which exalt the false sabbath, and lead men to trample underfoot God's memorial.

"Fallen angels upon earth form confederations with evil men. In this age antichrist will appear as the true Christ, and then the law of God will be fully made void in the nations of our world. Rebellion against God's holy law will be fully ripe. But the true leader of all this rebellion is Satan clothed as an angel of light. Men will be deceived and will exalt him to the place of God, and deify him. But Omnipotence will interpose, and to the apostate churches that unite in the exaltation of Satan, the sentence will go forth, 'Therefore shall her plagues come in one day, death, and mourning, and famine; and she shall be utterly burned with fire: for strong is the Lord God who judgeth her.'"

For further study: *Early Writings,* pages 278, 279; *Testimonies,* vol. 4, p. 13; vol. 5, pp. 81-84, 103-105, 202, 203; *Selected Messages,* b. 2, pp. 62-71; 396, 397.

The object of preaching is not alone to convey information, not merely to convince the intellect. The preaching of the word should appeal to the intellect, and should impart knowledge, but it should do more than this. The words of the minister should reach the hearts of the hearers.—*Review and Herald,* December 22, 1904.

Faithful, Earnest Warnings 2

Danger of Rejecting Truth

Cooranbong, Australia, May 30, 1896.

Dear Brother———:

I have returned from our season of prayer. The spirit of intercession came upon me, and I was drawn out in most earnest prayer for souls at Battle Creek. I know their peril. The Holy Spirit has in a special manner moved me to send up my petitions in their behalf.

God is not the author of anything sinful. None should fear to be singular if the fulfillment of duty requires it. If it makes us singular to avoid sin, then our singularity is merely the distinction between purity and impurity, righteousness and unrighteousness. Because the multitude prefer the path of transgression, shall we choose the same? We are plainly told by Inspiration, "Thou shalt not follow a multitude to do evil." Our position should be clearly stated, "As for me and my house, we will serve the Lord."

"In the beginning was the Word, and the Word was with God, and the Word was God. The same was in the beginning with God. All things were made by Him; and without Him was not anything made that was made. In Him was life; and the life was the light of men. And the light shineth in darkness; and the darkness comprehended it not." "And the Word was made flesh, and dwelt among us, (and we beheld His glory, the glory as of the Only-Begotten of the Father,) full of grace and truth." Would that everyone whose

---

The articles in this section are from *Special Testimony to Battle Creek Church* (1896). This article, pages 3-18.

name is written in the church books could from the heart utter these words. The church members need to know from experience what the Holy Spirit will do for them. It will bless the receiver, and make him a blessing. It is sad that every soul is not praying for the vital breath of the Spirit, for we are ready to die if it breathe not on us.

We are to pray for the impartation of the Spirit as the remedy for sin-sick souls. The church needs to be converted, and why should we not prostrate ourselves at the throne of grace, as representatives of the church, and from a broken heart and contrite spirit make earnest supplication that the Holy Spirit shall be poured out upon us from on high? Let us pray that when it shall be graciously bestowed our cold hearts may be revived, and we may have discernment to understand that it is from God, and receive it with joy. Some have treated the Spirit as an unwelcome guest, refusing to receive the rich gift, refusing to acknowledge it, turning from it, and condemning it as fanaticism.*

When the Holy Spirit works the human agent, it does not ask us in what way it shall operate. Often it moves in unexpected ways. Christ did not come as the Jews expected. He did not come in a manner to glorify them as a nation. His forerunner came to prepare the way for Him by calling upon the people to repent of their sins, and be converted, and be baptized. Christ's message was, "The kingdom of God is at hand: repent ye, and believe the gospel." The Jews refused to receive Christ, because He did not come in accordance with their expectations. The ideas of finite men were held as infallible, because hoary with age.

This is the danger to which the church is now exposed—that the inventions of finite men shall mark

---

*See Appendix.

out the precise way for the Holy Spirit to come. Though they would not care to acknowledge it, some have already done this. And because the Spirit is to come, not to praise men or to build up their erroneous theories, but to reprove the world of sin, and of righteousness, and of judgment, many turn away from it. They are not willing to be deprived of the garments of their own self-righteousness. They are not willing to exchange their own righteousness, which is unrighteousness, for the righteousness of Christ, which is pure, unadulterated truth. The Holy Spirit flatters no man, neither does it work according to the devising of any man. Finite, sinful men are not to work the Holy Spirit. When it shall come as a reprover, through any human agent whom God shall choose, it is man's place to hear and obey its voice.

MANIFEST WORKING OF THE HOLY SPIRIT

Just before He left them, Christ gave His disciples the promise, "Ye shall receive power, after that the Holy Ghost is come upon you: and ye shall be witnesses unto Me both in Jerusalem, and in all Judea, and in Samaria, and unto the uttermost part of the earth." "Go ye therefore, and teach all nations, baptizing them in the name of the Father, and of the Son, and of the Holy Ghost: teaching them to observe all things whatsoever I have commanded you: and, lo, I am with you alway, even unto the end of the world." While these words were upon His lips, He ascended, a cloud of angels received Him, and escorted Him to the City of God. The disciples returned to Jerusalem, knowing now for a certainty that Jesus was the Son of God. Their faith was unclouded, and they waited, preparing themselves by prayer and by humbling their hearts before God, until the baptism of the Holy Spirit came.

"And when the Day of Pentecost was fully come, they were all with one accord in one place. And suddenly there came a sound from heaven as of a rushing mighty wind, and it filled all the house where they were sitting. And there appeared unto them cloven tongues like as of fire, and it sat upon each of them. And they were all filled with the Holy Ghost, and began to speak with other tongues, as the Spirit gave them utterance." In that assembly there were mockers, who did not recognize the work of the Holy Spirit, and they said, "These men are full of new wine.

"But Peter, standing up with the eleven, lifted up his voice, and said unto them, Ye men of Judea, and all ye that dwell at Jerusalem, be this known unto you, and hearken to my words: for these are not drunken, as ye suppose, seeing it is but the third hour of the day. But this is that which was spoken by the prophet Joel." Read the history. The Lord was at work in His own way; but had there been such a manifestation among us, upon whom the ends of the world are come, would not some have mocked, as on that occasion? Those who did not come under the influence of the Holy Spirit knew it not. To this class the disciples seemed like drunken men.

WITNESSES OF THE CROSS

After the outpouring of the Holy Spirit, the disciples, clothed with the divine panoply, went forth as witnesses, to tell the wonderful story of the manger and the cross. They were humble men, but they went forth with the truth. After the death of their Lord they were a helpless, disappointed, discouraged company—as sheep without a shepherd; but now they go forth as witnesses for the truth, with no weapons but the word and Spirit of God, to triumph over all opposition.

Their Saviour had been rejected and condemned, and nailed to the ignominious cross. The Jewish priests and rulers had declared, in scorn, "He saved others; Himself He cannot save. If He be the King of Israel, let Him now come down from the cross, and we will believe Him." But that cross, that instrument of shame and torture, brought hope and salvation to the world. The believers rallied; their hopelessness and conscious helplessness had left them. They were transformed in character, and united in the bonds of Christian love. Although without wealth, though counted by the world as mere ignorant fishermen, they were made, by the Holy Spirit, witnesses for Christ. Without earthly honor or recognition, they were the heroes of faith. From their lips came words of divine eloquence and power that shook the world.

The third, fourth, and fifth chapters of Acts give an account of their witnessing. Those who had rejected and crucified the Saviour expected to find His disciples discouraged, crestfallen, and ready to disown their Lord. With amazement they heard the clear, bold testimony given under the power of the Holy Spirit. The words and works of the disciples represented the words and works of their Teacher; and all who heard them said, They have learned of Jesus, they talk as He talked. "And with great power gave the apostles witness of the resurrection of the Lord Jesus: and great grace was upon them all."

The chief priests and rulers thought themselves competent to decide what the apostles should do and teach. As they went forth preaching Jesus everywhere, the men who were worked by the Holy Spirit did many things that the Jews did not approve. There was danger that the ideas and doctrines of the rabbis would be brought into disrepute. The apostles were creating a wonderful excitement. The people were bringing their sick folk, and those that were vexed with unclean spirits, into the streets; crowds were collecting around them, and those that had been healed were shouting the praises of God and glorifying the name of Jesus, the very One whom the Jews had condemned, scorned, spit upon, crowned with thorns, and caused to be scourged and crucified. This Jesus was extolled above the priests and rulers. The apostles were even declaring that He had risen from the dead. The Jewish rulers decided that this work must and should be stopped, for it was proving them guilty of the blood of Jesus. They saw that converts to the faith were multiplying. "Believers were the more added to the Lord, multitudes both of men and women."

ARREST AND IMPRISONMENT OF THE APOSTLES

"Then the high priest rose up, and all they that were with him, (which is the sect of the Sadducees,)" who held that there would be no resurrection of the dead. The assertions made by the apostles that they had seen Jesus after His resurrection, and that He had ascended to heaven, were overthrowing the fundamental principles of the Sadducean doctrine. This was not to be allowed. The priests and rulers were filled with indignation, and laid their hands on the apostles, and put them in the common prison. The disciples were not intimidated or cast down. The words of Christ in His last lessons to them were brought to mind: "He that hath My commandments, and keepeth them, he it is that loveth Me: and he that loveth Me shall be loved of My Father, and I will love him, and will manifest

Myself to him." "But when the Comforter is come, whom I will send unto you from the Father, even the Spirit of truth, which proceedeth from the Father, He shall testify of Me: and ye also shall bear witness, because ye have been with Me from the beginning. These things have I spoken unto you, that ye should not be offended. They shall put you out of the synagogues: yea, the time cometh, that whosoever killeth you will think that he doeth God service. And these things will they do unto you, because they have not known the Father, nor Me. But these things have I told you, that when the time shall come, ye may remember that I told you of them."

PREACHING CONTRARY TO ESTABLISHED DOCTRINES

"The angel of the Lord by night opened the prison doors, and brought them forth, and said, Go, stand and speak in the temple to the people all the words of this life." We see here that the men in authority are not always to be obeyed, even though they may profess to be teachers of Bible doctrine. There are many today who feel indignant and aggrieved that any voice should be raised presenting ideas that differ from their own in regard to points of religious belief. Have they not long advocated their ideas as truth? So the priests and rabbis reasoned in apostolic days: What mean these men who are unlearned, some of them mere fishermen, who are presenting ideas contrary to the doctrines which the learned priests and rulers are teaching the people? They have no right to meddle with the fundamental principles of our faith.

But we see that the God of heaven sometimes commissions men to teach that which is regarded as contrary to the established doctrines. Because those who were once the depositaries of truth became unfaithful to their sacred trust, the Lord chose others who would receive the bright beams of the Sun of Righteousness, and would advocate truths that were not in accordance with the ideas of the religious leaders. And then these leaders, in the blindness of their minds, give full sway to what is supposed to be righteous indignation against the ones who have set aside cherished fables. They act like men who have lost their reason. They do not consider the possibility that they themselves have not rightly understood the word. They will not open their eyes to discern the fact that they have misinterpreted and misapplied the Scriptures, and have built up false theories, calling them fundamental doctrines of the faith.

But the Holy Spirit will, from time to time, reveal the truth through its own chosen agencies; and no man, not even a priest or ruler, has a right to say, You shall not give publicity to your opinions, because I do not believe them. That wonderful "I" may attempt to put down the Holy Spirit's teaching. Men may for a time attempt to smother it and kill it; but that will not make error truth, or truth error. The inventive minds of men have advanced speculative opinions in various lines, and when the Holy Spirit lets light shine into human minds, it does not respect every point of man's application of the word. God impressed His servants to speak the truth irrespective of what men had taken for granted as truth.

PRESENT DANGERS

Even Seventh-day Adventists are in danger of closing their eyes to truth as it is in Jesus, because it contradicts something which they have taken for granted as truth but which the Holy Spirit teaches is not truth. Let all be very modest, and seek most earnestly to put self out of the question, and to exalt Jesus. In most of the religious controversies the foundation of the trouble is that self is striving for the supremacy. About what? About matters which are not vital points at all, and which are regarded as such only because men have given importance to them. (See Matthew 12:31-37; Mark 14:56; Luke 5:21; Matthew 9:3.)

But let us follow the history of the men whom the Jewish priests and rulers thought so dangerous, because they were bringing in new and strange teaching on almost every theological subject. The command given by the Holy Spirit, "Go, stand and speak in the temple to the people all the words of this life," was obeyed by the apostles; "they entered into the temple early in the morning, and taught. But the high priest came, and they that were with him, and called the council together, and all the senate of the children of Israel, and sent to the prison to have them brought. But when the officers came, and found them not in the prison, they returned, and told, saying, The prison truly found we shut with all safety, and the keepers standing without before the doors: but when we had opened, we found no man within. Now when the high priest and the captain of the temple and the chief priests heard these things, they doubted of them whereunto this would grow. Then came one and told them, saying, Behold, the men whom ye put in prison are standing in the temple, and teaching the people. Then went the captain with the officers, and brought them without violence: for they feared the people, lest they should have been stoned." If the priests and rulers had dared act out their own feelings toward the apostles, there would have been a different record; for the angel of God was a watcher on that occasion, to magnify His name if any violence had been offered to His servants.

ANSWER OF THE APOSTLES

"And when they had brought them, they set them before the council: and the high priest asked them, saying, Did not we straitly command you that ye should not teach in this name? and, behold, ye have filled Jerusalem with your doctrine, and intend to bring this Man's blood upon us." (See Matthew 23:34, 35.) "Then Peter and the other apostles answered and said, We ought to obey God rather than men. The God of our fathers raised up Jesus, whom ye slew and hanged on a tree. Him hath God exalted with His right hand to be a Prince and a Saviour, for to give repentance to Israel, and forgiveness of sins. And we are His witnesses of these things; and so is also the Holy Ghost, whom God hath given to them that obey Him. When they heard that, they were cut to the heart, and took counsel to slay them."

Then the Holy Spirit moved upon Gamaliel, a Pharisee, "a doctor of the law, had in reputation among all the people." His advice was, "Refrain from these men, and let them alone: for if this counsel or this work be of men, it will come to nought: but if it be of God, ye cannot overthrow it; lest haply ye be found even to fight against God. And to him they agreed."

PREJUDICE OF THOSE IN AUTHORITY

Yet the attributes of Satan so controlled their minds that, notwithstanding the wonderful miracles that had been wrought in healing the sick and in releasing God's servants from prison, the priests and rulers were so filled with prejudice and hatred that they could hardly be restrained. "When they had called the apostles, and beaten them, they commanded that they should not speak in the name of Jesus, and let them go. And they departed from the presence of the council, rejoicing that they were counted worthy to suffer shame for His name. And daily in the temple, and in every house, they ceased not to teach and preach Jesus Christ."

MERCY OF GOD EXEMPLIFIED

We can see what evidence was given the priests and rulers, and how firmly they resisted the Spirit of God. Those who claim superior wisdom and piety may make most terrible and (to themselves) fatal mistakes if they allow their minds to be molded by another power, and pursue a course in resistance to the Holy Spirit. The Lord Jesus, represented by the Holy Spirit, was in the presence of that assembly, but they did not discern Him. For a moment they had felt the conviction of the Spirit, that Jesus was the Son of God; but they stifled conviction, and became more blind and hardened than before. Even after they had crucified the Saviour, God in His mercy had sent them additional evidence in the works wrought through the apostles. He was giving them another call to repentance, even in the terrible charge brought against them by the apostles, that they had killed the Prince of life.

It was not alone the sin of putting to death the Son of God that cut them off from salvation, but their persistence in rejecting light and the conviction of the Holy Spirit. The spirit that works in the children of disobedience worked in them, leading them to abuse the men through whom God was giving a testimony to them. The malignity of rebellion reappeared, and was intensified in every successive act of resistance against God's servants and the message He had given them to declare.

RESISTANCE OF TRUTH

Every act of resistance makes it harder to yield. Being the leaders of the people, the priests and rulers felt it incumbent on them to defend the course they had taken. They must prove that they had been in the right. Having committed themselves in opposition to Christ, every act of resistance became an additional incentive to persist in the same path. The events of their past career of opposition are as precious treasures to be jealously guarded. And the hatred and malignity that inspired those acts are concentrated against the apostles.

The Spirit of God revealed its presence unto those who, irrespective of the fear or favor of men, declared the truth which had been committed to them. Under the demonstration of the Holy Spirit's power, the Jews saw their guilt in refusing the evidence that God had sent; but they would not yield their wicked resistance. Their obstinacy became more and more determined, and worked the ruin of their souls. It was not that they could not yield, for they could, yet would not. It was not alone that they had been guilty, and deserving of wrath, but that they armed themselves with the attributes of Satan, and determinedly continued to be opposed to God. Every day, in their refusal to repent, they took up their rebellion afresh. They were preparing to reap that which they had sown. The wrath of God is not declared against men merely because of the sins which they have committed, but for choosing to continue in a state of resistance, and, although they have light and knowledge, repeating their sins of the past. If they would submit, they would be pardoned; but they are determined not to yield. They defy God by their obstinacy. These souls have given themselves to Satan, and he controls them according to his will.

How was it with the rebellious inhabitants of the antediluvian world? After rejecting the message of Noah, they plunged into sin with greater abandon than ever before, and doubled the enormity of their corrupting practices. Those who refuse to reform by accepting Christ find nothing reformative in sin; their minds are set to carry their spirit of revolt, and they are not, and never will be, forced to submission. The judgment which God brought upon the antediluvian world declared it incurable. The destruction of Sodom proclaimed the inhabitants of the most beautiful country in the world incorrigible in sin. The fire and brimstone from heaven consumed everything except Lot, his wife, and two daughters. The wife, looking back in disregard of God's command, became a pillar of salt.

How God bore with the Jewish nation while they were murmuring and rebellious, breaking the Sabbath and every other precept of the law! He repeatedly declared them worse than the heathen. Each generation surpassed the preceding in guilt. The Lord permitted them to go into captivity, but after their deliverance His requirements were forgotten. Everything that He committed to that people to be kept sacred was perverted or displaced by the inventions of rebellious men. Christ said to them in His day, "Did not Moses give you the law, and yet none of you keepeth the law?" And these were the men who set themselves up as judges and censors over those whom the Holy Spirit was moving to declare the word of God to the people. (See John 7:19-23, 27, 28; Luke 11:37-52.)

THE HOLY SPIRIT TO BE LEFT UNTRAMMELED

Read these scriptures to the people. Read carefully, solemnly, and the Holy Spirit will be by your side to impress minds as you read them. But do not fail to read with the true sense of the word in your own heart. If God has ever spoken by me, these scriptures mean very much to those who shall hear them.

Finite men should beware of seeking to control their fellowmen, taking the place assigned to the Holy Spirit. Let not men feel that it is their prerogative to give to the world what they suppose to be truth, and refuse that anything should be given contrary to their ideas. This is not their work. Many things will appear distinctly as truth which will not be acceptable to those who think their own interpretations of the Scripture always right. Most decided changes will have to be made in regard to ideas which some have accepted as without a flaw. These men give evidence of fallibility in very many ways; they work upon principles which the word of God condemns. That which makes me feel to the very depths of my being, and makes me know that their works are not the works of God, is that they suppose they have authority to rule their fellowmen. The Lord has given them no more right to rule others than He has given others to rule them. Those who assume the control of their fellowmen take into their finite hands a work that devolves upon God alone.

That men should keep alive the spirit which ran riot at Minneapolis* is an offense to God. All heaven is indignant at the spirit that for years has been revealed in our publishing institution at Battle Creek.* Unrighteous-

*See Appendix.

ness is practiced that God will not tolerate. He will visit for these things. A voice has been heard pointing out the errors and, in the name of the Lord, pleading for a decided change. But who have followed the instruction given? Who have humbled their hearts to put from them every vestige of their wicked, oppressive spirit? I have been greatly burdened to set these matters before the people as they are. I know they will see them. I know that those who read this matter will be convicted.

For further study: *Gospel Workers,* pages 297-315; *Testimonies,* vol. 5, pp. 706-709; *Selected Messages,* b. 1, pp. 155-208.

A Faithful Message

Hobart, Tasmania, May 1, 1895.

MANY HAVE OUTGROWN THEIR ADVENT FAITH

Because iniquity abounds, the love of many waxes cold. There are many who have outgrown their advent faith. They are living for the world, and while saying in their hearts, as they desire it shall be, "My Lord delayeth His coming," they are beating their fellow servants. They do this for the same reason that Cain killed Abel. Abel was determined to worship God according to the directions God had given. This displeased Cain. He thought that his own plans were best, and that the Lord would come to his terms. Cain in his offering did not acknowledge his dependence upon Christ. He thought that his father Adam had been treated harshly in being expelled from Eden. The idea of keeping that sin ever before the mind, and offering the blood of the slain lamb as a confession of entire dependence upon a power outside of himself, was torture to the high spirit of Cain. Being the eldest, he thought that Abel should follow his example. When Abel's offering was accepted of God, the holy fire consuming the sacrifice, Cain's anger was exceedingly great. The Lord condescended to explain matters to him; but he would not be reconciled to God, and he hated Abel because God showed him favor. He became so angry that he slew his brother.

The Lord has a controversy with all men who by their unbelief and doubt have been saying that He delays His coming, and who have been smiting their fellow servants, and eating and drinking with (working from the very same principle as) the drunken; they are drunken, but not with wine; they stagger, but not with strong drink. Satan has controlled their reason, and they know not at what they stumble.

RESULT OF SEPARATION FROM GOD

Just as soon as a man separates from God so that his heart is not under the subduing power of the Holy Spirit, the attributes of Satan will be revealed, and he will begin to oppress his fellowmen. An influence goes forth from him that is contrary to truth and justice and righteousness. This disposition is manifested in our institutions, not only in the relation of the workers to one another, but in the desire shown by one institution to control all others.* Men who are entrusted with weighty responsibilities, but who have no living connection with God, have been and are doing despite to His Holy Spirit. They are indulging the very same spirit as did Korah, Dathan, and Abiram, and as did the Jews in the days of Christ. (See Matthew 12:22-29, 31-37.) Warnings have come from God again and again for these men, but they have cast them aside and ventured on in the same course.

---

*See Appendix.

Read the words of Christ in Matthew 23:23: "Woe unto you, scribes and Pharisees, hypocrites! for ye pay tithe of mint and anise and cummin, and have omitted the weightier matters of the law, judgment, mercy, and faith: these ought ye to have done, and not to leave the other undone." These denunciations are given as a warning to all who "outwardly appear righteous unto men, but within" "are full of hypocrisy and iniquity." They say, We are delivered to do all these things. They also say, "If we had been in the days of our fathers, we would not have been partakers with them in the blood of the prophets. Wherefore," said Jesus, "ye be witnesses unto yourselves, that ye are the children of them which killed the prophets." What lessons are here; how fearful and decisive! Jesus said, "Wherefore, behold, I send unto you prophets, and wise men, and scribes: and some of them ye shall kill and crucify; and some of them shall ye scourge in your synagogues, and persecute them from city to city." This prophecy was literally fulfilled by the Jews in their treatment of Christ and of the messengers whom God sent to them. Will men in these last days follow the example of those whom Christ condemned?

These terrible predictions they have not as yet carried out to the full; but if God spares their lives, and they nourish the same spirit that marked their course of action both before and after the Minneapolis meeting,* they will fill up to the full the deeds of those whom Christ condemned when He was upon the earth.

The perils of the last days are upon us. *Satan takes the control of every mind that is not decidedly under the control of the Spirit of God.* Some have been cultivating hatred against the men whom God has commissioned to bear a special message to the world. They

---

*See Appendix.

began this satanic work at Minneapolis. Afterward, when they saw and felt the demonstration of the Holy Spirit testifying that the message was of God, they hated it the more, because it was a testimony against them. They would not humble their hearts to repent, to give God the glory, and vindicate the right. They went on in their own spirit, filled with envy, jealousy, and evil surmisings, as did the Jews. They opened their hearts to the enemy of God and man. Yet these men have been holding positions of trust, and have been molding the work after their own similitude, as far as they possibly could. . . .

EXHORTATION TO REPENTANCE

Those who are now first, who have been untrue to the cause of God, will soon be last, unless they repent. Unless they speedily fall upon the Rock and be broken, and be born again, the spirit that has been cherished will continue to be cherished. Mercy's sweet voice will not be recognized by them. Bible religion, in private and in public, is with them a thing of the past. They have been zealously declaiming against enthusiasm and fanaticism. Faith that calls upon God to relieve human suffering, faith that God has enjoined upon His people to exercise, is called fanaticism. But if there is anything upon the earth that should inspire men with sanctified zeal, it is the truth as it is in Jesus. It is the grand, great work of redemption. It is Christ, made unto us wisdom, and righteousness, and sanctification, and redemption.

The Lord has often made manifest in His providence that nothing less than revealed truth, the word of God, can reclaim man from sin or keep him from transgression. That word which reveals the guilt of sin has a power upon the human heart to make man right and keep him so. The Lord has said that His word is to be studied and obeyed; it is to be brought into the practical life; that word is as inflexible as the character of God—the same yesterday, today, and forever.

THE TRUE INSPIRATION TO ENTHUSIASM

If there is anything in our world that should inspire enthusiasm, it is the cross of Calvary. "Behold, what manner of love the Father hath bestowed upon us, that we should be called the sons of God: therefore the world knoweth us not, because it knew Him not." "For God so loved the world, that He gave His only-begotten Son, that whosoever believeth in Him should not perish, but have everlasting life." Christ is to be accepted, believed on, and exalted. This is to be the theme of conversation—the preciousness of Christ.

TRUTH TO BE ENTHRONED IN THE HEART

There is in Battle Creek a class that have the truth planted in the heart. It is to them the power of God unto salvation. But unless the truth is enthroned in the heart, and a thorough transition takes place from darkness to light, those who handle sacred responsibilities are ministers of darkness, blind leaders of the blind. "Clouds they are without water, carried about of winds; trees whose fruit withereth, without fruit, twice dead, plucked up by the roots." God requires that every soul that names His name shall have the truth enthroned in the heart. The time in which we live demands it. Eternity demands it. Pure religion demands it.

Worldly Amusements

PARTIES OF PLEASURE

While there has been so much fear of excitement and enthusiasm in the service of God, there has been manifest an enthusiasm in another line which to many seems wholly congenial. I refer to the parties of pleasure that have been held among our people. These occasions have taken much of the time and attention of people who profess to be servants of Christ; but have these assemblies tended to the glory of His name? Was Jesus invited to preside over them? Gatherings for social intercourse may be made in the highest degree profitable and instructive when those who meet together have the love of God glowing in their hearts, when they meet to exchange thoughts in regard to the word of God, or to consider methods for advancing His work, and doing good to their fellowmen. When nothing is said or done to grieve the Holy Spirit of God, but it is regarded as a welcome guest, then God is honored, and those who meet together will be refreshed and strengthened. "Then they that feared the Lord spake often one to another: and the Lord hearkened, and heard it, and a book of remembrance was written before Him for them that feared the Lord, and that thought upon His name. And they shall be Mine, saith the Lord of hosts, in that day when I make up My jewels."

But there has been a class of social gatherings in Battle Creek of an entirely different character, parties of pleasure that have been a disgrace to our institutions and to the church. They encourage pride of dress, pride of appearance, self-gratification, hilarity, and trifling. Satan

---

Special Testimony to Battle Creek Church (1896), pages 25-32.

is entertained as an honored guest, and he takes possession of those who patronize these gatherings. A view of one such company was presented to me, where were assembled those who profess to believe the truth. One was seated at the instrument of music, and such songs were poured forth as made the watching angels weep. There was mirth, there was coarse laughter, there was abundance of enthusiasm, and a kind of inspiration; but the joy was such as Satan only is able to create. This is an enthusiasm and infatuation of which all who love God will be ashamed. It prepares the participants for unholy thought and action. I have reason to think that some who were engaged in that scene heartily repented of the shameful performance.

EFFECT OF SUCH GATHERINGS

Many such gatherings have been presented to me. I have seen the gaiety, the display in dress, the personal adornment. All want to be thought brilliant, and give themselves up to hilarity, foolish jesting, cheap, coarse flattery, and uproarious laughter. The eyes sparkle, the cheek is flushed, conscience sleeps. With eating and drinking and merrymaking, they do their best to forget God. The scene of pleasure is their paradise. And heaven is looking on, seeing and hearing all.

BICYCLE SPORT

Turn to another scene. In the streets of the city is a party gathered for a bicycle race.* In this company also are those who profess to know God and Jesus Christ whom He has sent. But who that looks upon the exciting race would think that those who were thus exhibiting themselves were the followers of Christ? Who would suppose that any of that party felt their need of

---

*See Appendix.

Christ? Who would think they realized the value of their time and their physical powers as gifts from God, to be preserved for His service? Who thinks of the danger of accident, or that death may be the result of their wild chase? Who have prayed for the presence of Jesus, and the protection of the ministering angels? Is God glorified by these performances? Satan is playing the game of life for these souls, and he is well pleased with that which he sees and hears.

A PROFANATION OF RELIGION

The once earnest Christian who enters into these sports is on the downgrade. He has left the region pervaded by the vital atmosphere of heaven, and has plunged into an atmosphere of mist and fog. It may be some humble believer is induced to join in these sports. But if he maintains his connection with Christ, he cannot in heart participate in the exciting scene. The words he hears are not congenial, for they are not the language of Canaan. The speakers do not give evidence that they are making melody in their hearts to God. But there is unmistakable evidence that God is forgotten. He is not in all their thoughts. These parties of pleasure and gatherings for exciting sport, made up of those who profess to be Christians, are a profanation of religion and the name of God.

DECEPTIVE WORKING OF SATAN

The tenor of the conversation reveals the treasure of the heart. The cheap, common talk, the words of flattery, the foolish witticism, spoken to create a laugh, are the merchandise of Satan, and all who indulge in this talk are trading in his goods. Impressions are made upon those who hear these things similar to that made upon

Herod when the daughter of Herodias danced before him. All these transactions are recorded in the books of heaven; and at the last great day they will appear in their true light before the guilty ones. Then all will discern in them the alluring, deceptive workings of the devil, to lead them into the broad road and the wide gate that opens to their ruin.

PROFESSED CHRISTIANS AS DECOYS OF SATAN

Satan has been multiplying his snares in Battle Creek; and professed Christians who are superficial in character and religious experience are used by the tempter as his decoys. This class are always ready for the gatherings for pleasure or sport, and their influence attracts others. Young men and young women who have tried to be Bible Christians are persuaded to join the party, and they are drawn into the ring. They did not prayerfully consult the divine standard, to learn what Christ had said in regard to the fruit to be borne on the Christian tree. They do not discern that these entertainments are really Satan's banquet, prepared to keep souls from accepting the call to the marriage supper of the Lamb; they prevent them from receiving the white robe of character, which is the righteousness of Christ. They become confused as to what it is right for them as Christians to do. They do not want to be thought singular, and naturally incline to follow the example of others. Thus they come under the influence of those who have never had the divine touch on heart or mind.

In these exciting gatherings, carried away by the glamour and passion of human influence, youth that have been carefully instructed to obey the law of God, are led to form attachments for those whose education has been a mistake, and whose religious experience has been a fraud. They sell themselves to a lifelong bondage. As long as they live, they must be hampered by their union with a cheap, superficial character, one who lives for display, but who has not the precious, inward adorning, the ornament of a meek and quiet spirit, which in the sight of God is of great price. When sickness and death shall come to those who have lived to please themselves merely, they find that they have provided no oil in their vessels with their lamps, and they are utterly unfitted to close their life's history. This has been, this will continue to be.

We ask of those who have had great light in Battle Creek, Has the truth of God lost its hold upon the soul? Has the fine gold become dim? What has been the cause of this fanaticism and enthusiasm? A fearful accountability rests upon world-loving, selfish parents, for sin lies at their door. How much more favorable it would be if the school buildings that are now in Battle Creek were far off from the city, and separated from so large a colony of professed Sabbathkeepers!

DEPLORABLE CONVICTION GAINING GROUND

The conviction is gaining ground in the world that Seventh-day Adventists are giving the trumpet an uncertain sound, that they are following in the path of worldlings. Families in Battle Creek are departing from God, in planning contracts of marriage with those who have no love for God, with those who have lived a frivolous life, who have never practiced self-denial, and know not from experience what it means to be laborers together with God. Strange things are being transacted. False phases of Christianity are being received and taught, which bind souls in deception and delusion. Men are walking in the light of the sparks of their own kindling. Those who love and fear God will not descend to the world's level in choosing the society of the vain and trifling. They will not become charmed with men or women who are not converted. They are to stand up for Jesus, and then Jesus will stand up for them.

DISHONEST DEALINGS IN BUSINESS

Some of those who know the truth, but do not practice it, are trampling upon the law of God in their business transactions. We should have no intimate association with them, lest we catch their spirit, and share their doom. The patriarch Jacob, when speaking of certain deeds of his sons, which he contemplated with horror, exclaimed, "O my soul, come not thou into their secret; unto their assembly, mine honor, be not thou united." He felt that his own honor would be compromised if he associated with sinners in their doings. He lifts the danger signal to warn us away from such associations, lest we become partakers of their evil deeds. The Holy Spirit, through the apostle Paul, utters a similar warning, "Have no fellowship with the unfruitful works of darkness, but rather reprove them."

TRUE ATTITUDE OF THE CHRISTIAN

The eternal God has drawn the line of distinction between the saints and the sinners, the converted and the unconverted. The two classes do not blend into each other imperceptibly, like the colors of the rainbow. They are as distinct as midday and midnight.

Those who are seeking the righteousness of Christ will be dwelling upon the themes of the great salvation. The Bible is the storehouse that supplies their souls with nourishing food. They meditate upon the incarnation of Christ, they contemplate the great sacrifice made to save them from perdition, to bring in pardon, peace, and everlasting righteousness. The soul is aglow with these grand and elevating themes. Holiness and truth, grace and righteousness, occupy the thoughts. Self dies, and Christ lives in His servants. In contemplation of the word, their hearts burn within them, as did the hearts of the two disciples while they went to Emmaus, and Christ walked with them by the way, and opened to them the scriptures concerning Himself.

How few realize that Jesus, unseen, is walking by their side! How ashamed many would be to hear His voice speaking to them, and to know that He heard all their foolish, common talk! And how many hearts would burn with holy joy if they only knew that the Saviour was by their side, that the holy atmosphere of His presence was surrounding them, and they were feeding on the bread of life! How pleased the Saviour would be to hear His followers talking of His precious lessons of instruction, and to know that they had a relish for holy things! When the truth abides in the heart, there is no place for criticism of God's servants, or for picking flaws with the message He sends. That which is in the heart will flow from the lips. It cannot be repressed. The things that God has prepared for those that love Him will be the theme of conversation. The love of Christ is in the soul as a well of water, springing up into everlasting life, sending forth living streams that bring life and gladness wherever they flow.

For further study: *The Desire of Ages,* page 313; *Testimonies,* vol. 5, pp. 12-14, 74, 78, 206, 233, 505, 506, 542-549; vol. 2, pp. 289-292.

Rejecting the Light

God says to His servants, "Cry aloud, spare not, lift up thy voice like a trumpet, and show My people their transgression, and the house of Jacob their sins." But when the plain, straight testimony comes from lips under the moving of the Spirit of God, there are many who treat it with disdain. There are among us those who, in actions if not in words, "say to the seers, See not; and to the prophets, Prophesy not unto us right things, speak unto us smooth things, prophesy deceits: get you out of the way, turn aside out of the path, cause the Holy One of Israel to cease from before us. Wherefore thus saith the Holy One of Israel, Because ye despise this word, and trust in oppression and perverseness, and stay thereon: therefore this iniquity shall be to you as a breach ready to fall, swelling out in a high wall, whose breaking cometh suddenly at an instant. . . . For thus saith the Lord God, the Holy One of Israel; In returning and rest shall ye be saved; in quietness and in confidence shall be your strength: and ye would not."

CLEANSING OF THE HEART NEEDED

I inquire of those in responsible positions in Battle Creek, What are you doing? You have turned your back, and not your face, to the Lord. There needs to be a cleansing of the heart, the feelings, the sympathies, the words, in reference to the most momentous subjects—the Lord God, eternity, truth. What is the message to be given at this time? It is the third angel's message. But that light which is to fill the whole earth with its glory has been despised by some* who claim to believe the present truth. Be careful how you treat it. Take

---

Special Testimony to Battle Creek Church (1896), pages 32-42.

*See Appendix.

off the shoes from off your feet; for you are on holy ground. Beware how you indulge the attributes of Satan, and pour contempt upon the manifestation of the Holy Spirit. I know not but some have even now gone too far to return and to repent.

COMMUNICATION OF LIGHT

I state truth. The souls who love God, who believe in Christ, and who eagerly grasp every ray of light, will see light, and rejoice in the truth. They will communicate the light. They will grow in holiness. Those who receive the Holy Spirit will feel the chilling atmosphere that surrounds the souls of others by whom these great and solemn realities are unappreciated and spoken against. They feel that they are in the council of the ungodly, of men who stand in the way of sinners, and sit in the seat of the scornful.

The word of God speaketh truth, not a lie. In it is nothing strained, nothing extreme, nothing overdone. We are to accept it as the word of the living God. In obedience to that word, the church have duties to perform which they have not done. They are not to flee from the post of duty; but in trial and temptation they should lean more heavily upon God. There are difficulties to be met, but God's people as one must rise to the emergencies. There are duties to be discharged to the church and to our God.

The Spirit of God is departing from many among His people. Many have entered into dark, secret paths, and some will never return. They will continue to stumble to their ruin. They have tempted God, they have rejected light. All the evidence that will ever be given them they have received, and have not heeded. They have chosen darkness rather than light, and have defiled their souls. No man or church can associate with a pleasure-loving class, and reveal that they appreciate the rich current of truth which the Lord has sent to those who have simple faith in His word. The world is polluted, corrupted, as was the world in the days of Noah. The only remedy is belief in the truth, acceptance of the light. Yet many have listened to the truth spoken in demonstration of the Spirit, and they have not only refused to accept the message, but they have hated the light. These men are parties to the ruin of souls. They have interposed themselves between the heaven-sent light and the people. They have trampled upon the word of God and are doing despite to His Holy Spirit.

I call upon God's people to open their eyes. When you sanction or carry out the decisions of men who, as you know, are not in harmony with truth and righteousness, you weaken your own faith and lose your relish for communion with God. You seem to hear the voice which was addressed to Joshua: "Wherefore liest thou thus upon thy face? Israel hath sinned, and they have also transgressed My covenant which I commanded them. . . . There is an accursed thing in the midst of thee, O Israel." "Neither will I be with you anymore, except ye destroy the accursed from among you." Christ declares, "He that gathereth not with Me scattereth abroad."

THE MESSAGE OF JUSTIFICATION BY FAITH

The Lord in His great mercy sent a most precious message to His people through Elders Waggoner and Jones.* This message was to bring more prominently before the world the uplifted Saviour, the sacrifice for the sins of the whole world. It presented justification

*See Appendix.

through faith in the Surety; it invited the people to receive the righteousness of Christ, which is made manifest in obedience to all the commandments of God. Many had lost sight of Jesus. They needed to have their eyes directed to His divine person, His merits, and His changeless love for the human family. All power is given into His hands, that He may dispense rich gifts unto men, imparting the priceless gift of His own righteousness to the helpless human agent. This is the message that God commanded to be given to the world. It is the third angel's message, which is to be proclaimed with a loud voice, and attended with the outpouring of His Spirit in a large measure.

The uplifted Saviour is to appear in His efficacious work as the Lamb slain, sitting upon the throne, to dispense the priceless covenant blessings, the benefits He died to purchase for every soul who should believe on Him. John could not express that love in words; it was too deep, too broad; he calls upon the human family to behold it. Christ is pleading for the church in the heavenly courts above, pleading for those for whom He paid the redemption price of His own lifeblood. Centuries, ages, can never diminish the efficacy of this atoning sacrifice. The message of the gospel of His grace was to be given to the church in clear and distinct lines, that the world should no longer say that Seventh-day Adventists talk the law, the law, but do not teach or believe Christ.

The efficacy of the blood of Christ was to be presented to the people with freshness and power, that their faith might lay hold upon its merits. As the high priest sprinkled the warm blood upon the mercy seat, while the fragrant cloud of incense ascended before God, so while we confess our sins and plead the efficacy of Christ's atoning blood, our prayers are to ascend to heaven, fragrant with the merits of our Saviour's character. Notwithstanding our unworthiness, we are ever to bear in mind that there is One that can take away sin and save the sinner. Every sin acknowledged before God with a contrite heart, He will remove. This faith is the life of the church. As the serpent was lifted up in the wilderness by Moses, and all that had been bitten by the fiery serpents were bidden to look and live, so also the Son of man must be lifted up, that "whosoever believeth in Him should not perish, but have everlasting life."

Unless he makes it his life business to behold the uplifted Saviour, and by faith to accept the merits which it is his privilege to claim, the sinner can no more be saved than Peter could walk upon the water unless he kept his eyes fixed steadily upon Jesus. Now, it has been Satan's determined purpose to eclipse the view of Jesus and lead men to look to man, and trust to man, and be educated to expect help from man. For years the church has been looking to man and expecting much from man, but not looking to Jesus, in whom our hopes of eternal life are centered. Therefore God gave to His servants a testimony that presented the truth as it is in Jesus, which is the third angel's message, in clear, distinct lines. John's words are to be sounded by God's people, that all may discern the light and walk in the light: "He that cometh from above is above all: he that is of the earth is earthly, and speaketh of the earth: He that cometh from heaven is above all. And what He hath seen and heard, that He testifieth; and no man receiveth His testimony. He that hath received His testimony hath set to his seal that God is true. For He whom God hath sent speaketh the words of God: for God giveth not the Spirit by measure unto Him. The Father loveth the Son, and hath given all things into His hand. He that believeth on the Son hath everlasting life: and he that believeth not the Son shall not see life; but the wrath of God abideth on him."

This is the testimony that must go throughout the length and breadth of the world. It presents the law and the gospel, binding up the two in a perfect whole. (See Romans 5 and 1 John 3:9 to the close of the chapter.) These precious scriptures will be impressed upon every heart that is opened to receive them. "The entrance of Thy words giveth light; it giveth understanding unto the simple"—those who are contrite in heart. "As many as received Him, to them gave He power to become the sons of God, even to them that believe on His name." These have not a mere nominal faith, a theory of truth, a legal religion, but they believe to a purpose, appropriating to themselves the richest gifts of God. They plead for the gift, that they may give to others. They can say, "Of His fullness have all we received, and grace for grace."

"He that loveth not knoweth not God; for God is love. In this was manifested the love of God toward us, because that God sent His only-begotten Son into the world, that we might live through Him. Herein is love, not that we loved God, but that He loved us, and sent His Son to be the propitiation for our sins. Beloved, if God so loved us, we ought also to love one another. No man hath seen God at any time. If we love one another, God dwelleth in us, and His love is perfected in us. Hereby know we that we dwell in Him, and He in us, because He hath given us of His Spirit."

GOD'S MESSAGE FOR THE PRESENT TIME

This is the very work which the Lord designs that the message He has given His servants shall perform in the heart and mind of every human agent. It is the perpetual life of the church to love God supremely and to love others as they love themselves. There was but little love for God or man, and God gave to His messengers just what the people needed. Those who received the message were greatly blessed, for they saw the bright rays of the Sun of Righteousness, and life and hope sprang up in their hearts. They were beholding Christ. "Fear not," is His everlasting assurance; "I am He that liveth, and was dead; and, behold, I am alive forevermore." "Because I live, ye shall live also." The blood of the spotless Lamb of God the believers apply to their own hearts. Looking upon the great Antitype, we can say, "It is Christ that died, yea rather, that is risen again, who is even at the right hand of God, who also maketh intercession for us." The Sun of Righteousness shines into our hearts to give the knowledge of the glory of Jesus Christ. Of the Holy Spirit's office He says, "He shall glorify Me: for He shall receive of Mine, and shall show it unto you." The psalmist prays, "Purge me with hyssop, and I shall be clean: wash me, and I shall be whiter than snow. . . . Create in me a clean heart, O God; and renew a right spirit within me. Cast me not away from Thy presence; and take not Thy Holy Spirit from me. Restore unto me the joy of Thy salvation; and uphold me with Thy free Spirit. Then will I teach transgressors Thy ways; and sinners shall be converted unto Thee."

The Lord would have these grand themes studied

in our churches, and if every church member shall give entrance to the word of God, it will give light and understanding to the simple. "Who is among you that feareth the Lord, that obeyeth the voice of His servant, that walketh in darkness, and hath no light? let him trust in the name of the Lord, and stay upon his God. Behold, all ye that kindle a fire, that compass yourselves about with sparks: walk in the light of your fire, and in the sparks that ye have kindled. This shall ye have of Mine hand; ye shall lie down in sorrow." (See Isaiah 29:13-16, 18-21.) "Thus saith the Lord, Let not the wise man glory in his wisdom, neither let the mighty man glory in his might, let not the rich man glory in his riches: but let him that glorieth glory in this, that he understandeth and knoweth Me, that I am the Lord which exercise loving-kindness, judgment, and righteousness, in the earth: for in these things I delight, saith the Lord."

Never was there a time when the Lord would manifest His great grace unto His chosen ones more fully than in these last days when His law is made void. "The Lord is well pleased for His righteousness' sake; He will magnify the law, and make it honorable." What does God say in regard to His people? "But this is a people robbed and spoiled; they are all of them snared in holes, and they are hid in prison houses: they are for a prey, and none delivereth; for a spoil, and none saith, Restore." (See also Isaiah 43.) These are prophecies that will be fulfilled.

WARNING AGAINST DESPISING GOD'S MESSAGE

I would speak in warning to those who have stood for years resisting light* and cherishing the spirit of opposition. How long will you hate and despise the messengers of God's righteousness? God has given

*See Appendix.

them His message. They bear the word of the Lord. There is salvation for you, but only through the merits of Jesus Christ. The grace of the Holy Spirit has been offered you again and again. Light and power from on high have been shed abundantly in the midst of you. Here was evidence, that all might discern whom the Lord recognized as His servants. But there are those who despised the men and the message they bore. They have taunted them with being fanatics, extremists, and enthusiasts. Let me prophesy unto you: Unless you speedily humble your hearts before God, and confess your sins, which are many, you will, when it is too late, see that you have been fighting against God. Through the conviction of the Holy Spirit, no longer unto reformation and pardon, you will see that these men whom you have spoken against have been as signs in the world, as witnesses for God. Then you would give the whole world if you could redeem the past, and be just such zealous men, moved by the Spirit of God to lift your voice in solemn warning to the world; and, like them, to be in principle firm as a rock. Your turning things upside down is known of the Lord. Go on a little longer as you have gone, in rejection of the light from heaven, and you are lost. "The man that shall be unclean, and shall not purify himself, that soul shall be cut off from among the congregation."

I have no smooth message to bear to those who have been so long as false guideposts, pointing the wrong way. If you reject Christ's delegated messengers, you reject Christ. Neglect this great salvation, kept before you for years, despise this glorious offer of justification through the blood of Christ and sanctification through the cleansing power of the Holy Spirit, and there remaineth no more sacrifice for sins, but a certain fearful looking for of judgment and fiery indignation. I entreat you now to humble yourselves and cease your stubborn resistance of light and evidence. Say unto the Lord, Mine iniquities have separated between me and my God. O Lord, pardon my transgressions. Blot out my sins from the book of Thy remembrance. Praise His holy name, there is forgiveness with Him, and you can be converted, transformed.

"For if the blood of bulls and of goats, and the ashes of an heifer sprinkling the unclean, sanctifieth to the purifying of the flesh: how much more shall the blood of Christ, who through the eternal Spirit offered Himself without spot to God, purge your conscience from dead works to serve the living God?"

For further study: *Gospel Workers,* pages 297-304; *Selected Messages,* b. 1, pp. 350-400.

"Let Him That Thinketh He Standeth Take Heed Lest He Fall"

IDOLATRY OF THE CHILDREN OF ISRAEL

"Moreover, brethren, I would not that ye should be ignorant, how that all our fathers were under the cloud, and all passed through the sea; and were all baptized unto Moses in the cloud and in the sea; and did all eat the same spiritual meat; and did all drink the same spiritual drink: for they drank of that spiritual Rock that followed them: and that Rock was Christ. But with many of them God was not well pleased: for they were overthrown in the wilderness." The experience of Israel, referred to in the above words by the apostle, and as recorded in the one hundred fifth and one hundred sixth psalms, contains lessons of warning that the people of God in these last days especially need to study. I urge

Special Testimony to Battle Creek Church (1896), pages 43–48.

that these chapters be read at least once every week.

"Now these things were our examples, to the intent we should not lust after evil things, as they also lusted. Neither be ye idolaters, as were some of them; as it is written, The people sat down to eat and drink, and rose up to play."

In the hearing of all Israel, God had spoken in awful majesty upon Mount Sinai, declaring the precepts of His law. The people, overwhelmed with the sense of guilt, and fearing to be consumed by the glory of the presence of the Lord, had entreated Moses, "Speak thou with us, and we will hear: but let not God speak with us, lest we die." God called Moses up into the mount that He might communicate to him the laws for Israel, but how quickly the solemn impression made upon that people by the manifestation of God's presence passed away. Even the leaders of the host seemed to have lost their reason. The memory of their covenant with God, their terror when, falling upon their faces, they had exceedingly feared and quaked, all had vanished like smoke. Although the glory of God was still like devouring fire upon the top of the mount, yet when the presence of Moses was withdrawn, the old habits of thought and feeling began to assert their power. The people wearied of waiting for the return of Moses and began to clamor for some visible representation of God.

Aaron, who had been left in charge of the camp, yielded to their clamors. Instead of exercising faith in God, trusting to divine power to sustain him, he was tempted to believe that if he resisted the demands of the people, they would take his life; and he did as they desired. He collected the golden ornaments, made the molten calf, and fashioned it with a graving tool. Then the leaders of the people declared, "These be thy gods, O Israel, which brought thee up out of the land of

Egypt." When Aaron saw that the image he had graven pleased the people, he was proud of his workmanship. He built an altar before the idol, "made proclamation, and said, Tomorrow is a feast to the Lord. And they rose up early on the morrow, and offered burnt offerings, and brought peace offerings; and the people sat down to eat and to drink, and rose up to play." They drank and feasted, and gave themselves up to mirth and dancing, which ended in the shameful orgies that marked the heathen worship of false gods.

God in heaven beheld it all, and warned Moses of what was taking place in the camp, saying, "Now therefore let Me alone, that My wrath may wax hot against them, and that I may consume them: and I will make of thee a great nation. And Moses besought the Lord his God, and said, Lord, why doth Thy wrath wax hot against Thy people, which Thou has brought forth out of the land of Egypt with great power, and with a mighty hand? Wherefore should the Egyptians speak, and say, For mischief did He bring them out, to slay them in the mountains, and to consume them from the face of the earth? Turn from Thy fierce wrath, and repent of this evil against Thy people. Remember Abraham, Isaac, and Israel, Thy servants, to whom Thou swarest by Thine own self, and saidst unto them, I will multiply your seed as the stars of heaven, and all this land that I have spoken of will I give unto your seed, and they shall inherit it forever. And the Lord repented of the evil which He thought to do unto His people."

As Moses came down from the mountain with the two tables of the testimony in his hand, he heard the shouts of the people, and, as he came near, beheld the idol and the reveling multitude. Overwhelmed with horror and indignation that God had been dishonored, and that the people had broken their solemn covenant with Him, he cast the two tables of stone upon the ground and broke them beneath the mount. Though his love for Israel was so great that he was willing to lay down his own life for them, yet his zeal for the glory of God moved him to anger, which found expression in this act of such terrible significance. God did not rebuke him. The breaking of the tables of stone was but a representation of the fact that Israel had broken the covenant which they had so recently made with God. It is a righteous indignation against sin, which springs from zeal for the glory of God, not that anger prompted by self-love or wounded ambition, which is referred to in the scripture, "Be ye angry, and sin not." Such was the anger of Moses.

"And he took the calf which they had made, and burnt it in the fire, and ground it to powder, and strewed it upon the water, and made the children of Israel drink of it. And Moses said unto Aaron, What did this people unto thee, that thou hast brought so great a sin upon them? And Aaron said, Let not the anger of my lord wax hot: thou knowest the people, that they are set on mischief. For they said unto me, Make us gods, which shall go before us: for as for this Moses, the man that brought us up out of the land of Egypt, we wot not what is become of him." And "Moses saw that the people were naked; (for Aaron had made them naked unto their shame among their enemies)."

SPECIAL INFLUENCE OF SATAN'S WORK

To us the warning is given, "All these things happened unto them for ensamples: and they are written for our admonition, upon whom the ends of the world are come." Mark the influence of their extremes and fanaticism in the service of the great master worker, Satan. As soon as the wicked one had the people under his control, there were exhibitions of a satanic character. The people ate and drank without a thought of God and His mercy, without a thought of the necessity of resisting the devil, who was leading them on to the most shameful deeds. The same spirit was manifested as at the sacrilegious feast of Belshazzar. There was glee and dancing, hilarity and singing, carried to an infatuation that beguiled the senses; then the indulgence in inordinate, lustful affections—all this mingled in that disgraceful scene. God had been dishonored; His people had become a shame in the sight of the heathen. Judgments were about to fall on that infatuated, besotted multitude. Yet God in His mercy gave them opportunity to forsake their sins.

"Then Moses stood in the gate of the camp, and said, Who is on the Lord's side?" The trumpeters caught up the words, and sounded them through the trumpet, "Who is on the Lord's side? let him come unto me. And all the sons of Levi gathered themselves together unto him." All who were repentant had the privilege of taking their stand beside Moses. "And he said unto them, Thus saith the Lord God of Israel, Put every man his sword by his side, and go in and out from gate to gate throughout the camp, and slay every man his brother, and every man his companion, and every man his neighbor. And the children of Levi did according to the word of Moses: and there fell of the people that day about three thousand men." There was no partiality, no hypocrisy, no confederating to shield the guilty. For the terror of the Lord was upon the people.

Those who had shown so little sense of the presence and the greatness of God, and who, after the exhibition of His majesty, were ready to depart from the Lord, would be a continual snare to Israel. They were slain, as a rebuke to sin, and to put a fear upon the people to dishonor God.

DANGER OF SELF-PLEASING

I cannot now consider this history further, but I ask you in every city, in every town, in every household, I ask every individual, to study the lesson of this scripture, bearing in mind the words of inspiration, "Let him that thinketh he standeth take heed lest he fall." Here is presented the only election that is brought to view in the word of God. It is those who take heed lest they fall that will be accepted at last. There can be no presumption more fatal than that which leads men to venture upon a course of self-pleasing. In view of this solemn warning from God, should not fathers and mothers take heed? Should they not faithfully point out to the youth the dangers that are constantly arising to lead them away from God? Many allow the youth to attend parties of pleasure, thinking that amusement is essential for health and happiness; but what dangers are in that path! The more the desire for pleasure is gratified, the more it is cultivated and the stronger it becomes. The life experience is largely made up of self-gratification in amusement. God bids us to beware. "Let him that thinketh he standeth take heed lest he fall."

For further study: Consult "Youth" in the Index of *Testimonies,* vol. 2.

We should come into a position where every difference will be melted away. If I think I have light, I shall do my duty in presenting it. Suppose I consulted others concerning the message the Lord would have me give to the people; the door might be closed so that the light might not reach the ones to whom God had sent it. When Jesus rode into Jerusalem, "the whole multitude of the disciples began to rejoice and praise God with a loud voice for all the mighty works that they had seen; saying, Blessed be the King that cometh in the name of the Lord: peace in heaven, and glory in the highest. And some of the Pharisees from among the multitude said unto Him, Master, rebuke Thy disciples. And He answered and said unto them, I tell you that, if these should hold their peace, the stones would immediately cry out."—*Review and Herald,* February 18, 1890.

My brethren, in His great mercy and love God has given you great light, and Christ says to you, "Freely ye have received, freely give." Let the light bestowed on you shine forth to those in darkness. Let us rejoice and be glad that Christ has not only given us His word, but has given us also the spirit of wisdom and revelation in the knowledge of God, and that in His strength we may be more than conquerors. Christ is saying: "Come unto Me. To Me belong right counsel and sound judgment. I have understanding and strength for you." By faith we must rest in Christ, remembering the words of one who was inspired of God to write, "Thy gentleness hath made me great." Ask God to give you much of the oil of His grace. Carefully consider every word, whether it be written or spoken.—*Review and Herald,* December 22, 1904.

The Holy Scriptures 3

How Shall We Search the Scriptures?

How shall we search the Scriptures in order to understand what they teach? We should come to the investigation of God's word with a contrite heart, a teachable and prayerful spirit. We are not to think, as did the Jews, that our own ideas and opinions are infallible; nor with the papists, that certain individuals are the sole guardians of truth and knowledge, that men have no right to search the Scriptures for themselves, but must accept the explanations given by the fathers of the church. We should not study the Bible for the purpose of sustaining our preconceived opinions, but with the single object of learning what God has said.

Some have feared that if in even a single point they acknowledge themselves in error, other minds would be led to doubt the whole theory of truth. Therefore they have felt that investigation should not be permitted, that it would tend to dissension and disunion. But if such is to be the result of investigation, the sooner it comes the better. If there are those whose faith in God's word will not stand the test of an investigation of the Scriptures, the sooner they are revealed the better; for then the way will be opened to show them their error. We cannot hold that a position once taken, an idea once advocated, is not, under any circumstances, to be relinquished. There is but One who is infallible—He who is the way, the truth, and the life.

Those who allow prejudice to bar the mind against the reception of truth cannot receive the divine enlightenment. Yet, when a view of Scripture is presented,

---

Gospel Workers, 1893 edition, pages 125-131.

many do not ask, Is it true—in harmony with God's word? but, By whom is it advocated? and unless it comes through the very channel that pleases them, they do not accept it. So thoroughly satisfied are they with their own ideas that they will not examine the Scripture evidence with a desire to learn, but refuse to be interested, merely because of their prejudices.

The Lord often works where we least expect Him; He surprises us by revealing His power through instruments of His own choice, while He passes by the men to whom we have looked as those through whom light should come. God desires us to receive the truth upon its own merits—because it is truth.

The Bible must not be interpreted to suit the ideas of men, however long they may have held these ideas to be true. We are not to accept the opinion of commentators as the voice of God; they were erring mortals like ourselves. God has given reasoning powers to us as well as to them. We should make the Bible its own expositor.

CAREFULNESS IN PRESENTING NEW VIEWS

All should be careful about presenting new views of Scripture before they have given these points thorough study, and are fully prepared to sustain them from the Bible. Introduce nothing that will cause dissension, without clear evidence that in it God is giving a special message for this time.

But beware of rejecting that which is truth. The great danger with our people has been that of depending upon men and making flesh their arm. Those who have not been in the habit of searching the Bible for themselves, or weighing evidence, have confidence in the leading men and accept the decisions they make; and thus many will reject the very messages God sends to His people, if these leading brethren do not accept them.

No one should claim that he has all the light there is for God's people. The Lord will not tolerate this. He has said, "I have set before thee an open door, and no man can shut it." Even if all our leading men should refuse light and truth, that door will still remain open. The Lord will raise up men who will give the people the message for this time.

THE TRUTH WILL STAND

Truth is eternal, and conflict with error will only make manifest its strength. We should never refuse to examine the Scriptures with those who, we have reason to believe, desire to know what is truth. Suppose a brother held a view that differed from yours, and he should come to you, proposing that you sit down with him and make an investigation of that point in the Scriptures; should you rise up, filled with prejudice, and condemn his ideas, while refusing to give him a candid hearing? The only right way would be to sit down as Christians and investigate the position presented in the light of God's word, which will reveal truth and unmask error. To ridicule his ideas would not weaken his position in the least if it were false, or strengthen your position if it were true. If the pillars of our faith will not stand the test of investigation, it is time that we knew it. There must be no spirit of Pharisaism cherished among us.

THE SCRIPTURES TO BE STUDIED WITH REVERENCE

We should come with reverence to the study of the Bible, feeling that we are in the presence of God. All lightness and trifling should be laid aside. While some portions of the word are easily understood, the true meaning of other parts is not so readily discerned. There must be patient study and meditation and earnest prayer. Every student, as he opens the Scriptures, should ask for the enlightenment of the Holy Spirit; and the promise is sure that it will be given.

The spirit in which you come to the investigation of the Scriptures will determine the character of the assistant at your side. Angels from the world of light will be with those who in humility of heart seek for divine guidance. But if the Bible is opened with irreverence, with a feeling of self-sufficiency, if the heart is filled with prejudice, Satan is beside you, and he will set the plain statements of God's word in a perverted light.

There are some who indulge in levity, sarcasm, and even mockery toward those who differ with them. Others present an array of objections to any new view; and when these objections are plainly answered by the words of Scripture, they do not acknowledge the evidence presented, nor allow themselves to be convinced. Their questioning is not for the purpose of arriving at truth, but is intended merely to confuse the minds of others.

Some have thought it an evidence of intellectual keenness and superiority to perplex minds in regard to what is truth. They resort to subtlety of argument, to playing upon words; they take unjust advantage in asking questions. When their questions have been fairly answered, they will turn the subject [and] bring up another point to avoid acknowledging the truth. We should beware of indulging the spirit which controlled the Jews. They would not learn of Christ, because His explanation of the Scriptures did not agree with their ideas; therefore they became spies upon His track, "laying wait for Him, and seeking to catch something out of His mouth, that they might accuse Him." Let us not bring upon ourselves the fearful denunciation of the Saviour's words, "Woe unto you, lawyers! for ye have taken away the key of knowledge: ye entered not in yourselves, and them that were entering in ye hindered."

IN SIMPLICITY AND FAITH

It does not require much learning or ability to ask questions that are difficult to answer. A child may ask questions over which the wisest men may be puzzled. Let us not engage in a contest of this kind. The very same unbelief exists in our time as prevailed in the days of Christ. Now as then the desire for preferment and the praise of men leads people away from the simplicity of true godliness. There is no pride so dangerous as spiritual pride.

Young men should search the Scriptures for themselves. They are not to feel that it is sufficient for those older in experience to find out the truth; that the younger ones can accept it from them as authority. The Jews perished as a nation because they were drawn from the truth of the Bible by their rulers, priests, and elders. Had they heeded the lessons of Jesus, and searched the Scriptures for themselves, they would not have perished.

Young men in our ranks are watching to see in what spirit the ministers come to the investigation of the Scriptures; whether they have a teachable spirit, and are humble enough to accept evidence, and receive light from the messengers whom God chooses to send.

We must study the truth for ourselves. No man should be relied upon to think for us. No matter who he is, or in what position he may be placed, we are not to look upon any man as a criterion for us. We are to counsel together, and to be subject one to another; but at the same time we are to exercise the ability God has given us, in order to learn what is truth. Each one of us must look to God for divine enlightenment. We must individually develop a character that will stand the test in the day of God. We must not become set in our ideas, and think that no one should interfere with our opinions.

When a point of doctrine that you do not understand comes to your attention, go to God on your knees, that you may understand what is truth and not be found as were the Jews fighting against God. While warning men to beware of accepting anything unless it is truth, we should also warn them not to imperil their souls by rejecting messages of light, but to press out of the darkness by earnest study of the word of God.

When Nathanael came to Jesus, the Saviour exclaimed, "Behold an Israelite indeed, in whom is no guile!" Nathanael said, "Whence knowest Thou me?" Jesus answered, "When thou wast under the fig tree, I saw thee." And Jesus will see us also in the secret places of prayer, if we seek Him for light that we may know what is truth.

If a brother is teaching error, those who are in responsible positions ought to know it; and if he is teaching truth, they ought to take their stand at his side. We should all know what is being taught among us; for if it is truth, we need to know it. The Sabbath school teacher needs to know it, and every Sabbath school scholar ought to understand it. We are all under obligation to God to understand what He sends us. He has given directions by which we may test every doctrine—"To the law and to the testimony: if they speak not according to this word, it is because there is no light in them." But if it is according to this test, do not be so full of prejudice that you cannot acknowledge a point simply because it does not agree with your ideas.

It is impossible for any mind to comprehend all the richness and greatness of even one promise of God. One catches the glory of one point of view, another the beauty and grace from another point, and the soul is filled with the heavenly light. If we saw all the glory, the spirit would faint. But we can bear far greater revelations from God's abundant promises than we now enjoy. It makes my heart sad to think how we lose sight of the fullness of blessing designed for us. We content ourselves with momentary flashes of spiritual illumination, when we might walk day after day in the light of His presence.

Dear brethren, pray as you never before prayed for beams from the Sun of Righteousness to shine upon the word, that you may be able to understand its true meaning. Jesus pleaded that His disciples might be sanctified through the truth—the word of God. Then how earnestly should we pray that He who "searcheth all things, yea, the deep things of God," He whose office it is to bring all things to the remembrance of God's people, and to guide them into all truth, may be with us in the investigation of His Holy Word.

For further study: *Gospel Workers,* pages 98-100, 249-254.

God wants us to depend upon Him, and not upon man. He desires us to have a new heart; He would give us revealings of light from the throne of God.—*Review and Herald,* February 18, 1890.

The Study of the Books of Daniel and the Revelation

God's Spirit has illuminated every page of Holy Writ, but there are those upon whom it makes little impression, because it is imperfectly understood. When the shaking comes, by the introduction of false theories, these surface readers, anchored nowhere, are like shifting sand. They slide into any position to suit the tenor of their feelings of bitterness. . . . Daniel and Revelation must be studied, as well as the other prophecies of the Old and New Testaments. Let there be light, yes, light, in your dwellings. For this we need to pray. The Holy Spirit, shining upon the sacred page, will open our understanding, that we may know what is truth. . . .

There is need of a much closer study of the word of God; especially should Daniel and the Revelation have attention as never before in the history of our work. We may have less to say in some lines, in regard to the Roman power and the papacy; but we should call attention to what the prophets and apostles have written under the inspiration of the Holy Spirit of God. The Holy Spirit has so shaped matters, both in the giving of the prophecy and in the events portrayed, as to teach that the human agent is to be kept out of sight, hid in Christ, and that the Lord God of heaven and His law are to be exalted. Read the book of Daniel. Call up, point by point, the history of the kingdoms there represented. Behold statesmen, councils, powerful armies, and see how God wrought to abase the pride of men, and lay human glory in the dust. . . .

The light that Daniel received from God was given

Compiled from various publications, and from manuscripts of large circulation.

especially for these last days. The visions he saw by the banks of the Ulai and the Hiddekel, the great rivers of Shinar, are now in process of fulfillment, and all the events foretold will soon have come to pass.

Consider the circumstances of the Jewish nation when the prophecies of Daniel were given.

Let us give more time to the study of the Bible. We do not understand the word as we should. The book of Revelation opens with an injunction to us to understand the instruction that it contains. "Blessed is he that readeth, and they that hear the words of this prophecy," God declares, "and keep those things which are written therein: for the time is at hand." When we as a people understand what this book means to us, there will be seen among us a great revival. We do not understand fully the lessons that it teaches, notwithstanding the injunction given us to search and study it.

In the past teachers have declared Daniel and the Revelation to be sealed books, and the people have turned from them. The veil whose apparent mystery has kept many from lifting it, God's own hand has withdrawn from these portions of His word. The very name "Revelation" contradicts the statement that it is a sealed book. "Revelation" means that something of importance is revealed. The truths of this book are addressed to those living in these last days. We are standing with the veil removed in the holy place of sacred things. We are not to stand without. We are to enter, not with careless, irreverent thoughts, not with impetuous footsteps, but with reverence and godly fear. We are nearing the time when the prophecies of the book of Revelation are to be fulfilled. . . .

We have the commandments of God and the testimony of Jesus Christ, which is the spirit of prophecy. Priceless gems are to be found in the word of God. Those who search this word should keep the mind clear. Never should they indulge perverted appetite in eating or drinking.

If they do this, the brain will be confused; they will be unable to bear the strain of digging deep to find out the meaning of those things which relate to the closing scenes of this earth's history.

When the books of Daniel and Revelation are better understood, believers will have an entirely different religious experience. They will be given such glimpses of the open gates of heaven that heart and mind will be impressed with the character that all must develop in order to realize the blessedness which is to be the reward of the pure in heart.

The Lord will bless all who will seek humbly and meekly to understand that which is revealed in the Revelation. This book contains so much that is large with immortality and full of glory that all who read and search it earnestly receive the blessing to those "that hear the words of this prophecy, and keep those things which are written therein."

RESULT OF TRUE STUDY

One thing will certainly be understood from the study of Revelation—that the connection between God and His people is close and decided.

A wonderful connection is seen between the universe of heaven and this world. The things revealed to Daniel were afterward complemented by the revelation made to John on the Isle of Patmos. These two books should be carefully studied. Twice Daniel inquired, How long shall it be to the end of time?

"And I heard, but I understood not: then said I, O my Lord, what shall be the end of these things? And He said, Go thy way, Daniel: for the words are closed up and sealed till the time of the end. Many shall be purified, and made white, and tried; but the wicked shall do wickedly: and none of the wicked shall understand; but the wise shall understand. And from the time that the daily sacrifice shall be taken away, and the abomination that maketh desolate set up, there shall be a thousand two hundred and ninety days. Blessed is he that waiteth, and cometh to the thousand three hundred and five and thirty days. But go thou thy way till the end be: for thou shalt rest, and stand in thy lot at the end of the days."

It was the Lion of the tribe of Judah who unsealed the book and gave to John the revelation of what should be in these last days.

Daniel stood in his lot to bear his testimony which was sealed until the time of the end, when the first angel's message should be proclaimed to our world. These matters are of infinite importance in these last days; but while "many shall be purified, and made white, and tried," "the wicked shall do wickedly: and none of the wicked shall understand." How true this is! Sin is the transgression of the law of God; and those who will not accept the light in regard to the law of God will not understand the proclamation of the first, second, and third angels' messages. The book of Daniel is unsealed in the revelation to John, and carries us forward to the last scenes of this earth's history.

Will our brethren bear in mind that we are living amid the perils of the last days? Read Revelation in connection with Daniel. Teach these things.

UNCONQUERABLE FORCES WAITING

Those who eat the flesh and drink the blood of the Son of God will bring from the books of Daniel and Revelation truth that is inspired by the Holy Spirit. They will start into action forces that cannot be repressed. The lips of children will be opened to proclaim the mysteries that have been hidden from the minds of men.

We are standing on the threshold of great and solemn events. Many of the prophecies are about to be fulfilled in quick succession. Every element of power is about to be set to work. Past history will be repeated; old controversies will arouse to new life, and peril will beset God's people on every side. Intensity is taking hold of the human family. It is permeating everything upon the earth. . . .

Study Revelation in connection with Daniel, for history will be repeated. . . . We, with all our religious advantages, ought to know far more today than we do know.

Angels desire to look into the truths that are revealed to the people who with contrite hearts are searching the word of God and praying for greater lengths and breadths and depths and heights of the knowledge which He alone can give.

As we near the close of this world's history, the prophecies relating to the last days especially demand our study. The last book of the New Testament Scriptures is full of truth that we need to understand. Satan has blinded the minds of many so that they have been glad of any excuse for not making the Revelation their study. But Christ through His servant John has here declared what shall be in the last days; and He says, "Blessed is he that readeth, and they that hear the words of this prophecy, and keep those things which are written therein."

The books of Daniel and the Revelation should be bound together and published. A few explanations of certain portions might be added, but I am not sure that these would be needed.

This is the suggestion that I made to Elder Haskell* which resulted in the book he published. The need is not filled by this book. It was my idea to have the two books bound together, Revelation following Daniel, as giving fuller light on the subjects dealt with in Daniel. The object is to bring these books together, showing that they both relate to the same subjects.

A message that will arouse the churches is to be proclaimed. Every effort is to be made to give the light, not only to our people, but to the world. I have been instructed that the prophecies of Daniel and the Revelation should be printed in small books, with the necessary explanations, and should be sent all over the world. Our own people need to have the light placed before them in clearer lines.

The vision that Christ presented to John, presenting the commandments of God and the faith of Jesus, is to be definitely proclaimed to all nations, people, and tongues. The churches, represented by Babylon, are represented as having fallen from their spiritual state to become a persecuting power against those who keep the commandments of God and have the testimony of Jesus Christ. To John this persecuting power is represented as having horns like a lamb, but as speaking like a dragon. . . .

As we near the close of time, there will be greater and still greater external parade of heathen power; heathen deities will manifest their signal power, and

*See Appendix.

will exhibit themselves before the cities of the world; and this delineation has already begun to be fulfilled. By a variety of images the Lord Jesus represented to John the wicked character and seductive influence of those who have been distinguished for their persecution of God's people. All need wisdom carefully to search out the mystery of iniquity that figures so largely in the winding up of this earth's history. . . . In the very time in which we live, the Lord has called His people and has given them a message to bear. He has called them to expose the wickedness of the man of sin who has made the Sunday law a distinctive power, who has thought to change times and laws, and to oppress the people of God who stand firmly to honor Him by keeping the only true Sabbath, the Sabbath of creation, as holy unto the Lord.

The perils of the last days are upon us, and in our work we are to warn the people of the danger they are in. Let not the solemn scenes which prophecy has revealed be left untouched. If our people were half awake, if they realized the nearness of the events portrayed in the Revelation, a reformation would be wrought in our churches, and many more would believe the message. We have no time to lose; God calls upon us to watch for souls as they that must give an account. Advance new principles, and crowd in the clear-cut truth. It will be as a sword cutting both ways. But be not too ready to take a controversial attitude. There will be times when we must stand still and see the salvation of God. Let Daniel speak, let the Revelation speak, and tell what is truth. But whatever phase of the subject is presented, uplift Jesus as the center of all hope, "the Root and the Offspring of David, and the bright and morning Star."

Dig Deeper

We do not go deep enough in our search for truth. Every soul who believes present truth will be brought where he will be required to give a reason of the hope that is in him. The people of God will be called upon to stand before kings, princes, rulers, and great men of the earth, and they must know that they do know what is truth. They must be converted men and women. God can teach you more in one moment by His Holy Spirit than you could learn from the great men of the earth. The universe is looking upon the controversy that is going on upon the earth. At an infinite cost, God has provided for every man an opportunity to know that which will make him wise unto salvation. How eagerly do angels look to see who will avail himself of this opportunity! When a message is presented to God's people, they should not rise up in opposition to it; they should go to the Bible, comparing it with the law and the testimony, and if it does not bear this test, it is not true. God wants our minds to expand. He desires to put His grace upon us. We may have a feast of good things every day, for God can open the whole treasure of heaven to us.—*Review and Herald,* February 18, 1890.

For further study: *Gospel Workers,* pages 297-305, 311-315; *Fundamentals of Christian Education,* pages 305-307; *Testimonies,* vol. 5, pp. 706-708.

God's High Standard 4

True Education in Our Churches

FITTING SOULS FOR SERVICE

"The law of the Lord is perfect, converting the soul." "Blessed are the undefiled in the way, who walk in the law of the Lord. Blessed are they that keep His testimonies, and that seek Him with the whole heart. They also do no iniquity: they walk in His ways. Thou hast commanded us to keep Thy precepts diligently. O that my ways were directed to keep Thy statutes! Then shall I not be ashamed, when I have respect unto all Thy commandments."

Let us take this for our lesson. Study every word attentively. Upright principles and pure sentiments, cultivated and practiced, form a character after the divine similitude. A conscience void of offense toward God and man, a heart that feels the tenderest sympathy for human beings, especially that they may be won for Christ, will have the attributes that Christ had. All such will be imbued with His Spirit. They will have a reservoir of persuasion and a storehouse of simple eloquence.

As Christians, we are now to labor most earnestly to bring souls to Jesus Christ. There must be no cheap chapters of experience woven into our Christian life. All true experience costs every soul that obtains it an effort, because of Satan's temptations. God sees how the soul hungers for the knowledge of God, for salvation through Christ; and the promise is, "Blessed are they which do hunger and thirst after righteousness: for they shall be filled."

Special Testimony to Battle Creek Church (1898), pages 13-25.

CHARACTERISTICS OF THE TRUE SEEKER

God has commanded all men to obey His law. He sees not as man sees. His standard is elevated, pure, and holy; yet all may reach that standard. The Lord sees the soul want, the conscious soul hunger. He regards the disposition of the mind, from whence our actions proceed. He sees whether above everything else respect and faith are evidenced toward God. The true seeker, who is striving to be like Jesus in word, life, and character, will contemplate his Redeemer and, by beholding, become changed into His image, because he longs and prays for the same disposition and mind that was in Christ Jesus. He is not restrained from evil through fear of shame or through fear of loss, for he knows that all he enjoys comes from God, and he would improve his blessings that he may represent Christ. He is not hungry to stand the highest, to obtain praise from human beings. This is not his eager interest. By making a wise improvement of what he now has, he seeks to obtain more and still more ability, that he may give to God greater service. He longs after God. The history of his Redeemer, the immeasurable sacrifice that He made, becomes full of meaning to him. Christ, the Majesty of Heaven, became poor, that we through His poverty might become rich; not rich merely in endowments, but rich in attainments.

These are the riches that Christ earnestly longs that His followers shall possess. As the true seeker after the truth reads the word and opens his mind to receive the word, he longs after truth with his whole heart. The love, the pity, the tenderness, the courtesy, the Christian politeness, which will be the elements in the heavenly mansions that Christ has gone to prepare for those that love Him, take possession of his soul. His purpose is steadfast. He is determined to stand on the side of righteousness. Truth has found its way into the heart, and is planted there by the Holy Spirit, who is the truth. When truth takes hold of the heart, the man gives sure evidence of this by becoming a steward of the grace of Christ.

The heart of the true Christian is imbued with true love, with a most earnest hunger for souls. He is not at rest until he is doing all that is in his power to seek and to save that which is lost. Time and strength are spent; toilsome work is not shunned. Others must be given the truth which has brought to his own soul such gladness and peace and joy in the Holy Ghost.

When the truly converted soul enjoys the love of God, he will feel his obligation to yoke up with Christ and work in harmony with Him. The Spirit of Christ rests upon him. He reveals the Saviour's love, pity, and compassion, because he is one with Christ. He yearns to bring others to Jesus. His heart is melted with tenderness as he sees the peril of the souls that are out of Christ. He watches for souls as one that must give an account. With invitations and pleadings mingled with assurances of the promises of God, he seeks to win souls to Christ; and it is registered in the books of record. He is a laborer together with God.

Is not God the proper object of imitation? It should be the work of the Christian's life to put on Christ, and to bring himself to a more perfect likeness of Christ. The sons and daughters of God are to advance in their resemblance to Christ, our pattern. Daily they are to behold His glory, and contemplate His incomparable excellence. Tender, true, and full of compassion, they are to pull souls out of the fire, hating even the garment spotted by the flesh.

WE ARE NOT WORKING ALONE

There is a work to be done by God's people. What is true eloquence in the human life? It is a heart full of pure sentiments, a veneration for all God's commandments. But earnest work has not been done. A certain round of duties has been performed, but this is not enough. Step out of the common channel. If you cannot reach the members of the churches, do not become discouraged. Take the work into the highways, and if the self-righteousness of those for whom you labor will not be penetrated by the leaven of truth, go out of the usual round into the byways, and there do your missionary work.

God will not leave you to work alone. Ever since the proclamation of the third angel's message, angels of God have been waiting to cooperate with the human agent who is in earnest and determined to work. We must go deeper into the mines of truth than we have done.

"God so loved the world, that He gave His only-begotten Son, that whosoever believeth in Him should not perish, but have everlasting life." Oh, what love God hath shown for fallen man! Why do those who know the truth pass by on the other side so many who are in suffering need?

The whole worship of ancient Israel was a promise, in figures and symbols, of Christ; and it was not merely a promise, but an actual provision, designed by God to aid millions of people by lifting their thoughts to Him who was to manifest Himself to our world.

CHRIST THE REVELATION OF GOD

In Christ the world beheld the invisible God. "I am in the Father," He said, "and the Father in Me." "He that hath seen Me hath seen the Father." "If ye had known Me, ye should have known My Father also: and from henceforth ye know Him, and have seen Him." In all our acts of true devotion we fix our eye of faith upon our Advocate, who is standing between man and the eternal throne, waiting to meet our every effort and by His Spirit assist us to a more perfect knowledge of God.

The Lamb of God is represented before us as "in the midst of the throne" of God. He is the great ordinance by which man and God are united and commune together. Thus men are represented as sitting in heavenly places in Christ Jesus. This is the appointed place of meeting between God and humanity.

"And for their sakes I sanctify Myself, that they also might be sanctified through the truth. Neither pray I for these alone, but for them also which shall believe on Me through their word; that they all may be one; as Thou, Father, art in Me, and I in Thee, that they also may be one in Us: that the world may believe that Thou hast sent Me. And the glory which Thou gavest Me I have given them; that they may be one, even as We are one: I in them, and Thou in Me, that they may be made perfect in one; and that the world may know that Thou hast sent Me, and hast loved them, as Thou hast loved Me." Christ brought human nature into a personal relation with His own divinity. Thus He has given a center for the faith of the universe to fasten upon.

God designs that His law shall be obeyed by all who believe on Jesus Christ. Satan knew that if the human family could be induced to believe that God abolished His moral standard of character, man would not have a moral looking glass into which he could look and see what manner of person he was.

"If any be a hearer of the word, and not a doer, he is like unto a man beholding his natural face in a glass: for he beholdeth himself, and goeth his way, and straightway forgetteth what manner of man he was. But whoso looketh into the perfect law of liberty, and continueth therein, he being not a forgetful hearer, but a doer of the work, this man shall be blessed in his deed. If any man among you seem to be religious, and bridleth not his tongue, but deceiveth his own heart, this man's religion is vain. Pure religion and undefiled before God and the Father is this, To visit the fatherless and widows in their affliction, and to keep himself unspotted from the world."

This is the word of the living God. The law is God's great moral looking glass. He is to compare his words, his spirit, his actions, with the word of God. If we decide that in these last days we have no work assigned to us that is out of the common course of the nominal churches, we shall meet with great disappointment. The great question to be investigated, weighed, and decided is, What can I do to reach souls that are lost? God calls for a work to be done by Seventh-day Adventists that I need not define. Unless the work is first done in their own hearts, all the specific directions that might be given to point out their course of action will be labor in vain.

Read the second chapter of James. Practice the truth in your daily life and you will know the work that the Lord has given you to do. Read also the fourth chapter, especially verses 5-12; and chapter 5, especially verses 13-20. These chapters are a dead letter to the larger number of those who claim to be Seventh-day Adventists. I am directed to point you to these scriptures, and to the seventh chapter of Matthew. You need to study every word as for your life.

What the church in Battle Creek needs is to be doers of the word. This will lead a large number out of Battle Creek into other places, towns, and cities, where people have not had the light and opportunities that you have had. Many souls are now hanging in the balance. They are not with Christ. They are not gathering with Christ. Their influence is divided. They scatter abroad.

Especially give heed to these words: "Therefore whosoever heareth these sayings of Mine, and doeth them, I will liken him unto a wise man, which built his house upon a rock: and the rain descended, and the floods came, and the winds blew, and beat upon that house; and it fell not: for it was founded upon a rock. And everyone that heareth these sayings of Mine, and doeth them not, shall be likened unto a foolish man, which built his house upon the sand: and the rain descended, and the floods came, and the winds blew, and beat upon that house; and it fell: and great was the fall of it." Many houses now supposed to stand secure will fall. The Lord declares that He will not accept divided service.

PRECIOUS WORDS OF WARNING AND PROMISE

If you will take heed to the words of warning found in the chapters that I am directed to present before you, you will change your attitude, and become children of God. Thus you may save your souls through faith in Jesus Christ. You will receive the counsel given in the fifty-eighth chapter of Isaiah. If you will follow the directions marked out, the promise will be fulfilled: "Then shall thy light break forth as the morning, and thine health shall spring forth speedily: and thy righteousness shall go before thee; the glory of the Lord shall be thy rearward. Then shalt thou call, and the Lord shall answer; thou shalt cry, and He shall say, Here I am. If thou take away from the midst of thee the yoke, the putting forth of the finger, and speaking vanity; and if thou draw out thy soul to the hungry, and satisfy the afflicted soul; then shall thy light rise in obscurity, and thy darkness be as the noonday: and the Lord shall guide thee continually, and satisfy thy soul in drought, and make fat thy bones: and thou shalt be like a watered garden, and like a spring of water, whose waters fail not."

Take up your appointed work. The Lord will fulfill the promise on His part. These inspired scriptures would never have been given to you if the Lord had not had confidence that you could do all that He has required. You can heed the invitation, "Take My yoke upon you, and learn of Me; for I am meek and lowly in heart: and ye shall find rest unto your souls. For My yoke is easy, and My burden is light."

You may rise to the heights to which the Holy Spirit calls you. True religion means living the word in your practical life. Your profession is not of any value without the practical doing of the word. "If any man will come after Me, let him deny himself, and take up his cross daily, and follow Me." This is the condition of discipleship. "Behold My Servant, whom I have chosen; My Beloved, in whom My soul is well pleased: I will put My Spirit upon Him, and He shall show judgment to the Gentiles. He shall not strive, nor cry; neither shall any man hear His voice in the streets. A bruised reed shall He not break, and smoking flax shall He not quench, till He send forth judgment unto victory. And in His name shall the Gentiles trust."

Thank God that a work is being done outside of the church. The church has not been properly educated to work outside of their own people. Many souls out of the church might have been enlightened, and a great deal more light brought into the church, if every church member in every country, who claims to have the advanced light of truth, had worked with heart and soul and voice to win souls to the truth. Altogether too little work is being done by church members for those who need the light, those who are outside of the church of Seventh-day Adventists. The Lord declares: "A bruised reed shall He not break, and smoking flax shall He not quench, till He send forth judgment unto victory. And in His name shall the Gentiles trust." Those who cooperate with Jesus Christ will realize that all these promises are fulfilled in their own experience. The Lord has pointed out the duty of every soul. In the judgment no one will have any excuse to present for not doing his duty.

A CLOSER TEST OF DISCIPLESHIP

The test of discipleship is not brought to bear as closely as it should be upon those who present themselves for baptism. It should be understood whether those who profess to be converted are simply taking the name of Seventh-day Adventists, or whether they are taking their stand on the Lord's side to come out from the world and be separate and touch not the unclean thing. When they give evidence that they fully understand their position, they are to be accepted. But when they show that they are following the customs and fashions and sentiments of the world, they are to be faithfully dealt with. If they feel no burden to change their course of action, they should not be retained as members of the church. The Lord wants those who compose His church to be true, faithful stewards of the grace of Christ.

The sin of these last days is upon the professed people of God. Through selfishness, love of pleasure, and love of dress, they deny the Christ that their church membership says that they are following. I thank God that Jesus Christ knows every impulse in the heart of the believer. Many profess to be children of God who do not follow Christ. Their frivolity, their cheap conversation, their want of high-toned piety, their low aims, mislead others who would pursue a different course were it not for the example of these deceptive characters, those who do not love Christ or do His will but simply follow their own imaginations.

Jesus is acquainted with every heart that is humble, meek, and lowly. These have trials and make mistakes, but they are brokenhearted because they grieve the Saviour who loved them and died for them. They come humbly to His feet; they fight His battles. In meekness and lowliness of heart they seek to do good to others. They seek to advance the cause of truth in good and earnest endeavor.

The Lord Jesus loves those for whom He has given His life; and when worldly influences are allowed to come in between them and their Helper, when idols are chosen before Christ, when His appeals to the human soul are regarded with indifference and there is no response, Jesus is grieved. He knows that they are meeting with great losses, for they are stumbling blocks to sinners. They are not gathering with Christ, but scattering from Him. But when through great affliction the Spirit of God touches their hearts, and they turn to Him, He will hear their prayers. Christ knows the capabilities He has given to every soul to serve Him for his present and eternal good. He desires that these souls shall not disappoint Him. He wants them to shine in His kingdom. Those who will be the most highly honored are those who take up their cross daily, and follow Christ.

MAKE A REALITY OF TRUTH

The Lord Jesus demands that every soul make a reality of truth. Show that you believe that you are not half with Christ and half with the world. Of all such Christ says: "I would thou wert cold or hot. So then because thou art lukewarm, and neither cold nor hot, I will spew thee out of My mouth." He who appreciates the love of Christ will be an earnest worker with Christ to bring other souls as sheaves to the Master. Thorough work is always done by all who are connected with Christ. They bear fruit to His glory. But indolence and carelessness and frivolity separate the soul from Christ, and Satan comes in to work his will with the poor worldly subject. We have a great truth, but through careless indifference the truth has lost its force upon us. Satan has come in with his specious temptations, and has led the professed followers of Christ away from their Leader, classing them with the foolish virgins.

The Lord is coming, and we now need the oil of grace in our vessels with our lamps. I ask, Who will now be on the Lord's side? Before Jesus went away, He promised that He would return again, and receive us unto Himself, "that where I am," He said, "ye may be also." We are strangers and pilgrims in this world. We are to wait, watch, pray, and work. The whole mind, the whole soul, the whole heart, and the whole strength are purchased by the blood of the Son of God. We are not to feel it our duty to wear a pilgrim's dress of just such a color, just such a shape, but neat, modest apparel, that the word of inspiration teaches us we should wear. If our hearts are united with Christ's heart, we shall have a most intense desire to be clothed with His righteousness. Nothing will be put upon the person to attract attention or to create controversy.

Christianity—how many there are who do not know what it is! It is not something put on the outside. It is a life inwrought with the life of Jesus. It means that we are wearing the robe of Christ's righteousness. In regard to the world, Christians will say, We will not dabble in politics. They will say decidedly, We are pilgrims and strangers; our citizenship is above. They will not be seen choosing company for amusement. They will say, We have ceased to be infatuated by childish things. We are strangers and pilgrims, looking for a city which hath foundations, whose builder and maker is God.

For further study: *Fundamentals of Christian Education,* pages 107-112, 174-180; *Testimonies,* vol. 9, pp. 161-166, 169-172, 200, 201.

Sabbath Observance the Sign of Loyalty

Sunnyside, Cooranbong, January 12, 1898.

I call upon all who have united in a course of action that is wrong in principle to make a decided reformation, and forever after walk humbly with God. The world is soon to be judged. A righteous God must avenge the death of His Son. Today men are choosing Barabbas, and saying, Crucify Christ. They will do this in the person of His saints. They will go over the same ground as the Jewish priests and rulers did in their treatment of Christ. He, the Son of God, and an innocent man, was murdered because He told men truths that it did not please them to hear. Yet He was the Son of the infinite God.

Special Testimony to Battle Creek Church (1898), pages 29-40.

Those who today despise the law of Jehovah, showing no respect for His commandments, are taking sides with the great apostate. They proclaim to a sin-corrupted world that the law of God is null and void. Those who declare this as truth deceive the people, and have virtually nailed the law of Jehovah to the cross between two thieves. What a thought!

Before the worlds unfallen and the heavenly universe, the world will have to give an account to the Judge of the whole earth, the very One they condemned and crucified. What a reckoning day that will be! It is the great day of God's vengeance. Christ does not then stand at Pilate's bar. Pilate and Herod, and all that mocked, scourged, rejected, and crucified Him will then understand what it means to feel the wrath of the Lamb. Their deeds will appear before them in their true character.

A TERRIBLE DECEPTION

What a terrible deception is upon the minds of those who think that the world is growing better! Christ declares, "As it was in the days of Noah, so shall it be also in the days of the Son of man." "For as in the days that were before the Flood they were eating and drinking, marrying and giving in marriage, until the day that Noah entered into the ark, and knew not until the Flood came, and took them all away; so shall also the coming of the Son of man be." To just such a pass will the world come in rejecting the law of God.

"And the third angel followed them, saying with a loud voice, If any man worship the beast and his image, and receive his mark in his forehead, or in his hand, the same shall drink of the wine of the wrath of God, which is poured out without mixture into the cup of His indignation; and he shall be tormented with fire and brimstone in the presence of the holy angels, and in the presence of the Lamb: and the smoke of their torment ascendeth up forever and ever: and they have no rest day nor night, who worship the beast and his image, and whosoever receiveth the mark of his name."

John was called to behold a people distinct from those who worship the beast or his image by keeping the first day of the week. The observance of this day is the mark of the beast. John declares, "Here is the patience of the saints: here are they that keep the commandments of God, and the faith of Jesus."

"And the dragon was wroth with the woman, and went to make war with the remnant of her seed, which keep the commandments of God, and have the testimony of Jesus Christ." We are plainly shown that two parties will exist at the appearing of our Lord and Saviour Jesus Christ. In which party do we wish to be found? "Behold, I come quickly," Christ says, "and My reward is with Me, to give every man according as his work shall be. I am Alpha and Omega, the beginning and the end, the first and the last. Blessed are they that do His commandments, that they may have right to the tree of life, and may enter in through the gates into the city." This is the destination of commandment keepers. Should we not all wish to be among that number who have right to the tree of life, and who enter through the gates into the city?

Adam and Eve and their posterity lost their right to the tree of life because of their disobedience. "And the Lord God said, Behold, the man is become as one of Us, to know good and evil: and now, lest he put forth his hand, and take also of the tree of life, and eat, and live forever: therefore the Lord God sent him forth from the Garden of Eden, to till the ground from whence he was taken." Adam and Eve transgressed the law of God. This made it necessary for them to be driven from Eden and be separated from the tree of life, to eat of which after their transgression would perpetuate sin. "So He drove out the man; and He placed at the east of the Garden of Eden cherubims, and a flaming sword which turned every way, to keep the way of the tree of life." Man was dependent upon the tree of life for immortality, and the Lord took these precautions lest men should eat of that tree "and live forever"—become immortal sinners.

Death entered the world because of transgression. But Christ gave His life that man should have another trial. He did not die on the cross to abolish the law of God, but to secure for man a second probation. He did not die to make sin an immortal attribute; He died to secure the right to destroy him that had the power of death, that is, the devil. He suffered the full penalty of a broken law for the whole world. This He did, not that men might continue in transgression, but that they might return to their loyalty and keep God's commandments and His law as the apple of their eye.

A SIGN OF OBEDIENCE

The sign of obedience is the observance of the Sabbath of the fourth commandment. If men keep the fourth commandment, they will keep all the rest. It was no human voice that spoke to Moses, giving him the Sabbath as a sign. "The Lord spake unto Moses, saying, Speak thou also unto the children of Israel, saying, Verily My Sabbaths ye shall keep: for it is a sign between Me and you throughout your generations; that ye may know that I am the Lord that doth sanctify you. Ye shall keep the Sabbath therefore; for it is holy unto you: everyone that defileth it shall surely be put to death: for whosoever doeth any work therein, that soul shall be cut off from among his people."

The Lord does not leave so important a precept as this without definite specification. "Six days may work be done; but in the seventh is the Sabbath of rest, holy to the Lord: whosoever doeth any work in the Sabbath day, he shall surely be put to death. Wherefore the children of Israel shall keep the Sabbath, to observe the Sabbath throughout their generations, for a perpetual covenant."

HUMAN PHILOSOPHY VERSUS DIVINE REVELATION

Human philosophy declares that an indefinite period of time was taken in the creation of the world. Does God state the matter thus? No; He says, "It is a sign between Me and the children of Israel forever: for in six days [not six indefinite periods of time; for then there would be no possible way for man to observe the day specified in the fourth commandment] the Lord made heaven and earth, and on the seventh day He rested, and was refreshed." Please read carefully the fifth chapter of Deuteronomy. God says again, "Remember [do not forget] the Sabbath day, to keep it holy. . . . For in six days the Lord made heaven and earth, the sea, and all that in them is, and rested the seventh day: wherefore the Lord blessed the Sabbath day, and hallowed it."

Yet with the living oracles before them, those who claim to preach the word present the suppositions of human minds, the maxims and commandments of men. They make void the law of God by their traditions. The sophistry in regard to the world's being created in an indefinite period of time is one of Satan's falsehoods. God speaks to the human family in language they can comprehend. He does not leave the matter so indefinite that human beings can handle it according to their theories. When the Lord declares that He made the world in six days and rested on the seventh day, He means the day of twenty-four hours, which He has marked off by the rising and setting of the sun.

God would not present the death sentence for a disregard of the Sabbath unless He had presented before men a clear understanding of the Sabbath. After He had created our world and man, He looked upon the work that He had done, and pronounced it very good. And when the foundation of the earth was laid, the foundation of the Sabbath was laid also. "When the morning stars sang together, and all the sons of God shouted for joy," God saw that a Sabbath was essential for man, even in Paradise. In giving the Sabbath, God considered man's spiritual and physical health.

NOT ANY DAY IN SEVEN

God made the world in six literal days, and on the seventh literal day He rested from all His work which He had done, and was refreshed. So He has given man six days in which to labor. But He sanctified the day of His rest, and gave it to man to be kept, free from all secular labor. By thus setting apart the Sabbath, God gave the world a memorial. He did not set apart one day and any day in seven, but one particular day, the seventh day. And by observing the Sabbath, we show that we recognize God as the living God, the Creator of heaven and earth.

There is nothing in the Sabbath that restricts it to any particular class of people. It was given for all mankind. It is to be employed, not in indolence, but in the contemplation of the works of God. This men are to do that they may "know that I am the Lord that sanctify them."

The Lord draws very nigh to His people on the day that He has blessed and sanctified. "The heavens declare the glory of God; and the firmament showeth His handiwork. Day unto day uttereth speech, and night unto night showeth knowledge." The Sabbath is God's memorial, pointing men to their Creator, who made the world and all things that are therein. In the everlasting hills, in the lofty trees, in every opening bud and blooming flower, we may behold the work of the great Master Artist. All speak to us of God and His glory.

Every loyal child of God will seek to know the truth. John stated the truth so plainly that a child may understand it. "If ye love Me, keep My commandments. And I will pray the Father, and He shall give you another Comforter, that He may abide with you forever; even the Spirit of truth; whom the world cannot receive, because it seeth Him not, neither knoweth Him." Do we choose to be numbered with those who cannot discern the truth, who are so blinded by the deceptive power of the enemy that they see not Him who is the express image of the Father's person?

The followers of Christ are of another class altogether. "But ye know Him; for He dwelleth with you, and shall be in you. I will not leave you comfortless: I will come to you. Yet a little while, and the world seeth Me no more; but ye see Me: because I live, ye shall live also." "He that hath My commandments, and keepeth them, he it is that loveth Me: and he that loveth Me shall be loved of My Father, and I will love him, and will manifest Myself to him." "If a man love Me, he will keep My words: and My Father will love him, and We will come unto him, and make Our abode with him. He that loveth Me not keepeth not My sayings: and the word which ye hear is not Mine, but the Father's which sent Me." The word of a human being is not to be received and believed without question. We must first ask, Do they speak in harmony with the word? Do they refuse a plain "Thus saith the Lord" because they see that it involves a cross?

ON WHICH SIDE ARE YOU?

Are we on the side of those who refuse to be loyal to God? They have no interest in knowing God. They reject the divine Son of God, the personification of all human goodness. They place themselves with those who, although no fault could be preferred against Christ, chose instead a thief and a murderer. This testifies to the moral taste of the world. Shall we be on the side of the world, or on the side of Christ, who declared, "I have kept My Father's commandments"?

The word of Jehovah will stand forever. "In the beginning was the Word, and the Word was with God, and the Word was God. The same was in the beginning with God. All things were made by Him; and without Him was not anything made that was made. In Him was life; and the life was the light of men. And the light shineth in darkness; and the darkness comprehended it not. . . . He was in the world, and the world was made by Him, and the world knew Him not. He came unto His own, and His own received Him not. But as many as received Him, to them gave He power to become the sons of God, even to them that believe on His name: which were born, not of blood, nor of the will of the flesh, nor of the will of man, but of God. And the Word was made flesh, and dwelt among us, (and we beheld His glory, the glory as of the Only Begotten of the Father,) full of grace and truth."

Those who receive Christ by faith as their personal Saviour cannot be in harmony with the world. There are two distinct classes: One is loyal to God, keeping His commandments, while the other talks and acts like the world, casting away the word of God, which is truth, and accepting the words of the apostate, who rejected Jesus.

WHOM WILL YOU CHOOSE?

On whose side are we? The world cast Christ out; the heavens received Him. Man, finite man, rejected the Prince of life; God, our Sovereign Ruler, received Him into the heavens. God has exalted Him. Man crowned Him with a crown of thorns; God has crowned Him with a crown of royal majesty. We must all think candidly. Will you have this man Christ Jesus to rule over you, or will you have Barabbas? The death of Christ brings to the rejecter of His mercy the wrath and judgments of God, unmixed with mercy. This is the wrath of the Lamb. But the death of Christ is hope and eternal life to all who receive Him and believe in Him.

God will most assuredly call the world to judgment to avenge the death of His only-begotten Son, the One who stood at the bar of Pilate and Herod. That One is now in the heavenly courts making intercession for the people who refused Him. Shall we choose the stamp of the world, or shall we choose to be God's separate, peculiar people? Shall we receive a "Thus saith the Lord," for the "Thus saith" of man? The papal power, the man of sin, decides that the Roman Catholic Church has changed the law of God. In the place of the seventh day they have baptized and presented to the world a child of the papacy, the first day of the week, to be observed as a holy day of rest. The Protestant world has received this child of the papacy, has cradled it, and given to it the honor that God has placed on the seventh day.

"Behold, I have taught you statutes and judgments, even as the Lord my God commanded me, that ye should do so in the land whither ye go to possess it. Keep therefore and do them; for this is your wisdom and your understanding in the sight of the nations, which shall hear all these statutes, and say, Surely this great nation is a wise and understanding people. For what nation is there so great, who hath God so nigh unto them, as the Lord our God is in all things that we call upon Him for? And what nation is there so great, that hath statutes and judgments so righteous as all this law, which I set before you this day? Only take heed to thyself, and keep thy soul diligently, lest thou forget the things which thine eyes have seen, and lest they depart from thy heart all the days of thy life: but teach them thy sons, and thy sons' sons; specially the day that thou stoodest before the Lord thy God in Horeb, when the Lord said unto me, Gather Me the people together, and I will make them hear My words, that they may learn to fear Me all the days that they shall live upon the earth, and that they may teach their children. . . . And He declared unto you His covenant, which He commanded you to perform, even Ten Commandments; and He wrote them upon two tables of stone."

"Hear, O Israel: the Lord our God is one Lord: and

thou shalt love the Lord thy God with all thine heart, and with all thy soul, and with all thy might. And these words, which I command thee this day, shall be in thine heart: and thou shalt teach them diligently unto thy children, and shalt talk of them when thou sittest in thine house, and when thou walkest by the way, and when thou liest down, and when thou risest up. And thou shalt bind them for a sign upon thine hand, and they shall be as frontlets between thine eyes. And thou shalt write them upon the posts of thy house, and on thy gates."

"For thou art an holy people unto the Lord thy God: the Lord thy God hath chosen thee to be a special people unto Himself, above all people that are upon the face of the earth. The Lord did not set His love upon you, nor choose you, because ye were more in number than any people; for ye were the fewest of all people: but because the Lord loved you, and because He would keep the oath which He had sworn unto your fathers, hath the Lord brought you out with a mighty hand. . . . Thou shalt therefore keep the commandments, and the statutes, and the judgments, which I command thee this day, to do them." Please read carefully the whole of the seventh chapter of Deuteronomy, and think upon the word of the Lord.

Will you turn from a plain "Thus saith the Lord" after reading the history of Adam's sin and fall? He fell because he discarded the words of the Lord and heeded the words of Satan. Will it pay to transgress? By transgression Adam lost Eden. By the transgression of God's commandments man will lose heaven, and an eternity of bliss. These are no idle tales, but truth. Again I ask, On which side are you standing? "If the Lord be God, follow Him: but if Baal, then follow him."

A Solemn Appeal to Ministers 5

Call to a Higher Standard

Petoskey, Michigan, August 20, 1890.

Dear Brethren:

I cannot express to you my burden and distress of mind as the true condition of the cause has been presented before me. There are men working in the capacity of teachers of the truth who need to learn their first lessons in the school of Christ. The converting power of God must come upon the hearts of the ministers, or they should seek some other calling. If Christ's ambassadors realize the solemnity of presenting the truth to the people, they will be sober, thoughtful men, workers together with God. If they have a true sense of the commission which Christ gave to His disciples, they will with reverence open the word of God and listen for instruction from the Lord, asking for wisdom from heaven that, as they stand between the living and the dead, they may realize that they must render an account to God for the work coming forth from their hands.

A JOKING MINISTER

What can the minister do without Jesus? Verily, nothing. Then if he is a frivolous, joking man, he is not prepared to perform the duty laid upon him by the Lord. "Without Me," says Christ, "ye can do nothing." The flippant words that fall from his lips, the trifling anecdotes, the words spoken to create a laugh, are all

---

Special Testimonies to Ministers and Workers (Series A, No. 1, 1890), pages 1-15.

condemned by the word of God and are entirely out of place in the sacred desk.

I tell you plainly, brethren, unless the ministers are converted, our churches will be sickly and ready to die. God's power alone can change the human heart and imbue it with the love of Christ. God's power alone can correct and subdue the passions and sanctify the affections. All who minister must humble their proud hearts, submit their will to the will of God, and hide their life with Christ in God.

What is the object of the ministry? Is it to mix the comical with the religious? The theater is the place for such exhibitions. If Christ is formed within, if the truth with its sanctifying power is brought into the inner sanctuary of the soul, you will not have jolly men, neither will you have sour, cross, crabbed men to teach the precious lessons of Christ to perishing souls.

Our ministers need a transformation of character. They should feel that if their works are not wrought in God, if they are left to their own imperfect efforts, they are of all men the most miserable. Christ will be with every minister who, although he may not have attained to perfection of character, is seeking most earnestly to become Christlike. Such a minister will pray. He will weep between the porch and the altar, crying in soul anguish for the Lord's presence to be with him; else he cannot stand before the people, with all heaven looking upon him, and the angel's pen taking note of his words, his deportment, and his spirit.

Oh, that men would fear the Lord! Oh, that they would love the Lord! Oh, that the messengers of God would feel the burden of perishing souls! Then they would not merely speechify; but they would have the power of God vitalizing their souls, and their hearts would glow with the fire of God's love. Out of weakness they would become strong; for they would be doers of the word. They would hear the voice of Jesus: "Lo, I am with you alway." Jesus would be their teacher; and the word they minister would be quick and powerful, sharper than any two-edged sword, and a discerner of the thoughts and intents of the heart. Just in proportion as the speaker appreciates the divine presence and honors and trusts the power of God, is he acknowledged as a laborer together with God. Just in this proportion does he become mighty through God.

There needs to be an elevating, uplifting power, a constant growth in the knowledge of God and the truth, on the part of one who is seeking the salvation of souls. If the minister utters words drawn from the living oracles of God; if he believes in and expects the cooperation of Christ, whose servant he is; if he hides self and exalts Jesus, the world's Redeemer; his words will reach the hearts of his hearers, and his work will bear the divine credentials. The Holy Spirit must be the living agency to convince of sin. The divine agent presents to the speaker the benefits of the sacrifice made upon the cross; and as the truth is brought in contact with the souls present, Christ wins them to Himself, and works to transform their nature. He is ready to help our infirmities, to teach, to lead, to inspire us with ideas that are of heavenly birth.

How little can men do in the work of saving souls, and yet how much through Christ if they are imbued with His spirit! The human teacher cannot read the hearts of his hearers, but Jesus dispenses the grace that every soul needs. He understands the capabilities of man, his weakness, and his strength. The Lord is working on the human heart, and a minister can be to the souls who are listening to his words a savor of death unto death, turning them away from Christ; or, if he is consecrated, devotional, distrustful of self, but looking unto Jesus, he may be a savor of life unto life to souls who are already under the convicting power of the Holy Spirit, and in whose hearts the Lord is preparing the way for the messages which He has given to the human agent. Thus the heart of the unbeliever is touched, and it responds to the message of truth. "We are laborers together with God." The convictions implanted in the heart, and the enlightenment of the understanding by the entrance of the word, work in perfect harmony. The truth brought before the mind has power to arouse the dormant energies of the soul. The Spirit of God working in the heart cooperates with the working of God through His human instrumentalities. When ministers realize the necessity of thorough reformation in themselves, when they feel that they must reach a higher standard, their influence upon the churches will be uplifting and refining.

SECRET FAULTS TO BE OVERCOME

There are sinners in the ministry. They are not agonizing to enter in at the strait gate. God does not work with them, for He cannot endure the presence of sin. It is the thing that His soul hates. Even the angels that stood about His throne, whom He loved, but who kept not their first estate of loyalty, God cast out of heaven with their rebel leader. Holiness is the foundation of God's throne; sin is the opposite of holiness; sin crucified the Son of God. If men could see how hateful sin is, they would not tolerate it, nor educate themselves in it. They would reform in life and character. Secret faults would be overcome. If you are to be saints in heaven, you must first be saints upon the earth.

There is great need that our brethren overcome secret faults. The displeasure of God, like a cloud, hangs over many of them. The churches are weak. Selfishness, uncharitableness, covetousness, envy, evil-surmising, falsehood, theft, robbery, sensuality, licentiousness, and adultery,* stand registered against some who claim to believe the solemn, sacred truth for this time. How can these accursed things be cleansed out of the camp, when men who claim to be Christians are practicing them constantly? They are somewhat careful of their ways before men, but they are an offense to God. His pure eyes see, a witness records, all their sins, both open and secret; and unless they repent and confess their sins before God, unless they fall on the Rock and are broken, their sins will remain charged against them in the books of record. Oh, fearful histories will be opened to the world at the judgment—histories of sins never confessed, of sins not blotted out! Oh, that these poor souls might see that they are heaping up wrath against the day of wrath! Then the thoughts of the heart, as well as the actions, will be revealed. I tell you, my brethren and sisters, there is need of humbling your souls before God. "Cease to do evil," but do not stop here; "learn to do well." You can glorify God only by bearing fruit to His glory.

Ministers, for Christ's sake, begin the work for yourselves. By your unsanctified lives you have laid stumbling blocks before your own children and before unbelievers. Some of you move by impulse, act from passion and prejudice, and bring impure, tainted offerings to God. For Christ's sake cleanse the camp by beginning, through the grace of Christ, the personal work of purifying the soul from moral defilement. A jovial minister in the pulpit, or one who is stretching beyond his measure to win praise, is a spectacle that

*See Appendix.

crucifies the Son of God afresh and puts Him to open shame. There must be thorough repentance, faith in our Saviour Jesus Christ, vigilant watchfulness, unceasing prayer, and diligent searching of the Scriptures. God holds us responsible for all that we might be if we would improve our talents. We shall be judged according to what we ought to have been, but were not; what we might have done, but did not accomplish because we did not use our powers to glorify God. For all knowledge that we might have gained but did not, there will be an eternal loss, even if we do not lose our souls. All our influence belongs to God. All that we acquire is to be used to His glory. All the property that the Lord has entrusted to us is to be held on the altar of God, to be returned to Him again. We are working out our own destiny. May God help us all to be wise for eternity.

My brethren, we are living in a most solemn period of this earth's history. There is never time to sin; it is always perilous to continue in transgression; but in a special sense is this true at the present time. We are now upon the very borders of the eternal world and stand in a more solemn relation to time and to eternity than ever before. Now let every person search his own heart, and plead for the bright beams of the Sun of Righteousness to expel all spiritual darkness and cleanse from defilement. "If we confess our sins, He is faithful and just to forgive us our sins, and to cleanse us from all unrighteousness." Through faith, irrespective of feeling, Jesus, the Author of our salvation, the Finisher of our faith, will, by His precious grace, strengthen the moral powers, and the sinner may reckon himself "to be dead indeed unto sin, but alive unto God through Jesus Christ." Simple faith, with the love of Christ in the soul, unites the believer to God. While toiling in battle as a faithful soldier of Christ, he has the sympathy of the whole loyal universe. The ministering angels are round about him to aid in the conflict, so that he may boldly say, "The Lord is my helper," "the Lord is my strength and my shield;" I shall not be overcome. "By grace are ye saved through faith; and that not of yourselves: it is the gift of God."

The infinite wisdom and power of God are exerted in our behalf. The heavenly host are surely fighting our battles for us. They are always looking with intense interest upon the souls purchased by the Saviour's blood. They see, through the sacrifice of Christ, the value of the human soul. It is always safe to be on the Lord's side, not halfheartedly, but wholly. It is this halfhearted, indifferent, careless work that separates your souls from Jesus, the source of your strength. Let this be your prayer: "Take everything from me, let me lose property, worldly honor, everything, but let Thy presence be with me." It is safe to commit the keeping of the soul to God, who reigns over all heaven and earth.

SEARCH THE SCRIPTURES AND PRAY IN FAITH

Will my ministering brethren see that they work circumspectly, that they heed the charge of the apostle Paul to Titus: "Young men likewise exhort to be soberminded. In all things showing thyself a pattern of good works: in doctrine showing uncorruptness, gravity, sincerity, sound speech, that cannot be condemned; that he that is of the contrary part may be ashamed, having no evil thing to say of you"? Titus 2:6-8; read also verses 11-15.

It was shown to me that on the part of the ministers in all our conferences, there is a neglect to study the

Scriptures, to search for the truth. If their minds were properly disciplined, and were stored with the precious lessons of Christ, then at any time and in any emergency they could draw from the treasure house of knowledge things both new and old, to feed the church of God, giving to every man his portion of meat in due season. If Christ is abiding in the soul, He will be as a living fountain, "a well of water springing up into everlasting life."

I tell you the things which I have seen, and which are true, that by well-directed, persevering effort there might be many, very many, more souls brought to a knowledge of the truth. Oh, the end is near! Who is ready for Christ to rise from His throne to put on the garments of vengeance? Whose names are registered in the Lamb's book of life? The names of those only will be there who follow the Lamb whithersoever He goeth. Your erroneous ideas, your objectionable phases of character, must be given up, and you must be clothed with the garments of Christ's righteousness. *Faith and love*—how destitute are the churches of these! The heavenly Merchantman counsels you, "Buy of Me gold tried in the fire, that thou mayest be rich; and white raiment, that thou mayest be clothed; . . . and anoint thine eyes with eyesalve, that thou mayest see." God forbid that those who are preaching in our conferences should be like the foolish virgins, having lamps, but destitute of the oil of grace which makes the lamp burn and give forth light. Oh, we want more praying ministers—men who carry a solemn weight of souls—men who have a faith that works by love and purifies the soul. Without faith it is impossible to please God. How imperfect is faith in our churches! Why do we not believe the Lord will do just as He says He will?

We are God's servants, and to each of us He has given talents, both natural and spiritual. As children of God, we should be constantly gaining in fitness for the heavenly mansions which Christ told His disciples He was going away to prepare for them. He who lays hold upon the righteousness of Christ may become a perfect man in Christ Jesus. Working from a high standpoint, seeking to follow the example of Christ, we shall grow up into His likeness, possessing more and more refinement.

The Saviour prayed, "Sanctify them through Thy truth: Thy word is truth." Those who are disciplined by the truth will be doers of the word; they will be diligent Bible readers, searching the Scriptures with an earnest desire to understand the will of God, and to do His will intelligently.

BE COURTEOUS

The ministers in our conferences need to walk carefully before God. The apostle's injunction, "Be courteous," is greatly needed in their ministering, in watching for souls as those who must give account, in seeking to save the erring. You may be true to principle, you may be just, honest, and religious; but with it all you must cultivate true tenderness of heart, kindness, and courtesy. If a person is in error, be the more kind to him; if you are not courteous, you may drive him away from Christ. Let every word you speak, even the tones of your voice, express your interest in, and sympathy for, the souls that are in peril. If you are harsh, denunciatory, and impatient with them, you are doing the work of the enemy. You are opening a door of temptation to them, and Satan will represent you to them as one who knows not the Lord Jesus. They will think their own way is right, and that they are better than you. How, then, can you win the erring? They can recognize genuine piety, expressed in words and character. If you would teach repentance, faith, and humility, you must have the love of Jesus in your own hearts. The truth you believe is able to sanctify the soul and to fashion and mold the whole man, not only to change his words and deportment, but to abase pride and purify the soul temple from all defilement.

BIBLE RELIGION

Bible religion is very scarce, even among ministers. I mourn day and night for the coarseness, the harshness, the unkindness in words and spirit, that is manifested by those who claim to be children of the heavenly King, members of the royal family. Such hardness of heart, such a want of sympathy, such harshness is shown to those who are not special favorites, and it is registered in the books of heaven as a great sin. Many talk of the truth, they preach the theory of the truth, when the melting love of Jesus has not become a living, active element in their character.

This is an age of almost universal apostasy, and those who claim to hold advanced truth mislead the churches when they do not give evidence that their character and works harmonize with the divine truth. The goodness, the mercy, the compassion, the tenderness, the loving-kindness of God are to be expressed in the words, deportment, and character of all who claim to be children of God, especially in those who claim to be messengers sent by the Lord Jesus with the word of life to save the perishing. They are enjoined by the Bible to put away all that is harsh and coarse and rough in their character, and to be grafted into Christ, the living vine. They should bear the same quality of fruit that the vine bears. Thus only can the branch be a true representation of the preciousness of the vine.

Christ came to our world to reveal the Father amid the gross darkness of error and superstition which then prevailed. The disciples of Christ are to represent Him in their everyday life, and thus the true light from heaven will shine forth in clear, steady rays to the world; thus a character is revealed entirely different from that which is seen in those who do not make the word of God their guide and standard. A knowledge of God must be preserved amid the darkness that covers the world and the gross darkness that envelops the people. Age after age the pure character of Christ has been misrepresented by those who claimed to be believers in Him and in the word of God. Hardness of heart has been cultivated. Love and kindness and true courtesy have been fast disappearing from ministers and churches. What can the universe of God think of this? Those who claim to be representatives of Christ show rather the hardness of heart which is characteristic of Satan, which made him unfit for heaven, unsafe to be there. And just so it will be with those who know the truth and yet close the door of the heart against its sanctifying power. "It pleased God by the foolishness of preaching to save them that believe." The servants of Christ are not only to be instruments through the preaching of Jesus to lead men to repentance, but they are to continue their watchcare and interest by keeping before the people, by precept and example, the Lord and Saviour Jesus Christ. They are to sanctify themselves that their hearers also may be sanctified. Thus all will grow in godliness, going on from grace to grace, until the ambassador for God can present every man perfect in Christ Jesus. Then the ministerial office will be seen in its true, sacred character.

A LOWERED STANDARD

But the standard of the ministry has been greatly lowered, and the Minister of the true sanctuary is misrepresented before the world. God is ready to accept men as His colaborers, and to make them the light of the world, agents through whom He can graciously infuse light into the understanding. If the men who bear the message have not Christ abiding in them, if they are not true,—and some are not,—may the Lord awaken them from their deception before it shall be too late. God wants men to be tenderhearted, compassionate, and to love as brethren. Jesus is waiting for them to open the door, that He may come in and infuse into their hearts the warmth of His love, His goodness, His tender compassion; that the worker may in all his connection with humanity reveal the Saviour to the world.

Ministers too often act the part of critics, showing their aptness and sharpness in controversy. Sabbath after Sabbath passes away, and scarcely an impression of the grace of Christ is made upon the hearts and minds of the hearers. Thus the ministry comes to be regarded as unimportant. All heaven is working for the salvation of sinners; and when the poorest of the human family comes with repentance to his Father, as did the prodigal son, there is joy among the heavenly host. There is warmth and courtesy and love in heaven. Let ministers go before God in prayer, confessing their sins, and with all the simplicity of a little child ask for the blessings that they need. Plead for the warmth of

Christ's love, and then bring it into your discourses; and let no one have occasion to go away and say that the doctrines you believe unfit you for expressing sympathy with suffering humanity—that you have a loveless religion. The operations of the Holy Spirit will burn away the dross of selfishness, and reveal a love which is tried in the fire, a love that maketh rich. He who has these riches is in close sympathy with Him who so loved us that He gave His life for our redemption.

GIVE NOT GLORY TO MAN

Paul, when speaking to the Corinthians, says, "We have this treasure in earthen vessels, that the excellency of the power may be of God, and not of us." This is what Christ taught His disciples: "Without Me ye can do nothing." Paul would impress upon the minds of the ministers and people the reason why the gospel was committed to weak and erring men—that man might not receive the honor due to God only, but that God might receive all the glory. The ambassador is not to congratulate himself and take to himself the honor of success, or even to divide the honor with God, as if by his own power he had accomplished the work. Elaborate reasoning or argumentative demonstrations of doctrines seldom impress upon the hearer the sense of his need and his peril. Simple, brief statements, from a heart made soft and sympathetic by the love of Christ, will be as the grain of mustard seed, to which Christ Himself likened His utterances of divine truth. He throws into the soul the vital energy of His Spirit, to make the seed of truth germinate and bear fruit.

Will my brethren take heed that no glory is given to men? Will they acknowledge that Christ does the work upon the human heart, and not they themselves? Will my ministering brethren plead with God alone in secret prayer for His presence and His power? Dare not to preach another discourse until you know, by your own experience, what Christ is to you. With hearts made holy through faith in the righteousness of Christ, you can preach Christ, you can lift up the risen Saviour before your hearers; with hearts subdued and melted with the love of Jesus you can say, "Behold the Lamb of God, which taketh away the sin of the world."

CULTIVATE FAITH AND LOVE

There is a sad neglect of reading the Bible and searching it with humble hearts for yourselves. Take no man's explanation of Scripture, whatever his position, but go to the Bible and search for the truth yourselves. After hearing Jesus, the Samaritans said, "Now we believe, not because of thy saying: for we have heard Him ourselves, and know that this is indeed the Christ, the Saviour of the world." There is the mine of truth. Sink the shaft deep, and you will possess that knowledge which is of highest value to you. Many have become lazy and criminally neglectful in regard to the searching of the Scriptures, and they are as destitute of the Spirit of God as of the knowledge of His word. We read in the Revelation made to John, of some who had a name to live while they were dead. Yes, there are many such among us as a people, many who claim to be alive, while they are dead. My brethren, unless the Holy Spirit is actuating you as a vital principle, unless you are obeying its prompting, depending on its influences, laboring in the strength of God, my message to you from God is: "You are under a delusion which may prove fatal to your souls. You must be converted. You must receive light before you can give light. Place yourselves under the bright beams of the Sun of Righteousness." Then you can say with Isaiah, "Arise, shine; for thy light is come, and the glory of the Lord is risen upon thee." You must cultivate faith and love. "The Lord's hand is not shortened, that it cannot save; neither His ear heavy, that it cannot hear." Seek the Lord. Rest not until you know that Christ is your Saviour.

I wish you, my brethren, to bear in mind that Bible religion never destroys human sympathy. True Christian courtesy needs to be taught and acted, to be carried into all your intercourse with your brethren and with worldlings. There is need of far more love and courtesy in our families than is now revealed. When our ministering brethren shall drink in the spirit of Christ daily, they will be truly courteous, and will not consider it weakness to be tenderhearted and pitiful, for this is one of the principles of the gospel of Christ. Christ's teaching softened and subdued the soul. The truth received into the heart will work a renovation in the soul. Those who love Jesus will love the souls for whom He died. The truth planted in the heart will reveal the love of Jesus and its transforming power. Anything harsh, sour, critical, domineering, is not of Christ, but proceeds from Satan. Coldness, heartlessness, want of tender sympathy, are leavening the camp of Israel. If these evils are permitted to strengthen as they have done for some years in the past, our churches will be in a deplorable condition. Every teacher of the truth needs the Christlike principle in his character. There will be no frowns, no scolding, no expressions of contempt, on the part of any man who is cultivating the graces of Christianity. He feels that he must be a partaker of the divine nature, and he must be replenished from the exhaustless fountain of heavenly grace, else he will lose the milk of human kindness out of his soul. We must love men for Christ's sake. It is easy for the natural heart to love a few favorites, and to be partial to these special few; but Christ bids us love one another as He has loved us. "The wisdom that is from above is first pure, then peaceable, gentle, and easy to be entreated, full of mercy and good fruits, without partiality, and without hypocrisy. And the fruit of righteousness is sown in peace of them that make peace."

You have a serious, solemn work to do to prepare the way of the Lord. You need the heavenly unction, and you may have it. "Whatsoever ye shall ask the Father in My name, He will give it you. Hitherto have ye asked nothing in My name: ask, and ye shall receive, that your joy may be full." Who can be trifling, who can engage in frivolous, common talk, while by faith he sees the Lamb that was slain pleading before the Father as the intercessor of the church upon earth?

By faith let us look upon the rainbow round about the throne, the cloud of sins confessed behind it. The rainbow of promise is an assurance to every humble, contrite, believing soul, that his life is one with Christ, and that Christ is one with God. The wrath of God will not fall upon one soul that seeks refuge in Him. God Himself has declared, "When I see the blood, I will pass over you." "The bow shall be in the cloud; and I will look upon it, that I may remember the everlasting covenant."

It is Christ that loves the world with a love that is infinite. He gave His precious life. He was the Only Begotten of the Father. He is risen again from the dead, and is at the right hand of God, making intercession for us. That same Jesus, with His humanity glorified, with no cessation of His love, is our Saviour. He has enjoined upon us to love one another as He has loved us. Will we then cultivate this love? Shall we be like Jesus?

For further study: *Gospel Workers,* pages 20-23, 254-258, 271-276; *Fundamentals of Christian Education,* "Politics," pages 475-484.

Many of the Jews came and listened as Christ revealed the mysteries of salvation, but they came not to learn; they came to criticize, to catch Him in some inconsistency, that they might have something with which to prejudice the people. They were content with their knowledge, but the children of God must know the voice of the true Shepherd. Is not this a time when it would be highly proper to fast and pray before God? We are in danger of variance, in danger of taking sides on a controverted point; and should we not seek God in earnestness, with humiliation of soul, that we may know what is truth?—*Review and Herald,* February 18, 1890.

Take heed lest by your example you place other souls in peril. It is a terrible thing to lose our own soul, but to pursue a course that will cause the loss of other souls is still more terrible. That our influence should be a savor of death unto death is a terrible thought, and yet it is possible. With what earnestness, then, we should guard our thoughts, our words, our habits, our dispositions. God calls for personal holiness. Only by revealing the character of Christ can we cooperate with Him in saving souls.—*Review and Herald,* December 22, 1904.

Human Needs and Divine Supply 6

Reasons for Inefficiency, and the Remedy

Melbourne, Australia, July 3, 1892.

I would address those who preach the word: "The entrance of Thy words giveth light; it giveth understanding unto the simple." All the advantages and privileges that may be multiplied for your benefit, that you should be educated and trained, rooted and grounded in the truth, will be no real help to you personally unless the mind and heart are opened so that truth shall find entrance, and you make a conscientious surrender of every habit and practice, and every sin that has closed the door against Jesus. Let the light from Christ search every dark corner of the soul; with earnest determination adopt a right course of action. If you hold onto a wrong course, as many of you are now doing; if the truth does not work in you with transforming power, so that you obey it from the heart because you love its pure principles; be sure that for you the truth will lose its vitalizing power, and sin will strengthen.

This is why many are not efficient agents for the Master. They are constantly making provision to please and glorify themselves, or they cherish lust in the heart. True, they assent to the law of Ten Commandments, and many teach the law in theory, but they do not cherish its principles. They do not obey the command of God to be pure, to love God supremely, and their neighbor as themselves. While constantly living a lie, can such have strength, can they have confidence, will such become efficient workers for God?

The articles in this section are from *Special Testimonies to Ministers and Workers* (Series A, No. 2, 1892). This article, pages 9-12.

The Saviour prayed for His disciples, "Sanctify them through Thy truth: Thy word is truth." But if the receiver of Bible knowledge makes no change in his habits or practices to correspond to the light of truth, what then? The spirit is warring against the flesh, and the flesh against the spirit; and one of these must conquer. If the truth sanctifies the soul, sin is hated and shunned, because Christ is accepted as an honored guest. But Christ cannot share a divided heart; sin and Jesus are never in copartnership. He who accepts the truth in sincerity, who eats the flesh and drinks the blood of the Son of God, has eternal life. "The words that I speak unto you," said Jesus, "they are spirit, and they are life." When the receiver of truth cooperates with the Holy Spirit, he will go weighted with the burden of the message to souls; he will never be merely a sermonizer. He will enter heart and soul into the great work of seeking and saving that which is lost. Practicing the religion of Christ, he will accomplish a good work in winning souls.

UNDER BONDS TO GOD

Every believer is under bonds to God to be spiritually minded, keeping himself in the channel of light, that he may let his light shine to the world. When all those who are engaged in the sacred work of the ministry shall grow in grace and in the knowledge of our Lord and Saviour, they will hate sin and all selfishness. A moral renovation is constantly going on; as they continue looking to Jesus, they become conformed to His image, and are found complete in Him, not having their own righteousness, but the righteousness that is in Christ Jesus our Lord.

The great advantage of the ministerial institutes* is not

*See Appendix.

half appreciated. They are rich in opportunities, but do not accomplish half what they should because those who attend them do not practice the truth which is presented before them in clear lines. Many who are explaining the Scriptures to others have not conscientiously and entirely surrendered mind and heart and life to the control of the Holy Spirit. They love sin and cling to it. I have been shown that impure practices, pride, selfishness, self-glorying, have closed the door of the heart even of those who teach the truth to others, so that the frown of God is upon them. Cannot some renovating power take hold of them? Have they fallen a prey to a moral disease which is incurable because they themselves refuse to be cured? Oh, that everyone who labors in word and doctrine would heed the words of Paul, "I beseech you therefore, brethren, by the mercies of God, that ye present your bodies a living sacrifice, holy, acceptable unto God, which is your reasonable service."

How my heart goes out in rejoicing for those who walk in humility of mind, who love and fear God. They possess a power far more valuable than learning or eloquence. "The fear of the Lord is the beginning of wisdom;" and His love and fear are like a thread of gold uniting the human agent to the divine. Thus all the movements of life are simplified. When the children of God are struggling with temptation, battling against the passions of the natural heart, faith connects the soul with the only One who can give help, and they are overcomers.

May the Lord work upon the hearts of those who have received great light, that they may depart from all iniquity. Behold the cross of Calvary. There is Jesus, who gave His life, not that men might continue in sin, not that they may have license to break the law of God, but that through this infinite sacrifice they may be saved from all sin. Said Christ, "I sanctify Myself, that they also might be sanctified," by the perfection of His example. Will those who preach the truth to others be sanctified by the truth themselves? Will they love the Lord with heart and mind and soul, and their neighbor as themselves? Will they meet the highest standard of Christian character? Are their tastes elevated, their appetites controlled? Are they cherishing only noble sentiments, strong, deep sympathy, and pure purposes, that they may indeed be laborers together with God? We must have the Holy Spirit to sustain us in the conflict; "for we wrestle not against flesh and blood, but against principalities, against powers, against the rulers of the darkness of this world, against spiritual wickedness in high places."

For further study: *Gospel Workers,* pages 273, 284, 285, 288.

Need of Divine Power and Wisdom

Melbourne, Australia, July 3, 1892.

We have been asked why it is that there is so little power in the churches, why there is so little efficiency among our teachers. The answer is that it is because known sin in various forms is cherished among the professed followers of Christ, and the conscience becomes hardened by long violation. The answer is that men do not walk with God but separate company with Jesus, and as a result we see manifested in the church selfishness, covetousness, pride, strife, contention, hard-heartedness, licentiousness, and evil practices. Even among those who preach the sacred word of God, this

---

Special Testimonies to Ministers and Workers (Series A, No. 2, 1892), pages 12-16.

state of evil is found; and unless there is thorough reformation among those who are unholy and unsanctified, it would be better that such men should leave the ministry, and choose some other occupation, where their unregenerate thoughts would not bring disaster upon the people of God.

WAITING AND WATCHING

The apostle exhorts the brethren, saying, "Finally, my brethren, be strong in the Lord, and in the power of His might. Put on the whole armor of God, that ye may be able to stand . . . in the evil day, and having done all, to stand." Oh, what a day is before us! What sifting will there be among those who claim to be the children of God! The unjust will be found among the just. Those who have great light and who have not walked in it will have darkness corresponding to the light they have despised. We have need to heed the lesson contained in the words of Paul, "But I keep under my body, and bring it in subjection: lest that by any means, when I have preached to others, I myself should be a castaway." The enemy is diligently working to see whom he can add to the ranks of apostasy; but the Lord is soon coming, and erelong every case will be decided for eternity. Those whose works correspond with the light graciously given them will be numbered on the Lord's side.

We are waiting and watching for the grand and awful scene which will close up this earth's history. But we are not simply to be waiting; we are to be vigilantly working with reference to this solemn event. The living church of God will be waiting, watching, and working. None are to stand in a neutral position. All are to represent Christ in active, earnest effort to save perishing souls. Will the church fold her hands now? Shall we sleep as is represented in the parable of the foolish virgins? Every precaution is to be taken now; for haphazard work will result in spiritual declension, and that day will overtake us as a thief. The mind needs to be strengthened to look deep and discern the reasons of our faith. The soul-temple is to be purified by the truth, for only the pure in heart will be able to stand against the wiles of Satan.

OUR RELATION TO THE WORLD

We are not to copy the world's practices, and yet we are not to stand aloof from the people of the world; for our light must shine amid the moral darkness that covers the earth. There is a sad lack in the church, of Christian love one for another. This love is easily extinguished; and yet without it we cannot have Christian fellowship, nor love for those for whom Christ died.

Our brethren need to take heed to the injunction: "But foolish and unlearned questions avoid, knowing that they do gender strifes. And the servant of the Lord must not strive; but be gentle unto all men, apt to teach, patient, in meekness instructing those that oppose themselves; if God peradventure will give them repentance to the acknowledging of the truth; and that they may recover themselves out of the snare of the devil, who are taken captive by him at his will." We shall have to meet crooked elements in the world and in the church. Men will come claiming to have great light; but those who have experience in the cause of God will see that what they present as light is great darkness. Men of this class will have to be treated according to the specifications of the word of God. Those who are in error may become excited in advocating their views, but those who are walking in the light can afford to be calm, gentle with the erring, "apt to teach," making manifest the fact that they have asked and received wisdom of God. They will have no occasion to move excitedly, but occasion to move wisely, patiently, "in meekness instructing those that oppose themselves."

The time has come when those who are rooted and grounded in the truth may manifest their firmness and decision, may make known the fact that they are unmoved by the sophistry, maxims, or fables of the ignorant and wavering. Without foundation men will make statements with all the positiveness of truth; but it is of no use to argue with them concerning their spurious assertions. The best way to deal with error is to present the truth, and leave wild ideas to die out for want of notice. Contrasted with truth, the weakness of error is made apparent to every intelligent mind. The more the erroneous assertions of opposers, and of those who rise up among us to deceive souls, are repeated, the better the cause of error is served. The more publicity is given to the suggestions of Satan, the better pleased is his satanic majesty; for unsanctified hearts will be prepared to receive the chaff that he provides for them. We shall have to meet difficulties of this order even in the church. Men will make a world of an atom and an atom of a world.

USING GOD-GIVEN TALENTS

Cannot we do more for the churches, that they may be aroused to act upon the light already given? God has appointed to every man his work. The lowliest as well as the mightiest have been endowed with influence that should tell on the Lord's side, and they should devote their talent to Him, each working in his appointed place of duty. The Lord expects everyone to do his best. When light shines into the heart,

He expects our work to correspond with our light, to be in accordance with the measure of the fullness of Christ which we have received. The more we use our knowledge and exercise our powers, the more knowledge we shall have, the more power we shall acquire to do more and better work.

Our talents are not our own, they are the Lord's property with which we are to trade. We are responsible for the use or the abuse of the Lord's goods. God calls upon men to invest their entrusted talents, that when the Master cometh He may receive His own with usury. With His own blood Christ has purchased us as His servants. Shall we serve Him? Shall we now study to show ourselves approved unto God? Shall we show by our actions that we are stewards of His grace? Every effort put forth for the Master, prompted by a pure, sincere heart, will be a fragrant offering to Him.

We are walking in the sight of unseen intelligences. A witness is by our side constantly to see how we trade with the Lord's entrusted goods. When the good steward returns his talents with usury, he will claim nothing. He will realize that they are the talents that God delivered unto him, and will give glory to the Master. He knows that there would have been no gain without the deposit, no interest without the principal. He will say, "Lord, thou deliveredst unto me five talents: behold, I have gained beside them five talents more." Let the church now consider whether they are putting out to usury the capital the Lord has given. Without the grace of Christ every soul would have been bankrupt for eternity; therefore we can rightfully claim nothing. But while we can claim nothing, yet when we are faithful stewards, the Lord rewards us as if the merit were all our own. He says, "Well done, thou good and faithful servant: thou hast been faithful over a few things, I will make thee ruler over many things: enter thou into the joy of thy Lord."

How many will mourn for lost opportunities when it is eternally too late! Today we have talent and opportunity, but we know not how long these may be ours. Then let us work while it is day; for the night cometh, in which no man can work. "Blessed is that servant, whom his Lord when He cometh shall find so doing."

Return to the First Love

Melbourne, Australia, July 15, 1892.

The reason so many fail to have success is that they trust in themselves altogether too much, and do not feel the positive necessity of abiding in Christ as they go forth to seek and save that which is lost. Until they have the mind of Christ and teach the truth as it is in Jesus, they will not accomplish much. I walk with trembling before God. I know not how to speak or trace with pen the large subject of the atoning sacrifice. I know not how to present subjects in the living power in which they stand before me. I tremble for fear lest I shall belittle the great plan of salvation by cheap words. I bow my soul in awe and reverence before God, and say, Who is sufficient for these things? How can I talk, how can I write to my brethren, so that they will catch the beams of light flashing from heaven? What shall I say?

"REPENT, AND DO THE FIRST WORKS"

The atmosphere of the church is so frigid, its spirit is of such an order, that men and women cannot sus-

---

Special Testimonies to Ministers and Workers (Series A, No. 2, 1892), pages 17-22.

tain or endure the example of primitive and heaven-born piety. The warmth of their first love is frozen up, and unless they are watered over by the baptism of the Holy Spirit, their candlestick will be removed out of its place, except they repent and do their first works. The first works of the church were seen when the believers sought out friends, relatives, and acquaintances, and with hearts overflowing with love told the story of what Jesus was to them and what they were to Jesus. Oh, that the Lord would awaken those who are in responsible positions, lest they undertake to do work, relying upon their own smartness. The work that comes forth from their hands will lack the mold and superscription of Christ.

PERVERTING POWER OF SELFISHNESS

Selfishness mars all that unconsecrated workers do. They have need to pray always, but they do not. They need to watch unto prayer. They have need to feel the sacredness of the work, but they do not feel this. They handle sacred things as they do common things. Spiritual things are spiritually discerned, and until they can drink of the water of life, and Christ be in them as a well of water springing up unto everlasting life, they will refresh no one, bless no one; and except they repent, their candlestick will be removed out of its place. There is need of enduring patience, of invincible charity, of omnipotent faith in the work of saving souls. Self must not be prominent. Wisdom from Christ must be exercised in dealing with human minds.

Every worker who deals with souls successfully must come to the work divested of self. There can be no scolding or fretting, no arbitrary authority exercised, no putting forth of the finger and speaking vanity; but come to the work with hearts warmed with love for Jesus and for precious souls for whom He died. Those who are self-sufficient cannot conceal their weakness. They will come to the trial with overweening confidence in themselves, and make manifest the fact that Jesus is not with them. These self-sufficient souls are not few, and they have lessons to learn by hard experience of discomfiture and defeat. Few have the grace to welcome such an experience, and many backslide under the trial. They blame circumstances for their discomfiture, and think their talent is not appreciated by others. If they would humble themselves under the hand of God, He would teach them.

ESSENTIALS IN SERVICE

Those who do not learn every day in the school of Christ, who do not spend much time in earnest prayer, are not fit to handle the work of God in any of its branches; for if they do, human depravity will surely overcome them and they will lift up their souls unto vanity. Those who become co-workers with Jesus Christ, and who have spirituality to discern spiritual things, will feel their need of virtue and of wisdom from Heaven in handling His work. There are some who neither burn nor shine, yet are contented. They are in a wretchedly cold and indifferent condition, and a large number who know the truth manifestly neglect duty, for which the Lord will hold them accountable.

God has given us Jesus, and in Him is the revelation of God. Our Redeemer says: "If a man love Me, he will keep My words: and My Father will love him, and We will come unto him, and make Our abode with him." "Let that therefore abide in you, which ye have heard from the beginning. If that which ye have heard from the beginning shall remain in you, ye also shall continue in the Son, and in the Father." If we know God, and Jesus Christ whom He has sent, unspeakable gladness will come to the soul. Oh, how we need the divine presence! For the baptism of the Holy Spirit every worker should be breathing out his prayer to God. Companies should be gathered together to call upon God for special help, for heavenly wisdom, that the people of God may know how to plan and devise and execute the work.

Especially should men pray that the Lord will choose His agents, and baptize His missionaries with the Holy Spirit. For ten days the disciples prayed before the Pentecostal blessing came. It required all that time to bring them to an understanding of what it meant to offer effectual prayer, drawing nearer and nearer to God, confessing their sins, humbling their hearts before God, and by faith beholding Jesus, and becoming changed into His image. When the blessing did come, it filled all the place where they were assembled, and, endowed with power, they went forth to do effectual work for the Master.

CHOOSING MEN FOR THE MINISTRY

Altogether too light a matter is made of selecting men to do the sacred work committed to our hands. As a consequence of this carelessness, unconverted men are at work in missionary fields, who are full of passionate lusts, who are unthankful, who are unholy. Though some of them have been often reproved, they have not changed their course, and their lustful practices bring reproach upon the cause of God. What will be the fruit of such labor? Why do not all our workers remember that every word, good or evil, must be met again in the judgment? Every inspiration of the Holy Spirit leading men to goodness and to God is noted in the books of heaven, and the worker through whom the Lord has brought light will be commended in the day of God. If the workers realized the eternal responsibility that rests upon them, would they enter upon the work without a deep sense of its sacredness? Should we not expect to see the deep movings of the Spirit of God upon men who present themselves to enter the ministry?

The apostle says, "Put ye on the Lord Jesus Christ, and make not provision for the flesh, to fulfill the lusts thereof." Let every soul heed these words, and know that the Lord Jesus will accept of no compromise. In accepting and retaining workers who persist in retaining their imperfections of character, and do not give full proof of their ministry, the standard has been greatly lowered. There are many in responsible positions who do not heed the injunction of the apostle, but make provision for fulfilling the lust of the flesh. Unless the worker puts on the Lord Jesus Christ and finds in Him wisdom, sanctification, and redemption, how can he represent the religion of Jesus? All his efficiency, all his reward, is found in Christ. There must be evidence on the part of those who take the solemn position of shepherds that they have, without reservation, dedicated themselves to the work. They must take Christ as their personal Saviour. Why is it that those who have been long engaged in the ministry do not grow in grace and the knowledge of the Lord Jesus? I have been shown that they gratify their selfish propensities and do only such things as agree with their tastes and ideas. They make provision for indulgence in pride and sensuality and carry out their selfish ambitions and plans. They are full of self-esteem. But although their evil propensities may seem to them as precious as the right hand or the right eye, they must be separated from the worker, or he cannot be acceptable before God. Hands are laid upon men to ordain them for the ministry before they are thoroughly examined as to their qualifications for the sacred work; but how much better would it be to make thorough work before accepting them as ministers, than to have to go through this rigid examination after they have become established in their position and have put their mold upon the work.

A CONSECRATED LIFE

The following quotation shows what true consecration will do, and this is what we should require of our workers:

"Harlan Page consecrated himself to God, with a determination to live and labor to promote the Lord's glory, in the salvation of the perishing. 'When I first obtained hope,' he said on his dying bed, 'I felt that I must labor for souls. I prayed year after year that God would make me the means of saving some.' His prayers were signally answered. Never did Page lose an opportunity of holding up the lamp to souls. By letters, by conversation, by tracts, by prayers, by appeals and warnings, as well as by a holy and earnest example, did he try to reclaim the wandering, or edify the believer. In factories, in schools, and elsewhere did this mechanic labor, and only the mighty power of grace can explain how one so humble could achieve so much. His life is a speaking comment on the words, 'God hath chosen the foolish things of the world to confound the wise; and God hath chosen the weak things of the world to confound the things which are mighty; and base things of the world, and things which are despised, hath God chosen, yea, and things which are not, to bring to naught things that are.' 'Our faith in eternal realities is weak,' he cried, 'and our sense of duty faint, while we neglect the salvation of our fellow beings. Let us awake to our duties, and while we have tongue or pen, devote them to the service of the Most High, not in our own strength, but with strong faith and firm confidence.'"

We have increased light. We have a solemn, weighty message to bear to the world, and God designs that His chosen disciples shall have a deep experience, and be endowed with the power of the Holy Spirit. "The Lord seeth not as man seeth; for man looketh on the outward appearance, but the Lord looketh on the heart." This was a lesson that David never forgot, and in his dying testimony to Solomon he said, "And thou, Solomon my son, know thou the God of thy father, and serve Him with a perfect heart and with a willing mind: for the Lord searcheth all hearts, and understandeth all the imaginations of the thoughts: if thou seek Him, He will be found of thee; but if thou forsake Him, He will cast thee off forever."

We are living in an important period of this earth's history; and with the light of truth shining upon us, we cannot now be excused for a moment in meeting a low standard. As co-workers with Christ, we are privileged to share with Christ in His suffering. We are to look at His life, study His character, and copy the pattern. What Christ was in His perfect humanity, we must be; for we must form characters for eternity.

For further study: *Gospel Workers,* pages 437-445; *Testimonies,* vol. 4, pp. 315, 318, 320, 371-383, 437, 441, 442.

The Power of the Holy Spirit Awaits Our Demand and Reception

Melbourne, Australia, December 28, 1891.

Just prior to His leaving His disciples for the heavenly courts, Jesus encouraged them with the promise of the Holy Spirit. This promise belongs as much to us as it did to them, and yet how rarely it is presented before the people, and its reception spoken of in the church. In consequence of this silence upon this most important theme, what promise do we know less about by its practical fulfillment than this rich promise of the gift of the Holy Spirit, whereby efficiency is to be given to all our spiritual labor? The promise of the Holy Spirit is casually brought into our discourses, is incidentally touched upon, and that is all. Prophecies have been dwelt upon, doctrines have been expounded; but that which is essential to the church in order that they may grow in spiritual strength and efficiency, in order that the preaching may carry conviction with it, and souls be converted to God, has been largely left out of ministerial effort. This subject has been set aside, as if some time in the future would be given to its consideration. Other blessings and privileges have been presented before the people until a desire has been awakened in the church for the attainment of the blessing promised of God; but the impression concerning the Holy Spirit has been that this gift is not for the church now, but that at some time in the future it would be necessary for the church to receive it.

ALL OTHER BLESSINGS

This promised blessing, if claimed by faith, would

Special Testimonies to Ministers and Workers (Series A, No. 2, 1892), pages 23-25.

bring all other blessings in its train, and it is to be given liberally to the people of God. Through the cunning devices of the enemy the minds of God's people seem to be incapable of comprehending and appropriating the promises of God. They seem to think that only the scantiest showers of grace are to fall upon the thirsty soul. The people of God have accustomed themselves to think that they must rely upon their own efforts, that little help is to be received from heaven; and the result is that they have little light to communicate to other souls who are dying in error and darkness. The church has long been contented with little of the blessing of God; they have not felt the need of reaching up to the exalted privileges purchased for them at infinite cost. Their spiritual strength has been feeble, their experience of a dwarfed and crippled character, and they are disqualified for the work the Lord would have them to do. They are not able to present the great and glorious truths of God's Holy Word that would convict and convert souls through the agency of the Holy Spirit. The power of God awaits their demand and reception. A harvest of joy will be reaped by those who sow the holy seeds of truth. "He that goeth forth and weepeth, bearing precious seed, shall doubtless come again with rejoicing, bringing his sheaves with him."

The world have received the idea from the attitude of the church that God's people are indeed a joyless people, that the service of Christ is unattractive, that the blessing of God is bestowed at severe cost to the receivers. By dwelling upon our trials, and making much of difficulties, we misrepresent God and Jesus Christ whom He has sent; for the path to heaven is made unattractive by the gloom that gathers about the soul of the believer, and many turn in disappointment from the service of Christ. But are those who thus present Christ believers? No, for believers rely upon the divine promise, and the Holy Spirit is a comforter as well as a reprover.

The Christian must build all the foundation if he would build a strong, symmetrical character, if he would be well balanced in his religious experience. It is in this way that the man will be prepared to meet the demands of truth and righteousness as they are represented in the Bible; for he will be sustained and energized by the Holy Spirit of God. He who is a true Christian combines great tenderness of feeling with great firmness of purpose, with unswerving fidelity to God; he will in no case become the betrayer of sacred trusts. He who is endowed with the Holy Spirit has great capacities of heart and intellect, with strength of will and purpose that is unconquerable.

For further study: *Testimonies,* vol. 5, pp. 102, 103, 46, 69; *The Desire of Ages,* pages 302, 672, 412, 805, 821, 822, 827.

My brethren, you are required by our Saviour to take heed how you witness for Him. You need to go deeper and still deeper in the study of the word. You have all classes of minds to meet, and as you teach the truths of the sacred word, you are to manifest earnestness, respect, and reverence. Weed out storytelling from your discourses, and preach the word. You will then have more sheaves to bring to the Master. Remember that in your audience there are those who are constantly harassed by temptation. Some are wrestling with doubt, almost in despair, almost hopeless. Ask God to help you to speak words that will strengthen them for the conflict.—*Review and Herald,* December 22, 1904.

Economy 7

Economy to Be Practiced in All Things

Melbourne, Australia, August 3, 1892.

My dear Brethren and Sisters:

My mind has been very much exercised for several nights, sleeping and waking, in regard to the work to be done in this country. In this wide missionary field there is a great deal to be done in advancing the cause and work of the Master, and with the great want of means and of workers, we know not how it can be done. We must humble our hearts before God, and offer up sincere, fervent prayer that the Lord, who is rich in resources, will open our way. "The silver is Mine, and the gold is Mine, saith the Lord," "and the cattle upon a thousand hills."

The life of Christ, the Lord of glory, is our example. He came from heaven, where all was riches and splendor; but He laid aside His royal crown, His royal robe, and clothed His divinity with humanity. Why? That He might meet men where they were. He did not rank Himself with the wealthy, the lordly of earth. The mission of Christ was to reach the very poor of earth. He Himself worked from His earliest years as the Son of a carpenter. Self-denial, did He not know its meaning? The riches and glory of heaven were His own, but for our sakes He became poor, that we through His poverty might become rich. The very foundation of His mission was self-denial, self-sacrifice. The world was His, He made it; yet in a world of His own creating the Son of man had not where to lay His head. He said, "The foxes have

---

The articles in this section are from *Special Testimonies to Ministers and Workers* (Series A, No. 3, 1895). This article pages 3-7.

holes, and the birds of the air have nests; but the Son of man hath not where to lay His head."

STUDY THE PATTERN

Now in the establishment and broadening of the work in this country, means will be essential, that we may do a large work in a short time. And the only way we can do it is, in every movement, to keep the eye single to the glory of God, so that it may not be said of us, They began to build, and were not able to finish. In leading out to do a broader work, we need, at the very beginning, to put pride and worldly ambition entirely out of our hearts. Having before us the example of Christ, the greatest Teacher the world ever knew, we need not make a mistake. "He that followeth Me shall not walk in darkness, but shall have the light of life." "If any man will come after Me, let him deny himself, and take up his cross daily, and follow Me." We must study the Pattern, and inquire at every step, "Is this the way of the Lord?" We shall certainly make grave mistakes if we do not keep self-denial and self-sacrifice prominent before the people in every movement.

The work in this missionary field is yet in its infancy. The believers have made only a beginning in the Christian life; and the reason why we have felt so great a burden for this people is, that henceforth they may learn greater things. It doth not yet appear what they shall be through a practical belief in the truth and the sanctification of the entire being by the truth. The words and example of our Redeemer in His life of humility and self-denial will be the light and strength of His people if they follow Jesus fully, trusting in Him at every step. Let it be the language of our hearts, "Be Thou my pattern." He that "willeth to do His will, he shall know of the teaching." Nothing is so desirable as to live as Christ lived, to deny self as Christ denied Himself, and to labor with Him in seeking to save that which is lost.

AVOID EXTRAVAGANCE

In the line of furniture, do not purchase one article merely to make a show. Get things that will be useful, and that will bear handling. Educate the people to practice self-denial. Let it be considered that every dollar may represent a soul, for someone might be brought to a knowledge of the truth through the use of that dollar in the missionary work. We may have very nice taste, and enjoy that which is beautiful and artistic; but had not Christ the very finest, purest, holiest taste? His home was heaven, yet He denied Himself; humiliation marked all His life, from the manger to Calvary. In the beginning of the work, we must not reproduce the very things that the Lord has condemned in America, the needless, extravagant expenditure of money to gratify pride and love of display. Let everything of this order be scrupulously shunned.

MAINTAIN SIMPLICITY

In eating, dressing, and in the furnishing of our school building, we want to preserve the simplicity of true godliness. Many will deny themselves and sacrifice much in order to contribute toward making the missionary work a success, and should they see this means expended upon the finest linen and the more expensive furniture or articles for the table, it would have a most unfortunate influence upon these brethren and sisters. Nothing could militate more decidedly against our present and future usefulness in this country. The very first lesson to teach the students is self-denial. Let their eyes, their senses, take in the lesson; let all the appointments of the school convey practical instruction in this line, that the work can be carried forward only by a constant sacrifice.

In every movement let us follow closely the example of our Saviour. I feel deeply over these things. We must consider in what lines to work in order to secure success; we must come to the work with our hearts imbued with the spirit of Christ. Then we shall realize that our work must be carried forward in a humble way. Our ministers and their wives should be an example in plainness of dress; they should dress neatly, comfortably, wearing good material, but avoiding anything like extravagance and trimmings, even if not expensive; for these things tell to our disadvantage. We should educate the youth to simplicity of dress, plainness with neatness. Let the extra trimmings be left out, even though the cost be but a trifle.

THE WEDDING RING

Some have had a burden in regard to the wearing of a marriage ring, feeling that the wives of our ministers should conform to this custom. All this is unnecessary. Let the ministers' wives have the golden link which binds their souls to Jesus Christ, a pure and holy character, the true love and meekness and godliness that are the fruit borne upon the Christian tree, and their influence will be secure anywhere. The fact that a disregard of the custom occasions remark is no good reason for adopting it. Americans can make their position understood by plainly stating that the custom is not regarded as obligatory in our country. We need not wear the sign, for we are not untrue to our marriage vow, and the wearing of the ring would be no evidence that we were true. I feel deeply over this leavening process which seems to be going on among us, in the conformity to custom and fashion. Not one penny should be spent for a circlet of gold to testify that we are married. In countries where the custom is imperative, we have no burden to condemn those who have their marriage ring; let them wear it if they can do so conscientiously; but let not our missionaries feel that the wearing of the ring will increase their influence one jot or tittle. If they are Christians, it will be manifest in their Christlikeness of character, in their words, in their works, in the home, in association with others; it will be evinced by their patience and long-suffering and kindliness. They will manifest the spirit of the Master, they will possess His beauty of character, His loveliness of disposition, His sympathetic heart.

Improvement in the Work

April 23, 1894.

God calls for decided improvement to be made in the various branches of the work. The business done in connection with the cause of God must be marked with greater precision and exactitude. There have not been close, decided, firm efforts put forth to bring about essential reform. Some connected with the cause are drawing near to the close of their lives, and yet they have not so learned the lessons of the Bible as to feel the necessity of bringing them into their practical life. They have wasted opportunities, and gracious

---

Special Testimonies to Ministers and Workers (Series A, No. 3, 1895), pages 7, 8.

blessings have been unappreciated because they did not wish to make a change.

My Guide said: "Elevate the standard in all school education. You must set up no lower standard. Discipline must be maintained. Teach the youth by precept and example." There has not been too much strictness but too much laxness of action tolerated. But the workers must not despair. Work with the spirit of Christ, with the mind of Christ to correct existing evils. Expect that the wrongdoers will have the sympathy of wrongdoers; but faithful shepherds of the flock have lessons to learn in order to keep on an elevated standard and yet teach that the star of hope is still shining. Work on patiently; but rebuke sin firmly, and give it no sanction. The refuge of lies for the covering up of sin must be torn away in order that poor deluded souls may not sleep on to their everlasting ruin.

The world is soon to be left by the angel of mercy, and the seven last plagues are to be poured out. Sin, shame, sorrow, and darkness are on every side; but God still holds out to the souls of men the precious privilege of exchanging darkness for light, error for truth, sin for righteousness. But God's patience and mercy will not always wait. Let not one soul think that he can hide from God's wrath behind a lie, for God will strip from the soul the refuge of lies. The bolts of God's wrath are soon to fall, and when He shall begin to punish the transgressors, there will be no period of respite until the end. The storm of God's wrath is gathering, and those only will stand who are sanctified through the truth in the love of God. They shall be hid with Christ in God till the desolation shall be overpast. He shall come forth to punish the inhabitants of the world for their iniquity, and "the earth also shall disclose her blood, and shall no more cover her slain." Let the language of the soul be—

Hide me, O my Saviour, hide!
Till the storm of life is past;
Safe into the haven guide,
Oh, receive my soul at last!

Other refuge have I none,
Hangs my helpless soul on Thee;
Leave, oh, leave me not alone!
Still support and comfort me.

For further study: *Gospel Workers,* pages 98-100, 249-253; *Testimonies,* vol. 5, pp. 158, 159, 706, 708, 80; vol. 8, pp. 156, 157; vol. 6, pp. 34, 113; vol. 2, pp. 232-234.

Idleness

April 30, 1894.

"Not slothful in business; fervent in spirit; serving the Lord." There is but one remedy for indolence, and that is to throw off sluggishness as a sin that leads to perdition, and go to work using the physical ability that God has given you for this purpose. The only cure for a useless, inefficient life is effort, determined, persevering effort. The only cure for selfishness is to deny self, and work earnestly to be the blessing that you can be to your fellowmen. "He that observeth the wind shall not sow; and he that regardeth the clouds shall not reap."

As God's human agents we are to do the work that He has given us. To every man He has given his work, and we are not going to give ourselves up to conjecture as to whether or not our earnest endeavors will prove successful. All that we as individuals are re-

---

Special Testimonies to Ministers and Workers (Series A, No. 3, 1895), pages 8, 9.

sponsible for is the unwearied, conscientious discharge of duty that someone must do; and if we fail to do that which is placed in our way, we cannot be excused of God. But having done the best we can, then we are to leave all results with God. But it is required of us that we exercise more mental and spiritual power. It is your duty, and it has been your duty every day of the life God has graciously granted you, to pull at the oars of duty, for you are a responsible agent of God.

The command to you is, "Go work today in My vineyard." We are all God's workmen, and not one is to be idle; but I would ask, What are you doing for the Master in order that you may hear His words of approval, "Well done, thou good and faithful servant: thou hast been faithful over a few things, I will make thee ruler over many things"? God never makes a mistake; He will never call men good and faithful who are not good and faithful.

For further study: *Testimonies,* vol. 5, pp. 122, 180; vol. 2, pp. 349, 254, 498, 501, 529; *Gospel Workers,* pages 277-279.

The Spirit of Jesus

August 3, 1894.

Christ identifies His interest with that of humanity. The work that bears the divine credentials is that which manifests the spirit of Jesus, which reveals His love, His carefulness, His tenderness in dealing with the minds of men. What revelations would come to man if the curtain should be rolled back and you could see the result of your work in dealing with the erring who have needed most judicious treatment lest they should be turned out of the way. "Wherefore lift up the hands which hang down, and the feeble knees; and make straight paths for your

---

Special Testimonies to Ministers and Workers (Series A, No. 3, 1895), pages 9-12.

feet, lest that which is lame be turned out of the way; but let it rather be healed."

We will always have tried and tempted ones to deal with, and it is essential that we be converted to God every day and be vessels that can be used unto His name's honor and glory. The true value of the soul can be estimated only by the cross of Calvary. "For God so loved the world, that He gave His only-begotten Son, that whosoever believeth in Him should not perish, but have everlasting life." Those who are unconverted, who are unsanctified, will make manifest what manner of spirit they are of. They will show by their likes and dislikes that their natural feelings are not under the control of a sanctified will. The religion of Jesus Christ is one which will revolutionize the entire man. The truth of God has power to transform the character.

We are to have the faith that works by love and purifies the soul. A faith that does not result in this is of no value. The fruit of the branch will show what is the character of the parent stock. He who is planted in Christ will be elevated. In place of acting rashly, in place of cutting off the erring from faith and hope with your severity and harshness, the true Christian will teach the ignorant, reform the sinful, comfort those who mourn, restrain oppression and injustice, and work after a Christlike plan, even in all business transactions. Instead of stirring up strife, he will bring about peace and harmony.

A hard, unjust, critical spirit has been indulged among those who have held positions of trust in the work of God. Unless those who have indulged this spirit are converted, they will be relieved of the responsibility of acting a part in committees of counsel, even in the transaction of business. Unless they are converted, their voices must not be heard in the council, for the aggregate result is more injurious than beneficial. Wrong prevails, man is made an offender for a word, and suspicion, distrust, jealousy, evil-surmising, evilspeaking, and injustice reproduce themselves even in connection with the cause of God. A false zeal passes for jealousy for the cause of God; but the miserable, filthy garment of self must be destroyed, and in its place men must accept the righteousness of Christ. The persecution that is carried on among church members is a most terrible thing. It is true that some have committed errors and made mistakes, but it is equally true that these errors and mistakes are not nearly as grievous in the sight of God as is the harsh and unforgiving spirit of those who are criticizers and censors. Many of those who are free to pass judgment on others are committing errors which, although not made manifest, are tainted with deadly evil that is corrupting their spiritual life.

LOVE AND UNITY

God would open the eyes of His professed people in order that they may see that they must love God supremely, and their neighbors as themselves, if they would be saved in His kingdom. Many are making manifest that they are not controlled by the Spirit of Christ but by another spirit. The attributes they display are as unlike the attributes of Christ as are the characteristics of Satan. It is high time that believers should stand shoulder to shoulder and strive together for eternal life, in place of holding themselves aloof and expressing by word and action, "I am holier than thou." Those who would exert all their powers for the salvation of perishing souls must come heart to heart, and be bound together in cords of sympathy and love. The brethren should manifest the same spirit as that manifested by our merciful and faithful High Priest, who is touched with the feeling of our infirmities. We may inspire fainting, hopeless ones with new life. We may achieve victories which our own erroneous and misconceived opinions, our own defects of character, our own smallness of faith, have made to seem impossible. Faith! we scarcely know what it is.

The Lord Is Soon Coming

The end of all things is at hand. The Lord is soon coming. Already His judgments are abroad in our land. We are not only to talk of Christ's coming, but in every action we are to reveal the fact that He is soon to be manifested in the clouds of heaven with power and great glory. Have we the wedding garment on? Have we personal piety? Have we cooperated with divine agencies in a wholehearted, unreserved manner, in weaving into our life's practices the divine principles of God's holy law? It is one thing to talk the law, and it is another thing entirely to practice it. It is the doers of the law that shall be justified before God; for those who do the law represent the character of God, and lie not against the truth.

The Lord is coming. Oh, the time is short, and who in the Bible view are laborers together with God? Shall we not be filled with fear and awe lest we are still in our own natural tempers, lest we are unconverted and unholy, and seeking to pass off a counterfeit experience for a genuine one? Awake, brethren, awake, before it shall be forever too late.

Special Testimonies to Ministers and Workers (Series A, No. 3, 1895), pages 12, 13.

There are many who are laborers together with God whom we do not discern. The hands of ministers have never been laid upon them in ordination for the work; but nevertheless they are wearing the yoke of Christ, and exert a saving influence in working in different lines to win souls to Christ. The success of our work depends upon our love to God and our love to our fellowmen. When there is harmonious action among the individual members of the church, when there is love and confidence manifested by brother to brother, there will be proportionate force and power in our work for the salvation of men. Oh, how greatly we need a moral renovation! Without the faith that works by love, you can do nothing. May the Lord give you hearts to receive this testimony.

For further study: *The Desire of Ages,* pages 633-636.

Read and study the fourth chapter of Zechariah. The two olive trees empty the golden oil out of themselves through the golden pipes into the golden bowl from which the lamps of the sanctuary are fed. The golden oil represents the Holy Spirit. With this oil God's ministers are to be constantly supplied, that they, in turn, may impart it to the church. "Not by might, nor by power, but by My Spirit, saith the Lord of hosts." God's servants can obtain victories only by inward purity, by cleanness of heart, by holiness. It is of the utmost importance that ministers set a right example. If they follow lax, loose principles, their example is quoted by those who are doing wrong as a vindication of their course. The whole synagogue of Satan is watching for defects in the lives of God's representatives, and the most is made of every defect.—*Review and Herald,* December 22, 1904.

Workers With God 8

Love and Confidence Among Brethren

October 30, 1894.

When men will show confidence in their fellow-men they will come much nearer to possessing the mind of Christ. The Lord has revealed the estimate that He places upon man. "For God so loved the world, that He gave His only-begotten Son, that whosoever believeth in Him should not perish, but have everlasting life." But some minds are ever seeking to reshape the character of others according to their own ideas and measure. God has not given them this work to do.

Self will ever cherish a high estimate of self. As men lose their first love, they do not keep the commandments of God, and then they begin to criticize one another. This spirit will constantly be striving for the mastery to the close of time. Satan is seeking to foster it in order that brethren in their ignorance may seek to devour one another. God is not glorified but greatly dishonored; the Spirit of God is grieved. Satan exults, because he knows that if he can set brother to watch brother in the church and in the ministry some will be so disheartened and discouraged as to leave their posts of duty. This is not the work of the Holy Spirit; a power from beneath is working in the chambers of the mind and in the soul temple to place his attributes where the attributes of Christ should be.

He who has paid the infinite price to redeem men reads with unerring accuracy all the hidden workings of the human mind, and knows just how to deal with every soul. And in dealing with men, He mani-

---

The articles in this section are from *Special Testimonies to Ministers and Workers* (Series A, No. 3, 1895). This article pages 16-23.

fests the same principles that are manifest in the natural world. The beneficent operations of nature are not accomplished by abrupt and startling interpositions; men are not permitted to take her work into their own hands. God works through the calm, regular operation of His appointed laws. So it is in spiritual things. Satan is constantly seeking to produce effects by rude and violent thrusts; but Jesus found access to minds by the pathway of their most familiar associations. He disturbed as little as possible their accustomed train of thought by abrupt actions or prescribed rules. He honored man with His confidence, and thus placed him on his honor. He introduced old truths in a new and precious light. Thus when only twelve years old, He astonished the doctors of the law by His questions in the temple.

Jesus assumed humanity that He might meet humanity. He brings men under the transforming power of truth by meeting them where they are. He gains access to the heart by securing sympathy and confidence, making all feel that His identification with their nature and interest is complete. The truth came from His lips beautiful in its simplicity, yet clothed with dignity and power. What a teacher was our Lord Jesus Christ! How tenderly did He treat every honest inquirer after truth, that He might gain admission to his sympathies and find a home in his heart.

I must tell you, brethren, that you are far from what the Lord would have you be. The attributes of the enemy of God and man too often find expression in your spirit and attitude toward one another. You hurt one another because you are not partakers of the divine nature. And you work against your own perfection of character, you bring trouble to yourselves, make your work hard and toilsome, because you regard your own spirit and defects of character as precious virtues to be clung to and fostered.

Jesus points the highest minds, as well as the lowest, to the lily, in the freshness of the dew of the morning, and bids us, "Consider the lilies of the field, how they grow; they toil not, neither do they spin: and yet I say unto you, That even Solomon in all his glory was not arrayed like one of these." And He impresses the lesson: "If God so clothe the grass of the field, which today is, and tomorrow is cast into the oven, shall He not much more clothe you, O ye of little faith?"

ADVANCING THE TRUTH

Men make the work of advancing the truth tenfold harder than it really is by seeking to take God's work out of His hands into their own finite hands. They think that they must be constantly inventing something to make men do things which they suppose these persons ought to do. The time thus spent is all the while making the work more complicated, for the great chief Worker is left out of the question in the care of His own heritage. Men undertake the job of tinkering up the defective character of others, and only succeed in making the defects much worse. They would better leave God to do His own work, for He does not regard them as capable of reshaping character.

What they need is to be imbued with the spirit of Christ. If they take hold of His strength, they will make peace with Him; then they will be in a fair way to make peace with their fellow laborers. The less of the meekness and lowliness of Christ the human agent has in his spirit and character, the more he sees perfection in his own methods and imperfection in the methods of others. Our only safety is to watch unto prayer, and to counsel together, believing that God will keep our brethren as well as ourselves, for there is no respect of persons with Him. God will work for us when we are faithful students and the doers of His words.

But when there is, on the part of the laborers, so manifest a disregard of Christ's express command that we love one another as He has loved us, how can we expect that brethren will heed the commandments of finite men, and the regulations and definite specifications as to how each shall labor? The wisdom that prescribes for us must be supernatural, else it will prove a physician that cannot heal, but will only destroy. We would better seek God with the whole heart, and lay down self-importance; for "all ye are brethren."

CHRIST HAS MADE THE YOKE EASY

Instead of toiling to prepare set rules and regulations, you might better be praying and submitting your own will and ways to Christ. He is not pleased when you make hard the things He has made easy. He says: "Take My yoke upon you, and learn of Me; for I am meek and lowly in heart: and ye shall find rest unto your souls. For My yoke is easy, and My burden is light." The Lord Jesus loves His heritage; and if men will not think it their special prerogative to prescribe rules for their fellow laborers, but will bring Christ's rules into their life and copy His lessons, then each will be an example, and not a judge.

PATERNAL CHARACTER OF GOD

Christ's most favorite theme was the paternal character and abundant love of God. The curse of every church today is that men do not adopt Christ's methods. They think they can improve on the rules given in the gospel, and so are free to define them, hoping thus to reform the churches and the workmen. Let God be our one Master, our one Lord, full of goodness, compassion, and love.

God gives knowledge to His workmen; and He has left on record for us the rich, full promise: "If any of you lack wisdom, let him ask of God, that giveth to all men liberally, and upbraideth not; and it shall be given him. But let him ask in faith, nothing wavering. For he that wavereth is like a wave of the sea driven with the wind and tossed. For let not that man think that he shall receive anything of the Lord." Is it not best to obtain wisdom individually by going to God, and not to man? What saith the Great Teacher? "I have manifested Thy name unto the men which Thou gavest Me out of the world."

CRITICIZING DEFECTS IN OTHERS

There is among us an evil that needs to be corrected. Brethren feel free to look at, and speak of, the supposed defects of others, when that very liberty reveals a decided defect in themselves. They make it manifest that they are wise in their own conceits; and God cannot give them His special blessing, for they would exalt themselves and hurt the precious cause of truth. When the world was destitute of the knowledge of God, Jesus came to impart this inestimable blessing—a knowledge of the paternal character of our heavenly Father. This was His own gift to our world; and this gift He committed to His disciples, to be communicated by them to the world.

LABORERS SHOULD IMPROVE THEMSELVES

Having learned the simple rules, they [the ministers] should bend their minds to the acquisition of knowledge in connection with their labor, so that they may be workmen that need not be ashamed. They can master one branch of science after another, while they are engaged in the work of preaching the truth, if they will wisely employ their time. Golden moments are thrown away in unimportant conversation, in indolence, and in doing those things which are of little consequence, that ought to be used every day in useful employments that will fit us more nearly to approach the high standard.

The men who now stand before the people as representatives of Christ have generally more ability than they have training, but they do not put their faculties to use, making the most of their time and opportunities. Nearly every minister in the field, had he exerted his God-given energies, might not only be proficient in reading, writing, and grammar, but even in languages. It is essential for them to set their aim high. But there has been but little ambition to put their powers to the test to reach an elevated standard in knowledge and in religious intelligence.

Our ministers will have to render to God an account for the rusting of the talents He has given to improve by exercise. They might have done tenfold more work intelligently had they cared to become intellectual giants. Their whole experience in their high calling is cheapened because they are content to remain where they are. Their efforts to acquire knowledge will not in the least hinder their spiritual growth if they will study with right motives and proper aims.

NEED OF WORKERS

Workers are needed all over the world. The truth of God is to be carried to foreign lands, that those that are in darkness may be enlightened. Work should be done that will qualify the students to be laborers together with God.

God requires that a zeal be shown in this direction infinitely greater than has hitherto been manifested. As a people we are in some respects far behind in missionary work. We are not doing one twentieth part of the good we might accomplish in positions of trust, because selfishness prevails to a large extent among us. Some are envious of others, fearing that they will be more highly esteemed than themselves.

Cultivated intellects are now needed in every part of the work of God; for novices cannot do the work acceptably in unfolding the hidden treasure to enrich souls. God has devised that schools shall be an instrumentality for developing workers for Jesus Christ of whom He will not be ashamed, and this object must ever be kept in view. The height man may reach by proper culture has not hitherto been realized. We have among us more than an average of men of ability. If their capabilities were brought into use, we should have twenty ministers where we now have one. Physicians, too, would be educated to battle with disease.

Cities and towns are steeped in sin, yet there are Lots in every Sodom. The poison of sin is at work at the heart of society. God calls for reformers to stand in defense of the laws He has established to govern the physical system, and to maintain an elevated standard in the training of the mind and the culture of the heart.

HEART CULTURE

There is danger of pharisaical exactitude, burdening minds with worldly forms and customs which will, in many cases, become all-important, making a world of an atom and an atom of a world. The grace of Christ with its purifying, ennobling influence will do more for us than all the worldly education upon etiquette that is made so essential. To many the externals are the sum total of religion, and yet it will be evidenced that the heart has not that genuine courtesy which alone is of value with God. If they are spoken to about their faults, they have so little Christian politeness that the sacred position of the minister whom God has sent with His message of warning is lost sight of in their effort to criticize his attitude, his gestures, and the formation of his sentences. They think themselves paragons of wisdom, but they pay no heed to the words of God from the courts of heaven. To all such God says that they will have to become fools in order to know the true wisdom of Christ.

I was shown that our college was designed of God to accomplish the great and good work of saving souls. It is only when brought under the full control of the Spirit of God that the talents of an individual are rendered useful to the fullest extent. The precepts and principles of religion are the first steps in the acquisition of knowledge, and lie at the very foundation of true education. Knowledge and science must be vitalized by the Spirit of God in order to serve the noblest purposes. The Christian alone can make the right use of knowledge. Science, in order to be fully appreciated, must be viewed from a religious standpoint. Then all will worship the God of science. The heart which is ennobled by the grace of God can best comprehend the real value of education. The attributes of God as seen in His created works can be appreciated only as we have a knowledge of the Creator. The teachers must be acquainted, not only with the theory of the truth, but must have an experimental knowledge of the way of holiness in order to lead the youth to the fountains of truth, to the Lamb of God that taketh away the sins of the world. Knowledge is power only when united with true piety. A soul emptied of self will be noble. Christ abiding in the heart by faith will make us wise in God's sight.

For further study: *Testimonies,* vol. 2, pp. 133-136, 212-215; vol. 3, pp. 186-188; vol. 4, pp. 63-66; vol. 5, pp. 341-345.

Receiving Gifts

January 30, 1895.

You inquire with respect to the propriety of receiving gifts from Gentiles or the heathen.* The question is not strange; but I would ask you, Who is it that owns our world? Who are the real owners of houses and lands? Is it not God? He has an abundance in our world which He has placed in the hands of men, by which the hungry might be supplied with food, the naked with clothing, the homeless with homes. The Lord would move upon worldly men, even idolaters, to give of their abundance for the support of the work, if we would approach them wisely, and give them an opportunity of doing those things which it is their privilege to do. What they would give we should be privileged to receive.

We should become acquainted with men in high places and, by exercising the wisdom of the serpent and the harmlessness of the dove, we might obtain advantage from them, for God would move upon their minds to do many things in behalf of His people. If proper persons would set before those who have means and influence the needs of the work of God in a proper light, these men might do much to advance the cause of God in our world. We have put

---

Special Testimonies to Ministers and Workers (Series A, No. 3, 1895), pages 32-35.

*See Appendix.

away from us privileges and advantages that we might have had the benefit of, because we chose to stand independent of the world. But we need not sacrifice one principle of truth while taking advantage of every opportunity to advance the cause of God.

The Lord would have His people in the world, but not of the world. They should seek to bring the truth before the men in high places, and give them a fair chance to receive and weigh evidence. There are many who are unenlightened and uninformed, and as individuals we have a serious, solemn, wise work to do. We are to have travail of soul for those who are in high places, and go to them with the gracious invitation to come to the marriage feast. Very much more might have been done than has been done for those in high places. The last message that Christ gave to His disciples before He was parted from them and taken up into heaven was a message to carry the gospel to all the world, and was accompanied by the promise of the Holy Spirit. The Lord said, "Ye shall receive power, after that the Holy Ghost is come upon you: and ye shall be witnesses unto Me both in Jerusalem, and in all Judea, and in Samaria, and unto the uttermost part of the earth."

"The earth is the Lord's, and the fullness thereof." "The silver is Mine, and the gold is Mine, saith the Lord of hosts." "Every beast of the forest is Mine, and the cattle upon a thousand hills. I know all the fowls of the mountains: and the wild beasts of the field are Mine. If I were hungry, I would not tell thee: for the world is Mine, and the fullness thereof."

THE BURDEN FOR SOULS

There is a great work to be done in the earth, and the Lord Jesus has taken men into copartnership with

Himself, in order that heavenly agencies may cooperate with human agencies. Christ was in travail of soul for the redemption of the world, and those who are laborers together with God are representatives of Christ to our world and will have compassion for the lost and will travail in soul for the redemption of men. Unless the church awakes and attends to her post of duty, God will charge the loss of souls to her account. I have a deep interest that the work of God shall advance.

Those who are the chosen of God are required to multiply churches wherever they may be successful in bringing souls to the knowledge of the truth. But the people of God are never to collect together into a large community as they have done in Battle Creek. Those who know what it is to have travail of soul will never do this, for they will feel the burden that Christ carried for the salvation of men.

THE SPIRIT OF WISDOM

Everyone who is chosen of God should improve his intellectual powers. Jesus came to represent the character of the Father, and He sent His disciples into the world to represent the character of Christ. He has given us His word to point out the way of life, and He has not left us simply to carry that word, but has also promised to give it efficiency by the power of the Holy Spirit. Is there need, then, that any should walk in uncertainty, grieving that they do not know and experience the movings of the Holy Spirit upon their hearts? Are you hungering and thirsting for instruction in righteousness? Then you have the sure promise that you shall be filled. "And we know that the Son of God is come, and hath given us an understanding, that we may know Him that is true, and we are in Him that is true, even in His Son Jesus Christ. This is the true God, and eternal life."

The Lord would have us in possession of the spirit of heavenly wisdom. Are we all being impressed to pray to the Lord humbly and earnestly as our necessities require, importuning Him for the spirit of wisdom? Do we pray, saying, "Show me the secrets which I know not, teach Thou me"? Oh, for humble, earnest prayer to go forth from unfeigned lips praying for the counsel that is of God! He says, Counsel is Mine, and sound wisdom.

For further study: *The Desire of Ages,* pages 315-317.

Solemn Times

January 31, 1895.

Solemn, serious times are upon us, and perplexities will increase, to the very close of time. There may be a little respite in these matters, but it will not be for long. I have letters to write that must go in the next mail to Battle Creek. Our brethren there are not looking at everything in the right light. The movements they have made to pay taxes* on the property of the sanitarium and Tabernacle have manifested a zeal and conscientiousness that in all respects is not wise nor correct. Their ideas of religious liberty are being woven with suggestions that do not come from the Holy Spirit, and the religious liberty cause is sickening, and its sickness can only be healed by the grace and gentleness of Christ.

The hearts of those who advocate this cause must be filled by the spirit of Jesus. The Great Physician alone can apply the balm of Gilead. Let these men read the book of Nehemiah with humble hearts touched by the Holy Spirit, and their false ideas will be modified,

---

Special Testimonies to Ministers and Workers (Series A, No. 3, 1895), pages 32-35.

*See Appendix.

and correct principles will be seen, and the present order of things will be changed. Nehemiah prayed to God for help, and God heard his prayer. The Lord moved upon heathen kings to come to his help. When his enemies zealously worked against him, the Lord worked through kings to carry out His purpose, and to answer the many prayers that were ascending to Him for the help which they so much needed.

EXTREME POSITIONS

I am often greatly distressed when I see our leading men taking extreme positions, and burdening themselves over matters that should not be taken up or worried over, but left in the hands of God for Him to adjust. We are yet in the world, and God keeps for us a place in connection with the world, and works by His own right hand to prepare the way before us, in order that His work may progress along its various lines. The truth is to have a standing place, and the standard of truth is to be uplifted in many places in regions beyond.

Be sure that God has not laid upon those who remain away from these foreign fields of labor the burden of criticizing the ones on the ground where the work is being done. Those who are not on the ground know nothing about the necessities of the situation, and if they cannot say anything to help those who are on the ground, let them not hinder, but show their wisdom by the eloquence of silence, and attend to the work that is close at hand. I protest against the zeal that they manifest that is not according to knowledge, when they ventilate their ideas about foreign fields of labor.

Let the Lord work with the men who are on the ground, and let those who are not on the ground walk humbly with God, lest they get out of their place, and lose their bearings. The Lord has not placed the burden of criticizing the work upon those who have taken this burden, and He does not give them the sanction of His Holy Spirit. Many move according to their own human judgment, and zealously seek to adjust things that God has not placed in their hands. Just as long as we are in the world, we shall have to do a special work for the world; the message of warning is to go to all countries, tongues, and peoples.

The Lord does not move upon His workers to make them take a course which will bring on the time of trouble before the time. Let them not build up a wall of separation between themselves and the world, by advancing their own ideas and notions. There is now altogether too much of this throughout our borders. The message of warning has not reached large numbers of the world in the very cities that are right at hand, and to number Israel is not to work after God's order.

FAVORS TO BE RECEIVED AS WELL AS IMPARTED

Just as long as we are in this world, and the Spirit of God is striving with the world, we are to receive as well as to impart favors. We are to give to the world the light of truth as presented in the Sacred Scriptures, and we are to receive from the world that which God moves upon them to do in behalf of His cause. The Lord still moves upon the hearts of kings and rulers in behalf of His people, and it becomes those who are so deeply interested in the religious liberty question not to cut off any favors, or withdraw themselves from the help that God has moved men to give, for the advancement of His cause.

We find examples in the word of God concerning this very matter. Cyrus, king of Persia, made a proclamation throughout all his kingdom, and put it into writing, saying: "Thus saith Cyrus king of Persia, The Lord God of heaven hath given me all the kingdoms of the earth; and He hath charged me to build Him an house at Jerusalem, which is in Judah. Who is there among you of all His people? his God be with him, and let him go up to Jerusalem, which is in Judah, and build the house of the Lord God of Israel." A second commandment was issued by Darius for the building of the house of the Lord, and is recorded in the sixth chapter of Ezra.

The Lord God of Israel has placed His goods in the hands of unbelievers, but they are to be used in favor of doing the works that must be done for a fallen world. The agents through whom these gifts come may open up avenues through which the truth may go. They may have no sympathy with the work, and no faith in Christ, and no practice in His words; but their gifts are not to be refused on that account.

It is very strange that some of our brethren should feel that it is their duty to bring about a condition of things that would bind up the means that God would have set free. God has not laid upon them the responsibility of coming in conflict with the authorities and powers of the world in this matter. The withstraining hand of God has not yet been withdrawn from the earth. Let the leaders in the work bide their time, hide in Christ, and move and work with great wisdom. Let them be as wise as serpents, and as harmless as doves. I have repeatedly been shown that we might receive far more favors than we do in many ways if we would approach men in wisdom, acquaint them with our work, and give them an opportunity of doing those things which it is our privilege to induce them to do for the advancement of the work of God.

Activity in Our Churches

February 2, 1895.

The prevailing monotony of the religious round of service in our churches needs to be disturbed. The leaven of activity needs to be introduced, that our church members may work along new lines, and devise new methods. The Holy Spirit's power will move upon hearts when this dead, lifeless monotony is broken up, and many will begin to work in earnest who never before thought of being anything but idle spectators. A working church on earth is connected with the working church above. God works, angels work, and men should work for the conversion of souls. Efforts should be made to do something while the day lasts, and the grace of God will be revealed that souls may be saved to Christ. Everywhere souls are perishing in their sins, and God is saying to every believing soul, Hasten to their help with the message that I shall give you.

ECONOMY IN THE HOME

The Lord has made men His agents, and with heart filled with the love of Jesus, they are to cooperate with Him in turning men from error to truth. God blesses the earth with sunshine and showers. He causes the earth to bring forth its plenteous treasures for the use of man. The Lord has made man His almoner to dispense His heavenly gifts by bringing souls to the truth. Will my brethren in America inquire how the precious, saving truth reached them when they were in darkness? Men and women brought their tithes and offerings unto God, and as means filled the treasury, men were sent out to advance the work.

This same process must be repeated if souls in dark-

Special Testimonies to Ministers and Workers (Special A, No. 3, 1895), pages 35-39.

ness are reached in this day. But I have seen that there are many who are withholding their tithes altogether, and others are withholding a part, and yet the great missionary work increases year by year. We should learn to economize in our household expenditures. No needless expenses should be incurred; because want and wretchedness, poverty and misery of every description press upon our notice, and we are called upon to help those who are needy and distressed. We must see that those who need food and clothing are supplied, that those who are in soul poverty may understand the goodness of salvation.

EARNEST WORK

It is when we are engaged in earnest work, working according to our several abilities, that God manifests Himself to us, and gives us grace for grace. A working church in travail for souls will be a praying church, a believing church, and a receiving church. A church whose members are found upon their knees before God, supplicating His mercy, seeking Him daily, is a church that is feeding upon the bread of life, and drinking of the waters of life. The promise, "Whatsoever ye shall ask the Father in My name, He will give it you," will be verified to them.

Christlike activity pursued with persevering zeal will bring large returns. There will be an enlarged experience in love, and the human agents will have elevated views as to what God would do through them as they stand at their post of duty. Then will the church arise and shine, realizing that the glory of the Lord has risen upon her, and that darkness is receding.

Missionary success will be proportionate to wholehearted, thoroughly consecrated effort. Every departure from true missionary effort, every failure to cherish the missionary spirit, has reacted upon the church, and there has been a decline of spirituality. But every earnest effort that has been made in missionary lines has brought spiritual health to the church, and has not only increased the membership of the church, but has increased its holy zeal and gladness.

The commandment-keeping people of God erelong will be placed in a most trying position; but all those who have walked in the light, and diffused the light, will realize that God interposes in their behalf. When everything looks most forbidding, then the Lord will reveal His power to His faithful ones. When the nation for which God has worked in such a marvelous manner, and over which He has spread the shield of Omnipotence, abandons Protestant principles, and through its legislature gives countenance and support to Romanism in limiting religious liberty, then God will work in His own power for His people that are true. The tyranny of Rome will be exercised, but Christ is our refuge.

SELF-DENYING SACRIFICE

Many have been altogether too long in a sleepy condition. While some have worked intently, and have manifested unfailing energy, others have stood as spectators, and have been ready to make remarks of a critical character as to methods and results. This they are ready to do, though they have never exercised their minds in originating any plans whereby precious souls might be saved for Christ. They stand ready to find fault with those who do something. When these indolent souls awake and show some signs of returning consciousness, they are disappointed if others do not at once find them pleasant places in the work. It is a great shock to them to find out that work cannot be done without painstaking, self-denying, self-crucifying efforts. They expect success, and think that they must have the same order of success as did the apostles on the Day of Pentecost. This success they will have when they go through the experience of humble, self-denying sacrifice as did the apostles. When they present as earnest supplications from broken, contrite, believing hearts as did the apostles, then the same proportion of success will attend their labors. "For thus saith the high and lofty One that inhabiteth eternity, whose name is Holy; I dwell in the high and holy place, with him also that is of a contrite and humble spirit, to revive the spirit of the humble, and to revive the heart of the contrite ones." "To this man will I look, even to him that is poor and of a contrite spirit, and trembleth at My word."

HOME MISSIONARY WORK

The home missionary spirit is little known among us, and its manifestation is greatly needed in every line of work. A portion of the church has begun to exhibit some activity along missionary lines. But if we do not awake more generally and fully, then those who know not the truth for this time will advance before us and block up our way.

How long will it require to wake up the idlers who have for years loitered in Battle Creek? When will they become faithful witnesses for God? How long will it be before they yoke up with Christ? How much time each day is set apart for the worship of God? How many have seasons for contemplation and for fervent prayer? How many have educated themselves in economical habits, so that they may have gifts and offerings for the Lord's house? How many have had their hearts warmed by the practical exercise of benevolence? How many have made earnest efforts to inspire others to work for the Master? To work at home successfully will need a spirit, faith, and perseverance that will not fail nor be discouraged. There is not one inactive in heaven, and no one will enter the mansions of bliss who has failed to show love for Christ, who has put forth no efforts for the salvation of others.

Who can tell the work that might have been done in our churches, if those who had advocated the truth had not left these feeble churches, to crowd into Battle Creek? If all our people had been faithful, diligent, God-fearing servants of Christ, and had put forth efforts to make their influence as far-reaching as possible at home, where they were, how many souls might have been saved! One taper kindled in one place might have been the means of kindling many others, and the result would have been that the voice of praise and thanksgiving would have been heard, and many would have said: "What hath God wrought! He hath done exceedingly abundantly above all that we asked or thought."

For further study: *Testimonies,* vol. 6, pp. 24-29; vol. 9, pp. 43-48, 285-288.

Direct Dependence on God

February 19, 1895.

It is not in the order of God that any man, or any class of men, should assume that God has made them conscience for their brethren, or put forth their finite hand in a patronizing manner to control the Lord's delegated workers, thus endangering the safety of the Lord's heritage as well as their own, and

Special Testimonies to Ministers and Workers (Series A, No. 3, 1895), pages 39, 40.

retarding the work of God. God does not confine Himself to one man, or to a set of men, through whom to accomplish His work, but says of all, Ye "are laborers together with God." This means that every believing soul should have a part to act in His sacred work, and every individual believer in Jesus Christ is to manifest to the world a symbol of Christ's sufficiency, to represent to His church the higher laws of the future immortal world, and in obedience to the mandates of Heaven that are without a parallel, they should reveal a depth of knowledge independent of human inventions.

The Lord must be believed and served as the great "I AM," and we must trust implicitly in Him. Let not men prescribe laws to take the place of God's law. Never educate men to look to men, to trust in men; for man's wisdom is not sufficient to decide as to their right to engage in the Lord's work. When God lays a work upon individuals, men are not to reject His sanction. God must not be impeded in the working out of His plans by man's interference, but this has been done again and again.

If the church on earth is to resemble a temple, let it be built according to the pattern shown in heaven, and not according to man's genius. The invention of man often counteracts the working out of God's plans. The golden measuring rod has not been placed in the hands of any finite man or any class of men, whatever their position or calling, but is in the hand of the heavenly Architect. If men will not meddle with God's plan, and will let Him work upon minds and characters, building them up according to His plan, a work will be accomplished that will stand through the severest of trials.

For further study: *Testimonies,* vol. 6, pp. 247, 248; vol. 7, pp. 39, 152, 194-196; *Gospel Workers,* page 80.

Workers Under God 9

God the Master Worker

Times are growing hard, and money is difficult to obtain; but God will open the way for us from sources outside our own people. I cannot see how anyone can take exceptions to the receiving of gifts from those not of our faith. They can only do so by taking extreme views and by creating issues which they are not authorized to do. This is God's world, and if God could move upon human agents so that the land which has been in the hands of the enemy may be brought into our hands, so that the message may be proclaimed in regions beyond, shall men block up the way with their narrow notions? Such conscientiousness as this is anything but healthful. The Holy Spirit does not lead men to pursue such a course.

Let all be careful how they interpose themselves between God, the great Master Worker, and His people. We should see and acknowledge the workings of His providence, and bow to His authority. Let every messenger of God attend to his own specific work, and not rush into a work that is simply after his own wisdom and devising. Let the Lord's messengers go unto the mercy seat, that they may receive wisdom and grace to know God, to understand His workings. Knowledge of God will give them well-balanced minds and sound judgment, that they will not move impulsively at this critical, important time of earth's history.

DUE CONSIDERATION

It is not the will of God that any of His servants should move hastily and take shortsighted views. He

---

The articles in this section are from *Special Testimonies to Ministers and Workers* (Series A, Nos. 3 and 4, 1895). This article from No. 3, pp. 43-53.

would have them wait patiently, and manifest due consideration. Every movement should be made with judicious thoughtfulness, and after much prayer. Then our brethren will have a more even, tranquil experience, and will be able to be a greater benefit to the people; for the glory of the Lord will be their reward.

Our only safety will be found in constantly seeking wisdom from God, in carefully weighing every matter with much fear and trembling, lest there should be brought into the work not the light of heaven, but the weakness of man. But the Lord has promised to give light to those who seek Him with the whole heart. If we will but wait patiently and prayerfully upon God, and not follow our own impetuous plans, He will guide our decisions and open many doors of hope and labor.

The great General of armies will lead in every battle for the advancement of His cause. He will be the guide of His people in the perilous conflicts in which they have to engage, if the under leaders and undershepherds will do their appointed work, and listen to the voice which says: "This is the way, walk ye in it;" "He that followeth Me shall not walk in darkness." What a great comfort this promise should be to us! We may walk in the light as He is in the light.

Let the men to whom God has entrusted great responsibilities be perfectly sure that they are following their great Leader, even Christ, and are not moving under the impulse of their own natural tempers. We shall be safe only when we consecrate ourselves to God and look unto Jesus, earnestly longing to work out His plan. Men may follow many kinds of lights, but there is only one Light that it will be safe for them to follow. Be sure that you are following Jesus whithersoever He goeth. Let none run ahead of Christ, but wait for the word of command, "Follow Me." Let our leaders be distrustful of their own counsel, of their own ambitious fancies. Let them not suppose that the sparks of their own kindling are the true light, or after a while they will find that, instead of following the heavenly guiding Star, they are following an uncertain leader.

GOD ORDERS HIS WORK

I am grieved as I see men seeking to mark out the precise course that missionaries in far-off lands shall pursue. We must give matters more into the hands of Him whom we profess to follow, that He may work through His appointed agents as He shall see fit. We should not think that everything should be brought under the jurisdiction of a few finite men, who need to look constantly to God for wisdom or else they will make grave blunders. The Lord does not design to have everything center in Battle Creek.* He would have men stand aside, and not feel that His work depends wholly upon them and that every question must be referred to their judgment. It is difficult for me to express what I desire to, but in the name of the Lord I lift the danger signal. Responsible men should fear and tremble for themselves. They should not feel competent to run ahead of Him who has said, "Follow Me." God is not pleased that men in distant lands should have to wait before they can venture to make a move. We should believe in the power of the Lord to guide, for He has the ordering of His own work. He will give wisdom and understanding to His representative men in every part of His great moral vineyard. He says, "Ye have not chosen Me, but I have chosen you, and ordained you, that ye should go and bring forth fruit." To my brethren in Battle Creek I would say: The Lord does

*See Appendix.

not need to send His orders to His messengers in all parts of the world through Battle Creek. He does not lay this responsibility upon all those who assume to say to His workers, "Do this," and "Thou shalt not do that." God is dishonored when men are led to look to Battle Creek to so large a degree.

The people of every country have their own peculiar, distinctive characteristics, and it is necessary that men should be wise in order that they may know how to adapt themselves to the peculiar ideas of the people, and so introduce the truth that they may do them good. They must be able to understand and meet their wants. Circumstances will arise which demand immediate action, and it will be necessary that those who are right on the field should take hold of the interest, and do the thing that is necessary to be done under the guidance of the Holy Spirit. Should they wait in a time of crisis for direction to come from Battle Creek as to what they should do, they might lose much. The men who are handling the work should be faithful stewards of the grace of God. They should be men of faith, and they should be encouraged to look to God, and to trust in Him.

GOD'S ORGANIZATION

Let God's workmen study the sixth chapter of Isaiah, and the first and second chapters of Ezekiel.

To the prophet the wheel within a wheel, the appearances of living creatures connected with them, all seemed intricate and unexplainable. But the hand of Infinite Wisdom is seen among the wheels, and perfect order is the result of its work. Every wheel works in perfect harmony with every other.

I have been shown that human instrumentalities seek after too much power and try to control the work themselves. They leave the Lord God, the Mighty Worker, too much out of their methods and plans, and do not trust everything to Him in regard to the advancement of the work. No one should fancy that he is able to manage these things which belong to the great I AM. God in His providence is preparing a way so that the work may be done by human agents. Then let every man stand at his post of duty, to act his part for this time, and know that God is his instructor.

In the taking of Jericho the Lord God of hosts was the general of the army. He made the plan for the battle and united heavenly and human agencies to act a part in the work, but no human hand touched the walls of Jericho. God so arranged the plan that man could take no credit to himself for achieving the victory. God alone is to be glorified. So it shall be in the work in which we are engaged. The glory is not to be given to human agencies; the Lord alone is to be magnified. Please read carefully the third chapter of Ezekiel. We must learn to put our entire dependence upon God, and yet we must ever bear in mind that the Lord God has need of every agency that holds the truth in righteousness. As workers for Christ we are to stand in view of the cross of Calvary, proclaiming to the world, "Behold the Lamb of God, which taketh away the sin of the world." We are to proclaim the third angel's message with our human voices, and it is to go to the world with power and glory.

When men cease to depend upon men, when they make God their efficiency, then there will be more confidence manifested one in another. Our faith in God is altogether too feeble and our confidence in one another altogether too meager.

Christ breathed upon His disciples and said, "Receive

ye the Holy Ghost." Christ is represented by His Holy Spirit today in every part of His great moral vineyard. He will give the inspiration of His Holy Spirit to all those who are of a contrite spirit.

Let there be more dependence upon the efficiency of the Holy Spirit, and far less upon human agencies. I am sorry to say that at least some have not given evidence that they have learned the lesson of meekness and lowliness in the school of Christ. They do not abide in Christ, they have no vital connection with Him. They are not directed by the wisdom of Christ, through the impartation of His Holy Spirit. Then I ask you, How can we regard these men as faultless in judgment? They may be in responsible positions, but they are living separated from Christ. They have not the mind of Christ, and do not learn daily of Him. Yet in some cases their judgment is trusted, and their counsel is regarded as the wisdom of God.

When human agents choose the will of God and are conformed to the character of Christ, Jesus acts through their organs and faculties. They put aside all selfish pride, all manifestation of superiority, all arbitrary exactions, and manifest the meekness and lowliness of Christ. It is no more themselves that live and act, but it is Christ that lives and acts through them. They understand the precious words of the Saviour's prayer, "I in them, and Thou in Me, that they may be made perfect in one; and that the world may know that Thou hast sent Me, and hast loved them, as Thou hast loved Me."

God would have every individual look less to the finite, depend less upon men. We have counselors who make manifest that they have not a knowledge of the grace of Christ and do not understand the truth as it is in Christ. Those who are cooperating with God have humble opinions of themselves. They are not boastful, self-sufficient, and self-exalted. They are long-suffering, kind, full of mercy and good fruits. Human ambition takes the background with them. The righteousness of Christ goes before them, and the glory of the Lord is their reward.

COMMITTEES OF COUNSEL

In counseling for the advancement of the work no one individual is to be in controlling power, a voice for the whole, unless it is evident to all that the counsel given is the right one. All methods and plans are to be carefully considered so that all may become intelligent in regard to their relative merits and decide which one will be best to be followed in the missionary work that is to be done in the fields that open before us. It will be well not only to consider the fields to which duty seems to call us, but the difficulties that will be encountered. Committees of counsel, as far as possible, should let the people understand their plans, that the judgment of the church may sustain their efforts. Many of the church members are prudent, and have many other excellent qualities of mind. It is proper that their wisdom should be exercised, that others may become aroused in reference to the great questions to be considered. Many may be awakened to the fact that they should have deeper insight into the work of God.

Some are convinced that they are far behind in their knowledge of the message, but God will help those who earnestly seek Him for wisdom. None ever seek His mercy seat in vain. We should earnestly seek wisdom from above, realizing that souls are perishing for the word of life and that the kingdom of

Christ is to be extended. Men and women of noble minds will yet be added to the number of those of whom it is said, "Ye have not chosen Me, but I have chosen you, . . . that ye should go and bring forth fruit."

HOW TO SECURE NECESSARY FUNDS

From the beginning of our missionary work, we have been much perplexed to know how we could secure funds adequate to the support of missionary enterprises in the fields which Providence has opened before us. Missionary work is to be widely extended, and those who believe the truth should avoid using their means in purchasing that which is unnecessary. We are not to study our convenience but rather our necessities. We shall have to bind about our wants in order that there shall be means in the treasury to raise the standard of truth in new territory.

Seek God; believe in Him who has infinite resources. If we move wisely, putting our ability into the work, the good hand of God will be upon us. We must push forward the work, not waiting to see the funds in the treasury before we undertake it. God forbid that when His providence summons us to enter the fields white already to harvest, our steps should be retarded by the cry, "Our treasury is exhausted. We have no means to sustain the workers that are already in the field, and it is impossible for us to enlarge our operations."

We thank God that our Sabbath schools have contributed enough to advance many a precious enterprise. Children and youth have given their pennies, that like little rivulets have supplied a stream of beneficence. Children should be educated in such a way that they may perform unselfish acts which heaven will rejoice to see. When the dew of youth is upon them children should be trained how to do service for Christ. They should be taught self-denial.

The fields nigh and afar off belong to God; for the world is His. Usurpers have taken possession of God's earthly property, but He will make a way so that the truth may be presented in the dark corners of the earth. If men will only follow the leadings of the Holy Spirit they will find ways and means by which the message may go forth and gain a glorious victory.

POINT SOULS TO CHRIST

The servants of God who live in obedience to His requirements, who speak the truth in humility, will carry an influence with them which will work for the salvation of many souls. But we must not allow the people to hang helplessly upon us. We are human and finite. We must direct them to Christ, saying, "Behold the Lamb of God, which taketh away the sin of the world." Jesus pleads the case of His colaborers, but every hour they need to feel humble dependence upon the Captain of their salvation, and through the intercession of Christ our Advocate many souls will be saved unto eternal life. The Lord has provided for the descent of the Holy Spirit upon His workers, and everyone who sincerely seeks God will find Him. We are to come boldly to the throne of grace, and seek the footstool of mercy. We are to believe that the Lord hears and answers our prayers. Our great High Priest who has passed into the heavens says, "I will pray the Father, and He shall give you another Comforter, that He may abide with you forever." The Holy Spirit abides with consecrated laborers who in any locality are seeking to advance the cause.

CREATING UNNECESSARY OPPOSITION

I beg of you for Christ's sake, let no hasty, rash expressions fall from your lips, let no extravagant language be used, let nothing be uttered that will savor of railing, for all this is human. Christ has no part in it. Let the ready writers be careful how they use their pens, lest they may seem to cast ridicule upon the positions of believers or unbelievers. We shall find our only safety in preserving the lowly spirit of Christ, in making straight paths for our feet, lest the lame be turned out of the way. The meekness and lowliness of Christ must take possession of the soul.

Satan is putting forth his power in presenting masterly delusions, so that he may bring to pass that which is not in accordance with God's will. Let not those who believe the truth give occasion to our enemies to vindicate opposition, to give ground for the misrepresentation that men would use to oppose the advance of the truth. For the sake of Christ let every worker put forth efforts that will bring to naught Satan's assertions, and not engage in anything that God has not required at his hands. Under heavenly generalship we may work in accordance with God's will, and success will crown our efforts. Give God a chance to work, and leave men to do whatever He wishes them to do to advance His truth.

The question of religious liberty is very important, and it should be handled with great wisdom and discretion. Unless this is done there is danger that by our own course of action we shall bring upon ourselves a crisis before we are prepared for it. The burden of our message should be "the commandments of God, and the faith of Jesus." Our brethren should be cautioned to make moves that will not stir up and provoke the powers that be, so that they will make moves that will limit the work, and cut us off from proclaiming the message in different localities.

We need more of the working of the Infinite and far less trust in human agencies. We are to prepare a people to stand in the day of God's preparation; we are to call men's attention to the cross of Calvary, to make clear the reason why Christ made His great sacrifice. We are to show men that it is possible for them to come back to their allegiance to God and to their obedience to His commandments. When the sinner looks upon Christ as the propitiation for his sins, let men step aside. Let them declare to the sinner that Christ "is the propitiation for our sins: and not for ours only, but also for the sins of the whole world." Encourage him to seek wisdom from God; for through earnest prayer he will learn the way of the Lord more perfectly than if instructed by some human counselor. He will see that it was the transgression of the law that caused the death of the Son of the infinite God, and he will hate the sins that wounded Jesus. As he looks upon Christ as a compassionate, tender High Priest, his heart will be preserved in contrition.

For further study: *Testimonies,* vol. 5, pp. 749-754.

Humility

When he who is a colaborer with Christ presses home the truth to the sinner's heart in humility and love, the voice of love speaks through the human instrumentality. Heavenly intelligences work with a consecrated human agent, and the Spirit operates upon

Special Testimonies to Ministers and Workers (Series A, No. 3, 1895), pages 53-59.

the soul of the unbeliever. Efficiency to believe comes from God to the heart, and the sinner accepts the evidence of God's word. Through the gracious influence of the Holy Spirit he is changed and becomes one with Christ in spirit and purpose. His affection for God increases, he hungers after righteousness and longs to be more like his Master. By beholding Christ, he is changed from glory to glory, from character to character, and becomes more and more like Jesus. He is imbued with love for Christ and filled with a deep, unresting love for perishing souls, and Christ is formed within, the hope of glory. "As many as received Him, to them gave He power to become the sons of God, even to them that believe on His name."

Please read the second and third chapters of Philippians, and the first chapter of Colossians. There are lessons there that we all should study. Paul writes, "Let nothing be done through strife or vainglory; but in lowliness of mind let each esteem other better than themselves. Look not every man on his own things, but every man also on the things of others. Let this mind be in you, which was also in Christ Jesus: who, being in the form of God, thought it not robbery to be equal with God: but made Himself of no reputation, and took upon Him the form of a servant, and was made in the likeness of men: and being found in fashion as a man, He humbled Himself, and became obedient unto death, even the death of the cross. Wherefore God also hath highly exalted Him, and given Him a name which is above every name. . . . Work out your own salvation with fear and trembling. For it is God which worketh in you both to will and to do of His good pleasure. Do all things without murmurings and disputings: that ye may be blameless and harmless, the sons of God, without rebuke, in the midst of a crooked and perverse nation, among whom ye shine as lights in the world; holding forth the word of life; that I may rejoice in the day of Christ, that I have not run in vain, neither labored in vain." "I am made a minister, according to the dispensation of God which is given to me for you, to fulfill the word of God; even the mystery which hath been hid from ages and from generations, but now is made manifest to His saints: to whom God would make known what is the riches of the glory of this mystery among the Gentiles; which is Christ in you, the hope of glory: whom we preach, warning every man, and teaching every man in all wisdom; that we may present every man perfect in Christ Jesus."

AVOID PROVOCATION

Our workers should use the greatest wisdom, so that nothing shall be said to provoke the armies of Satan and to stir up his united confederacy of evil. Christ did not dare to bring a railing accusation against the prince of evil, and is it proper that we should bring such accusation as will set in operation the agencies of evil, the confederacies of men that are leagued with evil spirits? Christ was the only-begotten Son of the infinite God, He was the Commander in the heavenly courts, yet He refrained from bringing accusation against Satan. Speaking of Him, Isaiah says, "Unto us a Child is born, unto us a Son is given: and the government shall be upon His shoulder: and His name shall be called Wonderful, Counselor, The mighty God, The everlasting Father, The Prince of Peace."

Let those who speak and write concerning the third angel's message consider the fact that the Prince of Peace did not bring a railing accusation against the enemy, and let them learn the lesson they ought to have learned much earlier in their experience. They should wear Christ's yoke, they should practice the humility of Christ. The Great Teacher says, "Learn of Me [I am not boastful, I hide My glory]; for I am meek and lowly in heart." In learning of Me, "ye shall find rest unto your souls." Let such work be done by our missionaries as will lead to that repentance that needs not to be repented of. We need to learn much more of the meekness of Christ in order to be a savor of life unto life.

Let no one open the way for the enemy to do his work. Let no one help him to advance his oppressive powers, for we are not yet prepared to meet them. We need the softening, subduing, refining influence of the Holy Spirit, to mold our characters, and to bring every thought into captivity to Christ. It is the Holy Spirit that will enable us to overcome, that will lead us to sit at the feet of Jesus, as did Mary, and learn His meekness and lowliness of heart.

We need to be sanctified by the Holy Spirit every hour of the day, lest we be ensnared by the enemy and our souls be imperiled. There is constant temptation to exalt self, and we must watch much against this evil. We need to be on guard continually lest we manifest the spirit of overbearing, criticism, and condemnation. We should seek to avoid the very appearance of evil, and not reveal anything like the attributes of Satan that will dishearten and discourage those with whom we come in contact. We are to work as did Christ—to draw, to build up, not to tear down. It is natural for some to be sharp and dictatorial, to lord it over God's heritage; and because of the manifestation of these attributes, precious souls have been lost to the cause. The reason that men have manifested these unpleasant characteristics is because they have not been connected with God.

DEALING WITH PRECIOUS SOULS

Those who occupy important positions, who are brought in contact with souls for whom Christ has died, should place upon men the estimate God has placed upon them and regard them as precious. But many have treated the purchase of Christ's blood in a harsh manner, in harmony with the disposition of men instead of according to the mind and spirit of Christ. Of His disciples Christ says, "All ye are brethren." We should ever keep in mind the relation which we bear one to another, and remember that we must meet those with whom we associate here, around the judgment seat of Christ. God will be the Judge, and He will deal justly with every individual.

John says, "I saw the dead, small and great, stand before God; and the books were opened: and another book was opened, which is the book of life: and the dead were judged out of those things which were written in the books, according to their works." Let everyone who professes the name of Christ consider the fact that he must meet every act of injustice, give an account for every harsh word, at the judgment seat of Christ. It will not be pleasant to review the words that have been spoken that have wounded and bruised souls, to review the decisions that have worked against souls for whom Christ died. Every action will come into judgment, and the spirit that prompted it will be made manifest. The fruit of every selfish, arbitrary exaction will be made plain, and men will see the results of their doings even as God sees them. They will see that they have turned precious souls out of the right path by dealing with them in an un-Christlike manner. We are living in the great Day of Atonement, and it is now time that everyone should repent before God, confess his sins, and by living faith rest upon the merit of a crucified and living Saviour.

My brethren and sisters, will you bear in mind that in dealing with God's heritage you are not to act out your natural characteristics? The people of God are Christ's purchased possession, and what a price He has paid for them! Shall any of us be found aiding the enemy of God and man in discouraging and destroying souls? What will be the retribution brought upon us if we do this class of work? Every one of us should weed out of our conversation everything that is harsh and severe. We should not indulge in condemning others, and we will not do so if we are one with Christ. We are to represent Christ in our dealings with our fellowmen. We are to be laborers together with God in helping those who are tempted. We are not to encourage souls to sow seeds of doubt; for they will bear a baleful harvest. We are to learn of Christ, to practice His methods, to reveal His spirit. We are enjoined, "Let this mind be in you, which was also in Christ Jesus." We should educate ourselves to believe in the word of God which is being so wonderfully and gloriously fulfilled. If we have the full assurance of faith, we will not indulge in doubting our brethren and sisters.

CHARACTER OF CHRIST

We are privileged to see Jesus as He is, to know Him as One who is full of compassion, courteousness, and divine politeness. He is good and merciful, and will forgive our sins. Of Him it is written: "Wherefore in all things it behooved Him to be made like unto His brethren, that He might be a merciful and faithful high priest in things pertaining to God, to make reconciliation for the sins of the people. For in that He

Himself hath suffered being tempted, He is able to succor them that are tempted."

We should cherish love and gratitude, we should look unto Jesus and become transformed into His image. The result of this will be increased confidence, hope, patience, and courage. We shall be drinking of the water of life of which Christ spoke to the woman of Samaria. He said: "If thou knewest the gift of God, and who it is that saith to thee, Give Me to drink; thou wouldest have asked of Him, and He would have given thee living water. . . . Whosoever drinketh of the water that I shall give him shall never thirst; but the water that I shall give him shall be in him a well of water springing up into everlasting life." This water represents the life of Christ, and every soul must have it by coming into living connection with God. Then blessed, humble, grateful confidence will be an abiding principle in the soul. Unbelieving fear will be swept away before living faith. We shall contemplate the character of Him who first loved us.

By contemplation of God's matchless love, we take upon us His nature. Christ was a representative before men and before angels, of the character of the God of heaven. He demonstrated the fact that when humanity depends wholly upon God, men may keep God's commandments and live, and His law be as the apple of the eye.

Those who inquire after the way of life need not be rich, need not be wise, learned, or honored; yet God will quicken their perceptions so that they may understand what they may do to be saved. The light of heaven is shining upon the earth from the throne of God, and Christ says, "And I, if I be lifted up from the earth, will draw all men unto Me." His gracious invitation is going forth to all mankind, and those who respond to it will find life and salvation. Peter writes, "Grace and peace be multiplied unto you through the knowledge of God, and of Jesus our Lord, according as His divine power hath given unto us all things that pertain unto life and godliness, through the knowledge of Him that hath called us to glory and virtue: whereby are given unto us exceeding great and precious promises: that by these ye might be partakers of the divine nature, having escaped the corruption that is in the world through lust."

For further study: *Testimonies,* vol. 4, pp. 101, 338, 371-383, 527; *Gospel Workers,* pages 318-321.

Calmness and Consideration

January 14, 1894.

The Lord is soon to work in greater power among us, but there is danger of allowing our impulses to carry us where the Lord would not want us to go. We must not make one step that we will have to retrace. We must move solemnly, prudently, and not make use of extravagant expressions or allow our feelings to become overwrought. We must think calmly and work without excitement; for there will be those who become easily wrought up, who will catch up unguarded expressions and make use of extreme utterances to create excitement, and thus counteract the very work that God would do. There is a class of people who are always ready to go off on some tangent, who want to catch up something strange and wonderful and new; but God would have all move calmly, considerately, choosing our words in harmony with the solid truth for this time, which requires to be presented to the mind as free from that which is emotional as possible, while still bearing the intensity and solemnity

---

Special Testimonies to Ministers and Workers (Series A, No. 3, 1895), pages 59-62.

that it is proper it should bear. We must guard against creating extremes, guard against encouraging those who would either be in the fire or in the water.

I beseech you to weed out of your teachings every extravagant expression, everything that unbalanced minds and those who are inexperienced will catch up, and from which they will make wild, immature movements. It is necessary for you to cultivate caution in every statement you make, lest you start some on a wrong track, and make confusion that will require much sorrowful labor to set in order, thus diverting the strength and work of the laborers into lines which God does not design shall be entered. One fanatical streak exhibited among us will close many doors against the soundest principles of truth.

Oh, how careful should every worker be not to rush on before the Master, but to follow where He leads the way! How it would rejoice the enemies of our faith to get hold of some statement made by our people which will have to be retracted! We must move discreetly, sensibly, for this is our strength; for then God will work with us, and by us, and for us. . . . Oh, how Satan would rejoice to get in among this people and disorganize the work at a time when thorough organization is essential and will be the greatest power to keep out spurious uprisings and to refute claims not endorsed by the word of God! We want to hold the lines evenly, that there shall be no breaking down of the system of regulation and order. In this way license shall not be given to disorderly elements to control the work at this time. We are living in a time when order, system, and unity of action are most essential. And the truth must bind us together like strong cords in order that no distracted efforts may be witnessed among the workers. If disorderly manifestations appear, we must have clear discernment to distinguish the spurious from the genuine. Let no messages be proclaimed until they have borne a careful scrutiny in every jot and tittle.

AVOID SIDE ISSUES

My soul is much burdened, for I know what is before us. Every conceivable deception will be brought to bear upon those who have not a daily, living connection with God. In our work no side issues must be advanced until there has been a thorough examination of the ideas entertained, that it may be ascertained from what source they have originated. Satan's angels are wise to do evil, and they will create that which some will claim to be advanced light, will proclaim as new and wonderful things; and yet while in some respects the message is truth, it will be mingled with men's inventions and will teach for doctrines the commandments of men. If there was ever a time when we should watch and pray in real earnest, it is now. There may be supposable things that appear as good things, and yet they need to be carefully considered with much prayer, for they are specious devices of the enemy to lead souls in a path which lies so close to the path of truth that it will be scarcely distinguishable from the path which leads to holiness and heaven. But the eye of faith may discern that it is diverging from the right path, though almost imperceptibly. At first it may be thought positively right, but after a while it is seen to be widely divergent from the path of safety, from the path which leads to holiness and heaven. My brethren, I warn you to make straight paths for your feet, lest the lame be turned out of the way.

For further study: *Testimonies,* vol. 2, p. 186; vol. 9, pp. 147-149, 208, 209; *Gospel Workers,* pages 324-329, 372-376, 410.

Hovering Over the Churches

Cooranbong, Australia, September 1, 1895.

Dear Brother and Sister———:

Brother———laid out before me the plans for meetings to be held for weeks in different places among those who know the truth. Doubtless some who have newly come to the faith would be benefited, but I know you are not on the right track. Some of those called together will no doubt have their faith strengthened and confirmed; but this work is not bearing the message of warning to those who are still in darkness and error, who know not the truth. Time is passing, the perils of the last days are upon us; and how many will say to us in the last great day when every man shall receive according to his works: Why have you not warned us? You have not told us those things that we should have known.

Christ says, "I came not to call the righteous, but sinners to repentance." Let our ministers go forth weighted with the solemn message of warning. When men have had every advantage to obtain a knowledge of the truth, how shall plans be laid to keep our laborers from the work of saving souls in the darkness of error? The time is short. Let the message of warning be given clear and distinct. The Lord is coming to execute judgment upon all who obey not the gospel.

Enoch in his day sounded the proclamation of the coming of Christ and the execution of judgment upon the unrighteous; and we now see the fulfillment of Enoch's prophecy concerning the great wickedness that should abound. But these who have the light are the very ones commissioned of God to make constantly aggressive warfare. As the inquiry shall be

---

Special Testimonies to Ministers and Workers, (Series A, No. 4, 1895), pages 4-10.

made, "Watchman, what of the night?" the faithful message is to be heard in response, "The morning cometh, and also the night."

The influence of truth is too much restricted. Let men who know the truth be urged to communicate truth to those who are in darkness. Many are satisfied with a view of truth, but they have not yet stepped into their place to communicate that which they have received. God has let men feel the power of truth, but they are not all doing their appointed work in seeking to save that which was lost. Everyone is to have the armor on, prepared to win others to obedience to the law of God. I see so much given to those who already have; these wonderful meetings for those who wish to get more strength are depriving the world of the very work that should be done. Our ministers should now be working for the saving of the lost. The weeks spent in gatherings to fit men for work might better, far better, be spent in going to the highways and hedges with the proclamation, "Come; for all things are now ready."

MORE LIGHT TO THOSE WHO USE IT

To those who obey the light they have, illumination will come from on high; for the heavenly messengers are waiting to cooperate with men in warning a deceived, sinful world. When the people of God engage in this work with real travail of soul there will be manifest a decided change in cities and villages. This hovering about churches to keep them propped up makes them more dependent on human effort. They learn to lean on the experience of their fellowmen and do not make God their dependence and their efficiency. It is time that cities and villages everywhere were hearing the solemn note of warning, "Behold,

He cometh with clouds; and every eye shall see Him." Get ready that you may be found of Him in peace.

I entreat you whom God has favored with a knowledge of the truth, Go to work; there is work to do everywhere. The fields are all white unto the harvest. Sowers and reapers are needed just now. The time you devote to imparting constantly to those who understand the message of warning will not give one tithe of the strength which they would receive in taking hold of the work to communicate life to save perishing souls. Angels are waiting to bless the consecrated workers. The parable of the lost sheep should be a lesson to every soul who has been rescued from the snare of Satan. We are not to hover over the ninety and nine, but to go forth to save the lost, hunting them up in the wilderness of the large cities and towns. In this work the laborers will be led to feel their weakness and they will flee to the stronghold. The divine presence will be with them to give strength and courage and faith and hope. The truehearted workers will be laborers together with God.

The warnings that Christ gave to Jerusalem were not to end with them. The judgments upon Jerusalem were a symbol of the events of Christ's coming to judgment in the last day, when before Him shall be gathered all nations. "He shall send His angels with a great sound of a trumpet, and they shall gather together His elect from the four winds, from one end of heaven to the other."

WORK FOR EVERY TRUE DISCIPLE

Every true follower of Christ has a work to do. God has given to every man his work. A few are now pointing to the roll of fast-fulfilling prophecy and proclaiming, Get ready, show your obedience to God by keeping His commandments. This is no time for the messengers of God to stop to prop up those who know the truth, and who have every advantage. Let them go on to lift the standard and give the warning, "Behold, the Bridegroom cometh; go ye out to meet Him." Many who hear the message—by far the greatest number—will not credit the solemn warning. Many will be found disloyal to the commandments of God, which are a test of character. The Lord's servants will be called enthusiasts. Ministers will warn the people not to listen to them. Noah received the same treatment while the Spirit of God was urging him to give the message, whether men would hear or whether they would forbear.

Come when it may, the advent of Christ will surprise the false teachers who are saying, "Peace and safety;" "all things continue as they were from the beginning." Thus saith the word of Inspiration, "Sudden destruction cometh upon them." The day of God shall come as a snare upon all who dwell upon the face of the whole earth. It comes to them as a prowling thief. "If the goodman of the house had known in what watch the thief would come, he would have watched, and would not have suffered his house to be broken up." Habitual watching is our only safety. We must be ever ready, that that day may not overtake us as a thief.

Let everyone who loves God consider that now while it is day is the time to work, not among the sheep already in the fold, but to go out in search of the lost and perishing ones. These need to have special help to bring them back to the fold. Now is the time for the careless to arouse from their slumber. Now is the time to entreat that souls shall not only hear the word of God, but without delay secure oil in their vessels with their lamps. That oil is the righteousness of Christ. It represents character, and character is not transferable. No man can secure it for another. Each must obtain for himself a character purified from every stain of sin.

The Lord is coming in power and great glory. It will then be His work to make a complete separation between the righteous and the wicked. But the oil cannot then be transferred to the vessels of those who have it not. Then shall be fulfilled the words of Christ: "Two women shall be grinding together; the one shall be taken, and the other left. Two men shall be in the field; the one shall be taken, and the other left." The righteous and the wicked are to be associated together in the work of life. But the Lord reads the character; He discerns who are obedient children, who respect and love His commandments.

THE TARES AND THE WHEAT

The looker-on may discern no difference; but there is One who said that the tares were not to be plucked up by human hands lest the wheat be rooted up also. Let both grow together until the harvest. Then the Lord sends forth His reapers to gather out the tares and bind them in bundles to burn, while the wheat is gathered into the heavenly garner. The time of the judgment is a most solemn period, when the Lord gathers His own from among the tares. Those who have been members of the same family are separated. A mark is placed upon the righteous. "They shall be Mine, saith the Lord of hosts, in that day when I make up My jewels; and I will spare them, as a man spareth his own son that serveth him." Those who have been obedient to God's commandments will unite with the company of the saints in light; they shall enter in through the gates into the city, and have right to the tree of life. The one shall be taken. His name shall stand in the book of life, while those with whom he associated shall have the mark of eternal separation from God.

The tares and wheat are now commingled, but then the one hand that alone can separate them will give to everyone his true position. Those who have had the light of truth, and heard the warning message, heard the invitation to the marriage supper—farmer, merchant, lawyer, false shepherds who have quieted the convictions of the people, unfaithful watchmen who have not sounded the warning or known the time of night—all who have refused obedience to the laws of the kingdom of God, will have no right therein. Those who have sought an excuse to avoid the cross of separation from the world will, with the world, be taken in the snare. They mingled with the tares from choice. Like drew to like in transgression. It is a fearful assimilation. Men choose to stand with the first rebel, who tempted Adam and Eve in Eden to disobey God. The tares multiply themselves, for they sow tares, and they have their part with the root of all sin—the devil.

Upon those who keep the commandments of God the benediction is pronounced: "Blessed are they that do His commandments, that they may have right to the tree of life, and may enter in through the gates into the city." They are "a chosen generation, a royal priesthood, an holy nation, a peculiar people;" that they should show forth the praises of Him who hath called us out of darkness into His marvelous light. The obedient are called the just; they are drawn to the holy magnet, Jesus Christ; the holy attracts the holy. He that is unjust will be unjust still. Character cannot then be made or transformed. The oil of grace cannot be lent by one to another, neither have the foolish virgins time to buy oil for themselves. The righteous are those who keep the commandments of God, and they will be forever separated from the disobedient and unrighteous who trampled underfoot the law of God. The pure ore and the dross will no longer commingle.

WHO IS THAT FAITHFUL AND WISE SERVANT?

"Who then is a faithful and wise servant, whom his Lord hath made ruler over His household?" Can we answer? Am I the steward, faithful to the sacred trust which is committed to me? To every man is given an individual responsibility. The watchmen have their specific work to discern the approach of danger and sound the note of warning. The soldiers of the cross of Christ are to have ears keen to hear. In their position of responsibility they are to give the trumpet a certain sound, that everyone may gird on the armor for action.

What work are we individually doing for the Master? Who are unfolding the truth to those who are in the darkness of error? Who are holding forth the words of life? The enemies of Christ are many, who, while they claim to be righteous, have not the righteousness of Christ. They disguise themselves as angels of light, but they are ministers of sin. This fact should be sufficient to stir every soul to action. Who are faithful stewards of the grace of Christ? Who are making wise division of labor, calling into active service every soul that has an intelligent knowledge of the truth, and giving to all a work to do?

The outposts are to be kept guarded. There are to be men to hold the fort, while the advancing forces are engaged in active warfare. To every man is given his work. We are not to echo the words of those in error, but to inculcate ideas of truth. Our work is to benefit our fellowmen. We are not to travel over the track of opponents to the truth, but to sound the message of the third angel, who is flying in the midst of heaven proclaiming the note of warning, the commandments of God, and the testimony of Jesus Christ.

Those who are "do-nothings" now will have the superscription upon them, "Thou art weighed in the balances, and art found wanting." They knew their Master's will, but did it not. They had the light of truth, they had every advantage, but chose their own selfish interests, and they will be left with those whom they did not try to save. "But and if that evil servant shall say in his heart, My Lord delayeth His coming; and shall begin to smite his fellow servants, and to eat and drink with the drunken; the Lord of that servant shall come in a day when he looketh not for Him, and in an hour that he is not aware of, and shall cut him asunder, and appoint him his portion with the hypocrites: there shall be weeping and gnashing of teeth."

Let there be an earnest consideration of these words. Let none say, "That does not mean me; I am a Christian." Who says this, yourself or He who reads the heart? The unfaithful steward had solemn responsibilities entrusted to him; before the world he appeared as a servant of Christ; but, oh, how deplorable for himself, and for all connected with him; he is an evil servant! He is imperiling his Lord's goods. He is teaching souls to trample upon the holy law of God. He calls Christ, "My Lord." But he says, "My Lord delayeth His coming." He does not say that Christ will not come; he does not scoff at the idea of His second coming; but he tells the people that His coming is delayed. He is removing from the minds of others the conviction that the Lord is coming quickly. His influence leads men to presumptuous, careless delay. Thus they are off their watch and they echo the words of the unfaithful watcher; still others catch them up, and the evil spirit, and men are confirmed in their worldliness and stupor. Their course is downward, not upward; they are not looking for and hasting unto the day of God. Earthly passions, corrupt thoughts, take possession of the mind.

The evil servant smites his fellow servants who are seeking to do the will of his Lord. He eats and drinks with the drunken, those who are carnally minded, notwithstanding their profession of Christianity. They are opposed to Christ and the work He came to our world to do, which was to live the law of God in humanity, to be an example to all humanity.

Christ was surrounded by His disciples, and a vast congregation were listening to His words when He said, "Take heed to yourselves, lest at any time your hearts be overcharged with surfeiting, and drunkenness, and cares of this life, and so that day come upon you unawares." "Let him that thinketh he standeth take heed lest he fall."

For further study: *Testimonies,* vol. 2, pp. 151, 340; vol. 3, pp. 203, 210, 406; *Gospel Workers,* pages 318-323, 104-107.

Right Methods, Principles, and Motives 10

Proper Education

Cooranbong, Australia, August 27, 1895.

Dear Brother and Sister——:

The students of our manual training school at this place are doing their best to follow the light God has given to combine with mental training the proper use of brain and muscle. Thus far the results have exceeded our expectations. At the close of the first term, which was regarded as an experiment, opportunity was given for the students to have their vacation, and engage in whatever work they chose to do. But everyone begged that the school might be continued as before, with manual labor each day combined with certain hours of study. The students did not want to give up the present opportunity of learning how to labor and how to study. If this is their choice under the most disadvantageous circumstances, what influence will it have when the school buildings are up and there are more favorable surroundings for the students?

The building they now occupy, the only one at all fit for the purpose, was an old hotel which we rented and are using to its fullest capacity. Four tents pitched in an adjoining paddock are also occupied by students. Every morning at six o'clock the members of the school are called together for morning worship and Bible study. These occasions have proved a blessing. . . .

I spoke to the students eight mornings. The Lord Jesus was indeed in our assembly. The congregation

---

The articles in this section are from *Special Testimonies to Ministers and Workers* (Series A, Nos. 4-6, 1895-1896). This article is from No. 4, pp. 14-20.

averaged from twenty-six to thirty. In the first meetings the spirit of intercession came upon me, and all were sensible that the Lord heard our prayers. Then I spoke about thirty minutes, and the Lord gave me words for those assembled. These seasons were most profitable; the testimonies of the students following gave evidence that the Holy Spirit was giving to all glimpses of the things of God.

The spiritual impressions became more marked as the meetings progressed. The divine presence was with us. The sympathies and sentiments of those present became inspired with power and favor. Hearts were susceptible to the influence of the Holy Spirit, and decided changes were wrought in minds and character. The Spirit of God was working upon human agents. I praise the Lord for the encouraging influence of His Spirit upon my own heart. We all felt that the Lord was cooperating with us to lead us to will, to resolve, and act.

The Lord does not propose to perform for us either the willing or the doing. This is our proper work. As soon as we earnestly enter upon the work, God's grace is given to work in us to will and to do, but never as a substitute for our effort. Our souls are to be aroused to cooperate. The Holy Spirit works the human agent, to work out our own salvation. This is the practical lesson the Holy Spirit is striving to teach us. "For it is God which worketh in you both to will and to do of His good pleasure."

I never had a deeper sense of the precious truth and its power upon human minds than when addressing those students in the early meetings. Morning after morning I felt charged with a message from God. I also had special freedom in speaking twice upon the Sabbath. At every meeting several unbelievers were present, and they were much affected as the truth was presented. If we had a suitable place for meeting we could invite the neighbors to come in. But our long, narrow dining room crowded as closely as if packed is not a very suitable place for worship. I am assigned a little space in the corner of the room, and am packed up close to the wall. Nevertheless the Lord Jesus is in the assembly. We know it. Some souls are thinking very seriously now upon the subject of the truth.

We all know that the most severe and intense soul struggles belong to the hour of the great resolve to act out the convictions upon the human heart. The consecration of the soul to God is committing the keeping of the soul to One who has purchased its freedom at an infinite price, and then we are to follow on to know the Lord, that we may know His goings forth are prepared as the morning. "To obey is better than sacrifice." The whole work of the Christian is comprised in willing and doing.

BALANCED TRAINING

The students work hard and faithfully. They are gaining in strength of nerve and in solidity as well as activity of muscles. This is the proper education which will bring forth from our schools young men who are not weak and inefficient, who have not a one-sided education, but an all-round physical, mental, and moral training. The builders of character must not forget to lay the foundation which will make education of the greatest value. This will require self-sacrifice, but it must be done. The physical training will, if properly conducted, prepare for mental taxation. But the one alone always makes a deficient man. The physical taxation combined with mental effort keeps the mind and morals in a more healthful condition, and far better work is done. Under this training students will come forth from our schools educated for practical life, able to put their intellectual capabilities to the best use. Physical and mental exercise must be combined if we would do justice to our students. We have been working on this plan here with complete satisfaction, notwithstanding the inconvenience under which students have to labor.

I came here and began work on my place so earnestly that it inspired all with fresh zeal, and they have been working with a will, rejoicing that they have the privilege. We have provoked one another to zeal and good works. The school workers were afraid I would plant the first trees, and now both they and and I have the satisfaction of having the first genuine orchards in this vicinity. Some of our trees will yield fruit next year, and the peaches will bear quite a crop in two years. Mr. ——, from whom we bought our trees, lives about twenty miles from here. He has an extensive and beautiful orchard. He says that we have splendid fruit land.

Well, the school has made an excellent beginning. The students are learning how to plant trees, strawberries, etc.; how they must keep every sprangle and fiber of the roots uncramped in order to give them a chance to grow. Is not this a most precious lesson as to how to treat the human mind, and the body as well—not to cramp any of the organs of the body, but give them ample room to do their work? The mind must be called out, its energies taxed. We want men and women who can be energized by the Spirit of God to do a complete work under the Spirit's guidance. But these minds must be cultivated, employed, not lazy and dwarfed by inaction. Just so men and women and children are wanted who will work the land, and use their tact and skill, not with a feeling that they are menials, but that they are doing just such noble work as God gave to Adam and Eve in Eden, who loved to see the miracles wrought by the divine Husbandman. The human agent plants the seed, and God waters it and causes His sun to shine upon it, and up springs the tiny blade. Here is the lesson God gives to us concerning the resurrection of the body, and the renewing of the heart. We are to learn of spiritual things from the development of the earthly.

EDUCATION IN THE TILLING OF THE SOIL

We are not to be put about and discouraged about temporal things because of apparent failures, nor should we be disheartened by delay. We should work the soil cheerfully, hopefully, gratefully, believing that the earth holds in her bosom rich stores for the faithful worker to garner, richer than gold or silver. The niggardliness laid to her charge is false witness. With proper, intelligent cultivation the earth will yield its treasures for the benefit of man.

The spiritual lessons to be learned are of no mean order. The seeds of truth sown in the soil of the heart will not all be lost, but will spring up, first the blade, then the ear, and then the corn in the ear. God said in the beginning, "Let the earth bring forth grass, the herb yielding seed, and the fruit tree yielding fruit." God created the seed as He did the earth, by the divine word. We are to exercise our reasoning powers in the cultivation of the earth, and to have faith in the word of God that has created the fruit of the earth for the service of man.

The cultivation of our lands requires the exercise of all the brainpower and tact we possess. The lands around us testify to the indolence of men. We hope to arouse to action the dormant senses. We hope to see intelligent farmers, who will be rewarded for their earnest labor. The hand and heart must cooperate, bringing new and sensible plans into operation in the cultivation of the soil. We have here seen the giant trees felled and uprooted, we have seen the plowshare pressed into the earth, turning deep furrows for the planting of young trees and the sowing of the seed. The students are learning what plowing means, and that the hoe and the shovel, the rake and the harrow, are all implements of honorable and profitable industry. Mistakes will often be made, but error lies close beside truth. Wisdom will be learned by failures, and the energy that will make a beginning gives hope of success in the end. Hesitation will keep things back, precipitancy will alike retard, but all will serve as lessons if the human agents will have it so.

In the school that is started here in Cooranbong, we look to see real success in agricultural lines, combined with a study of the sciences. We mean for this place to be a center, from which shall irradiate light, precious advanced knowledge that shall result in the working of unimproved lands, so that hills and valleys shall blossom like the rose. For both children and men, labor combined with mental taxation will give the right kind of all-round education. The cultivation of the mind will bring tact and fresh incentives to the cultivation of the soil.

There will be a new presentation of men as breadwinners, possessing educated, trained ability to work the soil to advantage. Their minds will not be overtaxed and strained to the uttermost with the study of the sciences. Such men will break down the foolish sentiments that have prevailed in regard to manual labor. An influence will go forth, not in loud-voiced oratory, but in real inculcation of ideas. We shall see farmers who are not coarse and rough and slack, careless of their apparel and of the appearance of their homes; but they will bring taste into farmhouses. Rooms will be sunny and inviting. We shall not see blackened ceilings, covered with cloth full of dust and dirt. Science, genius, intelligence, will be manifest in the home. The cultivation of the soil will be regarded as elevating and ennobling. Pure, practical religion will be manifested in treating the earth as God's treasure-house. The more intelligent a man becomes, the more should religious influence be radiating from him. And the Lord would have us treat the earth as a precious treasure, lent us in trust.

For further study: *Fundamentals of Christian Education.*

Less of Self

Granville, Australia, September 13, 1895.

There must certainly be a change in our ministers. In heart and character there must be more of Christ and less of self. We are to be representatives of our Lord. Those who have had great light and precious opportunities are accountable to God, who has given to every man his work. They are never to betray the sacred trust, but are to be indeed the light of the world.

"Herein is love, not that we loved God, but that He loved us, and sent His Son to be the propitiation for our sins." Here is language that expresses His mind toward a corrupt and idolatrous people: "How shall I give thee up, Ephraim? how shall I deliver

---

Special Testimonies to Ministers and Workers (Series A, No. 4, 1895), pages 20-25.

thee, Israel? how shall I make thee as Admah? how shall I set thee as Zeboim? Mine heart is turned within Me, My repentings are kindled together." Must He give up the people for whom such a provision has been made, even His only-begotten Son, the express image of Himself? God permits His Son to be delivered up for our offenses. He Himself assumes toward the Sin Bearer the character of a judge, divesting Himself of the endearing qualities of a father.

Herein His love commends itself in the most marvelous manner to the rebellious race. What a sight for angels to behold! What a hope for man, "that, while we were yet sinners, Christ died for us"! The just suffered for the unjust; He bore our sins in His own body on the tree. "He that spared not His own Son, but delivered Him up for us all, how shall He not with Him also freely give us all things?"

As witnesses chosen of God, do we value Christ's purchased possession? Are we ready to make any and every sacrifice within our power, to place ourselves under Christ's yoke, to cooperate with Him and to be laborers together with God? All who are bearing the test of God, obeying His commandments, love the perishing human race as Christ loved them. They follow the example of Christ in most earnest, self-sacrificing labor, to seek out in the highways and hedges the high and the low, the rich and the poor, and to bear to all the message that they are the objects of Christ's special love and guardian care.

WORK FOR ALL

So great is the natural blindness and ignorance of men in regard to God and to the Saviour that everyone who loves Jesus may find work to do. Not one who has true love for Christ will remain indifferent and indolent. There is a marked difference between the character and life of those who are obedient to all the commandments of God, and of those who are disobedient.

Parents have not restrained the selfishness of their children. Self-indulgence has been the object of pursuit. Through self-serving, multitudes are bound in servitude to Satan. They are the slaves of their own impulses and passions, which are under the control of the wicked one. In calling them to His service, God offers them freedom. Obedience to God is liberty from the thralldom of sin, deliverance from human passion and impulse.

But we have to meet and contend with men who employ all their power in slandering those who are loyal to God. Their wit and their God-given reason are devoted to making it appear that obedience to the commandments of God is an irksome service. But those who advocate the claims of the law of God testify, "Great peace have they which love Thy law: and nothing shall offend them." "The law of the Lord is perfect, converting the soul." The Lord presents truth in contrast with error, and presents also the sure result of accepting truth, the experience that always follows willing obedience. It is peace and rest.

The work before the servants of God is to present Jesus. The work for the ministers of Christ is to hang their helpless souls upon His merit. Men who turn away from the path of obedience and make transgression of the law of God a virtue are under the inspiration of the archdeceiver. They are blinded by his power. They need to have before them a representation of what the truth can do in enabling men to preserve a Christlike temper when tempted to become imperious and impatient. The enemies of the truth want to provoke those who teach the binding claims of the law of God. If there is retaliation on our part, Satan's hosts triumph. He has found a weak place in the armor. By their mean course of action the agents of Satan try to tempt the advocates of truth to say and do things that will not be commendable.

TREATMENT OF OPPOSITION

Fine perceptions, nobility of soul, are to be cherished; the spirit of truth and righteousness is to control our deportment, our words, and our pens. "The natural man receiveth not the things of the Spirit of God: for they are foolishness unto him: neither can he know them, because they are spiritually discerned." If the minister when before his congregation sees a disbelieving smile upon the faces of opponents, let him be as one who sees not. If any should be so impolite as to laugh and sneer, let not the minister, by voice or attitude, reflect the same spirit. Show that you handle no such weapons. The pen so often traces words that are sharp, and by repeating the statements of the advocates of error, our brethren sometimes give currency to the error. This is a mistake. Let your pen trace advanced truth.

The Holy Spirit does not work with men who love to be sharp and critical. That spirit has been cherished in meeting debaters, and some have formed the habit of squaring for combat. God is dishonored in this. Keep back the sharp thrusts; do not learn in Satan's school his methods of warfare. The Holy Spirit does not inspire the words of censure. A time of trouble is before us, and every honest soul who has not had the light of truth will then take a stand for Christ. Those who believe the truth are to be newly converted every day. Then they will be vessels unto honor.

PROPER MANNER OF MEETING OPPONENTS

Do not repeat the words of your opponents, or enter into controversy with them. You meet not merely the men, but Satan and his angels. Christ did not bring against Satan a railing accusation concerning the body of Moses. If the world's Redeemer, who understood the crooked, deceptive arts of Satan, durst not bring against him a railing accusation, but in holiness and humility said, "The Lord rebuke thee, O Satan," is it not wise for His servants to follow His example? Will finite human beings take a course that Christ shunned because it would afford Satan occasion to pervert, misrepresent, and falsify the truth?

PERSONALITIES TO BE AVOIDED

In this period of the world's history we have altogether too great a work to begin a new kind of warfare in meeting the supernatural power of satanic agencies. We must put aside personalities, however we may be tempted to take advantage of words or actions. In patience we must possess our souls. Brethren, make it manifest that you are wholly on the Lord's side. Let the truth of God's Holy Word reveal transgression and sin and manifest the sanctifying power of truth upon human hearts. A haughty spirit must not come in to mar the work of God. We have reason for gratitude to God every moment that we have the privilege of connecting with God.

There is need of contrition of soul every day, and the Lord declares the great advantage of everyone who will humble his heart and hide in Jesus. "Thus saith the high and lofty One that inhabiteth eternity, whose name is Holy; I dwell in the high and holy place, with him also that is of a contrite and humble spirit, to revive the spirit of the humble, and to revive the heart of the contrite ones." "To this man will I look, even to him that is poor and of a contrite spirit, and trembleth at My word." "The Lord is nigh unto them that are of a broken heart; and saveth such as be of a contrite spirit." "This poor man cried, and the Lord heard him, and saved him out of all his troubles. The angel of the Lord encampeth round about them that fear Him, and delivereth them."

Let those who hate the law of the Lord rave and pour out their anathemas against such as have moral courage to receive and live the truth. The Lord is our strength. It is safe for us not to build up self, but to let the Lord work His will in and by and through us. Let us preserve a contrite, humble spirit, which the Lord will revive.

VALUE OF COUNSEL AND ADVICE

Self-esteem and self-flattery will be sure to stir up in the heart resentment against any who venture to question one's course of action. Everything like counsel or advice is resented with indignation as a design to bruise and wound. This spirit cherished will lead to numerous evils. None will venture to tell you when you err, because the faithful one would be regarded as an enemy. Thus the kindness that should exist between brethren in the faith is killed because of the jealous interpretation put upon the God-fearing cautions given. Undue stress is laid upon words, imagination exaggerates the matter and creates alienation.

Nevertheless we must not suffer wrong upon a brother. Self-sufficiency must be overcome. Love of applause must be seen as a snare. There is always danger of making grave blunders through conceit of our own wisdom and qualifications. Let these qualifications reveal their true value, and they will be appreciated.

SPIRIT OF UNION AND EQUALITY AMONG LABORERS

I am urged by the Spirit of God to counsel my brethren to unite with one another in labor. Love as brethren, be pitiful, be courteous, be true as steel to one another, but crush that feeling of superiority over your brother ministers which leads one to feel that he cannot link up with others in labor. No one man should feel that he must do the whole work. However experienced or well qualified he may be, there is need of other talents to unite with his. It is a mistake to think that one man's train of thought will accomplish the work for all hearts in a religious effort. Men of different minds are needed, men whose hearts are tenderly led out to win souls. Different methods of labor are really essential in sowing the seeds of truth and gathering in the harvest. It is often the case that men of the humblest ability will reach hearts that have been steeled against another man's labors. Much praying is essential. The soul's drawing nigh to God in communion means God's drawing nigh to the soul that is seeking Him. There needs to be greater devotion of heart and life in service to God.

For further study: *The Desire of Ages,* pages 19-26, 408, 409, 417, 435, 436, 439, 440.

Counsel Together

The greatest work is before us. The peril which threatens our usefulness, and which will prove our ruin if not seen and overcome, is selfishness—placing a higher estimate upon our plans, our opinions, and our labors, and moving independently of our brethren. "Counsel together" have been the words repeated by the angels again and again.

Satan may move through one man's mind to warp things out of their proper channel; he may succeed with two who view things in a similar light; but with several minds enlisted there is greater safety against his wiles. Every plan will be more liable to be viewed from all sides, every advance will be more carefully studied, so that no enterprise will be so likely to be entered upon which will bring confusion and perplexity and defeat to the work in which we are engaged. In union there is strength; in division there is weakness and defeat.

God is leading out a people and fitting them for translation. Are we who are acting a part in this work standing as sentinels for God? Are we uniting our forces? Are we willing to become servants of all? Are we imitating the great Pattern?

PROPER METHODS IN LABOR

The truth cannot be introduced in any haphazard way among the colored people, neither can advice be given to the believers and to those who teach the truth, to be presumptuous. When the period comes in the Southern States to do as did the three worthies who refused to bow to Nebuchadnezzar's image, that time will present decisions for or against the command-

Special Testimonies to Ministers and Workers (Series A, No. 5, 1896), pages 3-7.

ments of God. There is no need of closing up our own way wholly. It will be made more difficult to work the many fields that have not yet been touched. Our policy is, Do not make prominent the objectionable features of our faith, which strike most decidedly against the practices and customs of the people, until the Lord shall give the people a fair chance to know that we are believers in Christ, that we do believe in the divinity of Christ and in His preexistence. Let the testimony of the world's Redeemer be dwelt upon. "I Jesus have sent Mine angel to testify unto you these things in the churches." There is need of strictly guarding the word that the pen traces upon paper. The Lord help us to learn in the school of Christ His meekness and lowliness.

If the Majesty of heaven guarded *His* every word lest *He* should stir up the spirit of Satan and the fallen angels, how much more careful should *we* be in all things!

CORRECT PRINCIPLES

I must speak to my brethren, nigh and afar off. I cannot hold my peace. They are not working on correct principles. Those who stand in responsible positions must not feel that their position of importance makes them men of infallible judgment. All the works of men are under the Lord's jurisdiction. It will be altogether safe for men to consider that there is knowledge with the Most High. Those who trust in God and His wisdom, and not in their own, are walking in safe paths. They will never feel that they are authorized to muzzle even the ox that treads out the grain; and how offensive it is for men to control the human agent who is in partnership with God and to whom the Lord Jesus has said: "Come unto Me, all ye that *labor* and are *heavy-laden,* and I will give you rest. Take My yoke upon you, and learn of Me; for I am meek and lowly in heart: and ye shall find rest unto your souls. For My yoke is easy, and My burden is light." "We are laborers together with God: ye are God's husbandry, ye are God's building."

OUR DUTY TO EXTEND THE WORK

Let forces be set at work to clear new ground, to establish new, living interests wherever an opening can be found. Let men learn how to pray earnestly, short and right to the point. Let them learn to speak of the world's Redeemer, to lift up the Man of Calvary higher and still higher. Transplant trees out of your thickly planted nursery. God is not glorified in centering such immense advantages in one place. We need wise nurserymen who will transplant trees to different localities and give them advantages whereby they may grow. It is a positive duty to go into regions beyond. Rally workers who possess true missionary zeal, and let them go forth to diffuse light and knowledge far and near. Let them take the living principles of health reform into communities that to a large degree are ignorant of what they should do. Let men and women teach these principles to classes that cannot have the advantages of the large sanitarium at Battle Creek. It is a fact that the truth of heaven has come to the notice of thousands through the influence of the sanitarium, yet there is a work to be done that has been neglected. We are encouraged as we see the work that is being done in Chicago, and in a few other places. But years ago the large responsibility that is centered in Battle Creek should have been distributed.

The people are encouraged to center in Battle Creek, and they pay their tithe and give their influence to the building up of a modern Jerusalem that is not after God's order. In this work other places are cut off from facilities which they should have. Enlarge ye, spread, yes; but not in one place. Go out and establish centers of influence in places where nothing, or next to nothing, has been done. Break up your consolidated mass; diffuse the saving beams of light and shed light into the darkened corners of the earth. A work needs to be done something like that which is described as an eagle stirring up her nest. "Moab hath been at ease from his youth, and he hath settled on his lees, and hath not been emptied from vessel to vessel, neither hath he gone into captivity: therefore his taste remained in him, and his scent is not changed." This is true of many Christians who are coming into Battle Creek. Many have a spasmodic zeal, but it is like a meteor that flashes across the heavens and goes out.

Let God's own workmen who have His cause at heart do something for the Southern field. Let not God's stewards be content with just touching it with their fingers' ends. Let those at the heart of the work plan for the field in earnest. You have talked about it; but what are you doing as the stewards of God's means?

Has God given us a work to do? Has God bidden us to go amid opposing influences and convert men from error to truth? Why have not the men and women who have so frequently gathered to the large assemblies in Battle Creek put into practice the truth which they have heard? If they had imparted the light which they had received, what a transformation of character we would have seen! For every grace imparted God would have given grace. The work that has been done for them has not been prized as it should have been, or they would have gone forth into the darkened places of the earth and shed abroad the light which God has shed upon them. They would have given to the world the message of the righteousness of

Christ through faith, and their own light would have become clearer and clearer, for God would have worked with them. Many have gone into the grave in error, simply because those who professed the truth have failed to communicate the precious knowledge they have received. If the light that has shone in superabundance in Battle Creek had been diffused we would have seen many raised up to become laborers together with God.

For further study: *Testimonies,* vol. 5, p. 463; vol. 9, pp. 257-261.

The Evil of Long Sermons

Dear Brother———:

Those who shall be mouthpieces for God should know that their lips have been touched with a live coal from off the altar, and present the truth in the demonstration of the Spirit. But lengthy discourses are a taxation to the speaker and a taxation to the hearers who have to sit so long. One half the matter presented would be of more benefit to the hearer than the large mass poured forth by the speaker. That which is spoken in the first hour is of far more value if the sermon closes then than the words that are spoken in an added half hour. There is a burying up of the matter that has been presented.

This subject has been opened to me again and again that our ministers were making mistakes in talking so long as to wear away the first forcible impression made upon the hearers. So large a mass of matter is presented, which they cannot possibly retain and digest, that all seems confused.

Special Testimonies to Ministers and Workers (Series A, No. 5, 1896), pages 7-9.

I have kept this before our ministering brethren, and begged them not to lengthen out their discourses. Some improvement has been made on this ground with the very best results. But few discourses have exceeded an hour.

While in America the light was given me in the night season concerning yourself. You had been speaking at great length, and still felt that you had not said all you wished to say, and were asking for a little more time. One of dignity and authority stepped before you, as you stood in the pulpit, and said: You have given the people a large amount of matter to consider; one half of what you have given would be of much greater profit than the whole. If energized by the Holy Spirit, it must make an impression on the human hearer. The Holy Spirit works the man, but if there are vital points to be made which are essential to be carried away by the hearer, a train of words is effacing that strong impression, pouring into the vessel more than it can retain, and is so much effort lost. To reserve the last half to be presented when the mind is fresh to receive it will be gathering up the fragments that nothing be lost.

The truth is a precious, vitalizing power. It is the entrance of the word that giveth light and understanding unto the simple. The truth should be spoken clearly, slowly, forcibly, that it may impress the hearer. When the truth in any line is presented it is essential for it to be understood, that all its precious food, the bread of life, the manna from heaven, may be received. Let every fragment be gathered up, that nothing be lost. In the presentation of the truth in preaching the word it is of consequence that nothing should be lost to the receptive hearer. The Lord Jesus is represented by the Holy Spirit, and is seeking to secure admission to the mind, and conviction comes to the heart and conscience; but the overmuch matter that is given is detrimental in its effect, it effaces the impression previously made. Speak short, and you will create an interest to hear again and again.

It is especially true that new and startling themes should not be presented to the people at too great length. In every address given, let there be an application of truth to the heart that whosoever may hear shall understand, and that men, women, and youth may become alive unto God. Try to lead all, from the least to the greatest, to search the word; for the knowledge of His glory is to fill the whole earth as the waters cover the sea.

For further study: *Testimonies,* vol. 2, pp. 116-118, 616, 617, 672; vol. 3, p. 419; vol. 4, p. 261; vol. 5, pp. 251, 252; *Gospel Workers,* pages 167, 168, 171.

Knowing God

"Simon Peter, a servant and an apostle of Jesus Christ, to them that have obtained like precious faith with us through the righteousness of God and our Saviour Jesus Christ: Grace and peace be multiplied unto you through the knowledge of God, and of Jesus our Lord." These precious words are spoken to those who have obtained like precious faith with us through the righteousness of God and our Saviour Jesus Christ. In order to realize the greatness of the promise, we must know by experimental knowledge who is back of the promise. "Thus saith the Lord, Let not the wise man glory in his wisdom, neither let the mighty man glory in his might, let not the rich man glory in his riches: but let him that glorieth glory in this, that he understandeth and knoweth Me, that I am

---

Special Testimonies to Ministers and Workers (Series A, 1896), pages 15-20.

the Lord which exercise loving-kindness, judgment, and righteousness, in the earth: for in these things I delight, saith the Lord."

QUALIFICATIONS ESSENTIAL FOR THE WORK OF GOD

In His word the Lord enumerates the gifts and graces that are indispensable for all who connect with His work. He does not teach us to ignore learning or despise education; for when controlled by the love and fear of God, intellectual culture is a blessing; yet this is not presented as the most important qualification for the service of God. Jesus passed by the wise men of His time, the men of education and position, because they were so proud and self-sufficient in their boasted superiority that they could not sympathize with suffering humanity and become colaborers with the Man of Nazareth. In their bigotry they scorned to be taught by Christ. The Lord Jesus would have men connected with His work who appreciate that work as sacred; then they can cooperate with God. They will be unobstructed channels through which His grace can flow. The attributes of the character of Christ can be imparted to those only who distrust themselves. The highest scientific education cannot in itself develop a Christlike character. The fruits of true wisdom come from Christ alone.

Every worker should test his own qualifications by the word of God. Have the men who are handling sacred things a clear understanding, a right perception, of things of eternal interest? Will they consent to yield to the working of the Holy Spirit? or do they permit themselves to be controlled by their own hereditary and cultivated tendencies? It becomes all to examine themselves whether they be in the faith.

POSITION AND RESPONSIBILITY

Those who occupy positions of trust in the work of God should ever bear in mind that these positions involve great responsibility. The right performance of the solemn work for this time and the salvation of the souls connected with us in any way depend in a great degree upon our own spiritual condition. All should cultivate a vivid sense of their responsibility; for their own present well-being and their eternal destiny will be decided by the spirit they cherish. If self is woven into the work, it is as the offering of strange fire in the place of the sacred. Such workers incur the displeasure of the Lord. Brethren, remove your hands from the work, unless you can distinguish the sacred fire from the common.

Those who have stood as representative men are not all Christian gentlemen. There is prevalent a spirit that seeks the mastery over others. Men regard themselves as authority, they express their opinions and pass resolutions about matters of which they have no experimental knowledge. Some who are connected with the publishing house at —— pass through the office, speaking with different ones, giving directions which they suppose it proper for them to give, when they do not understand what they are talking about.

INJUSTICE AND DISHONESTY

Great injustice and even dishonesty have been committed in the board meetings in bringing matters before those who have not an experience that will enable them to be competent judges. Manuscripts have been placed in the hands of men for criticism, when the eyes of their understanding were so blinded that they could not discern the spiritual import of the subject with which they were dealing. More than this, they had no real knowledge of bookmaking. They had had neither study nor practice in the line of literary productions. Men have sat in judgment upon books and manuscripts unwisely placed in their hands when they should have declined to serve in any such capacity. It would have been only honest for them to say: "I have had no experience in this line of work, and should certainly do injustice to myself and to others in giving my opinion. Excuse me, brethren; instead of instructing others, I need that someone should teach me." But this was far from their thoughts. They expressed themselves freely in regard to subjects of which they knew nothing. Conclusions have been accepted as the opinions of wise men, when they were simply the opinions of novices.

The time has come when in the name and strength of God the church must act for the good of souls and for the honor of God. A lack of firm faith and of discernment in sacred things should be regarded as sufficient to debar any man from connection with the work of God. So also the indulgence of a quick temper, a harsh, overbearing spirit, reveals that its possessor should not be placed where he will be called to decide weighty questions that affect God's heritage. A passionate man should have no part to act in dealing with human minds. He cannot be trusted to shape matters which have a relation to those whom Christ has purchased at an infinite price. If he undertakes to manage men, he will hurt and bruise their souls; for he has not the fine touch, the delicate sensibility, which the grace of Christ imparts. His own heart needs to be softened, subdued by the Spirit of God; the heart of stone has not become a heart of flesh.

ALL ARE TO REPRESENT CHRIST

Those who are thus misrepresenting Christ are placing a wrong mold upon the work, for they encourage all who are connected with them to do as they do. For their souls' sake, for the sake of those who are in danger from their influence, they should resign their positions; for the record will appear in heaven that the wrongdoer has the blood of many souls upon his garments. He has caused some to become exasperated, so that they have given up the faith; others have been imbued with his own satanic attributes, and the evil done it is impossible to estimate. Those only who make it manifest that their hearts are being sanctified through the truth should be retained in positions of trust in the Lord's work.

Let all consider that whatever their employment, they are to represent Christ. With steadfast purpose let every man seek to have the mind of Christ. Especially should those who have accepted the position of directors or counselors feel that they are required to be in every respect Christian gentlemen. While in dealing with others we are always to be faithful, we should not be rude. The souls with whom we have to do are the Lord's purchased possession, and we are to permit no hasty, overbearing expression to escape the lips.

Brethren, treat men as men, not as servants to be ordered about at your pleasure. He who indulges a harsh, overbearing spirit might better become a tender of sheep as did Moses, and thus learn what it means to be a true shepherd. Moses gained in Egypt an experience as a mighty statesman and as a leader of the armies, but he did not there learn the lessons essential for true greatness. He needed an experience in more humble duties, that he might become a caretaker, tender toward every living thing. In keeping the flocks of Jethro his sympathies were called out to the sheep and lambs, and he learned to guard these creatures of God with the gentlest care. Although their voice could never complain of mistreatment, yet their attitude might show much. God cares for all the creatures He has made. In working for God in this lowly station, Moses learned to be a tender shepherd for Israel.

DEPENDING UPON GOD

The Lord would have us learn a lesson also from the experience of Daniel. There are many who might become mighty men if like this faithful Hebrew they would depend upon God for grace to be overcomers, and for strength and efficiency in their labors. Daniel manifested the most perfect courtesy, both toward his elders and toward the youth. He stood as a witness for God, and sought to take such a course that he might not be ashamed for heaven to hear his words or to behold his works. When Daniel was required to partake of the luxuries of the king's table, he did not fly into a passion, neither did he express a determination to eat and drink as he pleased. Without speaking one word of defiance, he took the matter to God. He and his companions sought wisdom from the Lord, and when they came forth from earnest prayer their decision was made. With true courage and Christian courtesy, Daniel presented the case to the officer who had them in charge, asking that they might be granted a simple diet. These youth felt that their religious principles were at stake, and they relied upon God, whom they loved and served. Their request was granted, for they had obtained favor with God and with men.

Men in every position of trust need to take their place in the school of Christ, and heed the injunction of the Great Teacher: "Learn of Me; for I am meek and lowly in heart: and ye shall find rest unto your souls. For My yoke is easy, and My burden is light." We have no excuse for manifesting one wrong trait of character. "Not by might, nor by power, but by My Spirit, saith the Lord of hosts." In your dealing with others, whatever you see or hear that needs to be corrected, first seek the Lord for wisdom and grace, that in trying to be faithful you may not be rude. Ask Him to give you the gentleness of Christ; then you will be true to your duty, true to your position of trust, and true to God, a faithful steward, overcoming natural and acquired tendencies to evil.

None but a wholehearted Christian can be a perfect gentleman; but if Christ is abiding in the soul His spirit will be revealed in the manner, the words, and the actions. Gentleness and love cherished in the heart will appear in self-denial, in true courtesy. Such workers will be the light of the world.

For further study: *Gospel Workers,* pages 36-39, 414-419; *Testimonies,* vol. 5, pp. 552-554, 503, 587, 32, 80, 81, 737-746, 11.

The Need of Spiritual Discernment

On the steamer "Alameda" on the broad ocean,

November 17, 1891.

Redemption is part of the divine nature. It is the prerogative of God to have to reconstruct, not to destroy. The Son of God was given to die before the foundation of the world. The existence of sin is unexplainable; therefore not a soul knows what God is until he sees himself in the light reflected from the cross of

Special Testimonies to Ministers and Workers (Series A, No. 6, 1896), pages 3-17.

Calvary, and detests himself as a sinner in the bitterness of his soul. When his soul cries out in great need for a sin-pardoning Saviour, then God is revealed as gracious, full of compassion and forgiveness and love, long-suffering and patience. Individually, as church members, we are, if faithful servants of Jesus Christ, laborers together with God. When one is bruised by the enemy and wounded and commits error, as faithful and true to the Master, as workers together with God, we must take up the missionary work next to us, we must work to heal, not to ruin and to destroy. The hope we have in Christ is because we are sinners. We have a right to claim a Saviour. Then when there are those in any of our institutions associated together who err, let not men act the part of denouncing, condemning, and destroying, as though they were faultless.

It is the work of the Christian to mend, to restore, to heal. This healing process saves many a soul and hides a multitude of sins. God is love; God is, in Himself, in His essence, love. He makes the very best of what appears an injury, and gives Satan no occasion for triumph by making the worst appear and exposing our weakness to our enemies. The world must not be introduced into the church, and married to the church, forming a bond of unity. Through this means the church will become indeed corrupt, and as stated in Revelation, "a cage of every unclean and hateful bird."

INFLUENCE OF UNION WITH WORLDLINGS

Through association with the world our institutions will become unsubstantial, unreliable; because these worldly elements, introduced and placed in positions of trust, are looked up to as teachers to be respected in their educating, directing, and official position, and they are sure to be worked upon by the spirit and power of darkness; so that the demarcation becomes not distinguished between him that serveth God and him that serveth Him not. The parable is given by Jesus Christ in regard to the field in which it was supposed had been sown pure wheat, but the entrusted ones look upon the field with disappointment, and inquire, "Didst not thou sow good seed in thy field? from whence then hath it tares?" The master of the vineyard answers, "An enemy hath done this."

ACCUSER OF THE BRETHREN

Thus hath it been presented to me in regard to the Rural Health Retreat.* I had a message of warning. I spoke with earnestness, and I know the Lord put His Holy Spirit upon me while I presented the danger of association with and love of the world. The worldling is ever on the watch to criticize and accuse those who serve God. This will reveal itself in the querulous complaining of professed Christians, who have never been transformed by the grace of Jesus Christ. They are deadly enemies to those who believe. They despise the Sabbath of the fourth commandment, and if they can make it appear that those who are striving to obey the commandments of God are faulty, Satan has cast his arrow, and now what? He has shown his accusing power; but his cruel thrusts will do little harm if the professed believers will stand true to the words of Christ, and be doers of His word and not hearers only. Those to whom these complaints are made are under bonds to Jesus Christ to love and respect and be faithful to one another who are united to Christ in church fellowship. To unite with the

*See Appendix.

faultfinding element, to be accusers of the brethren, to take up the reproach they lay at your door is seconding the work of the enemy by playing yourself into his hands to make his work a success.

WHY CHRIST WAS HATED

I presented the matter before the hearers that Jesus the Lord of life and glory was crucified to please the malice of the Jews because the principles He presented did not coincide with their own ideas and ambitious aims. He condemned all guile, all underhanded work of policy for supremacy, and every unholy practice. Pilate and Herod became friends in crucifying Christ. They pleased the Jews in making effective their enmity against One whom Pilate proclaimed innocent. I presented to them Judas, who betrayed his Lord for money value; Peter, who denied Him in His humiliation in the judgment hall. A few hours before, he had with great firmness assured his Master he would go with Him to prison and to death; and notwithstanding Jesus' declaration that he would, ere the cock crew, deny Him thrice, he was so self-confident that he took not the words of Christ as verity and truth. How little he knew himself! How soon circumstances tested his allegiance to his Master! He denied Jesus in the very hour he should have watched with Him in fervent prayer. When in the judgment hall he was accused of being one of this Man's disciples, he denied; and the third time he was accused, he emphasized his denial with cursing and swearing.

EFFECT OF GENUINE CONVERSION

Said Christ, "Ye shall receive power, after that the Holy Ghost is come upon you: and ye shall be witnesses unto Me." The look of grief and sadness which Jesus gave Peter was not a hopeless look; it broke the heart of Peter, who denied his Lord.

But Peter was converted, and then after the crucifixion and resurrection of Christ when before the rulers, he boldly declared for Jesus, and charged the rulers with these words: "But ye denied the Holy One and the Just, and desired a murderer to be granted unto you; and killed the Prince of life." There Peter shows himself entirely a different man after his conversion than the self-confident, boasting Peter prior to his conversion. I presented before them the voice of the world, the enemies of Christ, saying to Christ's messengers, "Ye should not teach in this name" and "bring this Man's blood upon us." Did this threatening succeed? did it make cowards of the witnesses of Christ? No; they proclaimed the message given them of God; and they were shut up in prison, and God sent His angel to release them. The angel of the Lord by night opened the prison doors and brought them forth, and said, "Go, stand and speak in the temple to the people all the words of this life." This voice from the heavenly angels was directly opposite to that voice from the authorities, and which should they obey? "Then Peter and the other apostles answered and said, We ought to obey God rather than men. The God of our fathers raised up Jesus, whom ye slew and hanged on a tree. Him hath God exalted with His right hand to be a Prince and a Saviour, for to give repentance to Israel, and forgiveness of sins. And we are His witnesses of these things; and so is also the Holy Ghost, whom God hath given to them that obey Him. When they heard that, they were cut to the heart, and took counsel to slay them." Then Gamaliel, a doctor of the law, pleaded in behalf of the apostles, and his words prevailed. Well, this is a little part of the words the Lord gave me to speak to the people.

HOW TO TREAT THE ERRING

The words given me were of that character that I knew the people needed, and which would benefit them if they would hear. One discourse was upon how to treat those united with us in church capacity if they erred. They were not to permit their minds to be affected to action by the words of the Lord's enemies against His children. If complaints or murmurings or charges are made they must study in Christ's school as to the course to be pursued toward the ones of whom complaints are made. Tell the matter between him and thee *alone,* and if he will not hear, then take two or three others; if he will not hear these, tell it to the church.

LOVE NOT THE WORLD

The world has no part with the believers in this work. They cannot discern the motives and principles by which God's people are bound in their relations and dealings with one another. We must be true, loyal soldiers in the army of Jesus Christ. All His followers are to keep step with their Leader. They should never introduce their secrets to, or make confidants of, the enemies of Jesus Christ in regard to their movements or what they purpose to do in their line of action; for it is a betrayal of sacred trusts, and is giving the enemy every advantage. Let the counsel of the people of God be within their own company. The enemies of Christ should not be made familiar with their secrets, while the children of God are kept in ignorance of the very things they ought to know. The secrets of the Lord are with them that fear Him.

The world is the chief enemy of religion. The satanic forces are constantly at work through the world, and those who are professed Christians, yet associated with the world in close fellowship, are so much one in spirit, aims, and principles of working, that they cannot discern between him who serveth God and him who serveth the world. The enemy works constantly to push the world to the front, to be looked upon as superior to those who believe in Jesus, and who seek to be doers of His word. Words of praise and flattery from worldlings are received as sweet morsels, but the judgment of those who love this sort of food is in accordance with the weakness which they show in this direction. Their spiritual life is composed of just the kind of material they feed upon. Their Christian experience is largely dependent on flattery and human appreciation. The fear and love of God are not interwoven in their experience.

How pitiable and sad to see men who have known something of the Spirit of God fall so completely into the arms of the world as to be swayed and influenced by its voice, and depend upon its favors for strength and success! How manifestly such are alienated from Christ, how full of self-confidence, how full of vaunting, of vanity, and how shortsighted in regard to spirituality! How little true discernment have they to distinguish between him who is a child of God, an heir of the kingdom, and him who is a child of the wicked one, who is a child of disobedience, and an enemy of God!

THE TWO CLASSES

There are only two classes in our world: those who are obedient to Jesus Christ, who seek the Master to do His will, and work for the attainment of the salvation of their own souls and the soul of everyone who is associated with them who names the name of Christ; and the children of disobedience. There are but two classes in our world. Then listen to the words of One who knows: "Ye are of God, little children, and have overcome them: because greater is He that is in you, than he that is in the world. They are of the world: therefore speak they of the world, and the world heareth them." 1 John 4:4, 5. Souls are being deluded. The fear and love of God have not a controlling power. The world is their master, and they chase after its delusive, flattering mirage. Listen to One who gave His life for the world, "that whosoever *believeth* in Him should not perish, but have everlasting life." He spake as never man spake. The whole of John 15 contains a most important lesson. Read it; obey it. Again, hear the voice of God, "Ye cannot serve God and mammon."

MINGLING OF BELIEVERS WITH UNBELIEVERS

Let not God's people in any of our institutions sign a truce with the enemy of God and man. The duty of the church to the world is not to come down to their ideas and accept their opinions, their suggestions, but to heed the words of Christ through His servant Paul, "Be ye not unequally yoked together with unbelievers: for what fellowship hath righteousness with unrighteousness? and what communion hath light with darkness? and what concord hath Christ with Belial? or what part hath he that believeth with an infidel?" This means in a special sense marriage with unbelievers, but it covers more ground than this: it means in our instrumentalities ordained of God, in our institutions for health, in our colleges, in our publishing houses.

The matter is placed before us in the correct light. The question is asked, "And what agreement hath the temple of God with idols? for ye are the temple of the living God; as God hath said, I will dwell in them, and walk in them; and I will be their God, and they shall be My people. Wherefore come out from among them, and be ye separate, saith the Lord, and touch not the unclean thing." What does this mean—the suggestions, the evil workings in the children of disobedience. You are not in any case to become contaminated with the spirit or influence of unbelievers. Be afraid of uniting or binding up in bundles with them. Be afraid of communicating the works connected with the Lord's cause to those who have no part with God, or sympathy with those who love the truth of God. "And I will receive you, and will be a Father unto you, and ye shall be My sons and daughters, saith the Lord Almighty."

I raise my voice of warning against the mingling in our institutions of the worldly element with those who believe; we have the danger signal to sound. If in our institutions persons are placed in positions of trust, they are educators. Others are taught to look to these persons for instruction, and in this is a snare to the unwary; their ideas become confused in regard to righteousness and truth. They hear those persons who have no respect for the truth sneer and speak disparagingly of the truth, which should be held firmly and sacredly as truth.

When the day's work on Friday should be planned with reference to the Sabbath of the Lord, there is Satan working with those children of disobedience to prolong the service into the sacred hours, and give their orders that those under their direction shall do work on the Sabbath, and then they exult and Satan triumphs.

And when men in the highest responsible positions make no difference between those who serve God and those who serve Him not, they evidence that their eyes are not single to the glory of God; therefore their whole body is full of darkness. When these men in authority have so mingled with the spirit of worldlings that the words of complaint from the lips of these unbelievers are gathered as verity and truth, they know not what spirit they are of. When they encourage this spirit, and complaints against the people of God, they evidence that they are working on the enemy's side to belittle and humiliate those whom the Lord loves, and that they strengthen the hands of the wicked, who are doing an evil work. When they feel free to suffer the accusers of God's children to plan for them against His chosen ones, they do not have Christ to plan with them.

DEAL JUSTLY WITH THE ERRING

If one of the children of the Lord errs, then if the men in authority are discerning spiritual things, they will understand that their position allows no betrayal of sacred trusts on their part, and they will not betray the cause of God into the enemy's hands. They will not be reticent to the very ones in whom they should have confidence, and work in silence and secrecy, and open their plans to those who have no sympathy with the chosen people of God. If any workers in our institutions for health are murmured against and accused by unbelievers or believers, let the following special directions given by our Master, Jesus Christ, be placed in mottoes all through the establishment: "Judge not, that ye be not judged. For with what judgment ye judge, ye shall be judged: and with what measure ye mete, it shall be measured to you again."

Go to those supposed to be in error, talk with them, not working with duplicity and hypocrisy, meeting them day by day with apparent friendship, and at the same time plotting against them in perfect unity with the satanic agencies at work to uproot, to tear down, to remove from the institution the ones the unbelieving element wants removed, while not a word is spoken with the brethren or sisters in the faith to redeem them, to heal them, if they are in error; and if they are not in the wrong, to vindicate the right, and put the rebuke where it belongs—upon the plotters of an evil work, because Satan is behind the scene. The Lord Jesus rebuked the Pharisees, likening them to sepulchers that do not appear, hidden from sight, but full of corruption. The Lord hates all deception, secrecy, and guile. This is Satan's work; the work of God is open and frank. No one will work against a child of God on the strength of the testimony of the Lord's enemy, and work after Satan's manner—concealing himself, yet suggesting, instigating, planning in perfect unity with the Lord's enemies.

How can the universe of heaven regard such underhanded, cowardly work against those who love God and keep His commandments? Members of the church may commit errors, and often make mistakes; but they are to be dealt with kindly, tenderly, as Christ has dealt with us. But the rebuke of God is upon all those who do the work of God deceitfully, professedly friends of Christ, yet working in an undercurrent style, in darkness, against those who love God. "Brethren, if a man be overtaken in a fault, ye which are spiritual, restore such an one in the spirit of meekness; considering thyself, lest thou also be tempted."

Here is our work, brethren; will we take it up? So little of this is done that the words of the True Witness come home to the church: "Nevertheless I have somewhat against thee, because thou hast left thy first love. Remember therefore from whence thou art fallen, and repent, and do the first works; or else I will come unto thee quickly, and will remove thy candlestick out of his place, except thou repent."

"And he showed me Joshua the high priest standing before the Angel of the Lord, and Satan standing at his right hand to resist him. And the Lord said unto Satan, The Lord rebuke thee, O Satan; even the Lord that hath chosen Jerusalem rebuke thee: is not this a brand plucked out of the fire? Now Joshua was clothed with filthy garments, and stood before the Angel." This was the appearance of Satan. He had deceived these souls by his delusions and devices. Now these souls had repented before God, and pardon was written against their names. Satan was accusing them of sins, and asserting his right to do as he pleased with them because of their transgression which he had caused them to commit. But Jesus looked upon these souls believing in Him, trusting in His righteousness, with the tenderest and most loving compassion. "And He answered and spake unto those that stood before Him, saying, Take away the filthy garments from him. And unto him He said, Behold, I have caused thine iniquity to pass from thee, and I will clothe thee with change of raiment. And I said, Let them set a fair miter upon his head. So they set a fair miter upon his head, and clothed him with garments. And the Angel of the Lord stood by." Shall the people of God who are placed in positions of trust voice the words of Satan against the children of God? Let us act as Christians, true as steel to God and

His holy work; quick to discern the devices of Satan in his hidden, deceptive workings through the children of disobedience.

OUR WORDS

"Your words have been stout against Me, saith the Lord. Yet ye say, What have we spoken so much against Thee? Ye have said, It is vain to serve God: and what profit is it that we have kept His ordinance, and that we have walked mournfully before the Lord of hosts? And now we call the proud happy; yea, they that work wickedness are set up; yea, they that tempt God are even delivered." These are the words of the unconsecrated who are separating from God, blinded by the enemy. They cannot discern the ways and works of God. Now is represented the opposite class: "Then they that feared the Lord spake often one to another." These words were not speaking evil of brethren, or making complaints of God, but were words spoken from sincere hearts, words in which were no deceit, no underhanded working, no guile. "And the Lord hearkened, and heard it, and a book of remembrance was written before Him for them that feared the Lord, and that thought upon His name. And they shall be Mine, saith the Lord of hosts, in that day when I make up My jewels; and I will spare them, as a man spareth his own son that serveth him. Then shall ye return, and discern between the righteous and the wicked, between him that serveth God and him that serveth Him not."

OUR STRENGTH IN UNION WITH CHRIST

May the Lord bless His people with spiritual eyesight, to see that the children of God and the world can never be in copartnership. Whosoever will be the friend of the world is the enemy of God. While every individual should work with Christ to transform the children of darkness by showing them the Lamb of God that taketh away the sins of the world, they cannot have overflowing sympathy with worldlings in such a degree that they lend them their influence to carry out their suggestions to weaken and do injustice to God's chosen ones. God does not work in this way. In perfect and complete unity there is strength. Not in numbers, but in the perfect trust and unity with Christ, one can chase a thousand, and two put ten thousand to flight. Let us not form unholy bonds of union with the friends of the world; for God has pronounced His curse upon all such unions. Let the people of God take their stand firmly for truth and for righteousness. Already we see the terrible consequences of uniting believers with unbelievers. The result is, the unbelievers are given the confidence that belongs to those only who love and revere God.

Already has the power of darkness placed its mold and superscription upon the work that should stand forth untainted, unpolluted from Satan's cunning devices. We lift our voice of warning upon the social attractions by worldly bids and worldly baits. Keep clear. Touch not the unclean thing. Let not the world's direction and propositions be given to God's people to control them. Woe be unto him whose wisdom is not from above but from beneath! Men of superficial piety, by their desire to receive patronage, to obtain fame, betray the most sacred interests into the hands of unbelievers.

Let not money be obtained by touching or sanctioning any unclean practices. Let the grace of Christ be brought into the heart, and if the workers be few and God can work with them in our institutions, they will prevail. There must be no deceiving power at work, for it is an unclean thing. There must be no hands that are defiled. Clean hands and a pure heart God will recognize. "For thus saith the high and lofty One that inhabiteth eternity, whose name is Holy; I dwell in the high and holy place, with him also that is of a contrite and humble spirit, to revive the spirit of the humble, and to revive the heart of the contrite ones."

For further study: *Testimonies,* vol. 5, pp. 396-398; vol. 4, pp. 309-312, 43-55, 617-619; vol. 6, pp. 17, 148; *The Desire of Ages,* pages 302, 313.

The light of the glory of God must fall upon us. We need the holy unction from on high. However intelligent, however learned a man may be, he is not qualified to teach unless he has a firm hold on the God of Israel. He who is connected with heaven will do the works of Christ. By faith in God he will have power to move upon humanity. He will seek for the lost sheep of the house of Israel. If divine power does not combine with human effort, I would not give a straw for all that the greatest man could do. The Holy Spirit is wanting in our work.—*Review and Herald,* February 18, 1890.

To Brethren in Responsible Positions 11

Connection With God's Work

Cooranbong, Australia, July 6, 1896.

Dear Brother———:

It has been revealed to me that the Lord proves and tries all who have named the name of Christ, but especially those who are stewards in any department of His cause. A connection with the special work of God for this time brings with it much responsibility, and the higher the position of trust, the greater the responsibility attached to it. How humble and sincere the one needs to be who is filling such a position! How fearful and mistrustful of himself! How careful to give all the praise and thanksgiving to God!

There is a watcher standing by the side of all those who are filling positions of trust, ready to reprove and convict of wrongdoing, or to answer the prayers for help. He watches to see if the men privileged to bear responsibilities will look to God for wisdom and avail themselves of every opportunity to perfect a character after the divine similitude. If they deviate from straightforward rectitude, God turns from them; if they do not earnestly strive to understand the will of God concerning them, He cannot bless or prosper or sustain them.

Those whom God has placed in positions of responsibility should never seek to exalt themselves or to turn the attention of men to their work. They must give all the glory to God. They must not seek for power that they may lord it over God's heritage; for only

The articles in this section are from *Special Testimonies to Ministers and Workers* (Series A, No. 6, 1896). This article, pages 27-46.

those who are under the rule of Satan will do this.

But the rule-or-ruin system* is too often seen in our institutions. This spirit is cherished and revealed by some in responsible positions, and because of this God cannot do the work He desires to do through them. By their course of action those who reveal this spirit make manifest what they would be in heaven if entrusted with responsibility.

Those who will look at human souls in the light of the cross of Calvary need not err regarding the estimate which should be placed upon them. The reason why God has permitted some of the human family to be so rich and some so poor will remain a mystery to men till eternity, unless they enter into right relations with God and carry out His plans, instead of acting on their own selfish ideas that because a man is rich he is to be more highly respected than his poor neighbor. God makes His sun to shine on the just and on the unjust, and this sun represents Christ, the Sun of Righteousness, who shines as the light of the world, giving His blessings and mercies, seen and unseen, to rich and poor alike. This principle is to guide our conduct toward our fellowmen. The Lord is the teacher of the highest moral sentiments, the loftiest principles; and no man can deviate from these and be guiltless. It is the highest insult to God's goodness to doubt whether He would be willing for us to impart to others the blessings, spiritual and temporal, which He has freely given us.

WHAT CONSTITUTES A CHRISTIAN

A pure religion, an upright, holy life, constitutes a man a Christian. But ever since his defection in heaven, Satan's course has been one of perpetual de-

*See Appendix.

ception and harshness; and there are professed Christians who are learning his methods and practices. While they claim to be serving the cause of God they turn their fellowmen from their rights, in order to serve themselves.

Every human being has been bought with a price, and as God's heritage he has certain rights, of which no one should deprive him. The Lord will not accept service from those who practice double-dealing. The least advantage gained in this way will dishonor God and the truth. Those who possess Bible religion will do justice, love mercy, and walk humbly with their God. These are the lines drawn by the God of justice on this matter.

Again I would urge that living faith in God be cultivated. There are those who, though thought to be serving God, are fast becoming girded about with infidelity. To them crooked paths seem straight; they are living in continual violation of God's truth; corrupt principles are interwoven into their life practice, and wherever they go they sow seeds of evil. In the place of leading others to Christ their influence causes them to question and doubt. They unsettle minds in the truth by entering into speculative theories which draw them away from the truth. They help to forge the fetters of doubt and unbelief, faultfinding and accusing; and souls stumble over them to perdition. The blood of souls will be upon those who, while they profess to be in the service of God, are doing the work of His enemy.

WHAT OUGHT WE TO BE?

Knowing this, what manner of persons ought we to be? Shall we exalt human wisdom and point to finite, changeable, erring men as a dependence in time of trouble? or shall we exemplify our faith by our trust in God's power, revealing the net of false theories, religions, and philosophies which Satan has spread to catch unwary souls? By thus doing the word of God, we shall be lights in the world; for if the word of God is practiced, we show to all those who come within the sphere of our influence that we reverence and respect God, and that we are working under His administration. By a humble, circumspect walk, by love, forbearance, long-suffering, and gentleness, God expects His servants to manifest Him to the world.

God requires those to whom He has given sacred trusts to rise to the full height of their responsibilities. Man is placed here in the world on test and trial, and those who are given positions of trust must decide whether they will exalt self, or their Maker; whether they will use their power to oppress their fellowmen, or to exalt and glorify God.

Increased responsibilities bring increased accountability. He who would be a faithful servant must give entire and willing service to the greatest teacher the world ever knew. His ideas and principles must be kept pure by the power of God. Every day he must learn to become worthy of the trust placed in him. His mind must be quickened by the divine power. His character must be uncontaminated by the influence of his relatives, his friends, or his neighbors. At times he must turn aside from active life to commune with God, and to hear His voice saying to him, "Be still, and know that I am God."

The fruits of the Spirit will be borne by the man who loves God and keeps the way of the Lord, as the rich clusters of grapes grow on the living vine. Christ is his stronghold. Christ lived the law of God in humanity, and so may man do if he will by faith take hold on the strong and mighty One for strength. If he realizes that he cannot do anything without Christ by his side, God will give him wisdom. But he must cherish the love of Christ in his heart, and practice His lessons; for is he not to love Christ as Christ loved God? Is he not to demonstrate to all with whom he associates that he has the abiding presence of Jesus Christ more than he has ever had it before? Because of his increased responsibilities he must have an increased knowledge of God, and must reveal that living faith that works by love and purifies the soul.

FREQUENT CAUSE OF FAILURE

But frequently when placed in high positions of trust, men fail to take time to pray; they think they have no time to train their every faculty to respond to the convictions of the Holy Spirit. But if these men would sit at the feet of the meek and lowly Jesus they would carry out sacred responsibilities, confident, not in themselves, but in their God. They would render to God the sacrifice of a noble, self-denying, cross-bearing life. Jesus would be enthroned in their hearts, giving them physical, mental, and moral power to make Him known.

God longs to work through those to whom He has given capabilities for great things. He longs to see those who occupy responsible places representing Him to the world. He desires that Christ be acknowledged as the greatest teacher the world has ever known, and that He shall shine through their minds as the Light of the world. "But as many as received Him, to them gave He power to become the sons of God, even to them that believe on His name." But in order that this may be, God demands that every intellectual and physical capability be offered as a consecrated oblation to Him.

But some men, as soon as they are placed in sacred positions of trust, regard themselves as great men; and this thought, if entertained, ends the desire for divine enlightenment, which is the only possible thing that can make men great. Those who take this view extinguish all chance of true greatness in themselves, because they will not become illuminated by the Sun of Righteousness.

But men cannot extinguish the light of life, even though they close their eyes tightly in order that they may not see it. The Sun of Righteousness shines none the less because the poor, foolish human agent surrounds himself with self-created darkness.

SPECIAL DANGERS OF THOSE IN POSITIONS OF RESPONSIBILITY

The men who close their eyes to the divine light are ignorant, deplorably ignorant, both of the Scriptures and of the power of God. The Holy Spirit's working is not agreeable to them, and they attribute its manifestations to fanaticism. They rebel against the light, and do all they can to shut it out, calling darkness light and light darkness. They complain that the teachings of Christ cause undue excitement and fanaticism, which spoil those who receive them for the proper duties of life.

Those who entertain and speak this belief do not know what they are talking about. They are cherishing a love of darkness; and just as long as these Christless souls are retained in positions of responsibility the cause of God is imperiled. They are in danger of fastening themselves so firmly with the dark leader of all rebellion that they will never see light; and the longer they are retained the more hopeless is their chance of receiving Christ or of having a knowledge of the true God. How uncertain they make everything that is spiritual and progressive in the truth! Under the influence of their leader they become more and more determined to work against Christ. But through good and bad report, through darkness, through all the antagonism of the agencies of Satan, the Sun of Righteousness calmly shines on, searching out evil, repressing sin, and reviving the spirit of the humble and contrite ones. "Lord, to whom shall we go? Thou hast the words of eternal life."

A DAILY CHRISTIAN EXPERIENCE ESSENTIAL

The evidence of true value and worth in men who are in responsible positions is the fact that they have a daily Christian experience in the things of God. They find music in the words spoken by Christ. "But when the Comforter is come, whom I will send unto you from the Father, even the Spirit of truth, which proceedeth from the Father, He shall testify of Me: and ye also shall bear witness, because ye have been with Me from the beginning." If men will receive the ministration of the Holy Spirit—the richest gift God can bestow—they will impart blessings to all who are connected with them.

But God cannot reveal Himself through some who are entrusted with responsibilities. He cannot make them channels through which His grace and compassion and love can flow; for they insult His goodness by exhibiting a masterful spirit toward those whom they regard as being in error and needing reproof, eclipsing Christ's love and mercy by their own unsanctified passions. The enemy of all good is allowed to rule in their hearts, and their lives will reveal his attributes. They claim that the word of God directs them, but by their actions they say, We want not Thy way, but our way.

By their words, their works, and their spirit those who pursue such a course are making a record in the books of heaven which they will not care to meet; for God does not value them as they value themselves. They are abusing their probationary opportunities and are grievously neglecting the high privileges conferred upon them. Though finding nothing in the word of God to vindicate their actions or countenance their opinions, yet they persist in their own way. In that day when judgment is passed upon all, the sentence will be pronounced against them, "Thou art weighed in the balances, and art found wanting."

THE STEWARDSHIP OF MEN

God may entrust men with money and possessions, but because of this they are not to lift themselves up. All they have they hold in trust; it is lent them by God that they may develop a character like His. They are on trial. God wants to see whether they will prove themselves worthy of the eternal riches. If they use their Lord's goods to set themselves above their fellowmen, they prove unworthy of a place in the kingdom of God. In the great reckoning day they will hear the words: "If therefore ye have not been faithful in the unrighteous mammon, who will commit to your trust the true riches? And if ye have not been faithful in that which is another man's, who shall give you that which is your own?"

But if those whom the Lord has made stewards regard their treasures as His gifts and seek to manifest compassion, sympathy, and love for their fellowmen, they are in harmony with the character of God, who gave His only-begotten Son to die for their salvation. If they value the souls of the human race according to the price paid for their redemption, they will not work out their natural impulses, but will manifest the attributes of the mind and will of God, and will be channels through which God's generous, loving sentiments may flow to humanity.

THE OFFICE OF MISFORTUNE AND ADVERSITY

The Lord has permitted misfortunes to come to men, poverty to press upon them, adversity to try them, that He may thus test those whom He has placed in more favored circumstances; and if those to whom He has entrusted His goods are faithful, He declares them to be worthy to walk with Him in white, to become kings and priests unto God. "He that is faithful in that which is least is faithful also in much: and he that is unjust in the least is unjust also in much."

"Wherefore laying aside all malice, and all guile, and hypocrisies, and envies, and all evilspeakings, as newborn babes, desire the sincere milk of the word, that ye may grow thereby: if so be ye have tasted that the Lord is gracious. To whom coming, as unto a living stone, disallowed indeed of men, but chosen of God, and precious, ye also, as lively stones, are built up a spiritual house, an holy priesthood, to offer up spiritual sacrifices, acceptable to God by Jesus Christ. Wherefore also it is contained in the Scripture, Behold, I lay in Sion a chief cornerstone, elect, precious: and he that believeth on Him shall not be confounded. Unto you therefore which believe He is precious: but unto them which be disobedient, the stone which the builders disallowed, the same is made the head of the corner, and a stone of stumbling, and a rock of offense, even to them which stumble at the word, being disobedient: whereunto also they were appointed. But ye are a chosen generation, a royal priesthood, an holy nation, a peculiar people; that ye should show forth the praises of Him who hath called you out of darkness into His marvelous light."

POSITION POWERLESS TO SANCTIFY

Are acceptable spiritual sacrifices made to God when men who are placed in positions of great responsibility magnify themselves and dishonor God? That has been done, and God looks upon their course with displeasure. Instead of growing up into Christ, their living head, manifesting His divine attributes to the world, they have grown earthward. Self has been regarded as of great importance, and selfishness has attached itself to their work. Devotion to God has not been seen; spiritual life in Jesus Christ has not been developed.

God cannot give His wisdom to men who look upon their position as sufficient excuse for turning from Bible principles to their own finite judgment, as if a position in the work of the Lord gave them liberty of speech, and power to pass resolutions and devise plans and methods that are not in accordance with God's will. Such need to learn that elevated position has no power to sanctify the heart. God permits them to hold these positions that He may prove whether they will reveal the character of God or the character of weak, finite humanity, which has never been fully under God's discipline; but positions have no power to develop a man's character. It rests wholly with the man himself to prove whether he will work himself, which means that Satan will work him, or whether he will be worked by the Holy Spirit.

"Unto you therefore which believe He is precious: but unto them which be disobedient, the stone which the builders disallowed, the same is made the head of the corner." Have we all made Christ our righteousness? Has He been placed as the honored memorial stone of the corner? Have His lessons of humility been cherished, and have they been acted upon? Have His lessons of mercy, justice, and the love of God been exemplified in our lives?

GOD THE SOURCE OF STRENGTH

Oh, what weakness men manifest when they separate from the Source of wisdom and power! Have not men been magnified? Have not human sentiments and imperfect traits of character been held up as if of great value, while Christ and His righteousness have been excluded? Have not men woven selfishness into everything they have touched, revealing it persistently and determinedly in their work? Have they not treated the message of God with disdain? Have they not handled means which was not theirs as though they had a right to do with it as they pleased? And when this means was used to open new fields, have they not acted as though it came from their own individual capital, which they deserved great credit for thus appropriating? Has not the money offered as an oblation to God been used to pile up large buildings in Battle Creek—to give character to the work, it is said, but really to give opportunity for men to show the genius and tact they manifest in managing these large business houses?

"But ye are a chosen generation, a royal priesthood, an holy nation, a peculiar people; that ye should show forth the praises of Him who hath called you out of darkness into His marvelous light: which in time past were not a people, but are now the people of God: which had not obtained mercy, but now have obtained mercy. Dearly beloved, I beseech you as strangers and pilgrims, abstain from fleshly lusts, which war against the soul; having your conversation honest among the Gentiles: that, whereas they speak against you as evildoers, they may by your good works, which they shall behold, glorify God in the day of visitation."

THE EVIL OF SELF-SERVING

How do men regard the work of the Lord when they feel themselves at liberty to be disobedient, unthankful, unholy, condemnatory, and harsh, loving to serve themselves rather than the Lord? Those who hold sacred trusts are forming their own destiny by the spirit and character they reveal; and do they ever think how their works will appear in the judgment? If the important truth for this time were an abiding principle in the souls of those who minister in the work of the Lord, how earnestly they would strive to obtain perfection of character, that they might surround the souls of those with whom they come in contact with a life-giving, holy atmosphere that would revive the hearts of the humble and contrite!

It is a law of God that whoever believes the truth as it is in Jesus will make it known. The ideas and convictions of the individual mind will seek for expression. Whoever cherishes unbelief and criticism, whoever feels capable of judging the work of the Holy Spirit, will diffuse the spirit by which he is animated. It is the nature of unbelief and infidelity and resistance of the grace of God to make themselves felt and heard. The mind actuated by these principles is always striving to make a place for itself and obtain adherents. All who walk by the side of an apostate will be imbued by his spirit to share with others their thoughts and the result of their own inquiries, and the feelings which prompted their action; for it is not an easy matter to repress the principles upon which we act.

Some who are supposed to be heart and soul devoted to God are acting contrary to Him and to His work. Others have placed confidence in them, but deception covers them as with a garment. Their minds are controlled by a restless, irrepressible energy, an eagerness to disclose their sentiments. Thus seeds are sown everywhere. By a partially expressed sentiment they cast doubt and unbelief of the truth. There are those who are not in harmony with the testimonies because men in high positions of trust have expressed themselves as not in harmony with them; for the testimonies do not coincide with their opinions, but rebuke every vestige of selfishness.

EVILS OF UNSANCTIFIED CONSOLIDATION*

Everything that has been planned in regard to consolidation shows that men are seeking to grasp the scepter of power and hold control over human minds. But God does not work with them in their devising, and the voice they now have in the cause of God is not the voice of God. They have proved themselves utterly unworthy of a place as wise managers; for their strength is used to turn men away from their rights, to benefit themselves. There have been acts of apparent liberality, but God knows the motive which governed them, and He will not accept their offerings until they repent and become conscientious doers of His word.

DIVINE UNITY NECESSARY

There is great necessity for unity in the work and cause of God; but for a long time influences have been

*See Appendix.

at work seeking to create disaffection, and the men who feel that they have the power in their hands care little. They say within themselves: When this consolidation is perfected, we will show them who is master. We will then bring things into line. But they will never have that work to do.

As individuals and as members of the church of God, we need to realize the special work which has been committed to us. Paul writes to Timothy, "Take heed unto thyself, and unto the doctrine; continue in them: for in doing this thou shalt both save thyself, and them that hear thee." We have a very important work before us. "Unto me, who am less than the least of all saints," writes Paul, "is this grace given, that I should preach among the Gentiles the unsearchable riches of Christ; and to make all men see what is the fellowship of the mystery, which from the beginning of the world hath been hid in God, who created all things by Jesus Christ: to the intent that now unto the principalities and powers in heavenly places might be known by the church the manifold wisdom of God, according to the eternal purpose which He purposed in Christ Jesus our Lord."

"So thou, O son of man, I have set thee a watchman unto the house of Israel; therefore thou shalt hear the word at My mouth, and warn them from Me. When I say unto the wicked, O wicked man, thou shalt surely die; if thou dost not speak to warn the wicked from his way, that wicked man shall die in his iniquity; but his blood will I require at thine hand. Nevertheless, if thou warn the wicked of his way to turn from it; if he do not turn from his way, he shall die in his iniquity; but thou hast delivered thy soul." "When I shall say to the righteous, that he shall surely live; if he trust to his own righteousness, and commit iniquity, all his righteousnesses shall not be remembered; but for his iniquity that he hath committed, he shall die for it. Again, when I say unto the wicked, Thou shalt surely die; if he turn from his sin, and do that which is lawful and right; if the wicked restore the pledge, give again that he had robbed, walk in the statutes of life, without committing iniquity; he shall surely live, he shall not die. None of his sins that he hath committed shall be mentioned unto him: he hath done that which is lawful and right; he shall surely live. Yet the children of thy people say, The way of the Lord is not equal: but as for them, their way is not equal. When the righteous turneth from his righteousness, and committeth iniquity, he shall even die thereby. But if the wicked turn from his wickedness, and do that which is lawful and right, he shall live thereby. Yet ye say, The way of the Lord is not equal. O ye house of Israel, I will judge you every one after his ways."

THE PREEMINENCE OF THE WORK OF SAVING SOULS

The saving of human souls is an interest infinitely above any other line of work in our world. Whoever is brought under the influences of the truth, and through faith is made partaker of Christ's love, is by that very fact appointed of God to save others. He has a mission in the world. He is to be a colaborer with Christ, making known the truth as it is in Jesus; and when men in any line of God's work seek to bring the minds and talents of the Lord's human agents under their control, they have assumed a jurisdiction over their fellowmen that they cannot maintain without injustice and iniquity. The Lord has placed no man as judge, either of the pen or the voice of God's workmen.

There are men whose character and life testify to the fact that they are false prophets and deceivers. These we are not to hear or tolerate. But those whom God is using are under His control, and He has not appointed men with human, shortsighted judgment to criticize and condemn, to pass judgment and reject their work because every idea does not coincide with that which they suppose to be truth.

THE FALLIBILITY OF HUMAN JUDGMENT

Men can become just as were the Pharisees—wide-awake to condemn the greatest teacher that the world ever knew. Christ gave unmistakable evidence that He was sent of God, yet the Jewish rulers took upon themselves the work the enemy prompted them to do, and charged Him who made the Sabbath, who was the Lord of the Sabbath, with being a Sabbath breaker. Oh, the foolishness of men! the weakness of men!

There are those who are today doing the very same things. In their counsels they venture to pronounce judgment upon the work of God; for they have become trained in doing that which the Lord has never required them to do. They would better humble their own hearts before God, and keep their hands off the ark of God, lest the wrath of God shall break forth upon them; for if God has ever spoken by me, I testify that they have undertaken a work in criticizing and pronouncing unsound judgment which I know is not right. They are but finite men and, being befogged themselves, suppose that other men are in error.

But these men who presume to judge others should take a little broader view and say, Suppose the statements of others do not agree with our ideas; shall we for this pronounce them heresy? Shall we, uninspired men, take the responsibility of placing our stakes, and saying, This shall not appear in print?

If they still persist in clinging to their own opinions, they will find that God will not sustain their action. Do they take the position that all they advance is infallible? that there is not a shadow of an error or mistake in their productions? Cannot other men who give just as much evidence that they are led and taught of God catch at an expression in their work which they do not entertain as their views in every particular, and command them to cut it out?

Has not our past experience in these things been sufficient? Will we ever learn the lessons which God designs we shall learn? Will we ever realize that the consciences of men are not given into our command? If you have appointed committees to do the work which has been going on for years in Battle Creek, dismiss them; and remember that God, the infinite God, has not placed men in any such positions as they occupied at Minneapolis, and have occupied since then.

NOT TO BE CONSCIENCE FOR OUR FELLOWMEN

I feel deeply over this matter of men being conscience for their fellowmen. Stand out of the way, and let God work His own instrumentalities. Some have done work for which God will call them to account. He will ask of them, Who hath required this at your hands?

I have not liberty to place my writing in the hands of men who feel that their work is to act the part of detectives over their brethren. My brethren in positions of trust, will you not discern your own deficiencies and put on the whole armor of righteousness yourselves? Will you not be just as watchful and critical over your own spirits and temperaments and words as you are over those of others, lest God should be dishonored, and His truth misrepresented? Your discernment would be greatly improved if you would do this. The truth, the living word, would be as a fire shut up in your bones, which would shine forth in clear, unmistakable distinctness, representing Christ to the world. "Let your light so shine before men, that they may see your good works, and glorify your Father which is in heaven."

Could none of those who have made themselves detectives see the tendency of the position they have taken in endeavoring to become a controlling power? Where was their clear spiritual eyesight? Why could they discern a mote in the eye of a brother, while a beam was in their own eye? Oh, if ever a temple upon earth needed purifying, the institutions in Battle Creek need it now! Will you not seek God most humbly, that you may give the Laodicean message with clear, distinct utterance? Where are God's watchmen who will see the peril and give the warning? Be assured that there are messages to come from human lips under the inspiration of the Holy Spirit. "Cry aloud, spare not, . . . show My people their transgression, and the house of Jacob their sins. Yet they seek Me daily, . . . as a nation that did righteousness, and forsook not the ordinance of their God."

We are soldiers of Christ. He is the Captain of our salvation, and we are under His orders and rules. We are to wear His armor; we are to be marshaled only under His banner. We are to subdue not our brother soldiers but our enemies, that we may build up Christ's kingdom. We are laborers together with God. We are to keep on the whole armor of God, and work as in view of the universe of heaven. Let every man do his duty, as given him of God.

For further study: *Testimonies,* vol. 2, p. 503; vol. 4, pp. 84-87, 413; vol. 9, pp. 19-29, 281-284.

The Need of Divine Guidance

Christiania, Norway, October 1, 1885.

Dear Brother——:

I was more sorry than I can express to learn that under your instruction Brethren——and——sought to restrict the work at the——camp meeting. You could not have advised them to do a worse thing, and you should not have put a work into their hands that they were not fitted to do in a wise manner. Be careful how you repress advancing work in any locality. There is little enough being done in any place, and it certainly is not proper to seek to curtail operations in missionary lines.

After looking matters over carefully and prayerfully, I wrote as I did in my notes of travel. I wanted to leave the matter in such a shape as not to discourage the laborers in——in their effort to do something, although I desired to give them caution so that they would not make any extreme moves in their plans. The workers were doing well, and ought to have been encouraged and advised to go on with their work. There are men in——who should have helped them by making needed donations to invest in the cause. They will have to give to the work before they will grow in grace and the knowledge of the truth.

You and your workers should have looked at this

Special Testimonies to Ministers and Workers (Series A, No. 6, 1896), pages 56-60.

matter from different points of view than you did. You should have investigated the work thoroughly, and asked yourselves if five thousand dollars was too large a debt to incur in the important work in which these workers were engaged. Your influence should have been exerted in such a way as to cause the people to see the importance of the work, and to realize that it was their duty to rise to the emergency. You should have done as I wrote of doing, in my notes of travel. But if our brethren feel at liberty to stop the work when they cannot see where money is coming from to sustain it, then the work will not only be contracted in —— and ——, but in every other state in the Union. If our workers are going forward in any place, do not put up the bars, and say, Thus far shalt thou go, and no farther. I feel sad that you have closed up the school at ——. I see that the brethren sent to look after this enterprise have not taken measures to advance the work by soliciting donations from men who could give. There are rich men in the conference, who have made complaints about the debt that has been incurred, who ought to have sustained these workers. While reproach and discouragement have been cast upon the workers, the impression has been left upon those who have means that they have a perfect right to question every enterprise that calls for money.

WHEN PERSONAL OVERSIGHT OF DETAILS IS INCONSISTENT

God does not require you to take such a course that the workers in —— or anywhere else shall not feel at liberty to make advance movements unless they can consult you, and ask what your judgment of the matter is, before they advance. I cannot sanction the idea that you must have a personal oversight of all the details of the work. If I did, the result would be that no worker would dare to exercise his own judgment in anything. The workers would have to rely upon one man's brain and one man's judgment, and the result would be that men would be left in inefficiency because of their inactivity. There are altogether too many of this class now, and they amount to next to nothing. I write this because I feel deeply on this point. We are not doing one half that we ought to do.

It is true that the —— school must be sustained, but this need not hinder us from sustaining other schools. We should have primary schools in different localities to prepare the youth for our higher schools. It may seem to you that it is wise to close the school in ——, but I fail to see the wisdom of it. To close up this school will seem to reflect discredit upon all that the people have done, and will discourage them from making further advancement. I cannot see that you have gained anything in making the move that you have, nor can I feel that it is in accordance with God's order. It will work nothing but injury, not only to those that have complained about the debt, but also to the workers. Men who have property and could have helped this enterprise will breathe more freely. These moneyed men will be encouraged, not to do more for the cause than they have done, but to do less. They will feel at liberty to complain concerning anything that calls for an outlay of means.

THE WORK NOT CIRCUMSCRIBED BY THE COUNSEL OF GOD

Oh, that the Lord might guide you! You should never in a single instance allow hearsay to move you to action, and yet you have sometimes done this. Never take action to narrow and circumscribe the work unless you know that you are moved to do so by the Spirit of the Lord. Our people are doing work for foreign missions, but there are home missions that need their help just as much as these foreign missions. We should make efforts to show our people the wants of the cause of God, and to open before them the need of using means that God has entrusted to them to advance the work of the Master both at home and abroad. Unless those who can help in ——— are aroused to a sense of their duty, they will not recognize the work of God when the loud cry of the third angel shall be heard. When light goes forth to lighten the earth, instead of coming up to the help of the Lord, they will want to bind about His work to meet their narrow ideas. Let me tell you that the Lord will work in this last work in a manner very much out of the common order of things, and in a way that will be contrary to any human planning. There will be those among us who will always want to control the work of God, to dictate even what movements shall be made when the work goes forward under the direction of the angel who joins the third angel in the message to be given to the world. God will use ways and means by which it will be seen that He is taking the reins in His own hands. The workers will be surprised by the simple means that He will use to bring about and perfect His work of righteousness. Those who are accounted good workers will need to draw nigh to God, they will need the divine touch. They will need to drink more deeply and continuously at the fountain of living water, in order that they may discern God's work at every point. Workers may make mistakes, but you should give them a chance to correct their errors, give them an opportunity to learn caution, by leaving the work in their hands.

Use of Individual Judgment

Orebro, Sweden, October 28, 1885.

Dear Brethren —— and ——:

My prayer is that the Lord may be with you in great power during the coming conference. Some may be absent that you might wish were present; but Jesus is your helper. I sincerely hope and pray that those who bear responsibilities in Michigan, New England, Ohio, Indiana, and other states will take broader views of the work than they have done. I hope Michigan will take a step in advance. I feel to regret the fact that there is such a dearth of breadth of mind and of far-seeing ability. Workers should be educated and trained for the fields of labor. We need missionaries everywhere. We need men and women who will give themselves without reserve to the work of God, bringing many sons and daughters to God.

INDIVIDUAL JUDGMENT TO BE EXERCISED

I have been shown that there is one practice which those in responsible places should avoid; for it is detrimental to the work of God. Men in position should not lord it over God's heritage, and command everything around them. Too many have marked out a prescribed line which they wish others to follow in the work. Workers have tried to do this with blind faith, without exercising their own judgment upon the matter which they had in hand. If those who were placed as directors were not present, they have followed their implicit directions just the same. But in the name of Christ, I would entreat you to stop this work. Give men a chance to exercise their individual judgment. Men

---

Special Testimonies to Ministers and Workers (Series A, No. 6, 1896), pages 61-65.

who follow the leading of another, and are willing that another should think for them, are unfit to be entrusted with responsibility. Our leading men are remiss in this matter. God has not given to special ones all the brain power there is in the world.

Men in responsible positions should credit others with some sense, with some ability of judgment and foresight, and look upon them as capable of doing the work committed to their hands. Our leading brethren have made a great mistake in marking out all the directions that the workers should follow, and this has resulted in deficiency, in a lack of a caretaking spirit in the worker, because they have relied upon others to do all their planning, and have themselves taken no responsibility. Should the men who have taken this responsibility upon themselves step out of our ranks, or die, what a state of things would be found in our institutions!

Leading men should place responsibilities upon others, and allow them to plan and devise and execute, so that they may obtain an experience. Give them a word of counsel when necessary, but do not take away the work because you think the brethren are making mistakes. May God pity the cause when one man's mind and one man's plan is followed without question. God would not be honored should such a state of things exist. All our workers must have room to exercise their own judgment and discretion. God has given men talents which He means that they should use. He has given them minds, and He means that they should become thinkers, and do their own thinking and planning, rather than depend upon others to think for them.

I think I have laid out this matter many times before you, but I see no change in your actions. We want every responsible man to drop responsibilities upon others. Set others at work that will require them to plan, and to use judgment. Do not educate them to rely upon your judgment. Young men must be trained up to be thinkers. My brethren, do not for a moment think that your way is perfection, and that those who are connected with you must be your shadows, must echo your words, repeat your ideas, and execute your plans.

EFFECTS OF CONSTANTLY FOLLOWING OTHERS

There are men who today might be men of breadth of thought, might be wise men, men to be depended upon, who are not such, because they have been educated to follow another man's plan. They have allowed others to tell them precisely what to do, and they have become dwarfed in intellect. Their minds are narrow, and they cannot comprehend the needs of the work. They are simply machines to be moved by another man's thought. Now do not think that these men who do follow out your ideas are the only ones that can be trusted. You have sometimes thought that because they do your will to the letter, they were the only ones in whom you could place dependence. If anyone exercised his own judgment, and differed with you, you have disconnected from him as one that could not be trusted. Take your hands off the work, and do not hold it fast in your grasp. You are not the only man whom God will use. Give the Lord room to use the talents He has entrusted to men, in order that the cause may grow. Give the Lord a chance to use men's minds. We are losing much by our narrow ideas and plans. Do not stand in the way of the advancement of the work, but let the Lord work by whom He will. Educate, encourage young men to think and act, to devise and plan, in order that we may have a multitude of counselors.

How my heart aches to see presidents of conferences taking the burden of selecting those whom they think they can mold to work with them in the field. They take those who will not differ with them, but will act like mere machines. No president has any right to do this. Leave others to plan; and if they fail in some things, do not take it as an evidence that they are unfitted to be thinkers. Our most responsible men had to learn by a long discipline how to use their judgment. In many things they have shown that their work ought to have been better. The fact that men make mistakes is no reason why we should think them unfit to be caretakers. Those who think that their ways are perfect, even now make many grave blunders, but others are none the wiser for it. They present their success, but their mistakes do not appear. Then be kind and considerate to every man who conscientiously enters the field as a worker for the Master. Our most responsible men have made some unwise plans, and have carried them out because they thought their plans were perfect. They have needed the mingling of other elements of mind and character. They should have associated with other men who could view matters from an entirely different point of view. Thus they would have helped them in their plans. . . . What folly it is to trust a great mission in the hands of one man, so that he shall mold and fashion it in accordance with his mind, and after his own diseased imagination! Men who have been narrow, who have served tables, who are not farseeing, are disqualified for putting their mold upon the work. Those who desire to control the work think that none can do it perfectly but themselves, and the cause bears the marks of their defects.

For further study: *Testimonies,* vol. 9, pp. 187, 284; *Gospel Workers,* pages 303, 304, 484, 485, 488.

Means and Methods 12

A Faithful Tithe

Cooranbong, Australia, September 10, 1896.

Many presidents of state conferences do not attend to that which is their work—to see that the elders and deacons of the churches do their work in the churches, by seeing that a faithful tithe is brought into the treasury. Malachi has specified that the condition of prosperity depends upon bringing to God's treasury that which is His own. This principle needs to be often brought before the men who are lax in their duty to God, and who are neglectful and careless in bringing in their tithes, gifts, and offerings to God. "Will a man rob God?" "Wherein have we robbed Thee?" is the question asked by the unfaithful stewards. The answer comes plain and positive: "In tithes and offerings. Ye are cursed with a curse: for ye have robbed Me, even this whole nation. Bring ye all the tithes into the storehouse, that there may be meat in Mine house, and prove Me now herewith, saith the Lord of hosts, if I will not open you the windows of heaven, and pour you out a blessing, that there shall not be room enough to receive it." Please read this whole chapter, and see if words could be spoken that would be more plain and positive than these. They are so positive that no one who desires to understand his whole duty to God needs to make any mistake in the matter. If men offer any excuse as to why they do not perform this duty, it is because they are selfish, and have not the love and fear of God in their hearts.

The articles in this section are from *Special Testimonies to Ministers and Workers* (Series A, No. 7, 1897). This article, pages 20-23.

NO EXCUSE FOR NEGLECT IN PAYMENT OF TITHES

The Lord has always required this response to His arrangements in carrying forward His work in our world. He has never changed His own devised plan. He lays claim to all as His own, and of that entrusted to man, He claims His portion. "For I am the Lord, I change not; therefore ye sons of Jacob are not consumed. Even from the days of your fathers ye are gone away from Mine ordinances, and have not kept them. Return unto Me, and I will return unto you, saith the Lord of hosts."

Those who plead that they cannot understand this plain and decisive statement—which, if they are obedient, means so much to them in blessings which will be received, when even the windows of heaven will be opened and blessings poured out to overflowing—are not honest before God. Their excuse that they did not know the will of God will be of no avail for them in the great day of judgment.

ALL TO DO THEIR DUTY

Let the neglected tithes be now brought in. Let the new year open upon you as men honest in their deal with God. Let those that have withheld their tithes send them in before the year 1896 shall close, that they may be right with God, and never, never again run any risk of being cursed of God. Presidents of our conferences, do your duty; speak not your words, but a plain "Thus saith the Lord." Elders of churches, do your duty. Labor from home to home, that the flock of God shall not be remiss in this great matter, which involves such a blessing or such a curse.

Let all who fear God come up to the help of the Lord, and show themselves faithful stewards. The truth must go to all parts of the world. I have been shown that many in our churches are robbing God in tithes and offerings. God will execute upon them just that which He has declared. To the obedient, He will give rich blessings; to the transgressor, a curse. Every man who bears the message of truth to our churches must do his duty by warning, educating, rebuking. Any neglect of duty which is a robbery toward God means a curse upon the delinquent.

The Lord will not hold guiltless those who are deficient in doing the work that He requires at their hands—in seeing that the church is kept wholesome and healthy spiritually, and doing all their duty in allowing no neglect which will bring the threatened curse upon His people. A curse is pronounced upon all who withhold their tithe from God. He says: "Will a man rob God? Yet ye have robbed Me. But ye say, Wherein have we robbed Thee? In tithes and offerings. Ye are cursed with a curse: for ye have robbed Me, even this whole nation. Bring ye all the tithes into the storehouse, that there may be meat in Mine house."

This is not a request of man; it is one of God's ordinances, whereby His work may be sustained and carried on in the world. God help us to repent. "Return unto Me," He says, "and I will return unto you." Men who have a desire to do their duty have it laid down in clear lines in this chapter. No one can excuse himself from paying his tithes and offerings to the Lord.

The Lord bestows His gifts abundantly upon us. He "so loved the world, that He gave His only-begotten Son, that whosoever believeth in Him should not perish, but have everlasting life." Every blessing we have comes through Jesus Christ. Then shall we not arouse, and do our duty toward God, upon whom we are dependent for life and health, for His blessing upon our crops and fields, our cattle, our herds, and our vineyards? We are assured if we give to the Lord's treasury, we shall receive of Him again; but if we withhold of our means, He will withhold His blessing from us, and send a curse upon the unfaithful.

God has said, "Prove Me now herewith, . . . if I will not open you the windows of heaven, and pour you out a blessing, that there shall not be room enough to receive it." What a wonderful presentation in promised blessings is He giving us! Who can venture to rob God in tithes and offerings with such a promise as this! "And I will rebuke the devourer for your sakes, and he shall not destroy the fruits of your ground; neither shall your vine cast her fruit before the time in the field, saith the Lord of hosts. And all nations shall call you blessed: for ye shall be a delightsome land, saith the Lord of hosts."

Another year has nearly passed into eternity, with its burden of record. Let us look over the past year, and if we have not done our full duty willingly, heartily unto the Lord, let us come up to the new year making a faithful record to our God.

For further study: *Testimonies,* vol. 3, pp. 381-413; vol. 4, pp. 462-476; vol. 5, pp. 148-157, 267-272, 281-285; vol. 6, pp. 135, 215.

Practical Instruction in Labor

Cooranbong, Australia, June 14, 1896.

Dear Brother and Sister ——:

Last Friday night I was conversing with you, telling you something with reference to your methods of labor. The heavenly Watcher stood beside us, and I wish I could write every word He uttered; but I fear that I cannot. You said: "I wish I knew in regard to my duty. In some way I do not feel satisfied with the result of my labor." The voice of the One beside us was then heard, saying: "Have faith in God; learn of Christ Jesus. When you handle the sacred truths of God's word, keep Christ uplifted. Your great need is to learn Christ's manner of teaching. When you are teaching the people, present only a few vital points, and keep your mind concentrated on these points. You bring unimportant ideas into your discourses. These are not always a 'savor of life unto life,' and have no real connection with your text. By wandering from straight lines, and bringing in that which calls the minds off the subject, you weaken all that you have previously said."

DISCONNECTED PRESENTATION OF TRUTH

God would not have you think that you are impressed by His Spirit when you fly from your subject, bringing in foreign matters which are designed as a reproof, and which should not be named in connection with the words of solemn and sacred truth. By doing this, you lose your bearings, and weaken the effect of that which is profitable for doctrine, for reproof, for correction, for instruction in righteousness. You have made of none effect many precious ideas, by mixing them with other thoughts which have come to your mind but

---

Special Testimonies to Ministers and Workers (Series A, No. 7, 1897), pages 42-52.

which had no bearing upon the subject. That which is far from the subject under consideration should find no place in your discourses.

There are in this world hearts that are crying aloud for the living God. But helpless human nature has been fed with distasteful food; discourses dissatisfying to hungry, starving souls have been given in the churches. In these discourses there is not that divine manifestation that touches the mind and creates a glow in the soul; the hearers cannot say, "Did not our heart burn within us, while he talked with us by the way, and while he opened to us the Scriptures?" An abundance of chaff is given to the people, but this will not awaken the transgressor or convict souls of sin. The souls who come to hear need a plain, straightforward presentation of truth. Those who have tasted of the word of God have dwelt long in an atmosphere where there is no God, and they long for the divine presence.

Gird up the loins of your mind, that you may present the truth of God acceptably. Preach the truth in its simplicity, but let your discourses be short. Dwell decidedly on a few important points. Realize every moment that you must have the presence of the Holy Spirit; for it can do a work that you cannot do of yourself. If you have any burden of a disagreeable character on your mind, get rid of it by personal labor or earnest prayer before you come before the people. Plead earnestly with God to remove that burden from your mind. Keep decidedly to a few points. Give the people pure wheat thoroughly winnowed from all chaff. Do not let your discourses embrace so much that weakness shall be seen in the place of solid argument. Present the truth as it is in Jesus, that those who hear may receive the very best impression.

EVILS OF LONG SERMONS

Speak short. Your discourses are generally double the length they should be. It is possible to handle a good thing in such a manner that it loses its flavor. When a discourse is too long, the last part of the preaching detracts from the force and interest of that which has preceded it. Do not wander, but come right to the point. Give the people the very manna from heaven, and the Spirit will bear witness with your spirit that it is not you that speaks, but the Holy Spirit speaking through you. The teacher of the word of God must first talk with God, and then he can stand before the people with the Holy Spirit working upon his mind. If he faithfully cooperates with Christ, the promise will be fulfilled, "Lo, I am with you alway."

Be careful never to lose a sense of the presence of the divine Watcher. Remember that you are speaking not only to an unenlightened assembly, but to One whom you should ever recognize. Speak as though the whole universe of heaven were before you, as well as the hungry, starving company of God's sheep and lambs, which must be fed.

PREACH THE WORD

Those who claim to preach the word should preach the word, ever remembering that they are laborers together with God. He is their efficiency, and if He is given opportunity He will work for them. If they are humble, if they do not rely upon their own supposed wisdom and ability, God will place arguments in their mind and speak through their lips. He will also impress the minds of the hearers, preparing their hearts to receive the seed which is sown.

My brother, a daily work must be done for you by the power of God, or else, instead of the Holy Spirit, the enemy of God and man will stand by your side. Under his influence, weakness will appear in your work. The most precious points of faith relative to the salvation of the soul will be marred and mutilated in your hands.

Unless you change your manner of labor, you will give a faulty education to those connected with you in the work. Let your heart struggle and break for the longing it has for God, the living God. Let nothing divert your mind from the work of God to unimportant matters. With all your God-given energies work earnestly and prayerfully, calling upon the church to cooperate with you. Put no trust in yourself, but rest in the assurance that God is the chief Worker. You are only His servant; and your work is to voice His words, "We are laborers together with God."

DENYING OF SELF

Take no glory whatever to yourself. Do not work with a divided mind, trying to serve self and God at the same time. Keep self out of sight. Let your words lead the weary and heavy-laden to carry their burdens to Jesus. Work as seeing Him who is at your right hand, ready to give you His efficiency and omnipotent power in any emergency.

The Lord is your Counselor, your Guide, the Captain of your salvation. He goes before your face, conquering and to conquer. Dedicate yourself, soul and body, to Him, banishing all self-indulgence. Deny self; take up your cross, and work earnestly for the Master. Do not needlessly expend your strength by giving long discourses. This uses up the vitality, so that insufficient strength is left to devote to the most important part of the work—house-to-house ministry.

THE WORK OF AN EVANGELIST

Teaching the Scriptures, praying in families—this is the work of an evangelist, and this work is to be mingled with your preaching. If it is omitted, preaching will be, to a great extent, a failure. You need to be jealous of yourself. You and your wife need to come close to the people by personal effort. Teach them that the love of God must come into the inner sanctuary of the homelife. If you so desire, you may have the indwelling power of the Holy Spirit to help in your work.

We are carrying the last message of mercy to a perishing world, and God calls upon us to bring freshness and power into our work. We can do this only by the aid of the Holy Spirit. Hereditary tendencies and wrong habits must be disciplined and oft crucified. Humble yourself under the hand of God; for your ways are not God's ways, and you both have much to learn in the school of Christ.

Last night these words of instruction were spoken to you: "Counsel with your brethren. Your plans need the careful consideration of other minds." Warnings have been given in regard to depending upon men and trusting in their wisdom. The tempter aims to lead men astray by persuading them to cease looking to Jesus for strength and efficiency, and to make flesh their arm. This has been done in many cases. Satan has laid his trap to catch men and win them to his side by trying to prevail upon them to depend upon their finite, erring fellowmen.

A SPECIAL DANGER OF EXTREMES

But when a reproof is given upon this point, the enemy takes the counsel given, and presents it in such a perverted light that those who desire to follow their own judgment feel at liberty to plan and devise important measures without counseling with their brethren. Thus another error strives for recognition. Men go to an extreme in one direction, and if corrected, go to an extreme in the opposite direction.

You will be in danger of making mistakes if you move out in your own supposed wisdom. You need counsel. You have not the efficiency for all classes of labor, and you should not commence work in important places if there is danger that you will lay a foundation which you cannot complete. Light must be expressly given by God, and duty must be clear and unmistakable before one or two men enter new and important fields. You need to counsel with your brethren; for there is danger that you will run too fast in devising plans and methods.

Words which never should have been uttered have been spoken to you with reference to your brethren. The misconceptions existing in other minds have been communicated to you, and your mind has been led in a train of speculative thought that is not safe or correct. Keep watch over your thoughts. Guard closely the impulses of your mind and heart. Words have been spoken that have led you to place more confidence in your own plans and methods than is right. Words slip from your lips, unbidden and unsanctioned by God. Take heed lest, when the time comes that you can prove yourself a friend and fill a friend's place by giving sound counsel, you are unprepared.

IMPORTANCE OF COUNSEL WITH BRETHREN

You must not walk independently of all counsel. It is your duty to counsel with your brethren. This may touch your pride, but the humility of a mind taught by the Holy Spirit will listen to counsel, and will banish all self-confidence. When counsel is given that conflicts with your personal wishes, you are not to think that your own wisdom is sufficient for you to give counsel to others, or that you can afford to neglect the counsel given.

Wherever you may labor, there is need that you blend your efforts with those of other efficient laborers. You are not a complete whole; you cannot successfully complete a series of meetings by yourself, but you can do your part with other laborers. This may be humiliating to you; but it should not be, for God has given a variety of gifts, and He desires that these gifts blend in perfect harmony.

You need to realize the danger of viewing matters from your own standpoint and with your own eyes or discernment. It would be well for you frankly to state your plans to your brethren, that you may know how they appear to them when seen from their standpoint; for circumstances may be so vividly impressed upon your mind, that it is impossible for you to give an all-sided judgment. Let your plans be closely investigated; and with earnest prayer commit your case to Him who knoweth all things. Counsel together. Let not the whisperings of your own mind or of other minds close the door of your heart against the counsel of the Lord's servants.

August 9, 1896. I have written this to you because it is a serious matter, involving serious consequences, which will affect future work in other localities. Brother ——— needs no flattering words from you; for he has a full estimation of his own abilities and makes them appear by demeriting others. He does not realize that he is seeking to be first. He is not prepared to take upon himself the responsibilities of a minister of the gospel; for he needs a humble and a contrite spirit. He needs to continue to give Bible readings, and when his brethren see that he is fitted to become a preacher of the gospel, this will be made manifest. You need caution.

THE CANVASSING WORK

I cannot see why the canvassing work is not as good and successful a work as can be done for the Lord. Canvassers can become acquainted with the people, they can pray with them, and can understand their true necessities. From the light which God has given me, there is much responsibility resting upon the canvassers. They should go to their work prepared to explain the Scriptures, and nothing should be said or done to bind their hands. If they put their trust in the Lord as they travel from place to place, the angels of God will be round about them, giving them words to speak which will bring light and hope and courage to many souls. Were it not for the work of the canvasser, many would never hear the truth.

The canvasser should carry with him books and pamphlets and tracts to give away to those who cannot buy books from him. In this way the truth can be introduced into many homes.

Of all the gifts which God has given to man, none is more noble or a greater blessing than the gift of speech, if it is sanctified by the Holy Spirit. It is with the tongue we convince and persuade; with it we offer prayer and praise to God; and with it we convey rich thoughts of the Redeemer's love. By this work, the canvasser can scatter the seeds of truth, causing the light from the word of God to shine into many minds.

DOES NOT BELITTLE THE GOSPEL MINISTER

I sincerely hope that no mind will receive the impression that it belittles a minister of the gospel to canvass. Hear the apostle Paul's testimony: "Ye know, from the first day that I came into Asia, after what manner I have been with you at all seasons, serving the Lord with humility of mind, and with many tears, and temptations, which befell me by the lying in wait of the Jews: and how I kept back nothing that was profitable unto you, but have showed you, and have taught you publicly, and from house to house, testifying both to the Jews, and also to the Greeks, repentance toward God, and faith toward our Lord Jesus Christ." The eloquent Paul, to whom God manifested Himself in a wonderful manner, went from house to house, with all humility of mind and with many tears and temptations.

A MOST PRECIOUS MINISTRY

I have been shown that the most precious ministry can be done by canvassing, and that by ministers. By doing this work, they will obtain a varied experience and will be doing the very work that the apostle Paul did. I copy an extract from an appeal made to our brethren in regard to canvassing for our periodicals and books: "The canvassing work is an important field for labor; and the intelligent, God-fearing, truth-loving canvasser occupies a position equal to that of the gospel minister. Then should the canvasser feel at liberty, any more than the ordained minister, to act from selfish motives? Should he be unfaithful to all the principles of missionary work, and sell only those books that are cheapest and easiest to handle, neglecting to place before the people the books which will give most light, because by so doing he can earn more money for himself? The canvassing work is a missionary work, and the field must be worked from a missionary standpoint. Selfish principles, love of dignity and position, should not be once named among us. The thought of seeking to become the greatest should never come into our minds."

For further study: *Gospel Workers,* pages 14, 16, 19, 29-39, 249-274.

Neither is it the object of preaching to amuse. Some ministers have adopted a style of preaching that has not the best influence. It has become a habit with them to weave anecdotes into their discourses. The impression thus made upon the hearers is not a savor of life unto life. Ministers should not bring amusing stories into their preaching. The people need pure provender, thoroughly winnowed from the chaff. "Preach the word," was the charge that Paul gave to Timothy, and this is our commission also. The minister who mixes story-telling with his discourses is using strange fire. God is offended, and the cause of truth is dishonored, when His representatives descend to the use of cheap, trifling words.—*Review and Herald,* Dec. 22, 1904.

Conference Officials 13

Counsel and Guidance

Cooranbong, Australia, March 13, 1896.

In the night season I was listening to one who spoke with authority. Words of counsel in regard to the responsibilities that are to be borne in the sacred work of God were spoken. The Teacher said, There should be no haphazard work. Much of this has been done. Men have assumed authority, but the people should not depend upon poor, finite, erring men. They should put their entire trust in the wisdom that finds its strength in the wisdom of God. The inconsistency of centering so many responsibilities in Battle Creek has been presented many times, but the counsels have not been acted upon. The reproofs and warnings from the Lord have been evaded and interpreted and made void by the devices of men. There has been counterworking against God, and the judgment of men has been received.

In Battle Creek, and in other places, building has been added to building, for the sake of making an imposing display. Men have supposed that this would give character to the work. Their own characters needed the transforming grace of Christ. This alone is sufficient to give character to the work. Nothing can be done without His grace.

The Lord suffers impediments to arise, that His wisdom and power may be humbly, earnestly, and perseveringly sought, and be distinctly manifest. Nothing will so quickly and decidedly separate the soul from God and bring defeat, as for man to lift up his soul unto

---

The articles in this section are from *Special Testimonies to Ministers and Workers* (Series A, No. 8, 1897). This article, pages 2-11.

vanity, and speak proudly and boastingly, and in a masterly manner to his fellowmen, who are the property of God. "Ye are not your own; . . . ye are bought with a price," even the precious blood of the Son of God. The Lord alone is to be exalted. Let every human agent keep in his place and not seek to get into the place where God should be. There has been altogether too much trusting in men.

In Battle Creek you have evidence that men who have had the most to say are not walking with God. There is abundant activity, but not many are working in partnership with Christ; and those who walk and work apart from Him have been the most active in planning and inaugurating their methods. If they had that wisdom that cometh from the Source of all wisdom, they would move considerately, and would study more earnestly the relation of cause to effect. They would discern that a few minds in Battle Creek are not to be the power to manage everything in connection with our work.

The state conferences must have men at their head who love and fear God—capable men, who will learn in the school of Christ to be laborers with Him, to wear His yoke and lift His burdens. They are to be partners with Christ in the sacred service of soulsaving. All the members of the church are to labor interestedly, zealously, not striving, as many have done, to see who shall be the greatest, and how to secure the highest wages, but striving to win souls for Christ, which means being a part of the firm, in partnership with Christ. Let all try to do their best.

The matter was laid before me, which I was trying to present before the brethren. There is altogether too much responsibility imparted to a few men in Battle

Creek, and these men need the transforming power of the Holy Spirit, else they will lead God's heritage in false paths. The conferences are watching every move made at the center of the work. The different conferences have been led to look to the leading men at Battle Creek, feeling that no important move can be made without their approval. This tendency has been growing stronger, until it is a serious hindrance to the advancement of the work. This arrangement should never have been. The Lord would have His people under His jurisdiction. They should look to God, inquiring of Him in faith, and follow on to know the working of His providence.

The arrangement that all moneys must go through Battle Creek and under the control of the few men in that place is a wrong way of managing. There are altogether too many weighty responsibilities given to a few men, and some do not make God their counselor. What do these men know of the necessities of the work in foreign countries? How can they know how to decide the questions which come to them asking for information? It would require three months for those in foreign countries to receive a response to their questions, even if there was no delay in writing.

In each country a man should be appointed to work in the general interests of the cause. He need not be a preacher, and he must not be a policy man. He should be unselfish, a man who loves, who honors, and fears his God. His whole time should be devoted to the work. He should plan unselfishly, and in the fear of God. Let him be general agent for that country, and let him be connected with a council composed of the very best men, that they may counsel together, and attend to the work within their borders. There should be businessmen appointed to do the same in the different states in America.

CARE IN SELECTION

The men who act as presidents of state conferences should be carefully selected. Then let these men bear the responsibilities of the conference in a most thorough, earnest, God-fearing manner. If they are not qualified to do the work thoroughly and successfully, do not keep them in that position.

A mass of matter is laid before the General Conference; every burden is carried to Battle Creek. This makes the presidents of the state conferences very irresponsible. Many are not growing in aptitude and in judgment. They make mismoves, when they should have advanced experience sufficient to enable them to make right moves, because they seek counsel of God. As presidents of their several conferences, they should realize that they must be faithful in positions of trust. These conferences are to be to them a school, in which they are to reveal managing ability. They are to learn, learn, and educate, educate. They are to do firm, Christlike work, binding it off, so that it shall not ravel out.

IMPARTIAL AND UNSELFISH

He who is selected as the president of the General Conference, should, in the fear of God, stand in his lot and place, without partiality, and with unselfish interests. He should be a faithful steward. He should be a priest and wise ruler over his own house. He should make manifest that he understands the work of governing his own family wisely, and in the fear of God. If this is neglected, he will carry his defects with him into his work. If any man evidences that the love and fear of

God is kept away from the center of his being lest the truth should control his life practice, while worldly things are made all and in all, he is not the man, even for local elder.

Advice is asked of those in Battle Creek regarding matters which could just as well be settled by men on the ground, if they would seek the Lord, and which ought to have been done within their own borders. The Lord declares He is nigh to all that call upon Him with a sincere heart. Said Christ, "Ask, and it shall be given you; seek, and ye shall find; knock, and it shall be opened unto you." This promise is made doubly and trebly sure. There is no failure with God. Today men who are presidents of conferences are less efficient and strong and able than they should be, because they place man where God should be, and they receive only that which man can give them.

SEEK COUNSEL OF GOD

Presidents of conferences, you will be wise if you will decide to come to God. Believe in Him. He will hear your prayers, and come to your assistance, in much less time than the public conveyances could take one, two, three, or four men from a long distance, at a great expense, to decide questions which the God of wisdom can decide far better for you. He has promised, "If any of you lack wisdom, let him ask of God, that giveth to all men liberally, and upbraideth not; and it shall be given him." If you will sincerely humble your hearts before Him, empty your souls of self-esteem, and put away the natural defects of your character, and overcome your love of supremacy, and come to God as little children, He will bestow on you His Holy Spirit. When two or three shall agree as touching anything, and shall ask the Lord, in the name of Jesus, it shall be done for them.

When it is deemed expedient to invest means in school buildings, in sanitariums, or in homes for the poor in any country, in order to establish the work there, the Lord would have those who are living in that locality walk humbly before Him, and show that they realize their personal dependence upon Him, and that they believe in His willingness to help them to plan, to devise, to arrange intelligently for His work. He is as willing to give wisdom to those who feel the value of divine grace, as to give wisdom to some other mind, who will then, at great expense, communicate the same to you. Where is your faith? Will men turn from the God of wisdom to seek wisdom from finite men, sending for men from a long distance to come and help them out of perplexity? How does the Lord look upon this?

Each one may entertain the idea that he believes in God. You are working in one part of His great moral vineyard, and He has told you that if any man lack wisdom, he is to ask of God, who giveth to all men liberally, and upbraideth not. This world is but a little atom in the vast domain over which God presides, and yet this little fallen world is more precious in His sight than the ninety and nine which went not astray from the fold. If we will make Him our trust, He will not leave us to become the sport of Satan's temptations. God would have every soul for whom Christ has died become a part of the vine, connected with the parent stock, drawing nourishment from it. Our dependence on God is absolute, and should keep us very humble; and because of our dependence on Him, our knowledge of Him should be greatly increased. God would have us put away every species of selfishness, and come to Him, not as the owner of ourselves, but as the Lord's purchased possession.

A SUCCESSFUL BUSINESSMAN

Daniel sought the Lord three times a day, in earnest prayer for wisdom and strength and courage to carry forward the enterprise of representing the only true God in wicked Babylon. You will often be perplexed to know what to do next; but do not get pen and paper and write your perplexities to Battle Creek. There may be disagreement upon some points, but your Counselor is nigh. Bow before Him, and tell Him of everything you need. Can the men in Battle Creek give you light? They cannot understand your necessity. Because they are not on the ground, they may say No to some things, when, had you asked of God, He would have answered, "Go forward, and I will be with you, and give you grace."

For many years an education has been given to the people which places God second, and man first. The people have been taught that everything must be brought before the council of a few men in Battle Creek. God has given you an opportunity to see the weakness of finite men. Are there not men in different states of America who walk right in the sight of God?

Are there not registered in the books of heaven the names of those who love and serve God? Cannot they plan? Have those in Battle Creek been given superior reason and wisdom that God will not give those in the churches and state conferences? "If any of you lack wisdom, let him ask of God, that giveth to all men liberally, and upbraideth not; and it shall be given him."

The churches would realize one hundredfold more of the workings of the Holy Spirit if ministers would educate all to bear in mind that they have a God nigh at hand, and not afar off, and that they can honor God by seeking Him for help and wisdom just where they are. They will then have ability which will strengthen the General Conference.

There is talent in every place, but it is not always recognized. This talent should be discerned and set to work. Under the operation of the Spirit of God, talent will grow by being used. But God is greatly dishonored when men are placed in the position where God should be. He alone can give unerring counsel.

Men have been in council in Battle Creek who cannot appreciate the situation of matters in the different localities, as those can who are right on the ground; and it is not wise for men to seek to men, and place such dependence in a few men at Battle Creek, some of whom have walked apart from God for years. To accept the judgment of these men, and to send for them from a long distance to sit in council, has done great dishonor to God. By this you show that you place men, who are unsanctified in heart, where God should be.

Supposing that some mistakes are made by those in different places. They may be of far less consequence than the errors made by those at the heart of the work. Cannot you go to the great Leader, who is mighty in counsel? and cannot He restore? Cannot He work in your behalf? Will He not do it if you go to Him as little children go to their parents? There is altogether too much lofty sufficiency in the human agent. God cannot work with such an element of pride. If this is not laid down, if self is not humbled, God cannot work. Those who send all their perplexities from the different parts of the world to Battle Creek show the wisdom of men, and not the wisdom of God.

For further study: *Testimonies,* vol. 4, pp. 309-312, 386, 387, 494; vol. 5, pp. 409-411.

Conference Presidents

August 2, 1896.

My attention has been called to the instruction the Lord has been pleased to give in *Gospel Workers.* I have arisen at three o'clock a.m., and have read the matter in the little book entitled *Conference Presidents,* page 232. The same things have been presented to me again and again. Will our brethren take heed to these things? Or will they turn aside from the light? The president of the General Conference should act upon the light given, not contrary to this light. If men close their eyes to the testimonies God has been pleased to give, and think it wisdom to walk in the light of the sparks of their own kindling, it will spoil the church. Such men are not qualified to become either ministers or presidents of conferences; they have not taken counsel from the Source of all wisdom.

He who is placed as a president of a conference must learn that the human heart is wayward, and that it needs to be strictly sentineled by watchfulness and prayer. As he seeks the Lord conscientiously and constantly, he is taught of God to grow into a representative man, and can be trusted as God trusted Abraham. He needs the whole armor of God; for he has to fight the good fight of faith, and having done all that the

---

Special Testimonies to Ministers and Workers (Series A, No. 8, 1897), pages 11-15.

Spirit of God has taught him to do, to stand. His enemies may be those of his own household, his wife and children, or they may be his own hereditary and cultivated tendencies, which continually seek for the mastery. Man is human and defective in character, and must battle for the victory. Everyone who begins aright must begin at his own heart. Let the fervent prayer go forth from unfeigned lips, "Create in me a clean heart, O God," and it will bring the response, "A new heart also will I give you."

Lessons need to be learned by all who shall step into places where they are to be proved and tested by God, to see whether they shall be registered day by day as faithful and true stewards of God's entrusted talents. Have they shown that they have the fear of God before them, whether they are dealing with superiors, inferiors, or equals? They need to cherish the truth as an abiding principle, that it may sanctify the soul. The creating, transforming power of God's Holy Spirit will make them copartners with Jesus Christ. Yoked up with Christ, they can be more than conquerors through Him.

The man who is fully sensible that he is in the service of Jesus Christ, will aspire for the friendship of God. He will lie low before God, that he may be nothing, and God everything. Such a man is a copartner with Christ, fitted to preside over a state conference. If he proves himself circumspect, he is prepared for any position, according to his experience and qualifications. Let the churches understand that such a man is to be trusted and sustained. They may go to him and talk with him. Such a man will never feel sufficient to carry the work, even of a state conference, without the constant grace which God will give. He will not choose to do the work and bear the responsibility alone. Through wise management, he will have the tact to recognize talent in others. He will use those who have this talent, and help them, while they help to share his burdens.

UNITE WITH BRETHREN

It is a selfish thing for men who feel that they have some service to do for the Master, to wish to be alone in their work, and to refuse to connect with those who would be a help to them, because they fear that they will not obtain all the credit for doing the good work which they flatter themselves they will do. This has greatly hindered the work of God. Let brother lay hold of brother. Link up a Peter and a John. Let each encourage his brother to stand by his side, doing zealous, interested service, as partners in the great work. Two or three can pray together, sing the praises of God together, and grow up into the full stature of workers together with God. Perfect harmony must be cherished. All must serve the Lord as little children, feeling that they are branches in the same parent stock.

Let the presidents of state conferences walk humbly with God, and they will not have occasion to write to the president of the General Conference to leave his work to settle little matters for them. Even many large matters may be carried to God, and God will give counsel in every state conference. The Lord can be approached by all. He is much more accessible than the president of the General Conference. Let the president of the General Conference educate the presidents of state conferences to take care of their portion of the moral vineyard where they are situated wisely, without laying their burdens upon him. Lead these men who have ability and talent to look to God, that they may be taught by Him. Teach them to go to the Fountainhead for instruction in righteousness. Search the Scriptures. "All Scripture is given by inspiration of God, and is profitable for doctrine, for reproof, for correction, for instruction in righteousness: that the man of God may be perfect, throughly furnished unto all good works." What, then, is your excuse for turning for counsel from One who is infinite in wisdom to finite men, who are as weak as yourselves? One has suffered for you, the Just for the unjust.

How many petty grievances man traces upon paper, and pours into the soul of his fellowmen! How unwise it is to perpetuate and communicate to others those things you had better have kept to yourself! Never trace a line of discouragement. If you do just as Jesus has told you to do, you will find help. "Come unto Me, all ye that labor and are heavy-laden, and I will give you rest. Take my yoke upon you, and learn of Me; for I am meek and lowly in heart: and ye shall find rest unto your souls." The Lord God has given abundant evidence of His willingness to carry our burdens. As you lift His burdens, He lifts you, and the burdens also. He invites all who labor and are heavy-laden, "Come unto Me." You are not told that you must go around the world to tell your troubles and unload your burdens to your fellowmen. "Lo, I am with you alway," Christ says, "even unto the end of the world."

A Warning Against Political Entanglements

December 27, 1896.

To the General Conference of 1897:

I have words to speak to our brethren who shall assemble in conference in 1897. The present financial controversy* has been presented to me as one of Satan's masterpieces for these last days. There is a power moving from beneath, which is after the working of the great enemy. I supposed our own people would step softly, and move very guardedly, and keep themselves aloof from all these new issues in regard to the circulating currency. This is not of the devising of God—the changing of the circulating currency. What will it effect? It will cause a state of things that will bring oppression to the poor, and create great distress. It is one of the devil's schemes, and I thought those who believed the truth would not be deceived in the least degree upon this matter. But within the year 1896 matters have been presented to me which have made me tremble for our people. I have been where I heard conversations from those in positions of trust in our institutions, and there was great warmth in controversy over the different positions taken. The light given me was, This is the policy Satan has arranged to bring distress.

Would we know how we may best please the Saviour? It is not engaging in political speeches, either in or out of the pulpit. It is in considering with fear and trembling every word we utter. Where the people assemble to worship God let not a word be spoken that shall divert the mind from the great central interest—Jesus Christ, and Him crucified. The third angel's message is to be our burden of warning. The side issues

---

Special Testimonies to Ministers and Workers (Series A, No. 8, 1897), pages 17-27. (Former title, "The General Conference.")

*See Appendix.

are not for us to meddle with. The burden of the work is, Preach the word. There are those who have had an experience in preaching and laboring for the salvation of souls for whom Christ has given His precious life. The work is the special enterprise to engross everyone who feeds the flock of God. It is a time now when voices will be heard: "Hear. This is the way, walk in this path." But the Lord Jesus says, "Follow thou Me." "He that followeth Me shall not walk in darkness." The saving of souls is to be our personal work, from which nothing is of sufficient moment to divert the mind. Christ came to our world to save souls, to diffuse light amid the moral darkness. A living voice is heard, "I am the way, the truth, and the life."

LET POLITICS ALONE

I was surprised as I saw men who claim to believe the truth for this time all excited in regard to matters—which relate to the Lord Jesus and eternal interests? No; but they seemed to be wonderfully excited in regard to the currency. Some ministers were distinguishing themselves by weaving these subjects into their discourses. They were excitably involving themselves, taking sides in regard to these questions that the Lord did not lay upon them the burden to engage in. These persons seemed to have a large share of self-sufficiency. But they themselves really did not know what they were advocating. They knew not whether they were defending principles that originated in the councils of heaven or in the councils of Satan.

The voice of one in authority spoke with great decision, Ye know not what manner of spirit ye are of. Read the directions given by the only-begotten Son of God when enshrouded in the cloudy pillar. When that voice is obeyed, ye will not give your voice or influence to any policy to enrich a few, to bring oppression and suffering to the poorer class of humanity. There is in this excitement just what separates those of the same faith. Is this bearing the divine credentials? Beware. See that your arm is not linked in the arm of a personal demon. He is in appearance as a man. He is walking about as a roaring lion, seeking whom he may devour, and he finds them among Seventh-day Adventists. He can terrify by his roaring; but, when it suits his purposes best, he has the sweet voice of an angel of light and speaks of heavenly things. Does he not know all about heavenly glory?

I inquired why those who could read their Bibles and see the perils of these last days were so ready to snatch up matters they had best let alone. How can they connect with men who are advancing principles that originated in the councils of demons? Why do they not see that this is no work the Lord has set them to do? The answer came, Because their hearts are lifted up unto vanity. They are beguiled. They do not know how weak they are. There are many who will be deluded, and who, by pen and voice, will cast their whole influence to create an evil condition of things (a condition that will exist just the same whatever they may do); but they should not be bound up with the evil workers. All who are longing for some engagement that will represent Jehu riding furiously will have opportunity enough to distinguish themselves. Their arm will be linked with his who was once an exalted angel, and who has not forgotten his manners in the heavenly courts. These manners he will assume; and in representing persons, he will lure many whose life is not hid with Christ in God.

WHY LOVE WAXES COLD

Because iniquity abounds, the love of many waxes cold. Why should their love wax cold? Because they have not humbled their hearts and fled to their refuge, Jesus Christ. They thought they knew so much that they became fools, and allowed themselves to become depraved. Thus many souls will be lost. Worldly plans and devisings and strange sentiments and principles will be put forth by the prince of the power of the air, which are directly opposed to the law of God. Here we should reserve all our influence to act in upholding the truth. The sentiments brought to the front by politicians will be voiced by some who claim to be Sabbath keepers. What angels attend these in the pulpit as they stand up to give the flock poison instead of pure wheat, thoroughly winnowed? Here is the working of satanic agencies to bring in confusion, to bewitch the minds of old and young. Those who have been walking humbly with God will not be engrossed in advocating either side of this question. They will place themselves under His guardianship, and reveal that they are learning lessons from the Great Teacher, who has said, "Come unto Me, all ye that labor and are heavy-laden, and I will give you rest."

All this excitement and unrest is placing the mind where it will not dwell on the truth. Do you suppose that the world, the flesh, and the devil would be able to link up those souls who are humble and lowly of heart, and blind their understanding, so that they cannot tell what sort of companions they are choosing? If the eyes of many could be opened in their heedless march, they would see a mighty procession of people of all classes, all kinds, all nations, passing in the same ranks, classing themselves as the companions of demons, rapidly moving on in a continually swelling procession to certain ruin.

What shall I say? The faith of many, including those who preach the word, must be something different from what it is now, else their future eternal destiny is settled. The word of God, studied carefully and obeyed, is the only thing that will make man pure and keep him pure. This alone can save him from meddling with all the iniquities that prevail. Christians are to bear the stamp of the King of kings. All in our world are taking sides. We are not to take part in this political money strife. It has come into our ranks.

There are those, even among Seventh-day Adventists, who are under the reproof of the word of God, because of the way they acquired their property and use it, acting as if they owned it and created it, without an eye to the glory of God, and without earnest prayer to direct them in acquiring or using it. They are grasping at a serpent, which will sting them as an adder.

THE SAFE WAY

Of God's people He says, "Her merchandise and her hire shall be holiness to the Lord: it shall not be treasured nor laid up." But many who profess to believe the truth do not want God in their thoughts, any more than did the antediluvians or Sodomites. One sensible thought of God, awakened by the Holy Spirit, would spoil all their schemes. Self, self, self, has been their god, their alpha and their omega.

Christians are safe only in acquiring money as God directs, and using it in channels which He can bless.

God permits us to use His goods with an eye single to His glory to bless ourselves that we may bless others. Those who have adopted the world's maxim, and discarded God's specifications, who grasp all they can obtain of wages or goods, are poor, poor indeed, because the frown of God is upon them. They walk in paths of their own choosing, and do dishonor to God, to truth, to His goodness, to His mercy, His character.

Now, in probationary time, we are all on test and trial. Satan is working with his deceiving enchantments and bribes, and some will think that by their schemes they have made a wonderful speculation. But lo, as they thought they were rising securely and were carrying themselves loftily in selfishness, they learned that God can scatter faster than they can gather.

"I have seen the wicked in great power, and spreading himself like a green bay tree. Yet he passed away, and, lo, he was not: yea, I sought him, but he could not be found." He who sees the end from the beginning, and who brings order out of confusion, is doing all things well. We will view another side of the picture: "Mark the perfect man, and behold the upright: for the end of that man is peace." The word of God is offering all the preparation for eternal life. Our faith must be a faith that works by love and purifies the soul, not defies faith and practice. Do we believe the word of God? Are all who profess the truth faithful and true, steadfast to principle? Are we doing missionary work in the spirit of Christ?

There are men who stand in the pulpits as shepherds, professing to feed the flock, while the sheep are starving for the bread of life. There are long-drawn-out discourses, largely made up of the relation of anecdotes; but the hearts of the hearers are not touched. The feelings of some may be moved, they may shed a few tears, but their hearts are not broken. The Lord Jesus has been present when they have been presenting that which was called sermons, but their words were destitute of the dew and rain of heaven. They evidenced that the anointed ones described by Zechariah (see chapter 4) had not ministered to them that they might minister to others. When the anointed ones empty themselves through the golden pipes, the golden oil flows out of themselves into the golden bowls, to flow forth into the lamps, the churches. This is the work of every true, devoted servant of the living God. The Lord God of heaven cannot approve much that is brought into the pulpit by those who are professedly speaking the word of the Lord. They do not inculcate ideas that will be a blessing to those who hear. There is cheap, very cheap fodder placed before the people.

STRANGE FIRE

When the speaker shall, in a haphazard way, strike in anywhere, as the fancy takes him, when he talks politics to the people, he is mingling the common fire with the sacred. He dishonors God. He has not real evidence from God that he is speaking the truth. He does his hearers a grievous wrong. He may plant seeds which may strike their fibrous roots deep, and they spring up and bear poisonous fruit. How dare men do this? How dare they advance ideas when they do not know certainly whence they came, or that they are the truth?

THE KIND OF SERMONS NEEDED

Will our brethren bear in mind that we are living amid the perils of the last days? Read Revelation in connection with Daniel. Teach these things. Let discourses be short, spiritual, elevated. Let the preacher be full of the word of the Lord. Let every man who enters the pulpit know that he has angels from heaven in his audience. And when these angels empty from themselves the golden oil of truth into the heart of him who is teaching the word, then the application of the truth will be a solemn, serious matter. The angel messengers will expel sin from the heart, unless the door of the heart is padlocked and Christ is refused admission. Christ will withdraw Himself from those who persist in refusing the heavenly blessings that are so freely offered them.

The Holy Spirit is doing its work on the hearts. But if the ministers have not first received their message from heaven, if they have not drawn their own supplies from the refreshing, life-giving stream, how can they let that flow forth which they have not received? What a thought, that hungry, thirsty souls are sent away empty! A man may lavish all the treasures of his learning, he may exhaust the moral energies of his nature, and yet accomplish nothing, because he himself has not received the golden oil from the heavenly messengers; therefore it cannot flow forth from him, imparting spiritual life to the needy. The tidings of joy and hope must come from heaven. Learn, oh, learn of Jesus what it means to abide in Christ!

If the Christian minister receives the golden oil, he has life; and where there is life, there is no stagnation, no dwarfed experience. There is constant growth to the full stature of Christ Jesus. If we have a deep, growing experience in heavenly things, we walk with the Lord, as did Enoch. Instead of consenting to the propositions of Satan, there is most earnest prayer for the heavenly anointing, that we may distinguish the right, the heaven-born, from the common.

If we are fighting in the strength of the Mighty One, we are on the side that will win at last. In the end we shall conquer. The greatest work, the most perilous scenes are before us. The deadly conflict we must meet. Are we prepared for it? God is still speaking to the children of men. He is speaking in many different ways. Will they hear His voice? Will we place our hands confidingly in His and say, "Lead me, guide me"?

There is cheap religion in abundance, but there is no such thing as cheap Christianity. Self may figure largely in a false religion, but it cannot appear in Christian experience. You are workers together with God. "Without Me," said Christ, "ye can do nothing." We cannot be shepherds of the flock unless we are divested of our own peculiar habits, manners, and customs, and come into Christ's likeness. When we eat His flesh and drink His blood, then the element of eternal life will be found in the ministry. There will not be a fund of stale, oft-repeated ideas. There will be a new perception of truth.

Some who stand in the pulpit make the heavenly messengers in the audience ashamed of them. The precious gospel, which it has cost so much to bring to the world, is abused. There is common, cheap talk; grotesque attitudes and workings of the features. There is, with some, rapid talking, with others a thick, indistinct utterance. Everyone who ministers before the people should feel it a solemn duty to take himself in hand. He should first give himself to the Lord in complete self-renunciation, determined that he will have none of self, but all of Jesus.

The word is the preacher's light, and as the golden

oil flows from the heavenly olive tree into the bowl, it makes the lamp of life flash with a clearness and power that all will discern. Those who have the privilege of sitting under such a ministry, if their hearts are susceptible to the Holy Spirit's influence, will feel an inner life. The fire of God's love will be kindled within them. The Bible, the word of God, is the bread of life. He who feeds the flock of God must himself first eat of the bread which came down from heaven. He will see the truth on every side. He will not venture to come before the people until he has first communed with God. Then he is led to work as Christ worked. He respects the varied minds that compose his audience. He has a word that touches the case of all, not worldly, confusing ideas. He has no right to introduce the worldly perplexities. The bread of life will satisfy every soul hunger.

For further study: *Gospel Workers,* pages 374, 391-396, 489, 490; *Testimonies,* vol. 3, pp. 492-509; vol. 9, pp. 216-218.

Conference Officers

Cooranbong, Australia, August, 1896.

Conference Presidents and Counselors:

God gave to Moses special direction for the management of his work. He directed Moses to associate men with him as counselors, that his burdens might be lightened. Through Jethro the message was given: "Hearken now unto my voice, I will give thee counsel, and God shall be with thee: Be thou for the people to Godward, that thou mayest bring the causes unto

Special Testimonies to Ministers and Workers (Series A, No. 8, 1897), pages 27-32.

God: and thou shalt teach them ordinances and laws, and shalt show them the way wherein they must walk, and the work that they must do. Moreover thou shalt provide out of all the people able men, such as fear God, men of truth, hating covetousness; and place such over them, to be rulers of thousands, and rulers of hundreds, rulers of fifties, and rulers of tens: and let them judge the people at all seasons: and it shall be, that every great matter they shall bring unto thee, but every small matter they shall judge: so shall it be easier for thyself, and they shall bear the burden with thee. If thou shalt do this thing, and God command thee so, then thou shalt be able to endure, and all this people shall also go to their place in peace."

This counsel is for us. It should be heeded by our responsible men. The president of our General Conference has been left to gather to himself burdens which God has not laid upon him, and the things that he has tried to do could not be done wisely and well. . . .

Moses said, "When they have a matter, they come unto me; and I judge between one and another, and I do make them know the statutes of God, and His laws." This work is still to be done, and if the men who bear responsibilities will not do it, then it must be committed to others. The Lord's work must be carried forward without guile, hypocrisy, or covetousness.

CHARACTER OF COUNSELORS

In His instruction to Moses the Lord very plainly set forth the character of those who were to fill important positions as counselors. They are to be "able men, such as fear God, men of truth, hating covetousness." The Lord's counsel has been strangely neglected. There are men in places of holy trust who, when reproved, have cared nought for it. Some who for years have stood as counselors have boldly stated that they would not receive the testimonies given.* In triumph they have declared that many of our most responsible men have lost faith in the message coming from Sister White. Thus the rejecters of light have been strengthened in their unbelief, feeling that they had quite a strong confederacy. Men who have had the light have walked contrary to the light. These words are appropriate: "Truth is fallen in the street, and equity cannot enter." The malaria of unbelief has been diffusing its deathly atmosphere throughout the ranks, nigh and afar off. All this has been stated plainly, yet for years matters have been left unchanged. Can the Lord's favor be expected under such circumstances?. . .

STUDY GOD'S METHODS

As a people we should study God's plans for conducting His work. Wherever He has given directions in regard to any point, we should carefully consider how to regard His expressed will. This work should have special attention. It is not wise to choose one man as president of the General Conference. The work of the General Conference has extended, and some things have been made unnecessarily complicated. A want of discernment has been shown. There should be a division of the field, or some other plan should be devised to change the present order of things. . . .

The president of the General Conference* should have the privilege of deciding who shall stand by his side as counselors. Those who will keep the way of the Lord, who will preserve clear, sharp discernment by cultivating home religion, are safe counselors. Of such a one

*See Appendix.

the Searcher of hearts saith, "I know him, that he will command his children and his household after him, and they shall keep the way of the Lord, to do justice and judgment." Counselors of the character that God chose for Moses are needed by the president of the General Conference. It was his privilege at least to express his preference as to the men who should be his counselors. It was his privilege to discern between him that serveth God and him that serveth Him not. But a strange blindness was upon him. There has been a leavening influence upon human minds, and it has been most painful. For years God has been dishonored. . . .

I have the word of the Lord for presidents of conferences. They should shoulder the responsibilities involved in the trusts reposed in them. In your work, do not try to meet a human standard, but the standard of God's work. If you will not do this, if you will not seek the Lord most earnestly, if you will not be burden bearers, but choose to lay your whole weight of responsibilities upon the president of the General Conference, then, week by week, month by month, you are disqualifying yourselves for the work. You should leave it, and engage in common business transactions, which do not so decidedly involve eternal responsibilities.

Presidents of conferences, I appeal to you in the name of the Lord Jesus: "Seek ye the Lord while He may be found, call ye upon Him while He is near: let the wicked forsake his way, and the unrighteous man his thoughts: and let him return unto the Lord, and He will have mercy upon him; and to our God, for He will abundantly pardon." You are to be self-denying missionaries, men of thought, men who will pray for divine enlightenment, and who will be faithful and true to responsibilities. Sit at the feet of Jesus, and learn His will. There must be zealous activity on your part. Teach not your ideas, your plans, your notions, your maxims, but teach the word of the Lord.

Your weekly seasons of prayer will not qualify any one of you for your great and solemn responsibilities, if, after these seasons, you feel that your work is done, and, having looked into the great moral looking glass, you go away and forget what manner of man you were. It is not merely one day of service that will suffice for the soul's need. You must be constantly coming to the storehouse to feed on the flesh and blood of the Son of God. Religion is not to be cheapened in 1896 or 1897.

COME OUT FROM WORLDLY INFLUENCES

Those who are partakers of the divine nature are to come out from worldly influences, from empty festivities, and sit down with Christ, in heart communion with their Redeemer. Cease your unbelieving worry. When the anxious disciples saw the hungry multitudes beside the sea, impossibilities arose in their minds, and they questioned, Shall we go to the villages and buy, to give them to eat? Just so in the several conferences many now ask, Shall we send to Battle Creek for someone to come and hold meetings with us and revive us and feed us? What said Christ? No. He commanded the multitude to sit down on the grass in companies of fifty and one hundred. They obeyed orders, seating themselves in long lines on the grass. Jesus took the five loaves and two fishes out of the hands of the lad, and, looking up to His Father, He asked His blessing upon the meager supply. Then He put into the hands of His disciples the food to be distributed. The scanty provision grew under the hand of Christ, and He had constantly a fresh supply for His servants to distribute to the hungry multitude, until all had a sufficiency. Then the word came, "Gather up the fragments that remain, that nothing be lost." There was a surplus of food gathered up.

This is a lesson to all in their spiritual experience. What an amount of worry would be saved if men would only trust in God. The bread of life is to be given to needy souls. And what a work is often made of the matter. There are long councils for devising plans, inventing new methods. There is a constant effort to get up entertainments to draw people to the church or the Sabbath school. Like the disciples, the workers raise the question, Shall we go to the villages and buy? What is the work to be done? Come unto Jesus. Humble faith and prayer will accomplish very much more than your long councils. Listen to the Saviour's invitation. Put your neck under His yoke. Accept His burdens. Receive that which He bestows. He says, "My yoke is easy, and My burden is light."

This anticipation of terrible difficulties need not be. We must eat and drink the word of life, which is represented as eating and drinking of the flesh and blood of Christ. Those who know the truth must be educated to receive it from their own shepherds, and pray over it, and practice it. Then souls will grow in faith and in intelligent knowledge. They would receive the bread of life and digest it. The entrance of Thy words giveth light; it giveth understanding unto the simple." The truth needs to enter into heart and mind. More, much more praying, and less long sermonizing will be for the health of the body and soul.

Money has been expended in sending men to Jerusalem, to see the place where Jesus traveled and taught, when we have the precious Saviour nigh us, His presence with us, and we may have a Jerusalem in our own houses and in the churches. We can discern His fresh footsteps, we can eat His words and have eternal life. We need more study, more earnest meditation and communion with Christ. We need to listen for the still small voice, and to rest by faith in the love of Christ. We should have a much more healthful experience, and become much more vigorous Christians.

We have a superabundance of sermons, but we need to learn to receive the word. All the help from abroad cannot supply this deficiency. The home missionary work must be entered into by home missionaries. God is not pleased with the selfish devisings to give so many advantages to those who know the truth, who had opportunities to understand far more of the truth than they practice. Thousands upon thousands are in ignorance, perishing out of Christ. Yet money and time and labor are devoted to the class who are ever learning, yet never able to come to the experimental knowledge of the truth because they will not practice the truth.

Those who are ready to do service are those who feed most on Christ. Read and study His word, drink in the inspiration of His Spirit, and receive of His grace, not to hoard, but to give to others. In order to instruct others, the teachers must first be learners of Christ. There are Marthas in every church. They are intensely busy in religious activities, and they do much good; but we need also Mary's side of character. The most zealous workers need to learn at the feet of Jesus.

For further study: *Gospel Workers,* pages 271-272, 446-448; *Testimonies,* vol. 5, pp. 370-381; vol. 7, pp. 91-93.

Appeals for Truth and Loyalty 14

"All Ye Are Brethren"

March 8, 1895.

I must speak to my brethren nigh and afar off. I cannot hold my peace. They are not working on correct principles. Those who stand in responsible positions must not feel that their position of importance makes them men of infallible judgment.

All the works of men are under the Lord's jurisdiction. It will be altogether safe for men to consider that there is knowledge with the Most High. Those who trust in God and His wisdom, and not in their own, are walking in safe paths. They will never feel that they are authorized to muzzle even the ox that treads out the grain; and how offensive it is for men to control the human agent who is in partnership with God, and whom the Lord Jesus has invited: "Come unto Me, all ye that *labor* and are *heavy-laden,* and I will give you rest. Take My yoke upon you, and learn of Me; for I am meek and lowly in heart: and ye shall find rest unto your souls. For My yoke is easy, and My burden is light." "We are laborers together with God: ye are God's husbandry, ye are God's building."

The Lord has not placed any one of His human agencies under the dictation and control of those who are themselves but erring mortals. He has not placed upon men the power to say, You shall do this, and you shall not do that. But there is a power exercised in Battle Creek that God has not given, and He will judge those who assume this authority. They have somewhat of the same spirit that led Uzzah to lay his

---

The articles in this section are from *Special Testimonies to Ministers and Workers* (Series A, No. 9, 1897). This article, pages 3-15.

hand on the ark to steady it, as though God was not able to care for His sacred symbols. Far less of man's power and authority should be exercised toward God's human agencies. Brethren, leave God to rule.

THE WORK FOR THIS TIME

The great work for this time demands that men shall go everywhere, nigh and afar off, into the highways and hedges, to diffuse light, holding forth the words of life. Has God laid upon one man or a council of men to take this work into their hands, as though the workers, God's own property, were to be under their control?

The business connected with the work of God in any and every branch requires men who are working in harmony with God, for power and success in the work can be attained only through the cooperation of the human and the divine. Without the best of evidence that one understands heavenly and eternal things, he should not be authorized to minister in matters connected with the work that concerns the salvation of souls for whom Christ has died. Unsanctified hands and brains have had altogether too much power entrusted to them, and very unwise moves have been made, that are not in accordance with the will and ways of God.

No man is a proper judge of another man's duty. Man is responsible to God; and as finite, erring men take into their hands the jurisdiction of their fellowmen, as if the Lord commissioned them to lift up and cast down, all heaven is filled with indignation. There are strange principles being established in regard to the control of the minds and works of men, by human judges, as though these finite men were gods.

And how is it with some who are bearing these sacred responsibilities? Men who are not spiritually minded, who are not consecrated to God, have no commission to perform, nor authority to exercise, in regard to the willing or doing of their fellowmen. But unless men are daily in communion with God, instead of seeking Him with all their heart for a fitness for the work, they will assume the power of dictation over the conscience of others. A sense of the divine presence would awe and subdue the soul, but this they have not. Without the love of God burning in the soul, love to men grows cold. Their hearts are not touched at the sight of human woe. Selfishness has left its defiling imprint on life and character, and some will never lose this image and superscription.

Is the working of the cause of God to be entrusted to such hands? Are souls for whom Christ has died, to be manipulated at the will of men who have refused the light given them of heaven? We should be afraid of man-made laws, and of plans and methods that are not in accordance with the principles of the word of God concerning man's relation to his fellow. "All ye are brethren."

THE PRESENT ORDER MUST CHANGE

The present order of things must change,* or the wrath of God will fall upon His instrumentalities that are not working in Christ's lines. Has God given any one of you a commission to lord it over His heritage? This kind of work has been coming in for years. God sees it all, and He is displeased with it. When men come in between God and His human agents, they dishonor God and wrong the souls of those who need true encouragement and sympathy and love. I am constrained

*See Appendix.

to appeal to our workers: Whatever your position, do not depend on men, or make flesh your arm.

I am urged by the Spirit of God to say to you who have a connection with the Lord's work, Never forget that you are wholly dependent upon God; and if you pass one hour or one moment without relying upon His grace, without keeping the heart open to receive the wisdom that is not earthborn, being sure that without Christ ye can do nothing, you will be unable to distinguish between the common and the sacred fire. Words of a very forbidden character will flash from your lips to destroy hope and courage and faith. Thus it is written in the books of heaven: Your words were not inspired of God, but of the enemy that wounded and bruised Christ in the person of His purchased possession. Souls of infinite value were treated indifferently, turned from, left to struggle under temptation, and forced on Satan's battleground.

Job's professed friends were miserable comforters, making his case more bitter and unbearable, and Job was not guilty as they supposed. Those who are under the pain and distress of their own wrongdoing, while Satan is seeking to drive them to despair, are the very ones who need help the most. The intense agony of the soul that has been overcome by Satan and is feeling worsted and helpless—how little is it comprehended by those who should meet the erring one with tender compassion!

Most pitiable is the condition of one who is suffering under remorse; he is as one stunned, staggering, sinking into the dust. And many who suppose themselves to be righteous, become exasperating comforters; they deal harshly with these souls. In manifesting this hardness of heart in offending and oppressing, they are doing the very same work which Satan delights in doing. The tried, tempted soul cannot see anything clearly. The mind is confused; he knows not just what steps to take. Oh, then, let no word be spoken to cause deeper pain!

HOW TO DEAL WITH THE ERRING

Our Saviour said: "Whoso shall offend one of these little ones which believe in Me, it were better for him that a millstone were hanged about his neck, and that he were drowned in the depth of the sea. Woe unto the world because of offenses! for it must needs be that offenses come; but woe to *that man* by whom the offense cometh! . . . Take heed that ye despise not one of these little ones; for I say unto you, That in heaven their angels do always behold the face of My Father which is in heaven. For the Son of man is come to save that which was lost. How think ye? if a man have an hundred sheep, and one of them be gone astray, doth he not leave the ninety and nine, and goeth into the mountains, and seeketh that which is gone astray? And if so be that he find it, verily I say unto you, he rejoiceth more of that sheep, than of the ninety and nine which went not astray. Even so it is not the will of your Father which is in heaven, that one of these little ones should perish."

"I came not," said Christ, "to call the righteous [you who feel no need of repentance], but sinners to repentance." Those who are laborers together with God will work in Christ's lines. There is many a poor soul who is misunderstood, unappreciated, full of distress and agony—a lost, straying sheep. His mind is beclouded, he cannot find God, and almost hopeless unbelief takes possession of him. Yet he has an intense, longing desire for pardon and peace.

As this picture is opened before you, the inquiry

may be made, Are there no Christians to whom such a one can go for relief? This question God answers: "I have somewhat against thee, because thou hast left thy first love. Remember therefore from whence thou art fallen, and repent, and do the first works; or else I will come unto thee quickly, and will remove thy candlestick out of his place, except thou repent." A cold, hardhearted Pharisaism has taken possession of many of the professed followers of Christ, and the love of Jesus is dead.

"And unto the angel of the church in Sardis write; These things saith He that hath the seven Spirits of God, and the seven stars; I know thy works, that thou hast a name that thou livest, and art dead. Be watchful, and strengthen the things which remain, that are ready to die: for I have not found thy works perfect before God." Here the problem is solved. The persons here described have had light that would have prompted them to altogether different works, if they had followed the light and had strengthened the things that remained that were ready to die. The light which was glowing in their own hearts when Jesus spoke to their souls, "Thy sins be forgiven thee," they might have kept alive by helping those who needed help.

The work to be done is plainly specified: "Be watchful, and strengthen the things which remain, that are ready to die: for I have not found thy works perfect before God. Remember therefore how thou hast received and heard, and hold fast, and repent. If therefore thou shalt not watch, I will come on thee as a thief, and thou shalt not know what hour I will come upon thee." Many have heard and received the word of life, and have been strongly moved by the truth, but have allowed their souls to become cold, their faith dim, through self-righteousness, self-importance, and pride in the possession of a knowledge of truth which they fail to practice. The truth which is not put in practice, loses its power. The heart is closed to its divine influence, and those who should be workers for Christ are idle, and souls whom they might help are left in discouragement and darkness and despair.

HELP THE SINKING SOULS

There are souls who are starving for sympathy, starving for the bread of life; but they have no confidence to make known their great need. Those who bear the responsibilities in connection with the work of God should understand that they are under the most solemn obligation to help these souls; and they would be prepared to help them, if they themselves had retained the soft, subduing influence of the love of Christ. Do these poor souls, ready to die, look to them for help? No; they did this until they could have no hope of help from that quarter. They see not a hand stretched out to save.

The matter has been presented to me thus: A drowning man, vainly struggling with the waves, discovers a boat, and with his last remaining strength succeeds in reaching it, and lays hold upon its side. In his weakness he cannot speak, but the agony upon his face would excite pity in any heart that was touched with human tenderness. But do the occupants of the boat stretch out their hands to lift him in? No! All heaven looks on as these men beat off the feeble, clinging hands, and a suffering fellow being sinks beneath the waves, to rise no more. This scene has been enacted over and over again. It has been witnessed by One who gave His life for the ransom of just such souls. The Lord has reached down His own hand to save. The Lord Himself has done the work which He left for man to do, in revealing the pity and compassion of Christ toward sinners. Jesus says, "A new commandment I give unto you, That ye love one another; as I have loved you, that ye also love one another." Calvary reveals to every one of us the depths of that love.

There are souls in their darkness, full of remorse and pain and anguish, who still feel that God is just and good. The Lord is keeping alive the spark of hope in their hearts. The poor, darkened soul feels, If I could only appear before God, and plead my case, He would pity for Christ's sake, and this horrible fear and agony would be relieved. He has tried to speak to men, and has been rudely repulsed, reproved, taunted by his supposed friends. Sometimes the reproaches heaped upon his head have well-nigh destroyed the last spark of hope. The soul that is conscious of sincere and honest intentions finds he has less to fear from God than from men who have hearts of steel. The soul wrenched with human agony turns away from the misjudgment and condemnation of men who cannot read the heart, yet have taken it upon them to judge their fellowmen. He turns to One who is without a shadow of misapprehension, One who knows all the impulses of the heart, who is acquainted with all the circumstances of temptation. God knows every deed of the past life, and yet in consideration of all this, the troubled soul is ready to trust his case with God, knowing that He is a God of mercy and compassion.

LET US FALL INTO THE HAND OF GOD

When David was bidden to choose the punishment for his sin, he said, "Let us fall now into the hand of the Lord; for His mercies are great: and let me not fall into the hand of man." He felt that God knew the struggle and anguish of the soul. When one is enabled to catch a glimpse of the character of God, he sees not in Him the heartless, vindictive spirit manifested by human agents; he sees that affliction and trial are God's appointed means of disciplining His children, and teaching them His way, that they may lay hold of His grace. "Who is among you that feareth the Lord, that obeyeth the voice of His servant, that walketh in darkness, and hath no light? let him trust in the name of the Lord, and stay upon his God." As the poor backsliding one is led to the river of God's love, he exclaims, When He hath tried me, I shall come forth as gold purified. The suffering soul is made patient, trustful, triumphant in God under adverse circumstances.

"Wherefore in all things it behooved Him to be made like unto His brethren, that He might be a merciful and faithful high priest in things pertaining to God, to make reconciliation for the sins of the people. For in that He Himself hath suffered being tempted, He is able to succor them that are tempted. "Seeing then that we have a great High Priest, that is passed into the heavens, Jesus the Son of God, let us hold fast our profession. For we have not an high priest which cannot be touched with the feeling of our infirmities; but was in all points tempted like as we are, yet without sin. Let us therefore come boldly unto the throne of grace, that we may obtain mercy, and find grace to help in time of need." "Take heed, brethren, lest there be in any of you an evil heart of unbelief, in departing from the living God."

When finite, erring man gives evidence that he regards himself as of greater importance than God, when he thinks himself righteous, yet does not manifest the tenderness of spirit that characterized the life of our Lord Jesus, we may know that unless he repents, the candlestick will quickly be removed out of its place. All heaven is astonished at the terrible indifference of the human agents. Men who are themselves tempted to fall into sin, and need pardon, are yet full of self-sufficiency, and are unfeeling toward a brother who is ensnared by the enemy, and whose need and peril should call out Christlike sympathy and effort to plant his feet on the solid Rock.

A FATAL DECEPTION

There is a most fearful, fatal deception upon human minds. Because men are in positions of trust, connected with the work of God, they are exalted in their own estimation, and do not discern that other souls, fully as precious in the sight of God as their own, are neglected, and handled roughly, and bruised, and wounded, and left to die.

The converting power of God must come upon men who handle sacred things, yet who are unable, through some cause best known to God, to distinguish between the sacred fire of God's own kindling and the strange fire which they offer. That strange fire is as dishonoring to God as was that presented by Nadab and Abihu. The sacred fire of God's love would make men tender and kind and sympathetic toward those in peril. Those who indulge in sharp, overbearing words, are really saying: I am holier than thou. Do you not see my exalted position?

But the position does not make the man. It is the integrity of character, the spirit of Christ, that makes him thankful, unselfish, without partiality and without hypocrisy—it is this that is of value with God. To those whose life is hid with Christ in God, the Lord says, "Behold, I have graven thee upon the palms of My hands; thy walls are continually before Me."

For all in responsible positions I have a message spoken by the mouth of the Lord—the fifty-fifth chapter of Isaiah. Study this chapter, and let not any human being consider that he is above his fellow workers because greater responsibilities are involved in his branch of the work. If he is like Daniel, seeking for the power that comes alone from God, that he may represent, not himself, not his imperfections in selfish and fraudulent practices, but the truth in righteousness, he will not possess a vestige of pride or self-importance; but will be weighted with the spirit of wisdom from God.

THE SACRED AND THE STRANGE FIRE

He will represent the sacredness of the work, he will magnify the truth, and will ever present before men and angels the holy perfume of the character of Christ. This is the sacred fire of God's own kindling. Anything aside from this is strange fire, abhorrent to God, and the more offensive as one's position in the work involves larger responsibilities.

I have a message from God to the sinners in Zion, the ones whom Christ addressed: "Be watchful, and strengthen the things which remain, that are ready to die: for I have not found thy works perfect before God." You need to offer always the sacred fire; for then Christ's works, His love, His mercy, His righteousness, will ascend before God, as a cloud of holy, fragrant incense, wholly acceptable.

But strange fire has been offered in the use of harsh words, in self-importance, in self-exaltation, in self-righteousness, in arbitrary authority, in domineering, in oppression, in restricting the liberty of God's people, binding them about by your plans and rules, which God has not framed, neither have they come into His mind. All these things are strange fire, unacknowledged by God, and are a continual misrepresentation of His character.

I have a message for you: "Seek ye the Lord while He may be found, call ye upon Him while He is near: let the wicked forsake his way, and the unrighteous man his thoughts: and let him return unto the Lord, and He will have mercy upon him; and to our God, for He will abundantly pardon. For My thoughts are not your thoughts, neither are your ways My ways, saith the Lord. For as the heavens are higher than the earth, so are My ways higher than your ways, and My thoughts than your thoughts. For as the rain cometh down, and the snow from heaven, and returneth not thither, but watereth the earth, and maketh it bring forth and bud, that it may give seed to the sower, and bread to the eater: so shall My word be that goeth forth out of My mouth: it shall not return unto Me void, but it shall accomplish that which I please, and it shall prosper in the thing whereto I sent it."

"Judgment is turned away backward, and justice standeth afar off: for truth is fallen in the street, and equity cannot enter. Yea, truth faileth; and he that departeth from evil maketh himself a prey: and the Lord saw it, and it displeased Him that there was no judgment. And He saw that there was no man, and wondered that there was no intercessor: therefore His arm brought salvation unto Him; and His righteousness, it sustained Him. For He put on righteousness as a breastplate, and an helmet of salvation upon His head; and He put on the garments of vengeance for clothing, and was clad with zeal as a cloak. . . . So shall they fear the name of the Lord from the west, and His glory from the rising of the sun. When the enemy shall come in like a flood, the Spirit of the Lord shall lift up a standard against him. And the Redeemer shall come to Zion, and unto them that turn from transgression in Jacob, saith the Lord."

"Thou Shalt Have No Other Gods Before Me"

Granville, Australia, September, 1895.

I do not find rest in spirit. Scene after scene is presented in symbols before me, and I find no rest until I begin to write out the matter. At the center of the work matters are being shaped so that every other institution is following in the same course. And the General Conference is itself becoming corrupted with wrong sentiments and principles.* In the working of plans, the same principles are manifest that have controlled matters at Battle Creek for quite a length of time.

I have been shown that the Jewish nation were not brought suddenly into their condition of thought and practice. From generation to generation they were working on false theories, carrying out principles opposed to the truth, and combining with their religion thoughts and plans that were the product of human minds. Human inventions were made supreme.

The holy principles that God has given are represented as the sacred fire, but common fire has been used in place of the sacred. Plans contrary to truth and righteousness are introduced in a subtle manner on the

---

Special Testimonies to Ministers and Workers (Series A, No. 9, 1897), pages 16-21.

*See Appendix.

plea that this must be done, and that must be done, "because it is for the advancement of the cause of God." But it is the devising of men that leads to oppression, injustice, and wickedness. The cause of God is free from every taint of injustice. It can gain no advantage by robbing the members of the family of God of their individuality or their rights. All such practices are abhorrent to God. He inspires no such practices as have been entered into by your councils in regard to the publication of books.

The Lord accepts no such transactions; prosperity will not attend these moves. Men connected with His work have been dealing unjustly, and it is time to call a halt. Let men deal with men upon the principles of the Ten Commandments, and not ignore these principles in business transactions. False propositions are assumed as truth and righteousness, and then everything is worked in such a way as to carry out these propositions, which are not in accordance with the will of God, but are a misrepresentation of His character.

The great and holy and merciful God will never be in league with dishonest practices; not a single touch of injustice will He vindicate. Men have taken unfair advantage of those whom they supposed to be under their jurisdiction. They were determined to bring the individuals to their terms; they would rule or ruin. There will be no material change until a decided movement is made to bring in a different order of things.

Let no plans or methods be adopted in any of our institutions that will bind mind or talent under the control of human judgment; for this is not in God's order. God has given to men talents of influence which belong to Him alone, and no greater dishonor can be done to God than for one finite agent to bring other men's talents under his absolute control, even though the benefits of the same be used to the advantage of the cause. In such arrangements one man's mind is ruled by another man's mind, and the human agency is separated from God and exposed to temptation. Satan's methods tend to one end—to make men the slaves of men. And when this is done, confusion and distrust, jealousies and evil surmisings, are the result. Such a course destroys faith in God and in the principles which are to control, to purge from guile and every species of selfishness and hypocrisy.

THE HIGH-HANDED POWER

The high-handed power that has been developed, as though position has made men gods, makes me afraid, and ought to cause fear. It is a curse wherever and by whomsoever it is exercised. This lording it over God's heritage will create such a disgust of man's jurisdiction that a state of insubordination will result. The people are learning that men in high positions of responsibility cannot be trusted to mold and fashion other men's minds and characters. The result will be a loss of confidence even in the management of faithful men. But the Lord will raise up laborers who realize their own nothingness without special help from God. Age after age Jesus has been delivering His goods to His church. At the time of the first advent of Christ to our world, the men who composed the Sanhedrin exercised their authority in controlling men according to their will. Thus the souls whom Christ had given His life to free from the bondage of Satan were brought under bondage to him in another form.

Do we individually realize our true position, that as God's hired servants we are not to bargain away our stewardship? We have an individual accountability before the heavenly universe, to administer the trust committed us of God. Our own hearts are to be stirred. Our hands are to have something to impart of the income that God entrusts to us. The humblest of us may be agents for God, using our gifts for His name's glory. He who improves his talents to the best of his ability may present to God his offering as a consecrated gift that shall be as fragrant incense before Him. It is the duty of everyone to see that his talents are turned to advantage as a gift that he must return, having done his best to improve it.

The spirit of domination is extending to the presidents of our conferences. If a man is sanguine of his own powers and seeks to exercise dominion over his brethren, feeling that he is invested with authority to make his will the ruling power, the best and only safe course is to remove him, lest great harm be done and he lose his own soul and imperil the souls of others. "All ye are brethren." This disposition to lord it over God's heritage will cause a reaction unless these men change their course. Those in authority should manifest the spirit of Christ. They should deal as He would deal with every case that requires attention. They should go weighted with the Holy Spirit. A man's position does not make him one jot or tittle greater in the sight of God; it is character alone that God values.

The goodness, mercy, and love of God were proclaimed by Christ to Moses. This was God's character. When men who profess to serve God ignore His parental character and depart from honor and righteousness in dealing with their fellowmen, Satan exults, for he has inspired them with his attributes. They are following in the track of Romanism.

IN THE TRACK OF ROMANISM

Those who are enjoined to represent the attributes of the Lord's character, step from the Bible platform, and in their own human judgment devise rules and resolutions to force the will of others. The devisings for forcing men to follow the prescriptions of other men are instituting an order of things that overrides sympathy and tender compassion, that blinds the eyes to mercy, justice, and the love of God. Moral influence and personal responsibility are trodden underfoot.

The righteousness of Christ by faith has been ignored by some; for it is contrary to their spirit and their whole life experience. Rule, rule, has been their course of action. Satan has had an opportunity of representing himself. When one who professes to be a representative of Christ engages in sharp dealing and in pressing men into hard places, those who are thus oppressed will either break every fetter of restraint, or they will be led to regard God as a hard master. They cherish hard feelings against God, and the soul is alienated from Him, just as Satan planned it should be.

This hardheartedness on the part of men who claim to believe the truth Satan charges to the influence of the truth itself, and thus men become disgusted and turn from the truth. For this reason no man should have a responsible connection with our institutions who thinks it no important matter whether he has a heart of flesh or a heart of steel.

Men think they are representing the justice of God, but they do not represent His tenderness and the great love wherewith He has loved us. Their human invention originating with the specious devices of Satan, appears fair enough to the blinded eyes of men, because it is inherent in their nature. A lie, believed, practiced, becomes a truth to them. Thus the purpose of the satanic agencies is accomplished, that men should reach these conclusions through the working of their own inventive minds.

But how do men fall into such error? By starting with false premises, and then bringing everything to bear to prove the error true. In some cases the first principles have a measure of truth interwoven with the error, but it does not lead to any just action, and this is why men are misled. In order to reign and become a power, they employ Satan's methods to justify their own principles. They exalt themselves as men of superior judgment, and they have stood as representatives of God. These are false gods.

Under Which Banner?

September 24.

Everything in our world is in agitation. Coming events cast their shadows before. The signs of the times are ominous, indeed. There is assurance in nothing that is human or earthly. The winds are held by the four angels; a moment of respite has been graciously given us of God. Every power lent us of God, whether physical, mental, or moral, is to be sacredly cherished to do the work assigned us for our fellowmen who are perishing in their ignorance. The warning is to go forth to all parts of the world. There must be no delay.

Rapidly are men ranging themselves under the banner they have chosen, restlessly waiting and watching the movements of their leaders. There are those who are

---

Special Testimonies to Ministers and Workers (Series A, No. 9, 1897), pages 21-31.

watching and waiting and working for our Lord's appearing; while the other party are rapidly falling into line under the generalship of the first great apostate. They look for a god in humanity, and Satan personifies the one they seek. Multitudes will be so deluded through their rejection of truth that they will accept the counterfeit. Humanity is hailed as God.

One has come from the heavenly courts to represent God in human form. The Son of God was made man, and dwelt among us. "In Him was life; and the life was the light of men. And the light shineth in darkness; and the darkness comprehended it not. . . . That was the true Light, which lighteth every man that cometh into the world. He was in the world, and the world was made by Him, and the world knew Him not. He came unto His own, and His own received Him not. But as many as received Him, to them gave He power to become the sons of God."

There are but two parties. Satan works with his crooked, deceiving power, and through strong delusions he catches all who do not abide in the truth, who have turned away their ears from the truth and have turned unto fables. Satan himself abode not in the truth; he is the mystery of iniquity. Through his subtlety he gives to his soul-destroying errors the appearance of truth. Herein is their power to deceive. It is because they are a counterfeit of the truth that spiritualism, theosophy, and the like deceptions gain such power over the minds of men. Herein is the masterly working of Satan. He pretends to be the savior of man, the benefactor of the human race, and thus he more readily lures his victims to destruction.

We are warned in the word of God that sleepless vigilance is the price of safety. Only in the straight path of truth and righteousness can we escape the tempter's power. But the world is ensnared. Satan's skill is exercised in devising plans and methods without number to accomplish his purposes. Dissimulation has become a fine art with him, and he works in the guise of an angel of light. God's eye alone discerns his schemes to contaminate the world with false and ruinous principles bearing on their face the appearance of genuine goodness. He works to restrict religious liberty, and to bring into the religious world a species of slavery.* Organizations, institutions, unless kept by the power of God, will work under Satan's dictation to bring men under the control of men; and fraud and guile will bear the semblance of zeal for truth and for the advancement of the kingdom of God. Whatever in our practice is not as open as day belongs to the methods of the prince of evil. His methods are practiced even among Seventh-day Adventists, who claim to have advanced truth.

If men resist the warnings the Lord sends them, they become even leaders in evil practice; such men assume to exercise the prerogatives of God—they presume to do that which God Himself will not do in seeking to control the minds of men. They introduce their own methods and plans, and through their misconceptions of God they weaken the faith of others in the truth, and bring in false principles that will work like leaven to taint and corrupt our institutions and churches. Anything that lowers man's conception of righteousness and equity and impartial judgment, any device or precept that brings God's human agents under the control of human minds, impairs their faith in God; it separates the soul from God; for it leads away from the path of strict integrity and righteousness.

God will not vindicate any device whereby man shall in the slightest degree rule or oppress his fellowmen.

---

*See Appendix.

The only hope for fallen man is to look to Jesus and receive Him as the only Saviour. As soon as man begins to make an iron rule for other men, as soon as he begins to harness up and drive men according to his own mind, he dishonors God and imperils his own soul and the souls of his brethren. Sinful man can find hope and righteousness only in God, and no human being is righteous any longer than he has faith in God and maintains a vital connection with Him. A flower of the field must have its root in the soil; it must have air, dew, showers, and sunshine. It will flourish only as it receives these advantages, and all are from God. So with men. We receive from God that which ministers to the life of the soul. We are warned not to trust in man, nor to make flesh our arm. A curse is pronounced upon all who do this.

JESUS AND NICODEMUS

Nicodemus sought an interview with Jesus at night, saying, "Rabbi, we know that Thou art a teacher come from God: for no man can do these miracles that Thou doest, except God be with him." All this was true, as far as it went; but what said Jesus? He "answered and said unto him, Verily, verily, I say unto thee, Except a man be born again, he cannot see the kingdom of God." Here was a man in a high position of trust, a man who was looked up to as one educated in Jewish customs, one whose mind was stored with wisdom. He was indeed in possession of talents of no ordinary character. He would not go to Jesus by day, for this would make him a subject of remark. It would be too humiliating for a ruler of the Jews to acknowledge himself in sympathy with the despised Nazarene. Nicodemus thinks, I will ascertain for myself the mission and claims of this Teacher, whether He is indeed the

Light to lighten the Gentiles, and the Glory of Israel.

Jesus virtually says to Nicodemus: It is not controversy that will help your case: it is not arguments that will bring light to the soul. You must have a new heart, or you cannot discern the kingdom of heaven. It is not greater evidence that will bring you into a right position, but new purposes, new springs of action. You must be born again. Until this change takes place, making all things new, the strongest evidences that could be presented would be useless. The want is in your own heart; everything must be changed, or you cannot see the kingdom of God.

This was a very humiliating statement to Nicodemus, and with a feeling of irritation he takes up the words of Christ, saying, "How can a man be born when he is old?" He was not spiritually minded enough to discern the meaning of the words of Christ. But the Saviour did not meet argument with argument. Raising His hand in solemn, quiet dignity, He presses home the truth with greater assurance: "Verily, verily, I say unto thee, Except a man be born of water and of the Spirit, he cannot enter into the kingdom of God. That which is born of the flesh is flesh; and that which is born of the Spirit is spirit. Marvel not that I said unto thee, Ye must be born again. The wind bloweth where it listeth, and thou hearest the sound thereof, but canst not tell whence it cometh, and whither it goeth: so is everyone that is born of the Spirit." Nicodemus said unto Him, "How can these things be?"

Some gleams of the truth were penetrating the ruler's mind. Christ's words filled him with awe, and led to the inquiry, "How can these things be?" With deep earnestness Jesus answered, "Art thou a master of Israel, and knowest not these things?" His words convey to Nicodemus the lesson that, instead of feeling irritated over the plain words of truth, and indulging irony, he should have a far more humble opinion of himself, because of his spiritual ignorance. Yet the words of Christ were spoken with such solemn dignity, and both look and tone expressed such earnest love to him, that he was not offended as he realized his humiliating position.

Surely one entrusted with the religious interests of the people should not be ignorant of truth so important for them to understand as the condition of entrance into the kingdom of heaven. "Verily, verily, I say unto thee," continued Jesus, "we speak that we do know, and testify that we have seen; and ye receive not our witness. If I have told you earthly things, and ye believe not, how shall ye believe, if I tell you of heavenly things?"

THIS LESSON IS FOR US TODAY

This lesson to Nicodemus I present as highly applicable to those who are today in responsible positions as rulers in Israel, and whose voices are often heard in council giving evidence of the same spirit that Nicodemus possessed. Will the lesson given to the chief ruler have the same influence upon their heart and life? Nicodemus was converted as the result of this interview. The words of Christ are spoken just as verily to presidents of conferences, elders of churches, and those occupying official positions in our institutions, "Verily, verily, I say unto thee, Except a man be born again, he cannot see the kingdom of God." "A new heart also will I give you."

If you have the Holy Spirit molding and fashioning your heart daily, then you will have divine insight to perceive the character of the kingdom of God. Nicodemus received the lesson of Christ and became a true believer. His voice was heard in the Sanhedrin council in opposition to their measures for compassing the death of Christ. "Doth our law judge any man, before it hear him?" he said. The scornful answer was returned: "Art thou also of Galilee? Search, and look: for out of Galilee ariseth no prophet."

Jesus had a disciple in Nicodemus. In that night conference with Jesus the convicted man stood before the Saviour under the softening, subduing influence of truth which was shining into the chambers of his mind and impressing his heart. Jesus said: "If I have told you earthly things, and ye believe not, how shall ye believe, if I tell you of heavenly things? And no man hath ascended up to heaven, but He that came down from heaven, even the Son of man which is in heaven." Jesus not only tells Nicodemus that he must have a new heart in order to see the kingdom of heaven, but tells him how to obtain a new heart. He reads the inquiring mind of a true seeker after truth, and presents before him the representation of Himself: "As Moses lifted up the serpent in the wilderness, even so must the Son of man be lifted up: that whosoever believeth in Him should not perish, but have eternal life." Good news! good news! ring throughout the world! "For God so loved the world, that He gave His only-begotten Son, that whosoever believeth in Him should not perish, but have everlasting life." This lesson is one of the greatest importance to every soul that lives; for the terms of salvation are here laid out in distinct lines. If one had no other text in the Bible, this alone would be a guide for the soul.

Especially to every man who accepts responsibilities as a counselor, everyone who is dealing with human souls, is this grand, beautiful truth to be a bright and shining light. It is no credit to one who has the word of God in his possession, to say: "I have no experience; I do not understand these things." He will never be wiser until he becomes of much less consequence in his own estimation. He must learn his lesson as a little child. He must make it his first duty to understand the work of God in the regeneration of the soul. This change should take place in every man before he accepts a position as a leader or ruler in connection with the sacred work of God. If one has not a vital connection with God, his own spirit and sentiments will prevail. These may be well represented as strange fire offered in the place of the sacred. Man has woven into the work of God his own defects of character, devices that are human and earthly, delusions ensnaring to himself and to all who accept them.

THE JUDGMENT OF AMALEK

God pledges His most holy word that He will bless you if you will walk in His way and do justice and judgment. "Thou shalt not have in thy bag divers weights, a great and a small. Thou shalt not have in thine house divers measures, a great and a small. But thou shalt have a perfect and just weight, a perfect and just measure shalt thou have: that thy days may be lengthened in the land which the Lord thy God giveth thee. For all that do such things, and all that do unrighteously, are an abomination unto the Lord thy God. Remember what Amalek did unto thee by the way, when ye were come forth out of Egypt; how he met thee by the way, and smote the hindmost of thee, even all that were feeble behind thee, when thou wast faint and weary; and he feared not God."

Notwithstanding that the children of Israel had often grieved the Lord by departing from His counsel, yet He still had a tender care for them. The Lord Jesus Christ saw their enemies taking advantage of their circumstances, to do them an injury; for that work was to bring suffering against the weary, who were journeying under God's leading. Hear the judgments which God pronounced: "Therefore it shall be, when the Lord thy God hath given thee rest from all thine enemies round about, in the land which the Lord thy God giveth thee for an inheritance to possess it, that thou shalt blot out the remembrance of Amalek from under heaven; thou shalt not forget it."

I pen these words of God that those who profess to be His children may not receive the curse pronounced upon Amalek because they have followed the practices of Amalek. If the heathen received this denunciation of their course for overcoming the faint and weary, what will the Lord express toward those who have had light, great opportunities, and privileges, but have not manifested the spirit of Christ toward their own brethren?

The Lord sees all the dealings of brother with brother, which weaken faith, and which destroy their own confidence in themselves as men dealing with justice and equity. In the most positive language He expresses His displeasure at the iniquity practiced in trade. He says, "Shall I count them pure with the wicked balances, and with the bag of deceitful weights?" The very wrong here mentioned may not have been committed in our institutions, but acts which these things represent have been, and are still being done.

Page after page might be written in regard to these things. Whole conferences are becoming leavened with the same perverted principles. "For the rich men thereof are full of violence, and the inhabitants thereof have spoken lies, and their tongue is deceitful in their mouth." The Lord will work to purify His church. I tell you in truth, the Lord is about to turn and overturn in the institutions* called by His name.

Just how soon this refining process will begin I cannot say, but it will not be long deferred. He whose fan is in His hand will cleanse His temple of its moral defilement. He will thoroughly purge His floor. God has a controversy with all who practice the least injustice; for in so doing they reject the authority of God and imperil their interest in the atonement, the redemption which Christ has undertaken for every son and daughter of Adam. Will it pay to take a course abhorrent to God? Will it pay to put upon your censers strange fire to offer before God, and say it makes no difference?

It has not been after God's order to center so much in Battle Creek. The state of things now exists that was presented before me as a warning. I am sick at heart at the representation. The Lord gave warnings to prevent this demoralizing condition of things, but they have not been heeded. "Ye are the salt of the earth: but if the salt have lost his savor, wherewith shall it be salted? it is thenceforth good for nothing, but to be cast out, and to be trodden underfoot of men."

I appeal to my brethren to wake up. Unless a change takes place speedily, I must give the facts to the people; for this state of things must change; unconverted men must no longer be managers and directors in so important and sacred work. With David we are forced to say, "It is time for Thee, Lord, to work: for they have made void Thy law."

For further study: *The Desire of Ages,* pages 167-176.

---

*See Appendix.

The Lord Has a Controversy With His People

Cooranbong, Australia, July 5, 1896.

Care should be given to teach every man his dependence upon God; for He is the source of all wisdom and power and efficiency. I have been shown that it is a mistake to suppose that the men in positions of special responsibility at Battle Creek have wisdom which is far superior to that of ordinary men. Those who think that they have, supposing them to have divine enlightenment, rely upon the human judgment of these men, taking their counsel as the voice of God.* But this is not safe; for unless men are wholly consecrated to God, Satan will work through them to impart that knowledge which will not be for the present and eternal good of those who hear.

Many have educated themselves to write or ask for counsel and advice when brought into difficult places. But it is a mistake for those who are placed in responsible positions in our different institutions to depend upon the men who have all too many burdens and responsibilities to bear. A weak, sickly experience will be the lot of those who are educated to depend wholly upon others. Those upon whom they depend may have less of the fear of God than they themselves have; and not more mental power and talent than it is their privilege to possess if they will but realize that they are not to be children, but firm, brave men, seeking to gain more ability by exercising that which they already have, by trading upon the talent God has lent them. We are individually responsible for the use of the talents God

---

Special Testimonies to Ministers and Workers (Series A, No. 9, 1897), pages 37-50.

*See Appendix.

has given us. Our intellect must be cultivated. Close, hard thinking must be given to the solution of difficulties.

The Lord has given to every man his appointed work, and if He places men in positions of responsibility, He will communicate His Holy Spirit to them, giving them efficiency for their work. But the men who are called upon to take long and expensive journeys in order to help others to devise and plan are not themselves in close connection with the God of all wisdom if they put confidence in their own strength and wisdom. If they have not been willing to bear the yoke of Christ, or to learn in His school to be meek and lowly in heart as He was; if they have not learned to lift the burdens God has given them, and to follow wherever He may lead them, what will their expensive trips amount to? What is their wisdom worth? Is it not accounted foolishness with God?

TEACH THIS TO THE PEOPLE

State conferences may depend upon the General Conference for light and knowledge and wisdom; but is it safe for them to do this? Battle Creek is not to be the center of God's work. God alone can fill this place. When our people in the different places have their special convocations, teach them, for Christ's sake and for their own soul's sake, not to make flesh their arm. There is no power in men to read the hearts of their fellowmen. The Lord is the only one upon whom we can with safety depend, and He is accessible in every place and to every church in the Union. To place men where God should be placed does not honor or glorify God. Is the president of the General Conference to be the god of the people? Are the men at Battle Creek to be regarded as infinite in wisdom? When the Lord shall work upon human hearts and human intellects, principles and practices different from this will be set before the people. "Cease ye from man."

The Lord has a controversy with His people over this matter. Why have they left the Lord their God, who so loved them "that He gave His only-begotten Son, that whosoever believeth in Him should not perish, but have everlasting life"? His love is not uncertain and fluctuating, but is as far above all other love as the heavens are above the earth. Ever He watches over His children with a love that is measureless and everlasting. "O the depth of the riches both of the wisdom and knowledge of God! how unsearchable are His judgments, and His ways past finding out!"

"If any of you lack wisdom, let him ask of God, that giveth to all men liberally, and upbraideth not; and it shall be given him." Mercy and love and wisdom are to be found in God; but many who profess to know Him have turned from the One in whom our hope of eternal life is centered, and have educated themselves to depend upon their erring and fallible fellowmen. They are crippled spiritually when they do this; for no man is infallible, and his influence may be misleading. He who trusts in man not only leans upon a broken reed, and gives Satan an opportunity to introduce himself, but he hurts the one in whom the trust is placed; he becomes lifted up in his estimation of himself, and loses the sense of his dependence upon God. Just as soon as man is placed where God should be, he loses his purity, his vigor, his confidence in God's power. Moral confusion results, because his powers become unsanctified and perverted. He feels competent to judge his fellowmen, and he strives unlawfully to be a god over them.

"LET THIS MIND BE IN YOU"

But there must be no self-exaltation in the work of God. However much we know, however great our mental endowments, none of us can boast; for what we possess is but an entrusted gift, lent us on trial. The faithful improvement of these endowments decides our destiny for eternity; but we have nothing whereby we should exalt self or lift us up, for that which we have is not our own.

We are to be courteous toward all men, tenderhearted and sympathetic; for this was the character Christ manifested when on earth. The more closely we are united with Jesus Christ, the more tender and affectionate will be our conduct toward one another. The redemption of the human race was planned that man, fallen though he was, might be partaker of the divine nature, having escaped the corruption that is in the world through lust. If by His grace we become partakers of the divine nature, our influence upon those around us is not dangerous but beneficial. Looking unto Jesus, the Author and Finisher of our faith, we can be a blessing to all with whom we associate; for the Holy Spirit's power upon the human heart can make and keep it pure.

Those who do not receive Christ as their personal Saviour, who do not feel the need of His grace upon heart and character, cannot influence those around them for good. Whatever their station in life, they will carry with them an influence that Satan will use in his service. Such lose all hope of eternal life themselves, and by their wrong example lead others astray.

STUDY THE CROSS

The cross of Calvary means everything to perishing souls. Through the suffering and death of the Son of man, the salvation of man was made possible. Through the agency of the Holy Spirit God designs that His image shall be restored in humanity, that a new and living principle of life shall be introduced into the minds that have become defiled by sin. The love of God is fully able to restore, rebuild, encourage, and strengthen every believing soul who will accept the truth as it is in Jesus. But in order that this may be accomplished, men must yoke up with Christ. The cross of Christ must be studied. It must rivet the attention and hold the affections. The blood which there was shed for sins will purify and cleanse mind and heart from every species of selfishness.

SANCTIFIED THROUGH THE TRUTH

God is the author of all truth; and truth practiced prepares the way for more advanced truth. When God's delegated servants proclaim fresh truth, the Holy Spirit moves upon the mind which has been prepared by walking in the light, quickening the perceptive faculties to discern the beauty and majesty of truth.

But the truth is no truth to the one who does not reveal, by his elevated spiritual character, a power beyond that which the world can give, an influence corresponding in its sacred, peculiar character to the truth itself. He who is sanctified by the truth will exert a saving, vital influence upon all with whom he comes in contact. This is Bible religion.

Men, saved only by the atoning sacrifice of Christ Jesus, have no right to seek to exalt themselves above their fellowmen. Let them sit at the feet of Jesus, and learn of Him, striving not to make themselves shine. If the love of Jesus Christ abides in them, they will shine unconsciously, diffusing the light of the glory of Christ through the world. "I, if I be lifted up," Christ said, "will draw all men unto Me." If a minister makes Christ his hope, his trust, his dependence, he is one with Christ, a laborer together with God; and by his ministry, souls are converted to Christ.

ALL ABILITY IS FROM GOD

There are those who are not learned and who have not a large endowment of gifts, but they need not become discouraged because of this. Let them use what they have, faithfully guarding every weak point in their characters, seeking by divine grace to make it strong. There is no man living that has any power or ability which he has not received from God, and the source from whence it came is open to the weakest human being. If he will draw near to God, the unfailing source of strength, he will realize that God fulfills His promise. But in this work, we need not call men thousands of miles to give us aid; for Christ has promised, "Ask, and it shall be given you; seek, and ye shall find."

God has not given talents to men capriciously, but according to their God-given ability to use them. The greater the talents lent to man, the greater the returns required. God requires every human agent to consult the living oracle, and become thoroughly acquainted with His expressed will in all matters, that by diligently using the talents lent him, he may gain others.

God would have us learn the solemn lesson that we are working out our own destiny. The character we form in this life decides whether or not we are fitted to live through the eternal ages. No man can with safety remain idle. He may not have many talents, but let him trade on those which he has; and in proportion as he exhibits integrity toward God and his fellowmen, so God will bless him.

The Holy Spirit waits to give aid to every believing soul, and Jesus declares, "Lo, I am with you alway, even unto the end of the world." Let those who believe in Jesus be strong, prayerful, and full of trust in Christ's power to save. "Call upon Me in the day of trouble: I will deliver thee, and thou shalt glorify Me."

THE LORD'S ENTREATY

Let me entreat our state conferences and our churches to cease putting their dependence upon men and making flesh their arm. Look not to other men to see how they conduct themselves under the conviction of the truth, or to ask them for aid. Look not to men in high positions of responsibility for strength, for they are the very men who are in danger of considering a position of responsibility as evidence of God's special power. Our churches are weak because the members are educated to look to and depend upon human resources, and thousands of dollars are needlessly expended in transporting finite men from one place to another, in order that they may settle little difficulties, when Jesus is ever near to help those who are needy and distressed.

The warnings given in the word of God to the children of Israel were meant, not merely for them, but for all who should live upon the earth. He says to them: "Woe to the rebellious children, . . . that take counsel, but not of Me; and that cover with a covering, but not of My Spirit, that they may add sin to sin: that walk to go down into Egypt, and have not asked at My mouth; to strengthen themselves in the strength of Pharaoh, and to trust in the shadow of Egypt!" If the Lord reproved His people anciently because they neglected to seek counsel of Him when in difficulty, will He not be displeased today if His people, instead of depending on the bright beams of the Sun of Righteousness to lighten their way, turn from Him in their test and trial for the aid of human beings who are as erring and inefficient as themselves? Where is our strength? Is it in men who are as helpless and dependent as ourselves, who need guidance from God even as we do?

THE PRESENT HELP

Christ says, "Without Me ye can do nothing," and He has provided the Holy Spirit as a present help in every time of need. But many have a feeble religious experience because, instead of seeking the Lord for the efficiency of the Holy Spirit, they make flesh their arm. Let the people of God be educated to turn to God when in trouble and gain strength from the promises that are yea and amen to every trusting soul.

The word of the Lord is to us, "Ask, and it shall be given you; seek, and ye shall find; knock, and it shall be opened unto you. For everyone that asketh receiveth; and he that seeketh findeth; and to him that knocketh it shall be opened. If a son shall ask bread of any of you that is a father, will he give him a stone? or if he ask a fish, will he for a fish give him a serpent? or if he shall ask an egg, will he offer him a scorpion? If ye then, being evil, know how to give good gifts unto your children: how much more shall your heavenly Father give the Holy Spirit to them that ask Him?"

The promises of God are full and abundant, and there is no need for anyone to depend upon humanity for strength. To all that call upon Him, God is near to help and succor. And He is greatly dishonored when, after inviting our confidence, we turn from Him—the only One who will not misunderstand us, the only One who can give unerring counsel—to men who in their human weakness are liable to lead us astray.

"Wherefore the Lord said, Forasmuch as this people draw near Me with their mouth, and with their lips do honor Me, but have removed their heart far from Me, and their fear toward Me is taught by the precept of men: therefore, behold, I will proceed to do a marvelous work among this people, even a marvelous work and a wonder: for the wisdom of their wise men shall perish, and the understanding of their prudent men shall be hid. Woe unto them that seek deep to hide their counsel from the Lord, and their works are in the dark, and they say, Who seeth us? and who knoweth us?"

The Lord has shown us His way; shall we walk in it? or shall we, finite and erring as we are, walk in our own counsel, and practice the principles which He has warned us against?

THE PRESENT WARNING

"Now go, write it before them in a table, and note it in a book, that it may be for the time to come forever and ever: that this is a rebellious people, lying children, children that will not hear the law of the Lord: which say to the seers, See not; and to the prophets, Prophesy not unto us right things, speak unto us smooth things, prophesy deceits: get you out of the way, turn aside out of the path, cause the Holy One of Israel to cease from before us. Wherefore thus saith the Holy One of Israel, Because ye despise this word, and trust in oppression and perverseness, and stay thereon: therefore this iniquity shall be to you as a breach ready to fall, swelling out in a high wall, whose breaking cometh suddenly at an instant."

"Whom shall He teach knowledge? and whom shall He make to understand doctrine? them that are weaned from the milk, and drawn from the breasts. For precept must be upon precept, precept upon precept; line upon line, line upon line; here a little, and there a little: for with stammering lips and another tongue will He speak to this people. To whom He said, This is the rest wherewith ye may cause the weary to rest; and this is the refreshing: yet they would not hear. But the word of the Lord was unto them precept upon precept, precept upon precept; line upon line, line upon line; here a little and there a little; that they might go, and fall backward, and be broken, and snared, and taken. Wherefore hear the word of the Lord, ye scornful men that rule this people which is in Jerusalem. Because ye have said, We have made a covenant with death, and with hell are we at agreement; when the overflowing scourge shall pass through, it shall not come unto us: for we have made lies our refuge, and under falsehood have we hid ourselves: therefore thus saith the Lord God, Behold, I lay in Zion for a foundation a stone, a tried stone, a precious cornerstone, a sure foundation: he that believeth shall not make haste. Judgment also will I lay to the line, and righteousness to the plummet: and the hail shall sweep away the refuge of lies, and the waters shall overflow the hiding place."

"Thus saith the Lord God, the Holy One of Israel; In returning and rest shall ye be saved; in quietness and in confidence shall be your strength: and ye would not." "And in that day shall the deaf hear the words of the book, and the eyes of the blind shall see out of obscurity, and out of darkness. The meek also shall increase their joy in the Lord, and the poor among men shall rejoice in the Holy One of Israel. For the terrible one is brought to nought, and the scorner is consumed, and all that watch for iniquity are cut off: that make a man an offender for a word, and lay a snare for him that reproveth in the gate, and turn aside the just for a thing of nought. Therefore thus saith the Lord, who redeemed Abraham, concerning the house of Jacob, Jacob shall not now be ashamed, neither shall his face now wax pale. But when he seeth his children, the work of Mine hands, in the midst of him, they shall sanctify My name, and sanctify the Holy One of Jacob, and shall fear the God of Israel. They also that erred in spirit shall come to understanding, and they that murmured shall learn doctrine."

Will these warnings be passed by as of no account? The Lord calls upon every teacher, every minister, everyone who has received the light of His truth, to mark well his spiritual standing. They have had great light, and if they would secure eternal life, they must no longer make finite men their dependence, but build upon the sure foundation.

HOLD FAST TO GOD'S PRINCIPLES

No council of men can with safety remove God's principles, and set up their own; for the word of God declares, "Judgment also will I lay to the line, and righteousness to the plummet: and the hail shall sweep away the refuge of lies, and the waters shall overflow the hiding place." "For the Lord shall rise up as in Mount Perazim, He shall be wroth as in the valley of Gibeon, that He may do His work, His strange work; and bring to pass His act, His strange act. Now therefore be ye not mockers, lest your bands be made strong: for I have heard from the Lord God of hosts a consumption, even determined upon the whole earth."

We are living in times full of importance to each one. Light is shining in clear, steady rays around us. If this light is rightly received and appreciated, it will be a blessing to us and to others; but if we trust in our own wisdom and strength, or in the wisdom and strength of our fellowmen, it will be turned into a poison. In the struggle for eternal life, we cannot lean upon one another. The bread of life must be eaten by each one. Individually we must partake of it, that soul, body, and mind may be revived and strengthened by its transforming power, thus becoming assimilated to the mind and character of Jesus Christ. God must be made first and last and best in everything.

Each one must hunger and thirst after rightousness for himself. Leaning upon men, and trusting in their wisdom, is dangerous to the spiritual life of any Christian. Those in whom confidence is placed may be honest and true, serving the Lord with all diligence. But if, individually, we are endeavoring to walk in the footsteps of Christ, we can follow Him as well as those whom we admire for their consistent, humble lives.

NOT MAN BUT THE LORD

It is too often the case that those who are looked up to are not what they are supposed to be. Often sin lurks in the heart, and wrong habits and deceptive practices are woven into the character. How does our heavenly Father regard this? His counsel is always reliable, and He has evidenced His great love for the human race, and He looks on with sadness when His children are encouraged to turn away from Him and place their dependence upon finite men, whom they know not, and whose judgment and experience may not be reliable. But this has been done, and God has been made secondary.

In the name of Jesus Christ of Nazareth, I beseech the people of God to depend upon the Lord for strength. Beware how you place men where God should be. We are not safe in taking men as our authority or our guide, for they will surely disappoint us. Individually, we are to work out our own salvation with fear and trembling, "for it is God which worketh in you both to will and to do of His good pleasure." We have a high calling in Christ Jesus; we are carrying forward a vast and holy work, and God calls upon each one to uplift His standard in the sight of this world and of the universe of heaven, by the power of the Lord Jehovah, in whom is "everlasting strength."

For further study: *Prophets and Kings,* pages 119-189.

We are to be one with Christ as He is one with the Father, and the Father will love us as He loves His Son. We may have the same help that Christ had, we may have strength for every emergency; for God will be our front guard and our rearward. He will shut us in on every side, and when we are brought before rulers, before the authorities of the earth, we need not meditate beforehand of what we shall say. God will teach us in the day of our need. Now may God help us to come to the feet of Jesus and learn of Him, before we seek to become teachers of others.—*Review and Herald,* Feb. 18, 1890.

The Preciousness of Christ to His Followers

Cooranbong, Australia, May 4, 1896.

I felt sorry when I read your letter breathing so depressed a spirit. Read Ephesians 2:4-22. This scripture has been given me for you. Read it carefully, as you never read it before. It is full of instruction. Christ dwelling in our hearts by faith means the contemplation of Christ, beholding Christ, ever cherishing the dear Saviour as our very best and honored Friend, so that we would not in any action grieve and offend Him. We have always this promise to comfort and help us: "For by grace are ye saved through faith; and that not of yourselves: it is the gift of God."

Bear in mind, the time will never come when the hellish shadow of Satan will not be cast athwart our pathway to obstruct our faith and eclipse the light emanating from the presence of Jesus, the Sun of Righteousness. Our faith must not stagger, but cleave through that shadow. We have an experience that is not to be buried in the darkness of doubt. Our faith is not in feeling, but in truth. The inspired apostle speaks of our being built upon the foundation of the apostles and prophets, Jesus Christ Himself being the Chief Cornerstone. The church of Christ is represented as being builded for "an habitation of God through the Spirit." If we are "rooted and grounded in love," we shall "be able to comprehend with all saints what is the breadth, and length, and depth, and height; and to know the love of Christ, which passeth knowledge." Oh, precious possibilities and encouragement! In the human heart cleansed from all moral impurity dwells

---

Special Testimonies to Ministers and Workers (Series A, No. 9, 1897), pages 75-80.

the precious Saviour, ennobling, sanctifying the whole nature, and making the man a temple for the Holy Spirit.

CHRIST A PERSONAL SAVIOUR

Then is Christ a personal Saviour? We bear about in our body the dying of the Lord Jesus, which is life and salvation and righteousness to us. Wherever we go, there is the recollection of One dear to us. We are abiding in Christ by a living faith. He is abiding in our hearts by our individual appropriating of faith. We have the companionship of the divine presence, and as we realize this presence, our thoughts are brought into captivity to Jesus Christ. Our spiritual exercises are in accordance with the vividness of our sense of this companionship. Enoch walked with God in this way; and Christ is dwelling in our hearts by faith when we will consider what He is to us, and what a work He has wrought out for us in the plan of redemption. We shall be most happy in cultivating a sense of this great gift of God to our world and to us personally.

These thoughts have a controlling power upon the whole character. I want to impress upon your mind that you may have a divine companion with you, if you will, always. "And what agreement hath the temple of God with idols? for ye are the temple of the living God; as God hath said, I will dwell in them, and walk in them; and I will be their God, and they shall be My people." As the mind dwells upon Christ, the character is molded after the divine similitude. The thoughts are pervaded with a sense of His goodness, His love. We contemplate His character, and thus He is in all our thoughts. His love encloses us. If we gaze even a moment upon the sun in its meridian glory, when we turn away our eyes, the image of the sun will appear in everything upon which we look. Thus it is when we behold Jesus; everything we look upon reflects His image, the Sun of Righteousness. We cannot see anything else, or talk of anything else. His image is imprinted upon the eye of the soul and affects every portion of our daily life, softening and subduing our whole nature. By beholding, we are conformed to the divine similitude, even the likeness of Christ. To all with whom we associate we reflect the bright and cheerful beams of His righteousness. We have become transformed in character; for heart, soul, mind, are irradiated by the reflection of Him who loved us and gave Himself for us. Here again there is the realization of a personal, living influence dwelling in our hearts by faith.

ABIDING PRESENCE OF JESUS

When His words of instruction have been received, and have taken possession of us, Jesus is to us an abiding presence, controlling our thoughts and ideas and actions. We are imbued with the instruction of the greatest Teacher the world ever knew. A sense of human accountability and of human influence gives character to our views of life and of daily duties. Jesus Christ is everything to us—the first, the last, the best in everything. Jesus Christ, His Spirit, His character, colors everything; it is the warp and the woof, the very texture of our entire being. The words of Christ are spirit and life. We cannot, then, center our thoughts upon self; it is no more we that live, but Christ that liveth in us, and He is the hope of glory. Self is dead, but Christ is a living Saviour. Continuing to look unto Jesus, we reflect His image to all around us.

We cannot stop to consider our disappointments, or even to talk of them; for a more pleasant picture attracts our sight—the precious love of Jesus. He dwells in us by the word of truth.

What said Christ to the Samaritan woman at Jacob's well? "If thou knewest the gift of God, and who it is that saith to thee, Give Me to drink; thou wouldest have asked of Him, and He would have given thee living water." "Whosoever drinketh of this water shall thirst again: but whosoever drinketh of the water that I shall give him shall never thirst; but the water that I shall give him shall be in him a well of water springing up into everlasting life." The water that Christ referred to was the revelation of His grace in His word; His Spirit, His teaching, is as a satisfying fountain to every soul. Every other source to which they shall resort will prove unsatisfying. But the word of truth is as cool streams, represented as the waters of Lebanon, which are always satisfying. In Christ is fullness of joy forevermore. The desires and pleasures and amusements of the world are never satisfying nor healing to the soul. But Jesus says, "Whoso eateth My flesh, and drinketh My blood, hath eternal life."

Christ's gracious presence in His word is ever speaking to the soul, representing Him as the well of living water to refresh the thirsting soul. It is our privilege to have a living, abiding Saviour. He is the source of spiritual power implanted within us, and His influence will flow forth in words and actions, refreshing all within the sphere of our influence, begetting in them desires and aspirations for strength and purity, for holiness and peace, and for that joy which brings no sorrow with it. This is the result of an indwelling Saviour.

THE INTERCESSION OF CHRIST

Jesus says, "Lo, I am with you alway, even unto the end of the world." He walked once a man on earth, His divinity clothed with humanity, a suffering, tempted man, beset with Satan's devices. He was tempted in all points like as we are, and He knows how to succor those that are tempted. Now He is at the right hand of God, He is in heaven as our advocate, to make intercession for us. We must always take comfort and hope as we think of this. He is thinking of those who are subject to temptations in this world. He thinks of us individually, and knows our every necessity. When tempted, just say, He cares for me, He makes intercession for me, He loves me, He has died for me. I will give myself unreservedly to Him. We grieve the heart of Christ when we go mourning over ourselves as though we were our own savior. No; we must commit the keeping of our souls to God as unto a faithful Creator. He ever lives to make intercession for the tried, tempted ones. Open your heart to the bright beams of the Sun of Righteousness, and let not one breath of doubt, one word of unbelief, escape your lips, lest you sow the seeds of doubt. There are rich blessings for us; let us grasp them by faith. I entreat you to have courage in the Lord. Divine strength is ours; and let us talk courage and strength and faith. Read the third chapter of Ephesians. Practice the instruction given. Bear a living testimony for God under all circumstances.

To God's Workmen 15

A Reproof for Selfishness

Cooranbong, Australia, February 6, 1896.

To My Brethren in America:

The great office work of the Holy Spirit is thus distinctly specified by our Saviour: "And when He is come, He will reprove the world of sin." Christ knew that this announcement was a wonderful trust. He was nearing the close of His ministry upon this earth, and was standing in view of the cross, with a full realization of the load of guilt that must be placed upon Him as the Sin Bearer. Yet His greatest anxiety was for His disciples. He was seeking to find solace for them, and He told them, "Nevertheless I tell you the truth; It is expedient for you that I go away: for if I go not away, the Comforter will not come unto you; but if I depart, I will send Him unto you."

Evil had been accumulating for centuries and could only be restrained and resisted by the mighty power of the Holy Spirit, the Third Person of the Godhead, who would come with no modified energy, but in the fullness of divine power. Another spirit must be met; for the essence of evil was working in all ways, and the submission of man to this satanic captivity was amazing.

SELFISHNESS BECLOUDS JUDGMENT

Today, as in Christ's day, Satan rules the minds of many. Oh, that his terrible, fearful work could be discerned and resisted! Selfishness has perverted principles, selfishness has confused the senses and clouded the

---

The articles in this section are from *Special Testimonies to Ministers and Workers* (Series A, Nos. 9-11, 1897-1898). This article is from No. 10, pp. 25-33.

judgment. It seems so strange that notwithstanding all the light that is shining from God's blessed word, there should be such strange ideas held, such a departure from the spirit and practice of truth. The desire to grasp large wages, with a determination to deprive others of their God-given rights, has its origin in Satan's mind; and by their obedience to his will and way, men place themselves under his banner. Little dependence can be placed on those that have been taken in this snare, unless they are thoroughly converted and renovated; for they have been leavened by wrong principles, which they could not perceive were deleterious in their effect.

Oh, if those in the various fields, in America and all over the world, were working according to the Bible rule, and were striving to uproot selfishness, what a work would be accomplished for the church! But sins which have from time to time been pointed out are lying at the door of many, sins which the Lord regards as of no light character. If men would only give up their spirit of resistance to the Holy Spirit,—the spirit which has long been leavening their religious experience,—God's Spirit would address itself to their hearts. It would convince of sin. What a work! But the Holy Spirit has been insulted, and light has been rejected. Is it possible for those who for years have been so blinded, to see? Is it possible that in this late stage of their resistance their eyes will be anointed? Will the voice of the Spirit of God be distinguished from the deceiving voice of the enemy?

There are men who will soon evidence which banner they are standing under, the banner of the Prince of life, or the banner of the prince of darkness. If they could only see these matters as they are presented to me, if they could see that, as far as their souls are concerned, they are as men standing on the brink of a precipice, ready to slide over to the depths below, I do not think they would stand trembling on the brink another instant, if they had any regard for their salvation.

It is not the will of God that any shall perish, but that all shall have everlasting life. Oh, could I be assured that in the coming conference my brethren would feel a sense of what pure principles mean to them and to all with whom they are associated, my heart would leap with joy! If those that have wandered so far from God and true righteousness would show that the Holy Spirit was striving with them, that they were conscious of their guiltiness in departing from the word of God and acting as blind leaders of the blind, I should have hope. When these do awake from their paralysis, they will be overwhelmed with a sense of lost time,—the Lord's precious talent,—lost opportunities, which were given to them that they might show their appreciation of the infinite compassion of God for fallen man.

A SOUL HUNGER FOR SERVICE

Every soul that accepts Jesus as his personal Saviour will pant for the privilege of serving God and will eagerly seize the opportunity to signalize his gratitude by devoting his abilities to God's service. He will long to show his love for Jesus and for His purchased possession. He will covet toil, hardship, sacrifice. He will think it a privilege to deny self, lift the cross, and follow in Christ's footsteps, thus showing his loyalty and love. His holy and beneficent works will testify to his conversion, and will give to the world the evidence that he is not a spurious, but a true, devoted, Christian.

Men are now earnestly plying every art and trade

in order to satisfy their desire for more gain. If they would use this tact and zeal and careful thoughtfulness in an effort to gain something for the Lord's treasury, how much would be accomplished! When men who are thoroughly selfish accept Christ, they will show that they have a new heart; and instead of grasping all they possibly can obtain to benefit themselves, instead of making little, stunted sacrifices for the Lord, they will cheerfully do all that they can to advance His work. The spirit of grasping, which has been so largely developed, will die, and they will heed the words of Christ, "Sell that ye have, and give alms." They will work as laboriously, with zeal and energy and earnestness, to build up the kingdom of God, as they have worked to obtain riches for themselves.

I tell you the truth. We are far behind our holy religion in our conception of duty. Oh, if those who have been blessed with such grand and solemn truth would arise and shake off the spell that has benumbed their senses and caused them to withhold from God their true service, what would not their well-organized efforts accomplish for the salvation of souls! What a change would be seen in the principles carried out! The world, the flesh, the devil, would not blind men and women as to what constitute pure, sacred, loyal principles.

The word of God appropriated is the preparation for eternal life. But men have placed such an interpretation upon this word that it has been made meaningless. Heart and conscience have become hardened and corrupted. Brethren, in the name of Jesus, I ask, Do you believe the word of God? Are you sons and daughters of God? If you are, it is because you have been converted, and have received Christ into your soul temple, and your minds have been brought under the new law, even the royal law of liberty. Oh, if I could have the joyful news that the will and minds of those in Battle Creek who have stood professedly as leaders, were emancipated from the teachings and slavery of Satan, whose captives they have been for so long, I would be willing to cross the broad Pacific to see your faces once more. But I am not anxious to see you with enfeebled perceptions and clouded minds because you have chosen darkness rather than light.

AWAKENING INFLUENCE OF THE HOLY SPIRIT

The divine Spirit reveals its working on the human heart. When the Holy Spirit operates upon the mind, the human agent will understand the statement made by Christ, "He shall receive of Mine, and shall show it unto you." Subjection to the word of God means the restoration of one's self. Let Christ work by His Holy Spirit, and awaken you as from the dead, and carry your minds along with His. Let Him employ your faculties. He has created your every capability that you may better honor and glorify His name. Consecrate yourself to Him, and all associated with you will see that your energies are inspired of God, that your noblest powers are called into exercise to do God's service. The faculties once used to serve self and advance unworthy principles, once serving as members of unrighteous purposes, will be brought into captivity to Jesus Christ and become one with the will of God.

YOUNG PEOPLE TO BE TRAINED FOR SERVICE

There is a work to be done in the churches. Young men and women must be trained and educated, and then places will be found for them in the work. You are worried and perplexed because Dr. —— is gathering in disproportionately in the medical missionary work, because his work far exceeds the work being done in the churches by the General Conference. What is the matter? It is plain that the light given by God has not been acted upon. Men have supplanted God's plans by their own plans. The prosperity of the medical missionary work is in God's order. This work must be done; the truth must be carried to the highways and the hedges.

A CALL TO REFORM

But the heart of the work, the great center, has been enfeebled by the mismanagement of men who have not kept pace with their Leader.* Satan has diverted their money and their capabilities into wrong channels. Their precious time has been passing into eternity. The earnest work that is now being done, the aggressive warfare that is being carried on, might long ago have been just as vigorously carried forward in obedience to the light of God. The whole body is sick because of mismanagement and miscalculation. The people to whom God has entrusted eternal interests, the depositaries of truth pregnant with eternal results, the keepers of light that is to illuminate the whole world, have lost their bearings. Has God made a mistake? Are those at the heart of the work chosen vessels that can receive the golden oil, which the heavenly messengers, represented as two olive trees, empty into the golden tubes to replenish the lamps? Are those in Battle Creek, the men and women that God has appointed to do the most solemn work ever given to mortals, in partnership with Jesus Christ in His great firm? Are those whom He has bidden to communicate the light from the burning lamps to others, that the regions of dark-

*See Appendix.

ness may have opportunity to hear the saving message, doing their duty? . . .

RESULTS OF SELF-SERVING

Oh, if those who profess to know the truth had the spirit of Christ, the self-sacrificing Redeemer, who gave up His riches, His splendor, His high command, and did all that a God could do to save souls, they would deny self, lift the cross and follow Jesus. How will you who love worldly treasure answer to God in the great day of judgment for your feeble and sleepy efforts to send the truth to regions beyond? The money expended in bicycles and dress and other needless things must be accounted for.* As God's people you should represent Jesus; but Christ is ashamed of the self-indulgent ones. My heart is pained, I can scarcely restrain my feelings, when I think of how easily our people are led away from practical Christian principles to self-pleasing. As yet many of you only partially believe the truth. The Lord Jesus says, "Ye cannot serve God and mammon," and we are to live by every word which proceedeth out of His mouth. How many believe His word?

The Lord abhors your selfish practices, and yet His hand is stretched out still. I urge you for your soul's sake to hear my plea now for those who are missionaries in foreign countries, whose hands are tied by your ways. Satan has been working with all his powers of deception to bring matters to that pass where the way will be hedged up for want of means in the treasury.

Do you realize that every year thousands and thousands and ten times ten thousand souls are perishing, dying in their sins? The plagues and judgments of God are already doing their work, and souls are going to ruin because the light of truth has not been flashed

*See Appendix.

upon their pathway. Do we fully believe that we are to carry the word of God to all the world? Who believes this? "How then shall they call on Him in whom they have not believed? and how shall they believe in Him of whom they have not heard? and how shall they hear without a preacher?" Who has the faith that will enable them to practice this word? Who believes in the light which God has given?

GOD CALLS FOR ACTION

The Lord calls for united action. Well-organized efforts must be made to secure laborers. There are poor, honest, humble souls whom the Lord will put in your place, who have never had the opportunities you have had, and who could not have them because you were not worked by the Holy Spirit. We may be sure that when the Holy Spirit is poured out those who did not receive and appreciate the early rain will not see or understand the value of the latter rain. When we are truly consecrated to God, His love will abide in our hearts by faith, and we will cheerfully do our duty in accordance with the will of God.

But the little interest that has been manifested in the work of God by our churches alarms me. I would ask all who have means to remember that God has entrusted this means to them to be used in the advancement of the work which Christ came to our world to do. The Lord tells every man that in the sight of God he is not the owner of what he possesses, but only a trustee. Not thine, but Mine, saith the Lord. God will call you to account for your stewardship. Whether you have one talent, or two, or five, not a farthing is to be squandered on your own selfish indulgences. Your accountability to Heaven should cause you to fear and tremble. The decisions of the last day turn upon our practical benevolence. Christ acknowledges every act of beneficence as done to Himself.

Zeal for Christ

All who name the name of Christ should work for Him with heart and mind and soul and strength; and *they will work* if they believe the great gospel of truth. The heartiness of their zeal for Christ's sake will testify to the measure of their faith. Self will be swallowed in Christ if they are truly united with Him. "I live," said the great apostle; "yet not I, but Christ liveth in me: and the life which I now live in the flesh I live by the faith of the Son of God, who loved me, and gave Himself for me."

The light given over and over again by the Spirit of God is, Do not colonize.* Enter the large cities, and create an interest among the high and the low. Make it your work to preach the gospel to the poor, but do not stop there. Seek to reach the higher classes also. Study your location with a view to letting your light shine forth to others. This work should have been done long since. Do not make the Sabbath question your first specialty. You must reach the people with practical subjects, upon which all can agree. . . .

God's people have a work to do which is not being done. The last message of mercy must be given to a world perishing in their sins. Those who are connected with our institutions have every facility and opportunity to work for the poor sinners that are out of Christ; but they are dumb. If our churches would only practice

---

Special Testimonies to Ministers and Workers (Series A, No. 10, 1897), pages 33-39.

*See Appendix.

the truth, and show that they believe that Christ came to our world to save sinners, the power of God would attend their labors. But they must keep in touch with the Source of all light and efficiency, and in touch with the world, not to imbibe the spirit of the world, but that they may do the work God has appointed them to do. . . .

MINISTERIAL INSTITUTES

"Go ye into all the world, and preach the gospel to every creature" is Christ's command to His workers.

But this plain declaration has been disregarded. Even though the light has been given again and again, men are called from the fields, where they should have continued working in the love and fear of God, seeking to save the lost, to spend weeks in attending a ministerial institute. There was a time when this work was made necessary, because our own people opposed the work of God by refusing the light of truth on the righteousness of Christ by faith. This they should have received and reechoed with heart and voice and pen, for it is their only efficiency. They should have labored under the Holy Spirit's dictation to give the light to others.

By devoting year after year to ministerial institutes,* fields have been neglected that are white already to harvest. Even the workers have been weakened instead of being strengthened. This has been a mistake. God calls upon His servants to communicate, not to be ever learning and never able to come to a knowledge of the truth.

THE WORK OF THE HOLY SPIRIT

The great object of the advent of the Holy Spirit is distinctly specified by Christ. "When He is come," He

---

*See Appendix.

said, "He will reprove the world of sin, and of righteousness, and of judgment." This light has been kept before our people for years. The power of the Holy Spirit has been largely manifested at Battle Creek, the great heart of the work, to be communicated to those in the highways and hedges, that the mass of human beings under Satan's sway of sin and death might be reformed and renovated by the Spirit's power. But when light has come to those at the center of the work, they have not known how to treat it. The testimonies God has given His people are in harmony with His word.

When Christ spoke these words, He was standing in the shadow of the shameful cross, the symbol of the guilt which made the sacrifice of Christ necessary in order to save the world from complete ruin. Christ looked forward to the time when the Holy Spirit, as His representative, should come to do a wonderful work in and through His merits; and He felt privileged to communicate His relief to His disciples. . . .

Those who have not a living connection with God have not an appreciation of the Holy Spirit's manifestation, and do not distinguish between the sacred and the common. They do not obey God's voice, because, as the Jewish nation, they know not the time of their visitation. There is no help for man, woman, or child who will not hear and obey the voice of duty, for the voice of duty is the voice of God. The eyes, the ears, and the heart will become unimpressible if men and women refuse to give heed to the divine counsel, and choose the way that is best pleasing to themselves.

Oh, how much better it would be if all who do this were connected with some other work than the sacred institutions appointed by God as His great centers! They are supposed to be under the guidance of the

Holy Spirit; but this is a mistake. They do not do the work of God faithfully; they do not give evidence that they realize its sacred character. Their influence misleads others, causing them to regard lightly God's instrumentalities ordained for the saving of souls, and leading them to think that they may bring in their own ideas and common thoughts and plans. Thus a low, cheap level is reached, and God is greatly dishonored.

God would have all who have such an experience ingrained in their religious life choose occupation elsewhere, in laborious, narrow spheres, where eternal interests will not be cheapened by their unconsecrated lives, where there is less room to encounter temptation. Strenuous, flesh-wearing toil may counteract and subdue their evil propensities, and others will not be leavened by their harmful tendencies and traits of character.

NO NEUTRAL GROUND

Those who have any connection with God's work in any of our institutions must have a connection with God, and must be committed to do right under all circumstances, that they may know where they will be found in the day of trial. No one connected with the sacred work of God can remain on neutral ground. If a man is divided, undecided, unsettled, until he is sure that he will lose nothing, he shows that he is a man God cannot use. But many are working in this line. They have not been appointed by God, or else they have decidedly failed to be worked by the mighty agency of the Holy Spirit.

The Lord will use educated men if their supposed knowledge does not lead them to desire to work the Holy Spirit, and to seek to teach the Lord that human policy is better than divine plans, because it accords better with popular opinion. Everyone in God's service is under bonds to stand forth boldly and meet prejudice, opposition, and human passion. They must ever remember that they are God's servants, and in His service.

For further study: *Testimonies,* vol. 6, pp. 89, 90, 137, 138, 442; vol. 8, pp. 28, 29, 36; *The Desire of Ages,* page 409.

God's Messengers

The Lord would have His people divested of everything unscriptural in regard to the ministry. The men called to the ministry should not be made idols of; they should not be looked upon with superstitious reverence; and because of the power vested in them through their office, sin in them should not lose its offensiveness. Their very office makes sin in them more exceedingly sinful, for in committing sin they make themselves the ministers of sin, the agents of Satan, through whom he can work with success to perpetuate sin.

All should bear in mind that Satan's special efforts are directed against the ministry. He knows that it is but a human instrumentality, possessing no grace or holiness of its own. He knows that it is an agent that God has ordained to be a powerful means for the salvation of souls and is efficacious only as God, the eternal Spirit, makes it so. He knows that the treasure of the gospel is in earthen vessels, that it is God's power alone that can make them vessels of honor. They may cultivate the vineyard, a Paul may plant and an Apollos water, but God alone can give the increase.

God has never left His church without a witness. In all the scenes of trial and proving, of opposition and

---

Special Testimonies to Ministers and Workers (Series A, No. 11, 1898), pages 2-13.

persecution amidst moral darkness, through which the church has passed, God has had men of opportunity who have been prepared to take up His work at different stages and carry it forward and upward. Through patriarchs and prophets He revealed His truth to His people. Christ was the teacher of His ancient people as verily as He was when He came to the world clothed in the garments of humanity. Hiding His glory in human form, He often appeared to His people and talked with them "face to face, as a man speaketh unto his friend." He, their invisible Leader, was enshrouded in the pillar of fire and of cloud, and spoke to His people through Moses. The voice of God was heard by the prophets whom He had appointed to a special work and to bear a special message. He sent them to repeat the same words over and over again. He had a message prepared for them that was not after the ways and will of men, and this He put in their mouths and had them proclaim. He assured them the Holy Spirit would give them language and utterance. He who knew the heart would give them words with which to reach the people.

The message might not please those to whom it was sent. They might not wish for anything new, but desire to go right on as they had been doing; but the Lord stirred them up with reproofs; He rebuked their course of action. He infused new life in those who were sleeping at their post of duty, who were not faithful sentinels. He showed them their responsibility, and that they would be held accountable for the safety of the people. They were watchmen who were not to sleep day nor night. They were to discern the enemy, and give the alarm to the people, that everyone might be at his post, that the watching foe might not obtain the least advantage.

RESPONSIBILITIES OF GOD'S WATCHMEN

And today the Lord declares to His watchmen that if they are unfaithful and do not warn the people who are in peril, they will be taken away in their sins. "His blood," He says, "will I require at thine hand." But if His messengers lift up their voices in reproof and warning, to turn men from their wicked ways, and those souls will not hear, then the watchman is clear; the offender against God will be taken in his sins; his blood will be upon his own soul.

These solemn matters are set before me in clear lines. God has appointed apostles, pastors, evangelists, and teachers, for the perfecting of the saints, for the work of the ministry, for the edifying of the body of Christ, till we all come to the unity of the faith. God declares to His people, "Ye are God's husbandry, ye are God's building." There must be a continual advancement. Step by step His followers must make straight paths for their feet, lest that which is lame be turned out of the way. Those who would labor for God must work intelligently to replenish the deficiencies in themselves and glorify the Lord God of Israel by standing in the light, working in the light of the Sun of Righteousness. Thus they will carry the church forward and upward and heavenward, making its separation from the world more and more distinct.

As they assimilate their character to the divine Pattern, men will not guard their own personal dignity. With jealous, sleepless, loving, devoted interest, they will guard the sacred interest of the church from the evil which threatens to dim and cloud the glory that God intends shall shine forth through her. They will see that Satan's devices have no place or countenance in her by encouraging faultfinding, gossiping, evilspeaking, and accusing of the brethren; for those things would weaken and overthrow her.

THE CONTROVERSY WAXES STRONGER

There never will be a time in the history of the church when God's worker can fold his hands and be at ease, saying, "All is peace and safety." Then it is that sudden destruction cometh. Everything may move forward amid apparent prosperity; but Satan is wide-awake, and is studying and counseling with his evil angels another mode of attack where he can be successful. The contest will wax more and more fierce on the part of Satan; for he is moved by a power from beneath. As the work of God's people moves forward with sanctified, resistless energy, planting the standard of Christ's righteousness in the church, moved by a power from the throne of God, the great controversy will wax stronger and stronger, and will become more and more determined. Mind will be arrayed against mind, plans against plans, principles of heavenly origin against principles of Satan. Truth in its varied phases will be in conflict with error in its ever-varying, increasing forms, and which, if possible, will deceive the very elect.

Our work must be an earnest one. We are not to fight as those that beat the air. The ministry, the pulpit, and the press demand men like Caleb, who will do and dare, men whose eyes are single to detect the truth from error, whose ears are consecrated to catch the words from the faithful Watcher. And the Spirit from the throne of God will make itself felt upon a degenerate Christianity, a corrupt world, ready to be consumed by the long-deferred judgments of an offended God.

HATRED OF REPROOF

There is danger now of men's losing sight of the important truths applicable for this period of time, and seeking for those things that are new and strange and entrancing. Many, if reproved by the Spirit of God through His appointed agencies, refuse to receive correction, and a root of bitterness is planted in their hearts against the Lord's servants who carry heavy, disagreeable burdens. There are men who teach the truth, but who are not perfecting their ways before God, who are trying to conceal their defections and encourage an estrangement from God. They have not the moral courage to do the things that it is for their special benefit to do. They see no necessity for reform, and so they reject the words of the Lord and hate him who reproveth at the gate.

This very refusal to heed the admonitions which the Lord sends gives Satan every advantage to make of them the bitterest enemies of those who have told them the truth. They become falsifiers of those who have borne to them the message from the Lord.

The man who rejects the word of the Lord, who endeavors to establish his own way and will, tears to pieces the messenger and message which God sends in order to discover to him his sin. His own inclinations have influenced his conduct, and he has built himself up in a wrong way. The divine rule is, "Whether therefore ye eat, or drink, or whatsoever ye do, do all to the glory of God." But he would not do this. As a man thinketh, so is he. From within, out of the heart, proceed evil thoughts inspired by Satan. He begins to quibble at technicalities and manners. The spirit of Satan links him up with the enemy to bear a word of criticism on less important themes. The truth becomes of less and still less value to him. He becomes an accuser of his brethren, etc., and changes leaders. The outside world has a greater weight with him than has the flood of light that God has poured in upon the world in messages that he has given, and which he once rejoiced in.

Oh, how many things have developed since he became so full of hatred against God because his dangers and wrongs were brought before him! He has allowed wicked thoughts to strengthen and prevail because, day by day, he has not eaten of the flesh and drunk of the blood of the Son of God, because he has not become a partaker of the divine nature. The things which come from within defile the man. How corrupt then must be the source from which these evils have taken their rise!

THE FATAL CHOICE

Unsanctified ministers are arraying themselves against God. They are praising Christ and the god of this world in the same breath. While professedly they receive Christ, they embrace Barabbas, and by their actions say, "Not this Man, but Barabbas." Let all who read these lines, take heed. Satan has made his boast of what he can do. He thinks to dissolve the unity which Christ prayed might exist in His church. He says, "I will go forth and be a lying spirit to deceive those that I can, to criticize, and condemn, and falsify." Let the son of deceit and false witness be entertained by a church that has had great light, great evidence, and that church will discard the message the Lord has sent, and receive the most unreasonable assertions and false suppositions and false theories. Satan laughs at their folly, for he knows what truth is.

Many will stand in our pulpits with the torch of false prophecy in their hands, kindled from the hellish torch of Satan. If doubts and unbelief are cherished, the faithful ministers will be removed from the people who think they know so much. "If thou hadst known," said Christ, "even thou, at least in this thy day, the things which belong unto thy peace! but now they are hid from thine eyes."

THE LIGHT OF TRUTH

Nevertheless, the foundation of God standeth sure. The Lord knoweth them that are His. The sanctified minister must have no guile in his mouth. He must be open as the day, free from every taint of evil. A sanctified ministry and press will be a power in flashing the light of truth on this untoward generation. Light, brethren, more light we need. Blow the trumpet in Zion; sound an alarm in the holy mountain. Gather the host of the Lord, with sanctified hearts, to hear what the Lord will say unto His people; for He has increased light for all who will hear. Let them be armed and equipped, and come up to the battle—to the help of the Lord against the mighty. God Himself will work for Israel. Every lying tongue will be silenced. Angels' hands will overthrow the deceptive schemes that are being formed. The bulwarks of Satan will never triumph. Victory will attend the third angel's message. As the Captain of the Lord's host tore down the walls of Jericho, so will the Lord's commandment-keeping people triumph, and all opposing elements be defeated. Let no soul complain of the servants of God who have come to them with a heaven-sent message. Do not any longer pick flaws in them, saying, "They are too positive; they talk too strongly." They may talk strongly; but is it not needed? God will make the ears of the hearers tingle if they will not heed His voice or His message. He will denounce those who resist the word of God.

MEN OF OPPORTUNITY

Satan has laid every measure possible that nothing shall come among us as a people to reprove and rebuke us, and exhort us to put away our errors. But there is a people who will bear the ark of God. Some will go out from among us who will bear the ark no longer. But these cannot make walls to obstruct the truth; for it will go onward and upward to the end. In the past God has raised up men, and He still has men of opportunity waiting, prepared to do His bidding—men who will go through restrictions which are only as walls daubed with untempered mortar. When God puts His Spirit upon men, they will work. They will proclaim the word of the Lord; they will lift up their voice like a trumpet. The truth will not be diminished or lose its power in their hands. They will show the people their transgressions, and the house of Jacob their sins.

SATAN'S VEHEMENT WORK

The conflict is to wax fiercer and fiercer. Satan will take the field and personate Christ. He will misrepresent, misapply, and pervert everything he possibly can, to deceive, if possible, the very elect. Even in our day there have been and will continue to be entire families who have once rejoiced in the truth, but who will lose faith because of calumnies and falsehoods brought to them in regard to those whom they have loved and with whom they have had sweet counsel. They opened their hearts to the sowing of tares; the tares sprang up among the wheat; they strengthened; the crop of wheat became less and less; and the precious truth lost its power to them. For a time a false zeal accompanied their new theories, which hardened their hearts against the advocates of truth as did the Jews against Christ.

Under the zeal of Satan, some have for a time the appearance of men in a flourishing condition; but it is only for a season. Satan carried them so far that they do despite to the Spirit of God. They spread themselves like a green bay tree. The Lord suffers them for a time. He allows them to manifest their envy and hatred against the people of God, as He has allowed Satan to develop his character, that he might stand before the heavenly universe, before the worlds unfallen, and the fallen world, in his true attributes, as a deceiver, an accuser of the brethren, a murderer at heart.

ERECT BARRIERS AGAINST THE ENEMY

Many who now claim to believe the truth, but who have no anchor, will be bound up with Satan's party. Those who have not worked on God's side of the question will be left to prove a stumbling block to those who have gained a living experience for themselves. Let every minister, in the place of standing to criticize and question, to doubt and oppose, if there is the semblance of a chance to do so, be now employed in erecting barriers against the wily foes. Rather than fight against those whom the Lord has sent to save these, let His people pray fervently and continually for the power of God's grace, and that the Captain of the Lord's host will take the field. Rather than sit in judgment upon men whom God has accepted to do Him service, let the burden of their prayer be, night and day, that the Lord may send forth more laborers into His vineyard. Ministers, do not dishonor your God and grieve His Holy Spirit, by casting reflections on the ways and manners of the men He would choose. God knows the character. He sees the temperament of the men He has chosen. He knows that none but earnest, firm, determined, strong-feeling men will view this work in its vital importance, and will put such firmness and decision into their testimonies that they will make a break against the barriers of Satan.

God gives men counsel and reproof for their good. He has sent His message, telling them what was needed for the time—1897. Did you accept the message? Did you heed the appeal? He gave you opportunity to come up armed and equipped to the help of the Lord. And having done all, He told you to stand. But did you make ready? Did you say, "Here am I; send me"? You sat still and did nothing. You left the word of the Lord to fall unheeded to the ground; and now the Lord has taken men who were boys when you were standing at the forefront of the battle, and has given to them the message and the work which you did not take upon you. Will you be stumbling blocks to them? Will you criticize? Will you say, "They are getting out of their place"? Yet you did not fill the place they are now called to fill.

Oh, why will men be hindrances, when they might be helps? Why will they block the wheels, when they might push with marked success? Why will they rob their own soul of good and deprive others of blessing that might come through them? These rejecters of light will remain barren deserts, where no refreshing, healing waters flow, and their ministrations as barren of moisture as were the hills of Gilboa, where there was neither dew nor rain. They are not clothed with divine unction and convey no blessing to others. They might humble their hearts and confess their wrongs, and break Satan's hold upon them. They might break the fetters which education, prejudice, or habits have forged. Would they only inquire of God, in the spirit of penitence, they would find Him. Then they would not set up their own will, but go where the Spirit of the Lord leads; they would be guided by Him.

GATHER UP THE LIGHTS

The purging and cleansing will surely pass through every church in our land that has had great opportunities and privileges, and has passed them by unheeded. More evidence is not what they want. They need pure and sanctified hearts to gather up and retain all the light that God has given, and then they will walk in that light.

We need not say, "The perils of the last days are soon to come upon us." Already they have come. We need now the sword of the Lord to cut the very soul and marrow of fleshly lusts, appetites, and passions. May it pierce and divide in a far greater degree than it has ever yet done. May all the proud be cast down. May the carnally secure be drawn from the refuge of lies with which they have sought to deceive the people of God. May it cut away their self-righteousness and open the eyes of the blind, that they may see that they are not whole in the sight of God.

I address the people of God who today are holding fast their confidence, who will not depart from the faith once delivered unto the saints, who stand amid the moral darkness of these days of corruption. The word of the Lord to you is: "I will rejoice in Jerusalem, and joy in My people." Can we not here see the paternal love of God expressed to those who hold fast to the faith in righteousness? The closest relationship exists between God and His people. Not only are we objects of His sparing mercy, His pardoning love; we are more than this. The Lord rejoices over His people. He delights in them. He is their surety. He will beautify all who are serving Him with a whole heart with the spirit of holiness. He clothes them with righteousness. He loves those who do His will, who express His image. All who are true and faithful are conformed to the image of His Son. In their mouth is found no guile, for they are without fault before the throne of God.

For further study: *Early Writings,* pages 61-64, "The Messengers."

Our Message

What is the message that we are to give? "Ho, everyone that thirsteth, come ye to the waters, and he that hath no money; come ye, buy, and eat; yea, come, buy wine and milk without money and without price. Wherefore do ye spend money for that which is not bread? and your labor for that which satisfieth not? hearken diligently unto Me, and eat ye that which is good, and let your soul delight itself in fatness. Incline your ear, and come unto Me: hear, and your soul shall live; and I will make an everlasting covenant with you, even the sure mercies of David. Behold, I have given him for a witness to the people, a leader and commander to the people. Behold, thou shalt call a nation that thou knowest not, and nations that knew not thee shall run unto thee because of the Lord thy God, and for the Holy One of Israel; for He hath glorified thee. Seek ye the Lord while He may be found, call ye upon Him while He is near: let the wicked forsake his way, and the unrighteous man his thoughts: and let him return unto the Lord, and He will have mercy upon him; and to our God, for He will abundantly pardon."

To my ministering brethren I would say, Prosecute

Special Testimonies to Ministers and Workers (Series A, No. 11, 1898), pages 18-20.

this work with tact and ability. Set to work the young men and the young women in our churches. Combine the medical missionary work with the proclamation of the third angel's message. Make regular, organized effort to lift the churches out of the dead level into which they have fallen and have remained for years. Send into the churches workers who will set the principles of health reform in their connection with the third angel's message before every family and individual. Encourage all to take a part in work for their fellowmen, and see if the breath of life will not quickly return to these churches.

Study faithfully the thirty-third chapter of Ezekiel. The work which is being done in medical missionary lines is the very work which Christ commanded His followers to do. Can you not clearly see that those who are engaged in this work are fulfilling the Saviour's commission? Can you not see that it would please your Saviour if you would lay aside all false dignity and learn in His school how to wear His yoke and carry His burdens?

SINCERE CHRISTIANITY NEEDED

The world needs evidences of sincere Christianity. Professed Christianity may be seen everywhere; but when the power of God's grace is seen in our churches, the members will work the works of Christ. Natural and hereditary traits of character will be transformed. The indwelling of His Spirit will enable them to reveal Christ's likeness, and in proportion to the purity of their piety will be the success of their work.

There are in our world many Christian workers who have not yet heard the grand and wonderful truths that have come to us. These are doing a good work in accordance with the light which they have, and many of them are more advanced in the knowledge of practical work than are those who have had great light and opportunities.

The indifference which has existed among our ministers in regard to health reform and medical missionary work is surprising. Some who do not profess to be Christians treat these matters with greater reverence than do some of our own people; and unless we arouse, they will go in advance of us.

The word which the Lord has given to me for our ministers and our churches is, "Go forward." "All power is given unto Me in heaven and in earth. Go ye therefore, and teach all nations, baptizing them in the name of the Father, and of the Son, and of the Holy Ghost: teaching them to observe all things whatsoever I have commanded you: and, lo, I am with you alway, even unto the end of the world."

God to Be Sought

Cooranbong, Australia, August 27, 1896.

Piety is needed. Less self-confidence and far more humility must be seen. The work of God has come to be looked upon as a common thing. It would have been much better to have changed the men on boards and committees than to have retained the very same men for years, until they supposed that their propositions were to be adopted without a question; and generally no voice has been lifted in an opposite direction. There are men who sit in council who have not the discernment that they should have. The comprehension is narrow and egotistical. A change is needed. It will not

---

Special Testimonies to Ministers and Workers (Series A, No. 9, 1897), pages 31, 32.

be wise to carry out one half or one quarter of the enterprises which have been planned.

Let each one who sits in council and in committee meetings write in his heart the words: I am working for time and for eternity. I must give an account to God for all the motives which prompt me to action. Let this be his motto. Let the prayer of the psalmist go up to God, "Set a watch, O Lord, before my mouth; keep the door of my lips. Incline not my heart to any evil thing, to practice wicked works with men that work iniquity: and let me not eat of their dainties."

"Give Me Thine Heart"

Adelaide, Australia, October 12, 1896.

Those who are in responsible positions are not to become converted to the self-indulgent, extravagant principles of the world, for they cannot afford it; and if they could, Christlike principles would not allow it. Manifold teaching needs to be given. "Whom shall He teach knowledge? and whom shall He make to understand doctrine? them that are weaned from the milk, and drawn from the breasts. For precept must be upon precept, precept upon precept; line upon line, line upon line; here a little, and there a little." Thus the word of the Lord is patiently to be brought before the children and kept before them, by parents who believe the word of God. "For with stammering lips and another tongue will He speak to this people. To whom He said, This is the rest wherewith ye may cause the weary to rest; and this is the refreshing: yet they would not hear. But the word of the Lord was unto them precept upon

Special Testimonies to Ministers and Workers (Series A, No. 9, 1897), pages 51-59.

precept, precept upon precept; line upon line, line upon line; here a little, and there a little; that they might go, and fall backward, and be broken, and snared, and taken." Why?—because they did not heed the word of the Lord that came unto them.

This means those who have not received instruction, but have cherished their own wisdom, and have chosen to work themselves according to their own ideas. The Lord gives these the test, that they shall either take their position to follow His counsel, or refuse and do according to their own ideas, and then the Lord will leave them to the sure result. In all our ways, in all our service to God, He speaks to us, "Give Me thine heart." It is the submissive, teachable spirit that God wants. That which gives to prayer its excellence is the fact that it is breathed from a loving, obedient heart.

God requires certain things of His people; if they say, I will not give up my heart to do this thing, the Lord lets them go on in their supposed wise judgment without heavenly wisdom, until this scripture [Isaiah 28:13] is fulfilled. You are not to say, I will follow the Lord's guidance up to a certain point that is in harmony with my judgment, and then hold fast to your own ideas, refusing to be molded after the Lord's similitude. Let the question be asked, Is this the will of the Lord? not, Is this the opinion or judgment of ———?

THE LORD'S STANDARD

Everything must be viewed in the light of the example of Christ. He is the truth. He is the true Light that lighteth every man who cometh into the world. Listen to His words, copy His example in self-denial and self-sacrifice, and look to the merits of Christ for the glory in character which He possesses to be bestowed on you. Those who follow Christ live not to please themselves. Human standards are like feeble reeds. The Lord's standard is perfection of character.

"For the Lord shall rise up as in Mount Perazim, He shall be wroth as in the valley of Gibeon, that He may do His work, His strange work; and bring to pass His act, His strange act. Now therefore be ye not mockers, lest your bands be made strong: for I have heard from the Lord God of hosts a consumption, even determined upon the whole earth." Read Deuteronomy 7:6. Read the whole chapter, also chapters 1 and 8. These were presented to me as the words of the Lord. These things are written for our admonition, upon whom the ends of the world are come.

We are to have only those connected with our institutions who will hear the word of the Lord and appreciate and obey His voice. When a man will plead and urge to have his mind and his judgment to be supreme in any one of our institutions, you can have no greater evidence that that man does not know himself and is not qualified to manage. He will make mistakes and injure rather than restore. He does not know what responsibilities are involved in his relation to God or to his fellowmen.

"Seeing then that all these things shall be dissolved, what manner of persons ought ye to be?" Those who walk humbly with God will not be striving to obtain greater responsibilities, but will consider that they have a special work to do, and will be faithful to their duty. In our institutions, great good can be done in educating by precept and example, in economy in all lines. If you, my brother, had learned in the school of Christ to be meek and lowly in heart, you would always stand on vantage ground. You have not an evenly balanced character. You cannot safely put confidence in your own judgment in all things. Man's way is to devise and scheme; God implants a principle. Man is striving to make duty soft and accommodating to his own natural character; but life is a battlefield; life is a race which he has to run if he is victor. . . .

EXCUSES ARE VALUELESS

The question for us to consider is, Have we the attributes of Christ? Excuses are valueless. All circumstances, all appetites and passions, are to be servants to the God-fearing man, not rulers over him. The Christian is not to be enslaved by any hereditary or cultivated habits or tendency. He is to rule the animal passions, rather than to be held in the bondage of habit.

We are not to be the servants of circumstances, but to control circumstances by an inwrought principle learned of the greatest Teacher the world ever knew. The solemn position in which we stand today toward the world, the solemn responsibilities and duties enjoined upon us by our Lord, are not to be ignored until our will and our circumstances are adjusted. The principle of self-denial and self-sacrifice, as revealed in the example of Christ, of John the Baptist, of Daniel and the three worthies, is to pass like a plowshare through hereditary and cultivated habits through all circumstances and surroundings.

I ask you, Is the kingdom of God within you? God's people are to be minutemen, always ready, always composed in Jesus Christ. The time is now come when one moment we may be on solid earth, the next the earth may be heaving beneath our feet. Earthquakes will take place where least expected.

Christianity has a much broader meaning than many have hitherto given it. It is not a creed. It is the word of Him who liveth and abideth forever. It is a living, animating principle, that takes possession of mind, heart, motives, and the entire man. Christianity—oh, that we might experience its operations! It is a vital, personal experience, that elevates and ennobles the whole man. Every man is responsible to God, who has made provision for all to receive this blessing. But many do not receive it, although Christ has purchased it for them at infinite cost. They have not grasped the blessing within their reach, and therefore they have retained their objectionable traits of character, and sin lieth at the door. While they profess piety, Satan has made them his agents to pull down and confuse where he thought best. They exert an influence deleterious to the souls of many who need an example that would help them heavenward.

Who are the subjects of the kingdom of God?—all those who do His will. They have righteousness, peace, and joy in the Holy Ghost. The members of Christ's kingdom are the sons of God, partners in His great firm. The elect of God are a chosen generation, a peculiar people, a holy nation, to show forth the praises of Him who hath called them out of darkness into His marvelous light. They are the salt of the earth, the light of the world. They are living stones, a royal priesthood. They are in copartnership with Jesus Christ. These are they that follow the Lamb whithersoever He goeth. . . .

OUR INDIVIDUALITY

There are rights which belong to every individual. We have an individuality and an identity that is our own. No one can submerge his identity in that of any other. All must act for themselves, according to the dictates of their own conscience. As regards our responsibility and influence, we are amenable to God as deriving our life from Him. This we do not obtain from humanity, but from God only. We are His by creation and by redemption. Our very bodies are not our own, to treat as we please, to cripple by habits that lead to decay, making it impossible to render to God perfect service. Our lives and all our faculties belong to Him. He is caring for us every moment; He keeps the living machinery in action; if we were left to run it for one moment; we should die. We are absolutely dependent upon God.

A great lesson is learned when we understand our relation to God and His relation to us. The words, "Ye are not your own, for ye are bought with a price," should be hung in memory's hall, that we may ever recognize God's right to our talents, our property, our influence, our individual selves. We are to learn how to treat this gift of God, in mind, in soul, in body, that as Christ's purchased possession, we may do Him healthful, savory service.

Sowing Beside All Waters

We must sow beside all waters, keeping our souls in the love of God, working while it is day, and using the means the Lord has given us to do whatever duty comes next. Whatever our hands find to do, we are to do it with cheerfulness; whatever sacrifice we are called upon to make, we are to make it cheerfully. As we sow beside all waters, we shall realize that "he which soweth bountifully shall reap also bountifully."

"Every man according as he purposeth in his heart, so let him give; not grudgingly, or of necessity: for God loveth a cheerful giver. And God is able to make

Special Testimonies to Ministers and Workers (Series A, No. 10, 1897), pages 13-16.

all grace abound toward you; that ye, always having all sufficiency in all things, may abound to every good work." Do not draw back after once the Holy Spirit has awakened in your mind a sense of duty. Act on the suggestion, for it was prompted by the Lord. "If any man draw back, My soul shall have no pleasure in him."

It means much to sow beside all waters; it means a continual imparting of gifts and offerings. God will furnish facilities, so that that faithful steward of His entrusted means shall be supplied with a sufficiency in all things, and be enabled to abound to every good work.

THE PREACHING OF CHRIST

There is a great work to be done. The world will not be converted by the gift of tongues, or by the working of miracles, but by preaching Christ crucified. The Holy Spirit must be allowed to work. God has placed instrumentalities in our hands, and we must use every one of them to do His will and way. As believers we are privileged to act a part in forwarding the truth for this time. As far as possible we are to employ the means and agencies that God has given us to introduce the truth into new localities. Churches must be built to accommodate the people of God, that they may stand as centers of light, shining amid the darkness of the world. . . .

This work God would have us do. Christ's example must be followed by those who claim to be His children. Relieve the physical necessities of your fellowmen, and their gratitude will break down the barriers and enable you to reach their hearts. Consider this matter earnestly. As churches you have had an opportunity to work as laborers together with God. Had you obeyed the word of God, had you entered upon this work, you would have been blessed and encouraged, and would have obtained a rich experience. You would have found yourselves, as the human agencies of God, earnestly advocating a scheme of saving, of restoration, of salvation. This scheme would not be fixed, but progressive, moving on from grace to grace, and from strength to strength.

Christ sought the people where they were and placed before them the great truths in regard to His kingdom. As He went from place to place, He blessed and comforted the suffering and healed the sick. This is our work. God would have us relieve the necessities of the destitute. The reason that the Lord does not manifest His power more decidedly is because there is so little spirituality among those who claim to believe the truth.

Elevate the Standard 16

Clean Hands and Pure Hearts

There is much preaching the truth, but few are sanctified through the truth. Piety and righteousness are not brought into the practical life, and the Lord is dishonored; and, having no vital connection with God, poor, weak human nature has no strength to resist temptation, and never will have till the converting power of God takes hold upon the soul.

We are nearing the judgment, and those who bear the message of warning to the world must have clean hands and pure hearts. They must have a living connection with God. The thoughts must be pure and holy, the soul untainted, the body, soul, and spirit be a pure, clean offering to God, or He will not accept it.

Recent painful developments of evil are one of the greatest evidences we have that the end is near. Satan, like a roaring lion, is going about, seeking whom he may devour; and if men and women, under the blazing light that now shines in this perilous time, will be found fornicators, I am afraid that God will separate them from the work forever.

DECIDED ACTION CALLED FOR

The youth, for misdemeanors of a comparatively light character, are treated with much severity; but when men and women of large experience, who have been considered patterns of piety, are revealed in their true character,—unsanctified, unholy, impure in thought, debased in conduct,—then it is time for such to be dealt with in a decided manner. The greater forbearance that

---

This section is a reprint of the tract, *The Sin of Licentiousness.*

is exercised toward them has only had, as far as my knowledge extends, the influence to cause them to regard their fornication and adultery as a very light matter, and all their pretense has proved to be like morning dew when the sun shines upon it.

No sooner are they placed in temptation than they reveal their moral defects—that they are not partakers of the divine nature, neither have they escaped the corruption that is in the world through lust; but that they are earthly, sensual, devilish. Satan finds in them something that he can work up into marked iniquity, and he improves his opportunity, and the result is, those who claim to be shepherds of the flock are carnally minded, leading the sheep of their care, whose purity, modesty, and virtue they should strictly guard, into licentiousness and lewdness. Angels of heaven are looking on with shame and grief and disgust. How can the pure angels of heaven minister unto this class? How can they bring heavenly light into the assemblies where such ministers are advocating the law of God, but breaking that law whenever a favorable opportunity presents itself; living a lie, pursuing an underhanded course, working in secret, nursing their polluted thoughts and inflaming their passions, and then taking advantage of women or men who are tempted, like themselves, to break down all barriers and debase their bodies and pollute their souls? How can they do this thing? How can they have any fear of God before them? How can they have any love for God in their souls? Of what value is their faith in the truth?

Cleanse the camp of this moral corruption, if it takes the highest men in the highest positions. God will not be trifled with. Fornication is in our ranks;* I know it, for it has been shown me to be strengthening and extending its pollutions. There is much we will

*See Appendix.

never know; but that which is revealed makes the church responsible and guilty unless they show a determined effort to eradicate the evil. Cleanse the camp, for there is an accursed thing in it.

The words of God to Joshua are: "Neither will I be with you anymore, except ye destroy the accursed from among you. Up, sanctify the people, and say, Sanctify yourselves against tomorrow: for thus saith the Lord God of Israel, There is an accursed thing in the midst of thee, O Israel: thou canst not stand before thine enemies, until ye take away the accursed thing from among you." These things are written for our benefit, upon whom the ends of the world are come.

FALSE SHEPHERDS

I have no real ground of hope for those who have stood as shepherds to the flock, and have for years been borne with by the merciful God, following them with reproof, with warnings, with entreaties, but who have hid their evil ways, and continued in them, thus defying the laws of the God of heaven by practicing fornication. We may leave them to work out their own salvation with fear and trembling, after all has been done to reform them; but in no case entrust to them the guardianship of souls. False shepherds! Oh, can it be that the men who have been engaged in this work for a long time will corrupt their ways before the Lord after great experience and special light?

He that is to come says, "Behold, I come quickly; and My reward is with Me, to give every man according as his work shall be." Every good deed done by the people of God as the fruit of their faith, will have its corresponding reward. As one star differeth from another star in glory, so will believers have their different spheres assigned them in the future life. Will the man who did not walk with God as did Enoch, but who walked by the side of Satan, listening to his suggestions, obeying his promptings, imperiling his own soul and souls for whom Christ died, to gratify the carnal mind, giving lenity to sin in his example—will such a man be found among the overcomers?

When a man dies, his influence does not die with him; but it lives on, reproducing itself. The influence of the man who was good and pure and holy lives on after his death, like the glow of the descending sun, casting its glories athwart the heavens, lighting up the mountain peaks long after the sun has sunk behind the hill. So will the works of the pure and the holy and the good reflect their light when they no longer live to speak and act themselves. Their works, their words, their example will forever live. "The righteous shall be in everlasting remembrance."

But what a contrast to this is the life of those who are earthly, sensual, devilish! The sensual pleasure was indulged. In the light of the judgment, the man appears as he is, stripped of the livery of heaven. He stands before others as he is in the sight of a holy God. Let every one of us think seriously whether the works following us will be the mellow light of heaven or the shadows of darkness, and whether the legacies we bequeath are those of blessings or curses.

Every passing hour of the present is shaping our future life. These moments spent in carelessness, in self-pleasing, as if of no value, are deciding our everlasting destinies. The words we utter today will go on echoing when time shall be no more. The deeds done today are transferred to the books of heaven, just as the features are transferred by the artist onto the polished plate. They will determine our destiny for eternity, for bliss or eternal loss and agonizing remorse. Character cannot be changed when Christ comes, nor just as a man is about to die. Character building must be done in this life. We fear that repentance will come to the self-indulgent, tainted soul all too late. A few resolves, a few tears, will never reverse a guilty past life nor blot out of the books of heaven the transgressions, the willful, knowing sins of those who have had the precious light of truth, and can explain the Scriptures to others, while sin and iniquity are drunk up like stolen waters. As though written with an iron pen, they may be found *lead* in the rock forever.

NEED OF ALARM

I would make my brethren alarmed if I could. I would urge upon them with pen and voice, Live in the Lord, walk with God, if you would die in the Lord, and enter by and by where the Lord abideth forever. Be not disobedient to the heavenly warnings; grasp the neglected appeals, the entreaties, the warnings, the rebukes, the threatenings of God, and let them correct your wayward, sinful heart. Let the transforming grace of Christ make you pure, true, holy, and lovely as the pure white lily which opens its blossom on the bosom of the lake. Transfer your love and affections to Him who died for you on Calvary's cross. Train your lips to speak forth His praises, and to offer up your prayers as holy incense.

I ask again, How can any who have the precious, solemn message for this time indulge in impure thoughts and unholy deeds, when they know that He that never slumbers and never sleeps sees every action and reads every thought of the mind? Oh, it is because iniquity is found in God's professed people that He can do so little for them.

TRUTH IN THE HEART SANCTIFIES

The truth, when received into the heart, sanctifies the receiver; kept apart from the life and practice, it is dead and useless to the receiver. How can you, oh, how can you grieve your Redeemer? How can you dishonor Him before His angels and before men? How can you grieve the Holy Spirit of God? How can you crucify the Lord of glory afresh, and put Him to open shame? How can you give occasion for Satan and his angels to exult and triumph over those who claim to be loyal subjects of Jesus Christ?

All fornicators will be outside the City of God. Already God's angels are at work in judgment, and the Spirit of God is gradually leaving the world. The triumph of the church is very near, the reward to be bestowed is almost within our reach, and yet iniquity is found among those who claim to have the full blaze of heaven's light.

He who presides over His church and the destinies of nations is carrying forward the last work to be accomplished for this world. To His angels He gives the commission to execute His judgments. Let the ministers awake, let them take in the situation. The work of judgment begins at the sanctuary. "And, behold, six men came from the way of the higher gate, which lieth toward the north, and every man a slaughter weapon in his hand; and one man among them was clothed with linen, with a writer's inkhorn by his side: and they went in, and stood beside the brazen altar." Read Ezekiel 9:2-7. The command is, "Slay utterly old and young, both maids, and little children, and women: but come not near any man upon whom is the mark; and begin at My sanctuary. Then they began at the ancient men which were before the house." Saith God, "I will recompense their way upon their head."

The words will soon be spoken, "Go your ways, and pour out the vials of the wrath of God upon the earth." One of the ministers of vengeance declares, "And I heard the angel of the waters say, Thou art righteous, O Lord, which art, and wast, and shalt be, because Thou hast judged thus." These heavenly beings, in executing the mandate of God, ask no questions, but do as they are bid. Jehovah of hosts, the Lord God Almighty, the just, the true, and the holy, has given them their work to do. With unswerving fidelity they go forth panoplied in pure white linen, having their breasts girded with golden girdles. And when their task is done, when the last vial of God's wrath is poured out, they return and lay their emptied vials at the feet of the Lord.

And the next scene is recorded, "After these things ... I heard as it were the voice of a great multitude, and as the voice of many waters, and as the voice of mighty thunderings, saying, Alleluia: for the Lord God Omnipotent reigneth." They sing the song of Moses and the song of the Lamb.

KEEP CLOSE TO THE LEADER

We must keep close to our great Leader, or we shall become bewildered, and lose sight of the Providence which presides over the church and the world, and over each individual. There will be profound mysteries in the divine dealings. We may lose the footsteps of God and follow our own bewilderment, and say, Thy judgments are not known; but if the heart is loyal to God everything will be made plain.

There is a day just about to burst upon us when God's mysteries will be seen, and all His ways vindicated; when justice, mercy, and love will be the attributes of His throne. When the earthly warfare is accomplished, and the saints are all gathered home, our first theme will be the song of Moses, the servant of God. The second theme will be the song of the Lamb, the song of grace and redemption. This song will be louder, loftier, and in sublimer strains, echoing and re-echoing through the heavenly courts. Thus the song of God's providence is sung, connecting the varying dispensations; for all is now seen without a veil between the legal, the prophetical, and the gospel. The church history upon the earth and the church redeemed in heaven all center around the cross of Calvary. This is the theme, this is the song,—Christ all and in all,—in anthems of praise resounding through heaven from thousands and ten thousand times ten thousand and an innumerable company of the redeemed host. All unite in this song of Moses and of the Lamb. It is a new song, for it was never before sung in heaven.

Again I ask, In view of the revelation made to John on the Isle of Patmos, which from the opening of the first chapter to the close of the last chapter is light, great light, revealed to us by Jesus Christ, who chose John to be the channel through whom this light was to shine forth to the world—with such wonderful, solemn truths revealed, with such grand truths unfolded before us in the events to transpire just prior to the second appearing of Christ in the clouds of heaven with power and great glory, how can those who claim to see wondrous things out of the law of God, be found in the list of the impure, of the fornicators and adulterers, constantly evading the truth, and secretly working out iniquity? Do you think that they can hide their ways from the Lord? that God seeth not? that God taketh no knowledge?

UNINVITED GUESTS

Belshazzar, while engaged in his sacrilegious feast, was not aware that he had guests he had not invited. The God of heaven heard the praises bestowed upon vessels of gold and silver. He saw the desecration of that which had been dedicated to Him by holy consecration applied to profane and licentious purposes. It is a truth which should make every one of us weep, that those living in these last days, upon whom the ends of the world are come, are far more guilty than was Belshazzar. This is possible in many ways. When men have taken upon themselves the vows of consecration, to devote all their powers to the sacred service of God; when they occupy the position of expositors of Bible truth, and have received the solemn charge; when God and angels are summoned as witnesses to the solemn dedication of soul, body, and spirit to God's service—then shall these men who minister in a most holy office desecrate their God-given powers to unholy purposes? Shall the sacred vessel, whom God is to use for a high and holy work, be dragged from its lofty, controlling sphere to administer to debasing lust? Is not this idol worship of the most degrading kind?—the lips uttering praises and adoring a sinful human being, pouring forth expressions of ravishing tenderness and adulation which belong alone to God—the powers given to God in solemn consecration administering to a harlot; for any woman who will allow the addresses of another man than her husband, who will listen to his advances, and whose ears will be pleased with the outpouring of lavish words of affection, of adoration, of endearment, is an adulteress and a harlot.

No misfortune is so great as to become the worshiper of a false god. No man is in such miserable darkness as he who has lost his way to heaven. It seems that an infatuation is upon him, for he has a false god. To turn this worship of the human, fallen, corrupt beings of earth to the only true object of worship seems a hopeless task. There are in our time continual repetitions of Belshazzar's feast and Belshazzar's worship; and Belshazzar's sin is repeated when the heart, which God requires to be given to Him in pure and holy devotion, is turned away from Him to worship a human being, and the lips are made to utter words of praise and adoration which belong alone to the Lord God of heaven. When the affections God claims to cluster about Him are made to center upon earthly objects,—a woman, a man, or any earthly things,—God is superseded by the object which enchains the senses and affections, and the powers which were solemnly dedicated to God are bestowed upon a human being who is defiled with sin. Men and women who once bore the image of God, but are lost by disobedience and sin, He means to restore again through their becoming partakers of the divine nature, having escaped the corruption which is in the world through lust. And when men and women devote their God-given powers to unholy purposes, to minister to lust, God is dishonored, and the actors are ruined.

When engaged in man-and-woman worship, remember that there is the same witness present as at the feast of Belshazzar. On that occasion, when in the very midst of their revelry, when God was forgotten, when the carnal senses were inflamed, a thrill of terror rushed through every soul. The cup that was being praised and idolized by the king fell from his nerveless hand, and in the language of the Spirit of God, his "countenance was changed, and his thoughts troubled him, so that the joints of his loins were loosed, and his knees smote one against another." A mysterious, bloodless hand was seen tracing characters on the wall. These mysterious fingers belonging to and guided by an unseen power wrote the fully as mysterious characters, which were unintelligible to the awe-stricken revelers. A light like the lightning followed the forming of every letter, and lingered there, making them living characters of awful and terrible significance to all who looked upon them. *"Mene, mene, tekel, upharsin."* Their very ignorance of those letters traced upon the wall, standing there flashing with light, sent terror to their sinful hearts. Their aroused consciences interpreted these letters to be a denunciation against them. Suspicion, fear, and alarm took hold upon king and princes.

Belshazzar, awed by this representation of God's power, showing that they had a witness, though they knew it not, had had great opportunities of knowing the works of the living God, and His power, and of doing His will. He had been privileged with much light. His grandfather, Nebuchadnezzar, had been warned of his danger in forgetting God and glorifying himself. Belshazzar had a knowledge of his banishment from the society of men, and his association with the beasts of the field; and these facts, which ought to have been a lesson to him, he disregarded, as if they had never occurred; and he went on repeating the sins of his grandfather. He dared to commit the crimes which brought God's judgments upon Nebuchadnezzar. He was condemned, not alone that he himself was doing wickedly, but that he had not availed himself of opportunities and capabilities, if cultivated, of being right.

WHY CONDEMNED

God will not condemn any at the judgment because they honestly believed a lie, or conscientiously cherished error; but it will be because they neglected the opportunities of making themselves acquainted with truth. The infidel will be condemned, not because he was an infidel, but because he did not take advantage of the means God has placed within his reach to enable him to become a Christian.

So it will be found in the judgment. God's reproof has been plainly uttered against men and women who have sinned by corrupting their bodies and defiling their souls by licentiousness. They have the warnings to others placed in similar circumstances, who have been overcome by the tempter, and they know that the displeasure of God rested upon them. They have the example of Joseph and Daniel, who feared God. Joseph, when tempted, looked up to heaven, and realized that God's eye was upon him, and he exclaimed, "How can I do this great wickedness, and sin against God?" He also urged his duty to his master, who trusted him so fully, as a reason against it.

God has flashed light upon the pathway of all. Reproofs and warnings and cautions are given to individuals in similar circumstances, and God has expressed condemnation of sin in all its forms. The sin of licentiousness is plainly rebuked and condemned. Men and women will be judged according to the light given them of God. Lessons that have been neglected, become awful judgments. The warnings of God, neglected, from which men turn to a course of their own choosing, will afford no practical lessons of instruction. These warnings will prove their condemnation in the judgment. The only safety for anyone is to turn to a practical account for himself every lesson that is given to another. When the message is given, then his individual duty begins.

SHOW FORTH GOD'S POWER

God calls upon those who claim to be delegated to bear the truth to the world, to show in all places, both high and low, in public life and in the bypaths of private life, that they are in connection with God, that Christianity has done a noble work for them, that they are holier, happier than those who do not acknowledge their allegiance to God's commandments. God demands nothing less of every one of His followers than that they reveal Christ's character to the world in their individual life, and that they bear testimony by precept and example that it is not in vain that Christ has suffered and died, that the image of God might be restored in them through His redeeming grace.

God is represented as weighing all men, their words, their deeds, their motives, that which determines character. "The Lord is a God of knowledge, and by Him actions are weighed." "Men of low degree are vanity, and men of high degree are a lie: to be laid in the balance, they are altogether lighter than vanity." "Thou, most upright, dost weigh the path of the just." "All the ways of a man are clean in his own eyes; but the Lord weigheth the spirits." Important lessons are suggested to us in these scriptures. There is not a thought or motive in the heart that God is not acquainted with. He sees all as clearly as if it stood out registered in living characters, and He weighs individual motives and actions.

GOD MUST HAVE ALL THE HEART

Let our ministers and workers realize that it is not increased light that they need from the pulpit, so much as it is to live out the light they already have. Preaching the solemn truth to the people today, and then falling into the most abominable practices on the morrow, or pursuing a crooked course next week, will not answer. The Searcher of hearts, the One who weighs character, will denounce every unrighteous action at His great tribunal. "Lord, Thou hast searched me, and known me. Thou . . . art acquainted with all my ways." "Thou understandest my thought afar off." Now consider this. There is a witness to all your most secret actions, which you would never do in the presence of men; but because God is unseen by human eyes, you do before Him things which are an abomination in His sight, as though He had no knowledge. Now read the claims of God upon every man and woman: "Thou shalt love the Lord thy God with all thy heart, and with all thy soul, and with all thy strength, and with all thy mind; and thy neighbor as thyself." He will not release one atom of His claim; He will not accept half worship while half the heart is given to some idol. *All* the heart, God requires, *all* the mind. You are not allowed to have the mind diverted from God and centered upon any other object.

WEIGHING OF CHARACTER

God's claim is placed in one scale, and man's character in the other; and by the balances of the heavenly sanctuary every man's doom is fixed for eternity. Look at this, you that have lived carelessly and have regarded sin lightly. For years you have continued without a sense of your responsibility to God—years of selfish indulgence in a forbidden course. Consider the perfect, unchanging character of the law whose claims you have verbally vindicated. The law demands perfect, unswerving obedience. In the latter scale is also placed the sin, the folly, the deception, the unclean thoughts, the unholy actions; and the preponderance or the lightness of the weight determines the weal or woe of individuals; and the inscription is written upon the scale of many, "Thou art weighed in the balances, and art found wanting."

Will those before whom this letter shall come, consider their own individual cases, pass judgment upon no one else, but consider their own character in the light of God's law?

Has your character been transformed? Has darkness been exchanged for light, the love of sin for the love of purity and holiness? Have you been converted, who are engaged in teaching the truth to others? Has there been in you a thorough, radical change? Have you woven Christ into your character? You need not be in uncertainty in this matter. Has the Sun of Righteousness risen and been shining in your soul? If so, you know it; and if you do not know whether you are converted or not, never preach another discourse from the pulpit until you do. How can you lead souls to the fountain of life of which you have not drunk yourself? Are you a sham, or are you really a son of God? Are you serving God, or are you serving idols? Are you transformed by the Spirit of God, or are you yet dead in your trespasses and sins? To be sons of God means more than many dream of, because they have not been converted. Men are weighed in the balance and found wanting when they are living in the practice of any known sin. It is the privilege of every son of God to be a true Christian moment by moment; then he has all heaven enlisted on his side. He has Christ abiding in his heart by faith.

A soul united with Christ, eating His flesh and drinking His blood, in accepting and living by every word that proceedeth out of the mouth of God will war against all transgression and every approach of sin. He becomes every day more like a bright and shining light, and more victorious. He goes on from strength to strength, not from weakness to weakness.

Let no one deceive his own soul in this matter. If you harbor pride, self-esteem, a love for the supremacy, vainglory, unholy ambition, murmuring, discontent, bitterness, evil speaking, lying, deception, slandering, you have not Christ abiding in your heart, and the evidence shows that you have the mind and character of Satan, not of Jesus Christ, who was meek and lowly of heart. You must have a Christian character that will stand. You may have good intentions, good impulses, can speak the truth understandingly, but you are not fit for the kingdom of heaven. Your character has in it base material, which destroys the value of the gold. You have not reached the standard. The impress of the divine is not upon you. The furnace fires would consume you, because you are worthless, counterfeit gold.

There must be thorough conversions among those who claim to believe the truth, or they will fall in the day of trial. God's people must reach a high standard. They must be a holy nation, a peculiar people, a chosen generation—zealous of good works.

SET THE HEART ZIONWARD

Christ has not died for you that you may possess the passions, tastes, and habits of men of the world.

It is difficult to distinguish between those who serve God and those who serve Him not, because there is so little difference in character between believers and unbelievers. Ye cannot serve God and Belial. The sons of God belong to a different nation—the empire of purity and holiness. They are the nobility of heaven. The stamp of God is upon them. So evident and perceptible is this that the enmity of the world is aroused against them by the contrast. I call upon everyone who claims to be a son of God never to forget this great truth, that we need the Spirit of God within us in order to reach heaven, and the work of Christ without us in order to give us a title to the immortal inheritance.

Those who can have such an overpowering, gushing love for human objects, men or women, have an idol which they worship, devoting their heart's affection to it. One of the convincing characteristics of the sons of God is, their conversation, their sympathies, their outflowing love and affection are all in heaven. What is the predominating tone of your feelings, your tastes, your inclinations? Where is the main current of your sympathies, your affections, your conversation, your desires?

No man enters the portals of glory but he who sets his heart thitherward. Then let the questions come home, Do you mind earthly things? Are your thoughts pure? Are you breathing the atmosphere of heaven? Do you carry with you the miasma of pollution? Is your heart loving and worshiping a woman whom you have no right to love? Where is your heart? Where is your treasure? Where is your god? Have you been washing your robes of character, and making them white in the blood of the Lamb; or are you defiling your robes of character with moral pollution? Let the ministers of the gospel apply this to themselves. You are blessed with an understanding of the Scriptures, but is your eye single to the glory of God? Are you earnest and devoted, serving God with purity and in the beauty of holiness? Ask sincerely, Am I a child of God, or am I not?

"Ye are the light of the world." What an impression was produced upon Darius by the conduct of Daniel! Daniel lived a pure and holy life. God was first with him. Whenever real Christianity reigns in the heart, it will be revealed in the character. All will take knowledge of such, that they have been with Jesus. The undivided affections must be given to God.

A THOROUGH REFORMATION NEEDED

We need a thorough reformation in all our churches. The converting power of God must come into the church. Seek the Lord most earnestly, put away your sins, and tarry in Jerusalem till ye be endowed with power from on high. Let God set you apart to the work. Purify your souls by *obeying* the truth. Faith without works is dead. Put not off the day of preparation. Slumber not in a state of unpreparedness, having no oil in your vessels with your lamps. Let none leave their safety for eternity to hang upon a peradventure. Let not the question remain in perilous uncertainty. Ask yourselves earnestly, Am I among the saved, or the unsaved? Shall I stand, or shall I not stand? He only that hath clean hands and a pure heart shall stand in that day.

"Be Ye Clean"

I call upon ministers who have been handling the word of God, "Be ye clean, that bear the vessels of the Lord." I ask the people who have listened to the truths from the pulpit, What are your feelings in anticipation of that great day? In that day you have each an individual, personal interest. Be assured, God will not be mocked with pretensions. Have you the wedding garment on?

We hear now of earthquakes in divers places, of fires, of tempests, of disasters by sea and land, of pestilence, of famine. What weight do these signs have upon you? This is only the beginning of what shall be. The description of the day of God is given through John by the Revelator. The cry of the terror-stricken myriads has fallen upon the ear of John. "The great day of His wrath is come; and who shall be able to stand?" The apostle himself was awed and overwhelmed.

WHAT IS YOUR REFUGE IN THAT DAY?

If such scenes as this are to come, such tremendous judgments on a guilty world, where will be the refuge for God's people? How will they be sheltered until the indignation be overpast? John sees the elements of nature—earthquake, tempest, and political strife—represented as being held by four angels. These winds are under control until God gives the word to let them go. There is the safety of God's church. The angels of God do His bidding, holding back the winds of the earth, that the winds should not blow on the earth, nor on the sea, nor on any tree, until the servants of God should be sealed in their foreheads. The mighty angel is seen ascending from the east (or sunrising). This mightiest of angels has in his hand the seal of the living God, or of

---

From the tract *The Sin of Licentiousness.*

Him who alone can give life, who can inscribe upon the foreheads the mark or inscription, to whom shall be granted immortality, eternal life. It is the voice of this highest angel that had authority to command the four angels to keep in check the four winds until this work was performed, and until he should give the summons to let them loose.

Those that overcome the world, the flesh, and the devil, will be the favored ones who shall receive the seal of the living God. Those whose hands are not clean, whose hearts are not pure, will not have the seal of the living God. Those who are planning sin and acting it will be passed by. Only those who, in their attitude before God, are filling the position of those who are repenting and confessing their sins in the great antitypical day of atonement, will be recognized and marked as worthy of God's protection. The names of those who are steadfastly looking and waiting and watching for the appearing of their Saviour—more earnestly and wishfully than they who wait for the morning—will be numbered with those who are sealed. Those who, while having all the light of truth flashing upon their souls, should have works corresponding to their avowed faith, but are allured by sin, setting up idols in their hearts, corrupting their souls before God, and polluting those who unite with them in sin, will have their names blotted out of the book of life, and be left in midnight darkness, having no oil in their vessels with their lamps. "Unto you that fear My name shall the Sun of Righteousness arise with healing in His wings."

This sealing of the servants of God is the same that was shown to Ezekiel in vision. John also had been a witness of this most startling revelation. He saw the sea and the waves roaring, and men's hearts failing them for fear. He beheld the earth moved, and the mountains carried into the midst of the sea (which is literally taking place), the water thereof roaring and troubled, and the mountains shaking with the swelling thereof. He was shown plagues, pestilence, famine, and death performing their terrible mission.

"ESCAPE FOR THY LIFE"

The same angel who visited Sodom is sounding the note of warning, "Escape for thy life." The bottles of God's wrath cannot be poured out to destroy the wicked and their works until all the people of God have been judged, and the cases of the living as well as the dead are decided. And even after the saints are sealed with the seal of the living God, His elect will have trials individually. Personal afflictions will come; but the furnace is closely watched by an eye that will not suffer the gold to be consumed. The indelible mark of God is upon them. God can plead that His own name is written there. The Lord has shut them in. Their destination is inscribed—"GOD, NEW JERUSALEM." They are God's property, His possession.

Will this seal be put upon the impure in mind, the fornicator, the adulterer, the man who covets his neighbor's wife? Let your souls answer the question, Does my character correspond to the qualifications essential that I may receive a passport to the mansions Christ has prepared for those who are fitted for them? Holiness must be inwrought in our character.

God has shown me that at the very time that the signs of the times are being fulfilled around us, when we hear, as it were, the tread of the hosts of heaven fulfilling their mission, men of intelligence, men in responsible positions, will be putting rotten timbers in their character building—material which is consumable in the day of God, and which will decide them to be unfit to enter the mansions above. They have refused to let go the filthy garments; they have clung to them as if they were of precious value. They will lose heaven and an eternity of bliss on account of them.

BE CONVERTED MEN

I call upon you who minister in sacred things to be converted men before you go forth to act any part in the cause of my Master. Now is your time to seek a preparation and readiness for the fearful test which is before us—that holiness without which no man shall see God. Let none say, My way is hid from the Lord; God taketh no knowledge of my ways. Now it may be it is not too late. Now it may be you can repent. But even if pardon is written against your names, you will sustain terrible loss; for the scars you have made upon your souls will remain.

Oh, how can any who have the light of truth, the great light given them of God, defy the wrath and judgments of God by sinning against Him and doing the very things God has told them in His word not to do? How can they be so blinded by Satan as to dishonor God to His face, and defile their souls by sinning knowingly? Says the apostle, "We are made a spectacle unto the world, and to angels, and to men." Will these sinners—shall I call them hypocrites?—in Zion inquire, In what manner am I a spectacle to the world, to angels, and to men? Answer for yourselves, By my abuse of the light and privileges and mercies God has given me, by unseemly actions which corrupt and defile the soul. Professing to know God, do I put Him out of my thoughts, and substitute an idol? Do I lead other minds to regard sin lightly by my example? Am I a spectacle to the world of moral looseness? Am I a spectacle to angels in indecent actions and moral defilement of the body? The apostle exhorts us: "I beseech you, . . . brethren, by the mercies of God, that ye present your bodies a living sacrifice, holy, acceptable unto God, which is your reasonable service. And be not conformed to this world: but be ye transformed by the renewing of your mind, that ye may prove what is that good, and acceptable, and perfect, will of God." "Having therefore these promises, dearly beloved, let us cleanse ourselves from all filthiness of the flesh and spirit, perfecting holiness in the fear of God."

GOD'S STANDARD

God has a law, and it is the great standard of righteousness. Everyone who has presumed upon the mercy of God, and practiced iniquity, will be judged according to his works. God has warned you to depart from all iniquity. He has commanded you individually to resist the devil, not to entertain him as an honored guest. The time has come when Jerusalem is being searched as with lighted candles. God is at work investigating character, weighing moral worth, and pronouncing decisions on individual cases. It may not be too late for those who have sinned to be zealous and repent; "for godly sorrow worketh repentance to salvation not to be repented of: but the sorrow of the world worketh death." This sorrow is a deceptive kind. It has no real virtue in it. There is no sense of the aggravated character of sin; but there is a sorrow and regret that the sin has come to the knowledge of others; and so no confessions are made, except in acknowledgment of the things thus revealed which cannot be denied.

This is the sorrow of the world, which worketh death, and pacifies the conscience, while the sin is still cherished, and would be carried on just the same if there were an opportunity, and they could not be discovered. "For behold this selfsame thing, that ye sorrowed after a godly sort, what carefulness it wrought in you, yea, what clearing of yourselves, yea, what indignation, yea, what fear, yea, what vehement desire, yea, what zeal, yea, what revenge! In all things ye have approved yourselves to be clear in this matter." Here we can see the duty that rests upon the church to deal with those whose course of action is entirely contrary to the light which they have received. Will the people of God take their stand upon the Bible, or will they be worse than infidels, and give arguments to this class to reproach Christ and the truth, because they do not obey the claims of the gospel in faith and obedience by a circumspect life and a holy character?

Those who claim to have the light of truth have not met the conditions on which the fulfillment of the promises is suspended, neither have they been worthy of the grace of Christ. The character and service of the church are required to be according to the talents received. Her faith and obedience should be equal to the amount which a faithful improvement of her light and opportunities would have gained for her in moral and spiritual elevation.

But many—not a few, but *many*—have been losing their spiritual zeal and consecration, and turning away from the light that has been constantly growing brighter and brighter, and have refused to walk in the truth because its sanctifying power upon the soul was not what they desired. They might have been renewed in holiness and have reached the elevated standard that God's word demands; but condemnation is upon them. Many ministers and many people are in darkness. They have lost sight of the Leader, the Light of the world;

and their guilt is proportionate to the grace and truth opened to their understanding, which has been abundant and powerful.

LIFT UP THE STANDARD

God calls His people to elevate the standard. The church must show their zeal for God in dealing with those who have, while professing great faith, been putting Christ to open shame. They have imperiled the truth. They have been unfaithful sentinels. They have brought reproach and dishonor upon the cause of God. The time has come for earnest and powerful efforts to rid the church of the slime and filth which is tarnishing her purity. The church of Christ is called to be a holy, powerful people, a name and praise in all the earth. There has been opened a fountain for Judah and Jerusalem, to wash from all uncleanness and sin. There is an astonishing backsliding with God's people, to whom has been entrusted sacred, holy truth. Her faith, her service, her works, must be compared to what they would have been if her course had been continually onward and upward, according to grace and holy truth given her.

In this balance of the sanctuary, the individual members of the Christian church will be weighed; and if her moral character and spiritual state do not correspond to the benefits and blessings conferred upon her, she will be found wanting. If the fruit does not appear, then God is not glorified.

"Remember therefore from whence thou art fallen, and repent, and do the first works; or else I will come unto thee quickly, and will remove thy candlestick out of his place, except thou repent."

A knowledge of the state of the backslider from God

seems to be hidden from him. Has the candlestick been removed out of its place? I call upon all who are resting unconcerned in their present state of spiritual deadness, to arouse and arise from the dead, and Christ will give them light. Many rest as content as though the cloud by day and the pillar of fire by night were sheltering and guiding them. Many profess to know God, and yet deny Him in their works. They reckon themselves among God's peculiar, chosen people, who have a special, solemn message entrusted to their keeping to sanctify their lives and to give to the world, and yet the power of the truth is scarcely felt or manifested in our midst in zealous work for God. How great is our darkness, and we know it not! The light has not diminished, but we walk not in its rays.

A FEARFUL DELUSION

What greater delusion can deceive the human mind than that in which individuals flatter themselves that they have the truth, that they are on the only sure foundation, and that God accepts their works because they are actively engaged in some work in the cause of God, when they are sinning against Him by walking contrary to the expressed will of God? They work mechanically, like machinery; but preparation of heart, the sanctification of the character, is wanting. Sacred and holy things are brought down to the level of common things, and a commonness, a cheapness, is working itself into our churches. The service is degenerating into little else than form.

The standard must be elevated. The work must have a higher mold. There must be a coming out from the customs and practices of the world and being separate. There must be a coming up upon a higher platform by both ministers and people. There must be much more of Jesus and His meekness, His lowliness, His humility, His self-denial, His purity, His true goodness and nobility of character, brought into the experience and characters of all who claim to be acting any part in the sacred work of God.

Let God's word be the guide and the rule of life. Let that word, expressing His revealed commands, be obeyed. God summons everyone to put forth all his powers as a responsible being, to do His plainly specified will. If you do this, you will show it. Grappling with your own inherent defects of character, which are at war with spiritual advancement, is proof that you are doing your part of the work.

Let none say a state of feeling is upon them in undue attachments, unlawful love, that they cannot break away from. It is a deception. You cherish the evil; you strengthen it. You love it better than you love truth, purity, righteousness. You do not take hold of divine help, wrenching yourselves from hurtful and dangerous associations. You tamely give yourselves to the working of an evil way, as though you had no free moral agency. Study God's word prayerfully, meet its demands firmly, resolutely, as did Joseph and Daniel. Lay hold upon the help God has promised you.

YOU MUST CHOOSE

Will God compel your obedience, will He compel your will? Never. The Lord has furnished you with capacities, with intelligence, with reason. He has sent from heaven His only-begotten Son to open the way for you, and to place within your reach immortality. What account can you render to God for your weakness, your disobedience, your impurity, your evil thoughts and evil works?

God has appointed means, if we will use them diligently and prayerfully, that no vessel shall be shipwrecked, but outride the tempest and storm, and anchor in the haven of bliss at last. But if we despise and neglect these appointments and privileges, God will not work a miracle to save any of us, and we will be lost as were Judas and Satan.

Do not think that God will work a miracle to save those weak souls who cherish evil, who practice sin; or that some supernatural element will be brought into their lives, lifting them out of self into a higher sphere, where it will be comparatively easy work, without any special effort, any special fighting, without any crucifixion of self; because all who dally on Satan's ground for this to be done will perish with the evildoers. They will be suddenly destroyed, and that without remedy.

HOLINESS NOW

If God has made provision for man to have eternal life, He has means to meet the requirement that man shall practice holiness in this life. All who would evidence that they have a hold on the future life will give practical demonstrations in their life, their character, that they are living in newness of life, in purity and holiness here, following that which is revealed.

The way to heaven has been laid open at infinite cost to the Father and the Son. Are we individually walking in that way, complying with the conditions? Are you in the way? Are you following the Leader, the Light of life?

CHOSEN FOR WHAT?

There is an election of individuals and a people, the only election found in the word of God, where man is elected to be saved. Many have looked at the end, thinking they were surely elected to have heavenly bliss;

but this is not the election the Bible reveals. Man is elected to work out his own salvation with fear and trembling. He is elected to put on the armor, to fight the good fight of faith. He is elected to use the means God has placed within his reach to war against every unholy lust, while Satan is playing the game of life for his soul. He is elected to watch unto prayer, to search the Scriptures, and to avoid entering into temptation. He is elected to have faith continually. He is elected to be obedient to every word that proceedeth out of the mouth of God, that he may be, not a hearer only, but a doer of the word. This is Bible election.

Because great light has been given, because men have, as did the princes of Israel, ascended to the mount and been privileged to have communion with God, and been allowed to dwell in the light of His glory—for these thus favored to think that they can afterward sin, and corrupt their ways before God, and still keep on as though doing God's will, as though God would not mark sin against them because they have been thus honored of God, is a fatal deception. The great light and privileges bestowed require returns of virtue and holiness corresponding with the light given them. Anything short of this, God will not accept.

But these great manifestations by God should never lull to security or carelessness. They should never give license to licentiousness, or cause the recipients to feel that God will not be critical with them, because they think He is dependent on their ability and knowledge to act a part in the great work. All these advantages given by God are His means to throw ardor into the spirit, zeal into effort, and rigor into the carrying out of His holy will.

You, my brethren, fold your hands, and drift into evil practices, and then wait for God to work a miracle to change your characters and compel you to be pure and holy men. Will you expose yourselves wantonly to temptation, expecting God to force your mind and inclinations that you may not be corrupted? Will you take the viper to your bosom, expecting God to put a spell upon it so it will not poison you with its venomous sting? Will you drink poison, expecting God to provide an antidote?

BE GOD'S MEN

While, under God, we are to use means in the saving of our own souls, we are not to depend on what we can do alone, thinking that will be able to save us. While we must work with heart and soul and might, we must do it all in and through Jesus. But truth as it is in Jesus must be brought into the heart and into the life, into the home and into the church. God will use the channels He has provided for the flowing through of His grace.

Oh, that my brethren would be *men* according to God's estimate of men, and take their places in the great web of humanity, realizing that they are a part of God's great whole in creation, in redemption! *Only be men,* and then you make a decided advance in being Christians.

The means is provided, and no one will have any excuse for sin. If you fail of overcoming, there are reasons for this. Ye will not obey God's revealed will; ye will not pray; ye will not strive; ye will not fight evil habits and unholy thoughts. Are ye stronger than God? Can ye, dare ye, contend with the Eternal? If you are not proof against God's judgments, proof against His vengeance, then go on no longer in your own evil ways. Arise and make a stand against Satan. Be doing something, and do it now. Repent now, confess, forsake. A day of fire and storm is about to burst on our world. Conform your life to the simple prescriptions of the word of God. Seek the aid of God's Spirit by prayer, by watching thereunto, and ye will come off more than conquerors through Him who hath loved us. Read 1 John 4:10.

For further study: *Testimonies,* vol. 5, pp. 207-216; *Selected Messages,* b. 2, pp. 376-383.

All the Lord's

The very flesh in which the soul tabernacles and through which it works is the Lord's. We have no right to neglect any part of the living machinery. Every portion of the living organism is the Lord's. The knowledge of our own physical organism should teach us that every member is to do God's service, as an instrument of righteousness.

None but God can subdue the pride of man's heart. We cannot save ourselves. We cannot regenerate ourselves. In the heavenly courts there will be no song sung, To me that loved myself, and washed myself, redeemed myself, unto me be glory and honor, blessing and praise. But this is the keynote of the song that is sung by many here in this world. They do not know what it means to be meek and lowly in heart; and they do not mean to know this, if they can avoid it. The whole gospel is comprised in learning of Christ, His meekness and lowliness.

What is justification by faith? It is the work of God in laying the glory of man in the dust, and doing for man that which it is not in his power to do for himself.—*Special Testimonies to Ministers and Workers* (Series A, No. 9, 1897), pages 61, 62.

Appeal and Warning 17

The World's Need

In this age of boasted enlightenment, the Christian church is confronted with a world lying in midnight darkness, almost wholly given over to idolatry. A well-nigh universal disregard of the law of Jehovah is rapidly making the world like the cities of Sodom and Gomorrah. As in the days before the Flood, violence is filling the land. Gambling and robbery are coming to be common evils. The use of intoxicating liquors is on the increase. Many who have followed their own unsanctified will seek to end their unprofitable lives by suicide. Iniquity and crime of every order are found in the high places of the earth, and those who assent to these wrongs are seeking to shield the guilty ones from punishment. Not one hundredth part of the corruptions that exist is being made plain to the world. Little of the cruelty that is carried on is known. The wickedness of men has almost reached its limit.

In many ways Satan is revealing that he rules the world. He is influencing the hearts of men and corrupting their minds. Men in high places are giving evidence that their thoughts are evil continually. Many are seeking after riches and scruple not to add to their wealth through fraudulent transactions. The Lord is permitting these men to expose one another in their evil deeds. Some of their iniquitous practices are being laid open before the world, that thinking men who still have a desire in their hearts to be honest and just with their fellowmen may understand why God is beginning to

---

Review and Herald, March 31, 1910.

send His judgments on the earth. The Lord will surely punish the world for its iniquity; "the earth also shall disclose her blood, and shall no more cover her slain." . . .

The Lord in compassion is seeking to enlighten the understanding of those who are now groping in the darkness of error. He is delaying His judgments upon an impenitent world, in order that His light bearers may seek and save that which is lost. He is now calling upon His church on the earth to awake from the lethargy that Satan has sought to bring upon them, and fulfill their heaven-appointed work of enlightening the world. His message to His church at this time is, "Arise, shine; for thy light is come, and the glory of the Lord is risen upon thee." To meet the conditions existing at the time when darkness covers the earth, and gross darkness the people, the church of God has been commissioned to cooperate with God in shedding abroad the light of Bible truth. To those who seek to do their part faithfully as bearers of precious light, is given the assurance: "The Lord shall arise upon thee, and His glory shall be seen upon thee. And the Gentiles shall come to thy light, and kings to the brightness of thy rising."

The world today is in crying need of a revelation of Christ Jesus in the person of His saints. God desires that His people shall stand before the world a holy people. Why?—because there is a world to be saved by the light of gospel truth; and as the message of truth that is to call men out of darkness into God's marvelous light is given by the church, the lives of its members, sanctified by the Spirit of truth, are to bear witness to the verity of the messages proclaimed.

God desires His people to place themselves in right

relation to Him, that they may understand what He requires of them above all things else. They are to reveal to every struggling soul in the world what it means "to do justly, and to love mercy, and to walk humbly" with their God. Wherever they are, at home or abroad, they are to be His commandment-keeping people. They are to have the assurance that their sins are forgiven, and that they are accepted as children of the Most High. . . .

SUCCESS ASSURED

The world is in need of the saving truth that God has entrusted to His people. The world will perish unless it be given a knowledge of God through His chosen agencies. In the power of the Holy Spirit, those who are laborers together with God are to labor with unflagging zeal, and shed abroad in the world the light of precious truth. As they enter the highways and the byways, as they labor in the waste places of the earth, at home and in the regions beyond, they will see the salvation of God revealed in a remarkable manner.

God's faithful messengers are to seek to carry forward the Lord's work in His appointed way. They are to place themselves in close connection with the Great Teacher, that they may be daily taught of God. They are to wrestle with God in earnest prayer for a baptism of the Holy Spirit that they may meet the needs of a world perishing in sin. All power is promised those who go forth in faith to proclaim the everlasting gospel. As the servants of God bear to the world a living message fresh from the throne of glory, the light of truth will shine forth as a lamp that burneth, reaching to all parts of the world. Thus the darkness of error and unbelief will be dispelled from the minds of the honest in heart in all lands, who are now seeking after God, "If haply they might feel after Him, and find Him."

Danger in Adopting Worldly Policy in the Work of God

November 3, 1890, while laboring at Salamanca, New York,* as I was in communion with God in the night season, I was taken out of and away from myself to assemblies in different states, where I bore a decided testimony of reproof and warning. In Battle Creek a council of ministers and responsible men from the publishing house and other institutions was convened, and I heard those assembled, in no gentle spirit, advance sentiments and urge measures for adoption that filled me with apprehension and distress.

Years before, I had been called to pass through a similar experience, and the Lord then revealed to me many things of vital importance, and gave me warnings that must be delivered to those in peril. On the night of November 3, these warnings were brought to my mind, and I was commanded to present them before those in responsible offices of trust, and to fail not, nor be discouraged. There were laid out before me some things which I could not comprehend; but the assurance was given me that the Lord would not allow His people to be enshrouded in the fogs of worldly skepticism and infidelity, bound up in bundles with the world; but if they would only hear and follow His voice, rendering obedience to His commandments, He would lead them above the mists of skepticism and un-

Reprint from a testimony published in tract form.

*See Appendix.

belief, and place their feet upon the Rock, where they might breathe the atmosphere of security and triumph.

While engaged in earnest prayer, I was lost to everything around me; the room was filled with light, and I was bearing a message to an assembly that seemed to be the General Conference. I was moved by the Spirit of God to make a most earnest appeal; for I was impressed that great danger was before us at the heart of the work. I had been, and still was, bowed down with distress of mind and body, burdened with the thought that I must bear a message to our people at Battle Creek to warn them against a line of action that would separate God from the publishing house.

REPROOF FOR THE CHURCH

The eyes of the Lord were bent upon the people in sorrow mingled with displeasure, and the words were spoken: "I have somewhat against thee, because thou hast left thy first love. Remember therefore from whence thou art fallen, and repent, and do the first works; or else I will come unto thee quickly, and will remove thy candlestick out of his place, except thou repent."

He who wept over impenitent Israel, noting their ignorance of God and of Christ their Redeemer, looked upon the heart of the work at Battle Creek. Great peril was about the people, but some knew it not. Unbelief and impenitence blinded their eyes, and they trusted to human wisdom in the guidance of the most important interests of the cause of God relating to the publishing work. In the weakness of human judgment, men were gathering into their finite hands the lines of control, while God's will, God's way and counsel, were not sought as indispensable. Men of stubborn, ironlike will, both in and out of the office, were confederating together,* determined to drive certain measures through in accordance with their own judgment.

NEED OF SPIRITUAL DISCERNMENT

I said to them: "You cannot do this. The control of these large interests cannot be vested wholly in those who make it manifest that they have little experience in the things of God, and have not spiritual discernment. The people of God throughout our ranks must not, because of mismanagement on the part of erring men, have their confidence shaken in the important interests at the great heart of the work, which have a decided influence upon our churches in the United States and in foreign lands. If you lay your hand upon the publishing work, this great instrumentality of God, to place your mold and superscription upon it, you will find that it will be dangerous to your own souls, and disastrous to the work of God. It will be as great a sin in the sight of God as was the sin of Uzzah when he put forth his hand to steady the ark. There are those who have entered into other men's labors, and all that God requires of them is to deal justly, to love mercy, and walk humbly with God, to labor conscientiously as men employed by the people to do the work entrusted to their hands. Some have failed to do this, as their works testify. Whatever may be their position, whatever their responsibility, if they have as much authority even as had Ahab they will find that God is above them, that His sovereignty is supreme." . . .

No confederacy should be formed with unbelievers, neither should you call together a certain chosen number who think as you do, and who will say Amen to all that you propose, while others are excluded who you think

*See Appendix.

will not be in harmony. I was shown that there was great danger of doing this.

"For the Lord spake thus to me with a strong hand, and instructed me that I should not walk in the way of this people, saying, Say ye not, A confederacy, to all them to whom this people shall say, A confederacy; neither fear ye their fear, nor be afraid. Sanctify the Lord of hosts Himself; and let Him be your fear, and let Him be your dread. . . . To the law and to the testimony: if they speak not according to this word, it is because there is no light in them." The world is not to be our criterion. Let the Lord work, let the Lord's voice be heard.

NO ALLIANCE WITH UNBELIEVERS

Those employed in any department of the work whereby the world may be transformed, must not enter into alliance with those who know not the truth. The world know not the Father or the Son, and they have no spiritual discernment as to the character of our work, as to what we shall do or shall not do. We must obey the orders that come from above. We are not to hear the counsel or follow the plans suggested by unbelievers. Suggestions made by those who know not the work that God is doing for this time will be such as to weaken the power of the instrumentalities of God. By accepting such suggestions, the counsel of Christ is set at nought. . . .

The eye of the Lord is upon all the work, all the plans, all the imaginings of every mind; He sees beneath the surface of things, discerning the thoughts and intents of the heart. There is not a deed of darkness, not a plan, not an imagination of the heart, not a thought of the mind, but that He reads it as an open book. Every act, every word, every motive, is faithfully chronicled in the records by the great Heart Searcher who said, "I know thy works."

I was shown that the follies of Israel in the days of Samuel will be repeated among the people of God today unless there is greater humility, less confidence in self, and more trust in the Lord God of Israel, the Ruler of the people. It is only as divine power is combined with human effort that the work will abide the test. When men lean no longer on men or on their own judgment, but make God their trust, it will be made manifest in every instance by meekness of spirit, by less talking and much more praying, by the exercise of caution in their plans and movements. Such men will reveal the fact that their dependence is in God, that they have the mind of Christ.

TRUSTING IN MEN

Again and again I have been shown that the people of God in these last days could not be safe in trusting in men, and making flesh their arm. The mighty cleaver of truth has taken them out of the world as rough stones that are to be hewed and squared and polished for the heavenly building. They must be hewed by the prophets with reproof, warning, admonition, and advice, that they may be fashioned after the divine Pattern; this is the specified work of the Comforter, to transform heart and character, that men may keep the way of the Lord. . . .

Since 1845 the dangers of the people of God have from time to time been laid open before me, and I have been shown the perils that would thicken about the remnant in the last days. These perils have been revealed to me down to the present time. Great scenes are soon to open before us. The Lord is coming with power and great glory. And Satan knows that his usurped authority will soon be forever at an end. His last opportunity to gain control of the world is now before him, and he will make most decided efforts to accomplish the destruction of the inhabitants of the earth. Those who believe the truth must be as faithful sentinels on the watchtower, or Satan will suggest specious reasonings to them, and they will give utterance to opinions that will betray sacred, holy trusts. The enmity of Satan against good will be manifested more and more as he brings his forces into activity in his last work of rebellion; and every soul that is not fully surrendered to God, and kept by divine power, will form an alliance with Satan against heaven, and join in battle against the Ruler of the universe.

In a vision given in 1880 I asked, "Where is the security for the people of God in these days of peril?" The answer was, "Jesus maketh intercession for His people, though Satan standeth at His right hand to resist Him." "And the Lord said unto Satan, The Lord rebuke thee, O Satan; even the Lord that hath chosen Jerusalem rebuke thee: is not this a brand plucked out of the fire?" As man's Intercessor and Advocate, Jesus will lead all who are willing to be led, saying, "Follow Me upward, step by step, where the clear light of the Sun of Righteousness shines."

But not all are following the light. Some are moving away from the safe path, which at every step is a path of humility. God has committed to His servants a message for this time; but this message does not in every particular coincide with the ideas of all the leading men, and some criticize the message and the messengers. They dare even to reject the words of reproof sent to them from God through His Holy Spirit.

What reserve power has the Lord with which to

reach those who have cast aside His warnings and reproofs, and have accredited the testimonies of the Spirit of God to no higher source than human wisdom? In the judgment what can you who have done this offer to God as an excuse for turning from the evidences He has given you that God was in the work? "By their fruits ye shall know them." I would not now rehearse before you the evidences given in the past two years of the dealings of God by His chosen servants; but the present evidence of His working is revealed to you, and you are now under obligation to believe. You cannot neglect God's messages of warning, and cannot reject them or treat them lightly, but at the peril of infinite loss.

DEBASING THE SOUL

Caviling, ridicule, and misrepresentation can be indulged in only at the expense of the debasement of your own souls. The use of such weapons does not gain precious victories for you, but rather cheapens the mind and separates the soul from God. Sacred things are brought down to the level of the common, and a condition of things is created that pleases the prince of darkness and grieves away the Spirit of God. Caviling and criticism leave the soul as devoid of the dew of grace as the hills of Gilboa were destitute of rain. Confidence cannot be placed in the judgment of those who indulge in ridicule and misrepresentation. No weight can be attached to their advice or resolutions. You must bear the divine credentials before you make decided movements to shape the working of God's cause.

To accuse and criticize those whom God is using is to accuse and criticize the Lord who has sent them.

All need to cultivate their religious faculties, that they may have a right discernment of religious things. Some have failed to distinguish between pure gold and mere glitter, between the substance and the shadow.

The prejudices and opinions that prevailed at Minneapolis* are not dead by any means; the seeds sown there in some hearts are ready to spring into life and bear a like harvest. The tops have been cut down, but the roots have never been eradicated, and they still bear their unholy fruit to poison the judgment, pervert the perceptions, and blind the understanding of those with whom you connect, in regard to the message and the messengers. When, by thorough confession, you destroy the root of bitterness, you will see light in God's light. Without this thorough work you will never clear your souls. You need to study the word of God with a purpose, not to confirm your own ideas, but to bring them to be trimmed, to be condemned or approved as they are or are not in harmony with the word of God. The Bible should be your constant companion. You should study the testimonies, not to pick out certain sentences to use as you see fit, to strengthen your assertions, while you disregard the plainest statements given to correct your course of action.

TRUE RELIGION SLIGHTED

There has been a departure from God among us, and the zealous work of repentance and return to our first love essential to restoration to God and regeneration of heart has not yet been done. Infidelity has been making its inroads into our ranks; for it is the fashion to depart from Christ, and give place to skepticism. With many the cry of the heart has been, "We will not have this man to reign over us." Baal, Baal, is the

---

*See Appendix.

choice. The religion of many among us will be the religion of apostate Israel, because they love their own way, and forsake the way of the Lord. The true religion, the only religion of the Bible, that teaches forgiveness only through the merits of a crucified and risen Saviour, that advocates righteousness by the faith of the Son of God, has been slighted, spoken against, ridiculed, and rejected.* It has been denounced as leading to enthusiasm and fanaticism. But it is the life of Jesus Christ in the soul, it is the active principle of love imparted by the Holy Spirit, that alone will make the soul fruitful unto good works. The love of Christ is the force and power of every message for God that ever fell from human lips. What kind of a future is before us if we shall fail to come into the unity of the faith?

When we are united in the unity for which Christ prayed, this long controversy that has been kept up through satanic agency will end, and we shall not see men framing plans after the order of the world because they have not spiritual eyesight to discern spiritual things. They now see men as trees walking, and they need the divine touch, that they may see as God sees, and work as Christ worked. Then will Zion's watchmen unitedly sound the trumpet in clearer, louder notes; for they will see the sword coming, and realize the danger in which the people of God are placed.

You will need to make straight paths for your feet, lest the lame be turned out of the way. We are surrounded by the lame and halting in the faith, and you are to help them, not by halting yourselves, but by standing, like men who have been tried and proven, in principle firm as a rock. I know that a work must be done for the people, or many will not be prepared to receive the light of the angel sent down from heaven to

---

*See Appendix.

lighten the whole earth with his glory. Do not think that you will be found as vessels unto honor in the time of the latter rain, to receive the glory of God, if you are lifting up your souls unto vanity, speaking perverse things, in secret cherishing roots of bitterness. The frown of God will certainly be upon every soul who cherishes and nurtures these roots of dissension and possesses a spirit so unlike the spirit of Christ.

As the Spirit of the Lord rested upon me, I seemed to be present in one of your councils. One of your number rose; his manner was very decided and earnest as he held up a paper before you. I could read plainly the heading of the paper; it was the *American Sentinel.** Criticisms were then passed upon the paper and the character of the articles therein published. Those in council pointed to certain passages, declaring that this must be cut out, and that must be changed. Strong words were uttered in criticism of the methods of the paper, and a strong, un-Christlike spirit prevailed. Voices were decided and defiant.

My guide gave me words of warning and reproof to speak to those who took part in this proceeding, who were not slow to utter their accusations and condemnation. In substance this was the reproof given: The Lord has not presided at this council, and there is a spirit of strife among the counselors. The minds and hearts of these men are not under the controlling influence of the Spirit of God. Let the adversaries of our faith be the ones to suggest and develop such plans as you are now discussing. From the world's point of view some of these plans are not objectionable; but they are not to be adopted by those who have had the light of heaven. The light which God has given should be respected, not only for your own safety, but also for

*See Appendix.

the safety of the church of God. The steps now being taken by the few cannot be followed by the remnant people of God. Your course cannot be sustained by the Lord. It is made evident by your course of action that you have laid your plans without the aid of Him who is mighty in counsel; but the Lord will work. Those who have criticized the work of God need to have their eyes anointed, for they have felt mighty in their own strength; but there is One who can bind the arm of the mighty, and bring to nought the counsels of the prudent.

BEAR GOD'S MESSAGE

The message we have to bear is not a message that men need cringe to declare. They are not to seek to cover it, to conceal its origin and purpose. Its advocates must be men who will not hold their peace day nor night. As those who have made solemn vows to God, and who have been commissioned as the messengers of Christ, as stewards of the mysteries of the grace of God, we are under obligation to declare faithfully the whole counsel of God. We are not to make less prominent the special truths that have separated us from the world, and made us what we are; for they are fraught with eternal interests. God has given us light in regard to the things that are now taking place in the last remnant of time, and with pen and voice we are to proclaim the truth to the world, not in a tame, spiritless way, but in demonstration of the Spirit and power of God. The mightiest conflicts are involved in the furtherance of the message, and the results of its promulgation are of moment to both heaven and earth.

The controversy between the two great powers of good and evil is soon to be ended; but to the time of its close there will be continual and sharp contests. We should now purpose, as did Daniel and his fellows in Babylon, that we will be true to principle, come what may. The flaming fiery furnace heated seven times hotter than it was wont to be heated did not cause these faithful servants of God to turn aside from allegiance to the truth. They stood firm in the time of trial and were cast into the furnace, and they were not forsaken of God. The form of the fourth was seen walking with them in the flames, and they came forth not having even the smell of fire upon their garments. . . .

Today the world is full of flatterers and dissemblers; but God forbid that those who claim to be guardians of sacred trusts shall betray the interests of God's cause through the insinuating suggestions and devices of the enemy of all righteousness.

There is no time now to range ourselves on the side of the transgressors of God's law, to see with their eyes, to hear with their ears, and to understand with their perverted senses. We must press together. We must labor to become a unit, to be holy in life and pure in character. Let those who profess to be servants of the living God no longer bow down to the idol of men's opinions, no longer be slaves to any shameful lust, no longer bring a polluted offering to the Lord, a sin-stained soul.

As diligent students, read the word, be doers of the word, and the Holy Spirit will be close by every worker, and the love of God will be kindled in the soul of the one who is ministering, in doing the very work the Lord has appointed to be done in missionary lines.—*Special Testimonies to Ministers and Workers* (Series A, No. 11, 1898), page 31.

The Snares of Satan*

As the people of God approach the perils of the last days, Satan holds earnest consultation with his angels as to the most successful plan of overthrowing their faith. He sees that the popular churches are already lulled to sleep by his deceptive power. By pleasing sophistry and lying wonders he can continue to hold them under his control. Therefore he directs his angels to lay their snares especially for those who are looking for the second advent of Christ and endeavoring to keep all the commandments of God.

Says the great deceiver: "We must watch those who are calling the attention of the people to the Sabbath of Jehovah; they will lead many to see the claims of the law of God; and the same light which reveals the true Sabbath reveals also the ministration of Christ in the heavenly sanctuary, and shows that the last work for man's salvation is now going forward. Hold the minds of the people in darkness till that work is ended, and we shall secure the world and the church also.

"The Sabbath is the great question which is to decide the destiny of souls. We must exalt the sabbath of our creating. We have caused it to be accepted by both worldlings and church members; now the church must be led to unite with the world in its support. We must work by signs and wonders to blind their eyes to the truth, and lead them to lay aside reason and the fear of God and follow custom and tradition.

"I will influence popular ministers to turn the attention of their hearers from the commandments of God. That which the Scriptures declare to be a perfect

---

From the fourth volume of *Spirit of Prophecy*, or *The Great Controversy* (1884), ch. 27, pp. 337-340.

*See Appendix.

law of liberty shall be represented as a yoke of bondage. The people accept their minister's explanations of Scripture and do not investigate for themselves. Therefore, by working through the ministers, I can control the people according to my will.

"But our principal concern is to silence this sect of Sabbath keepers. We must excite popular indignation against them. We will enlist great men and worldly-wise men upon our side, and induce those in authority to carry out our purposes. Then the sabbath which I have set up shall be enforced by laws the most severe and exacting. Those who disregard them shall be driven out from the cities and villages, and made to suffer hunger and privation. When once we have the power, we will show what we can do with those who will not swerve from their allegiance to God. We led the Romish church to inflict imprisonment, torture, and death upon those who refused to yield to her decrees; and now that we are bringing the Protestant churches and the world into harmony with this right arm of our strength, we will finally have a law to exterminate all who will not submit to our authority. When death shall be made the penalty of violating our sabbath, then many who are now ranked with commandment keepers will come over to our side.

"But before proceeding to these extreme measures, we must exert all our wisdom and subtlety to deceive and ensnare those who honor the true Sabbath. We can separate many from Christ by worldliness, lust, and pride. They may think themselves safe because they believe the truth, but indulgence of appetite or the lower passions, which will confuse judgment and destroy discrimination, will cause their fall.

"Go, make the possessors of lands and money drunk

with the cares of this life. Present the world before them in its most attractive light, that they may lay up their treasure here and fix their affections upon earthly things. We must do our utmost to prevent those who labor in God's cause from obtaining means to use against us. Keep the money in our own ranks. The more means they obtain, the more they will injure our kingdom by taking from us our subjects. Make them care more for money than for the upbuilding of Christ's kingdom and the spread of the truths we hate, and we need not fear their influence; for we know that every selfish, covetous person will fall under our power, and will finally be separated from God's people.

"Through those that have a form of godliness but know not the power, we can gain many who would otherwise do us harm. Lovers of pleasure more than lovers of God will be our most effective helpers. Those of this class who are apt and intelligent will serve as decoys to draw others into our snares. Many will not fear their influence, because they profess the same faith. We will thus lead them to conclude that the requirements of Christ are less strict than they once believed, and that by conformity to the world they would exert a greater influence with worldlings. Thus they will separate from Christ; then they will have no strength to resist our power, and erelong they will be ready to ridicule their former zeal and devotion.

"Until the great decisive blow shall be struck, our efforts against commandment keepers must be untiring. We must be present at all their gatherings. In their large meetings especially our cause will suffer much, and we must exercise great vigilance, and employ all our seductive arts to prevent souls from hearing the truth and becoming impressed by it.

"I will have upon the ground, as my agents, men holding false doctrines mingled with just enough truth to deceive souls. I will also have unbelieving ones present who will express doubts in regard to the Lord's messages of warning to His church. Should the people read and believe these admonitions, we could have little hope of overcoming them. But if we can divert their attention from these warnings, they will remain ignorant of our power and cunning, and we shall secure them in our ranks at last. God will not permit His words to be slighted with impunity. If we can keep souls deceived for a time, God's mercy will be withdrawn, and He will give them up to our full control.

"We must cause distraction and division. We must destroy their anxiety for their own souls, and lead them to criticize, to judge, and to accuse and condemn one another, and to cherish selfishness and enmity. For these sins, God banished us from His presence; and all who follow our example will meet a similar fate."

For further study: *The Great Controversy,* ch. 37, pp. 593-602; *Early Writings,* pages 71-73.

Let Heaven Guide

Prophecy must be fulfilled. The Lord says: "Behold, I will send you Elijah the prophet before the coming of the great and dreadful day of the Lord." Somebody is to come in the spirit and power of Elijah,* and when he appears, men may say: "You are too earnest, you do not interpret the Scriptures in the proper way. Let me tell you how to teach your message."

There are many who cannot distinguish between the

---

*See Appendix.

work of God and that of man. I shall tell the truth as God gives it to me, and I say now, If you continue to find fault, to have a spirit of variance, you will never know the truth. Jesus said to His disciples, "I have yet many things to say unto you, but ye cannot bear them now." They were not in a condition to appreciate sacred and eternal things; but Jesus promised to send the Comforter, who would teach them all things, and bring all things to their remembrance, whatsoever He had said unto them.

Brethren, we must not put our dependence in man. "Cease ye from man, whose breath is in his nostrils: for wherein is he to be accounted of?" You must hang your helpless souls upon Jesus. It does not become us to drink from the fountain of the valley when there is a fountain in the mountain. Let us leave the lower streams; let us come to the higher springs. If there is a point of truth that you do not understand, upon which you do not agree, investigate, compare scripture with scripture, sink the shaft of truth down deep into the mine of God's word. You must lay yourselves and your opinions on the altar of God, put away your preconceived ideas, and let the Spirit of heaven guide into all truth.—*Review and Herald,* Feb. 18, 1890.

Vital Principles of Relationship 18

Jehovah Is Our King

God has revealed many things to me which He has bidden me give to His people by pen and voice. Through this message of the Holy Spirit, God's people are given sacred instruction concerning their duty to God and to their fellowmen.

A strange thing has come into our churches. Men who are placed in positions of responsibility that they may be wise helpers to their fellow workers have come to suppose that they were set as kings and rulers in the churches, to say to one brother, Do this; to another, Do that; and to another, Be sure to labor in such and such a way. There have been places where the workers have been told that if they did not follow the instruction of these men of responsibility, their pay from the conference would be withheld.

It is right for the workers to counsel together as brethren; but that man who endeavors to lead his fellow workers to seek his individual counsel and advice regarding the details of their work, and to learn their duty from him, is in a dangerous position and needs to learn what responsibilities are really comprehended in his office. God has appointed no man to be conscience for his fellowman. It is not wise to lay so much responsibility upon an officer that he will feel that he is forced to become a dictator.

A CONSTANT PERIL

For years there has been a growing tendency for men placed in positions of responsibility to lord it over God's heritage, thus removing from church members their

---

From *Special Testimonies,* Series B, No. 10 (1909), pp. 12-20.

keen sense of the need of divine instruction and an appreciation of the privilege to counsel with God regarding their duty. This order of things must be changed. There must be a reform. Men who have not a rich measure of that wisdom which cometh from above should not be called to serve in positions where their influence means so much to church members.

In my earlier experiences in the message, I was called to meet this evil. During my labors in Europe and Australia, and more recently at the San Jose camp meeting in 1905, I had to bear my testimony of warning against it, because souls were being led to look to man for wisdom, instead of looking to God, who is our wisdom, our sanctification, and our righteousness. And now the same message has again been given me, more definite and decisive, because there has been a deeper offense to the Spirit of God.

AN EXALTED PRIVILEGE

God is the Teacher of His people. All who humble their hearts before Him will be taught of God. "If any of you lack wisdom, let him ask of God, that giveth to all men liberally, and upbraideth not; and it shall be given him." The Lord wants every church member to pray earnestly for wisdom, that he may know what the Lord would have him do. It is the privilege of every believer to obtain an individual experience, learning to carry his cares and perplexities to God. It is written, "Draw nigh to God, and He will draw nigh to you."

Through His servant Isaiah, God is calling His church to appreciate her exalted privilege in having the wisdom of the Infinite at her command: "O Zion, that bringest good tidings, get thee up into the high mountain; O Jerusalem, that bringest good tidings, lift up thy voice with strength; lift it up, be not afraid; say unto the cities of Judah, Behold your God! Behold, the Lord God will come with strong hand, and His arm shall rule for Him: behold, His reward is with Him, and His work before Him. He shall feed His flock like a shepherd: He shall gather the lambs with His arm, and carry them in His bosom, and shall gently lead those that are with young.

"Who hath measured the waters in the hollow of His hand, and meted out heaven with the span, and comprehended the dust of the earth in a measure, and weighed the mountains in scales, and the hills in a balance? Who hath directed the Spirit of the Lord, or being His counselor hath taught Him? With whom took He counsel, and who instructed Him, and taught Him in the path of judgment, and taught Him knowledge, and showed to Him the way of understanding? Behold, the nations are as a drop of a bucket, and are counted as the small dust of the balance: behold, He taketh up the isles as a very little thing. And Lebanon is not sufficient to burn, nor the beasts thereof sufficient for a burnt offering. All nations before Him are as nothing; and they are counted to Him less than nothing, and vanity."

"Hast thou not known? hast thou not heard, that the everlasting God, the Lord, the Creator of the ends of the earth, fainteth not, neither is weary? there is no searching of His understanding. He giveth power to the faint; and to them that have no might He increaseth strength. Even the youths shall faint and be weary, and the young men shall utterly fall: but they that wait upon the Lord shall renew their strength; they shall mount up with wings as eagles; they shall run, and not be weary; and they shall walk, and not faint."

In the forty-first to the forty-fifth chapters of Isaiah, God very fully reveals His purpose for His people, and these chapters should be prayerfully studied. God does not here instruct His people to turn away from His wisdom and look to finite man for wisdom. "Remember these, O Jacob and Israel," He declares, "for thou art *My* servant: . . . O Israel, thou shalt not be forgotten of Me. I have blotted out, as a thick cloud, thy transgressions, and, as a cloud, thy sins: return unto Me; for I have redeemed thee. Sing, O ye heavens; for the Lord hath done it: shout, ye lower parts of the earth: break forth into singing, ye mountains, O forest, and every tree therein: for the Lord hath redeemed Jacob, and glorified Himself in Israel."

"Tell ye, and bring them near; yea, let them take counsel together: who hath declared this from ancient time? who hath told it from that time? have not I the Lord? and there is no God else beside Me. . . . *Look unto Me,* and be ye saved, all the ends of the earth: for I am God, and there is none else. I have sworn by Myself, the word is gone out of My mouth in righteousness, and shall not return, That unto Me every knee shall bow, every tongue shall swear. Surely, shall one say, in the Lord have I righteousness and strength: even to Him shall men come; and all that are incensed against Him shall be ashamed. In the Lord shall all the seed of Israel be justified, and shall glory."

EVERY YOKE TO BE BROKEN

I write thus fully, because I have been shown that ministers and people are tempted more and more to trust in finite man for wisdom, and to make flesh their arm. To conference presidents, and men in responsible places, I bear this message: Break the bands and fetters that have been placed upon God's people. To you the word is spoken, "Break every yoke." Unless you cease the work of making man amenable to man, unless you become humble in heart, and yourselves learn the way of the Lord as little children, the Lord will divorce you from His work. We are to treat one another as brethren, as fellow laborers, as men and women who are, with us, seeking for light and understanding of the way of the Lord, and who are jealous for His glory.

God declares, "I will be glorified in My people;" but the self-confident management of men has resulted in putting God aside, and accepting the devisings of men. If you allow this to continue, your faith will soon become extinct. God is in every place, beholding the conduct of the people who profess to represent the principles of His word. He asks that a change be made. He wants His people to be molded and fashioned, not after man's ideas, but after the similitude of God. I entreat of you to search the Scriptures as you have never yet searched them that you may know the way and will of God. Oh, that every soul might be impressed with this message, and put away the wrong!

PAUL'S EXPERIENCE

We would do well to study carefully the first and second chapters of 1 Corinthians. "We preach Christ crucified," the apostle declared, "unto the Jews a stumbling block, and unto the Greeks foolishness; but unto them which are called, both Jews and Greeks, Christ the power of God, and the wisdom of God. Because the foolishness of God is wiser than men; and the weakness of God is stronger than men. For ye see your calling, brethren, how that not many wise men after the flesh, not many mighty, not many noble, are called:

but God hath chosen the foolish things of the world to confound the wise; and God hath chosen the weak things of the world to confound the things which are mighty; and base things of the world, and things which are despised, hath God chosen, yea, and things which are not, to bring to nought things that are: that no flesh should glory in His presence. But of Him are ye in Christ Jesus, who of God is made unto us wisdom, and righteousness, and sanctification, and redemption: that, according as it is written, He that glorieth, let him glory in the Lord." The human being who undertakes to become wisdom for another will find himself coming short.

"I was with you," Paul continues, "in weakness, and in fear, and in much trembling. And my speech and my preaching was not with enticing words of man's wisdom, but in demonstration of the Spirit and of power: that your faith should not stand in the wisdom of men, but in the power of God. Howbeit we speak wisdom among them that are perfect: yet not the wisdom of this world, nor of the princes of this world, that come to nought: but we speak the wisdom of God in a mystery, even the hidden wisdom, which God ordained before the world unto our glory: which none of the princes of this world knew: for had they known it, they would not have crucified the Lord of glory."

TAUGHT BY THE SPIRIT

In the next words the apostle brings to view the true source of wisdom for the believer: "God hath revealed them unto us by His Spirit: for the Spirit searcheth all things, yea, the deep things of God. For what man knoweth the things of a man, save the spirit of man which is in him? even so the things of God knoweth no man, but the Spirit of God. . . . Which things also we speak, not in the words which man's wisdom teacheth, but which the Holy Ghost teacheth; comparing spiritual things with spiritual."

These words mean very much to the soul that is trying to run the race set before him in the gospel. "The natural man receiveth not the things of the Spirit of God: for they are foolishness unto him: neither can he know them, because they are spiritually discerned. But he that is spiritual judgeth all things, yet he himself is judged of no man. For who hath known the mind of the Lord, that he may instruct Him? But we have the mind of Christ."

Read also the third chapter of this book, and study and pray over these words. As a people our faith and practice need to be energized by the Holy Spirit. No ruling power that would compel man to obey the dictates of the finite mind should be exercised. "Cease ye from man, whose breath is in his nostrils," the Lord commands. By turning the minds of men to lean on human wisdom, we place a veil between God and man, so that there is not a seeing of Him who is invisible.

In our individual experience we are to be taught of God. When we seek Him with a sincere heart, we will confess to Him our defects of character; and He has promised to receive all who come to Him in humble dependence. The one who yields to the claims of God will have the abiding presence of Christ, and this companionship will be to him a very precious thing. Taking hold of divine wisdom, he will escape the corruptions that are in the world through lust. Day by day he will learn more fully how to carry his infirmities to the One who has promised to be a very present help in every time of need.

This message is spoken to our churches in every place. In the false experience that has been coming in, a decided influence is at work to exalt human agencies, and to lead some to depend on human judgment, and to follow the control of human minds. This influence is diverting the mind from God. God forbid that any such experience should deepen and grow in our ranks as Seventh-day Adventists. Our petitions are to reach higher than erring man—to God. God does not confine Himself to one place or person. He looks down from heaven upon the children of men; He sees their perplexities, and is acquainted with the circumstances of every experience of life. He understands His own work upon the human heart, and needs not that any man should direct the workings of His Spirit.

"This is the confidence that we have in Him, that, if we ask anything according to His will, He heareth us: and if we know that He hear us, whatsoever we ask, we know that we have the petitions that we desired of Him." God has appointed the angels that do His will to respond to the prayers of the meek of the earth, and to guide His ministers with counsel and judgment. Heavenly agencies are constantly seeking to impart grace and strength and counsel to God's faithful children, that they may act their part in the work of communicating light to the world. The wonderful sacrifice of Christ has made it possible for every man to do a special work. When the worker receives wisdom from the only true source, he will become a pure channel of light and blessing; for he will receive his capability for service in rich currents of grace and light from the throne of God.

Individual Responsibility and Christian Unity

Sanitarium, California, January 16, 1907.

We are living in a time when every true Christian must maintain a living connection with God. The world is flooded with sophistries of the enemy, and we are safe only as we learn lessons of truth from the Great Teacher. The solemn work in which we are engaged demands of us a strong, united effort under divine leadership.

The Lord desires His workers to counsel together, not to move independently. Those who are set as ministers and guides to the people should pray much when they meet together. This will give wonderful help and courage, binding heart to heart and soul to soul, leading every man to unity and peace and strength in his endeavors.

Our strength lies in taking our burdens to the great Burden Bearer. God confers honor on those who come to Him and ask Him for help, in faith believing that they will receive.

Human help is feeble. But we may unite in seeking help and favor from Him who has said, "Ask, and it shall be given you; seek, and ye shall find; knock, and it shall be opened unto you." Divine power is infallible. Then let us come to God, pleading for the guidance of His Holy Spirit. Let our united prayers ascend to the throne of grace. Let our requests be mingled with praise and thanksgiving.

NEED FOR RELIGIOUS EDUCATION

Christ, our Advocate with the Father, knows how to sympathize with every soul. To those who receive Him

From *Special Testimonies,* Series B, No. 9 (1907), pp. 14-36.

as their Saviour, He gives power to become sons and daughters of God. His life of perfect freedom from sin has prepared the way for us; through Him the entrance into the holiest of all is made manifest.

"For God so loved the world, that He gave His only-begotten Son, that whosoever believeth in Him should not perish, but have everlasting life." "He that hath received His testimony hath set to his seal that God is true. For He whom God hath sent speaketh the words of God: for God giveth not the Spirit by measure unto Him. The Father loveth the Son, and hath given all things into His hand. He that believeth on the Son hath everlasting life: and he that believeth not the Son shall not see life; but the wrath of God abideth on him."

A religious education is greatly needed by all who act a part in the work of Jesus Christ. They are to be laborers together with God, engaged in a sacred, solemn work. Each is to have an individual experience in being taught by the Great Teacher, and individual communion with God. There is to be imparted a new life, and that life is to be nourished by the Holy Spirit. When there is a spiritual union with the Lord Jesus, He will move and impress the heart. He will lead, and in the life there will be a growth of fellowship with Christ.

Christ is our only hope. We may look to Him, for He is our Saviour. We may take Him at His word, and make Him our dependence. He knows just the help we need, and we can safely put our trust in Him. If we depend on merely human wisdom to guide us, we shall find ourselves on the losing side. But we may come direct to the Lord Jesus, for He has said: "Come unto Me, all ye that labor and are heavy-laden, and I will give you rest. Take My yoke upon you, and learn of Me; for I am meek and lowly in heart: and ye shall find rest unto your souls." It is our privilege to be taught of Him who said, "Except ye eat the flesh of the Son of man, and drink His blood, ye have no life in you."

We have a divine audience to which to present our requests. Then let nothing prevent us from offering our petitions in the name of Jesus, believing with unwavering faith that God hears us, and that He will answer us. Let us carry our difficulties to God, humbling ourselves before Him. There is a great work to be done; and while it is our privilege to counsel together, we must be very sure, in every matter, to counsel with God, for He will never mislead us. We are not to make flesh our arm. If we do, depending chiefly upon human help, human guidance, unbelief will steal in, and our faith will die.

Frequently I receive letters from individuals telling me of their troubles and perplexities, and asking me to inquire of God as to what is their duty. To those for whom the Lord has given me no light, I have often replied: I have not been appointed by God to do such a work as you ask me to do. The Lord Jesus has invited you to bring your troubles to One who understands every circumstance of your life.

"What things soever ye desire, when ye pray, believe that ye receive them, and ye shall have them. And when ye stand praying, forgive, if ye have aught against any: that your Father also which is in heaven may forgive you your trespasses. But if ye do not forgive, neither will your Father which is in heaven forgive your trespasses."

I shall not dishonor my Lord by encouraging people to come to me for counsel, when they have a standing invitation to go to the One who is able to carry them and all their burdens.

"It is written in the prophets, And they shall be all taught of God. Every man therefore that hath heard, and hath learned of the Father, cometh unto Me. . . . I am the living bread which came down from heaven: if any man eat of this bread, he shall live forever: and the bread that I will give is My flesh, which I will give for the life of the world."

God deals with men as individuals, giving to everyone his work. All are to be taught of God. Through the grace of Christ every soul must work out his own righteousness, maintaining a living connection with the Father and the Son. This is a genuine experience that is of value.

NECESSITY OF HARMONIOUS ACTION

While it is true that the Lord guides individuals, it is also true that He is leading out a people, not a few separate individuals here and there, one believing this thing, another that. Angels of God are doing the work committed to their trust. The third angel is leading out and purifying a people, and they should move with him unitedly.

Those who were in our work at the beginning are passing away. Only a few of the pioneers of the cause now remain among us. Many of the heavy burdens formerly borne by men of long experience are now falling upon younger men.

This transfer of responsibilities to laborers whose experience is more or less limited is attended with some dangers against which we need to guard. The world is filled with strife for the supremacy. The spirit of pulling away from our fellow laborers, the spirit of disorganization, is in the very air we breathe. By some, all efforts to establish order are regarded as dangerous—as a restriction of personal liberty, and hence to be feared as popery. They declare that they will not take any man's say-so; that they are amenable to no man. I have been instructed that it is Satan's special effort to lead men to feel that God is pleased to have them choose their own course, independent of the counsel of their brethren.

Herein lies a grave danger to the prosperity of our work. We must move discreetly, sensibly, in harmony with the judgment of God-fearing counselors; for in this course alone lies our safety and strength. Otherwise God cannot work with us and by us and for us.

Oh, how Satan would rejoice if he could succeed in his efforts to get in among this people and disorganize the work at a time when thorough organization is essential and will be the greatest power to keep out spurious uprisings and to refute claims not endorsed by the word of God! We want to hold the lines evenly, that there shall be no breaking down of the system of organization and order that has been built up by wise, careful labor. License must not be given to disorderly elements that desire to control the work at this time.

UNITY OF EFFORT

Some have advanced the thought that as we near the close of time, every child of God will act independently of any religious organization. But I have been instructed by the Lord that in this work there is no such thing as every man's being independent. The stars of heaven are all under law, each influencing the other to do the will of God, yielding their common obedience to the law that controls their action. And in order that the Lord's work may advance healthfully and solidly, His people must draw together.

The spasmodic, fitful movements of some who claim to be Christians is well represented by the work of strong but untrained horses. When one pulls forward, another pulls back; and at the voice of their master, one plunges ahead, and the other stands immovable. If men will not move in concert in the great and grand work for this time, there will be confusion. It is not a good sign when men refuse to unite with their brethren and prefer to act alone. Instead of isolating themselves, let them draw in harmony with their fellow laborers. Unless they do this, their activity will work at the wrong time and in the wrong way. They will often work counter to that which God would have done, and thus their labor is worse than wasted.

MEN TO BE COUNSELORS, NOT RULERS

"Wait on the Lord: be of good courage, and He shall strengthen thine heart." Let us each wait on the Lord, and He will teach us how to labor. He will reveal to us the work that we are best adapted to perform. This will not lead men to start out in an independent spirit, to promulgate new theories. In this time when Satan is seeking to make void the law of God through the exaltation of false science, we need to guard most carefully against everything that would tend to lessen our faith and scatter our forces. As laborers together with God, we should be in harmony with the truth, and with our brethren. There should be counsel and cooperation.

Even in the midst of the great deceptions of the last days, when delusive miracles will be performed in the sight of men in behalf of satanic theories, it is our privilege to hide ourselves in Christ Jesus. It is possible for us to seek and to obtain salvation. And in this time of unusual peril, we must learn to stand alone, our faith fixed, not on the word of man, but on the sure promises of God.

Among all God's workers there should be a spirit of unity and harmony. The Lord has especially blessed some with an experience that has fitted them to be wise counselors. In our several callings there is to be a mutual dependence on one another for assistance. Of this, Peter says:

"Likewise, ye younger, submit yourselves unto the elder. Yea, all of you be subject one to another, and be clothed with humility: for God resisteth the proud, and giveth grace to the humble."

But this does not authorize any one man to undertake the work of ordering his brethren arbitrarily to do as he thinks advisable, irrespective of their own personal convictions of duty. Nor are God's chosen laborers to feel that at every step they must wait to ask some officer in authority whether they may do this or that. While cooperating heartily with their brethren in carrying out general plans that have been laid for the prosecution of the work, they are constantly to look to the God of Israel for personal guidance.

Sometimes a man who has been placed in responsibility as a leader gains the idea that he is in a position of supreme authority, and that all his brethren, before making advance moves, must first come to him for permission to do that which they feel should be done. Such a man is in a dangerous position. He has lost sight of the work of a true leader among God's people. Instead of acting as a wise counselor, he assumes the prerogatives of an exacting ruler. God is dishonored by every such display of authority and self-exaltation. No man standing in his own strength is ever to be mind and judgment for another man whom the Lord is using in His work. No one is to lay down man-made rules and regulations to govern arbitrarily his fellow laborers who have a living experience in the truth.

God calls upon those who have exercised undue authority to take off from His workers every dominating hand. Let everyone to whom has been entrusted sacred responsibilities seek to understand his individual duty before God, and do that duty humbly and faithfully. Let no one regard himself as a master, with controlling power to exercise over his brethren. The principles of the word of God are to be taught and practiced.

AMENABLE TO GOD

While respecting authority and laboring in accordance with wisely laid plans, every worker is amenable to the Great Teacher for the proper exercise of his God-given judgment and of his right to look to the God of heaven for wisdom and guidance. God is Commander and Ruler over all. We have a personal Saviour, and we are not to exchange His word for the word of any man. In the Scriptures the Lord has given instruction for every worker. The words of the Master Worker should be diligently studied; for they are spirit and life. Laborers who are striving to work in harmony with this instruction are under the leadership and guidance of the Holy Spirit, and need not always, before they make any advance move, first ask permission of someone else. No precise lines are to be laid down. Let the Holy Spirit direct the workers. As they keep looking unto Jesus, the Author and Finisher of their faith, the gifts of grace will increase by wise use.

God desires that we shall come into right relation with Him. He desires that every voice shall be sanctified. He wants all there is of us—soul, body, and spirit—to be fully sanctified to do His will. It is time that we begin to know that we are fastened to the Lord Jesus

Christ by a living, working faith; it is time for us to lay hold of the help proffered by the Spirit of God, and let our words reveal that we are under divine control. Let us believe in God, and trust in Him; and we shall see His mighty power working among us.

In 1895 I wrote to my brethren in the ministry, as follows:

"I must speak to my brethren nigh and afar off. I cannot hold my peace. They are not working on correct principles. Those who stand in responsible positions must not feel that their position of importance makes them men of infallible judgment.

"All the works of men are under the Lord's jurisdiction. It will be altogether safe for men to consider that there is knowledge with the Most High. Those who trust in God and His wisdom, and not in their own, are walking in safe paths. They will never feel that they are authorized to muzzle even the ox that treads out the grain; and how offensive it is for men to control the human agent who is in partnership with God, and whom the Lord Jesus has invited: 'Come unto Me, all ye that labor and are heavy-laden, and I will give you rest. Take My yoke upon you, and learn of Me; for I am meek and lowly in heart: and ye shall find rest unto your souls. For My yoke is easy, and My burden is light.' 'We are laborers together with God: ye are God's husbandry, ye are God's building.'

"The Lord has not placed any one of His human agencies under the dictation and control of those who are themselves but erring mortals. He has not placed upon men the power to say, You shall do this, and you shall not do that. . . .

"No man is a proper judge of another man's duty. Man is responsible to God; and as finite, erring men take into their hands the jurisdiction of their fellowmen, as if the Lord commissioned them to lift up and cast down, all heaven is filled with indignation. There are strange principles being established in regard to the control of the minds and works of men, by human judges, as though these finite men were gods. . . .

"Organizations, institutions, unless kept by the power of God, will work under Satan's dictation to bring men under the control of men; and fraud and guile will bear the semblance of zeal for truth, and for the advancement of the kingdom of God. . . .

"God will not vindicate any device whereby man shall in the slightest degree rule or oppress his fellowmen. The only hope for fallen man is to look to Jesus, and receive Him as the only Saviour. As soon as a man begins to make an iron rule for other men, as soon as he begins to harness up and drive men according to his own mind, he dishonors God, and imperils his own soul and the souls of his brethren. Sinful man can find hope and righteousness only in God; and no human being is righteous any longer than he has faith in God and maintains a vital connection with Him. A flower of the field must have its root in the soil; it must have air, dew, showers, and sunshine. It will flourish only as it receives these advantages, and all are from God. So with men. We receive from God that which ministers to the life of the soul. We are warned not to trust in man, nor to make flesh our arm."

The foregoing was printed in *Special Testimonies to Ministers and Workers* (Series A, No. 9, 1897).

In 1903, I wrote to the president of a conference:

"By means of one agency, Christ Jesus, God has mysteriously linked all men together. To every man He has assigned some special line of service; and we should be quick to comprehend that we are to guard against leaving the work given us in order that we may interfere with other human agencies who are doing a work not precisely the same as our own. To no man has been assigned the work of interfering with the work of one of his fellow laborers, trying to take it in hand himself; for he would so handle it that he would spoil it. To one God gives a work different from the work that He gives another.

"Let us all remember that we are not dealing with ideal men, but with real men of God's appointment, men precisely like ourselves, men who fall into the same errors that we do, men of like ambitions and infirmities. No man has been made a master, to rule the mind and conscience of a fellow being. Let us be very careful how we deal with God's blood-bought heritage.

"To no man has been appointed the work of being a ruler over his fellowmen. Every man is to bear his own burden. He may speak words of encouragement, faith, and hope to his fellow workers; he may help them to bear their special burdens by suggesting to them improved methods of labor; but in no case is he to discourage and enfeeble them, lest the enemy shall obtain an advantage over their minds—an advantage that in time would react upon himself.

"By the cords of tender love and sympathy the Lord linked all men to Himself. Of us He says, Ye 'are laborers together with God: ye are God's husbandry, ye are God's building.' This relationship we should recognize. If we are bound up with Christ, we shall constantly manifest Christlike sympathy and forbearance toward those who are striving with all their God-given ability to bear their burdens, even as we endeavor to bear our appointed burdens.

"In our several callings there is to be a mutual dependence on one another for assistance. A spirit of authority is not to be exercised, even by the president of a conference; for position does not change a man into a creature that cannot err. Every laborer entrusted with the management of a conference is to work as Christ worked, wearing His yoke and learning of Him His meekness and lowliness. A conference president's spirit and demeanor in word and in deed reveal whether he realizes his weakness and places his dependence on God, or whether he thinks that his position of influence has given him superior wisdom. If he loves and fears God, if he realizes the value of souls, if he appreciates every jot of the help that the Lord has qualified a brother worker to render, he will be able to bind heart to heart by the love that Christ revealed during His ministry. He will speak words of comfort to the sick and the sorrowing.

"If he does not cultivate a masterly manner, but bears in mind always that One is his Master, even Christ, he can counsel the inexperienced, encouraging them to be God's helping hand.

"The feeble hands are not to be deterred from doing something for the Master. Those whose knees are weak are not to be caused to stumble. God desires us to encourage those whose hands are weak, to grasp more firmly the hand of Christ, and to work hopefully. Every hand should be outstretched to help the hand that is doing something for the Master. The time may come when the hands that have upheld the feeble hands of another may, in turn, be upheld by the hands to whom they ministered. God has so ordered matters that no man is absolutely independent of his fellowmen."

COUNSEL TO MEN IN OFFICIAL POSITIONS

Among God's people are some who have had long experience in His work, men who have not departed from the faith. Notwithstanding the great trials through which they have passed, they have remained faithful. These men should be regarded as tried and chosen counselors. They should be respected, and their judgment should be honored by those who are younger or who have had less experience, even though these younger men may be in official positions.

We are engaged in a great work, and there are many opportunities for service in various lines. Let all pray earnestly that God may guide them into the right channels of service. God's workmen should not neglect any opportunity to help others in every possible way. If they seek God unselfishly for counsel, His word, which bringeth salvation, will lead them. They will engage in labor on the right hand and on the left, doing their best to remove from the minds of others every doubt and every difficulty in understanding the truth. The Spirit of God will make their labors effectual.

The Lord calls for minutemen, men who will be prepared to speak words in season and out of season that will arrest the attention and convict the heart. The kingdom of God consisteth not in outward show. Light will not be received by following selfish plans, but by looking unto Jesus, following Christ's leadings, not the suppositions of men. The kingdom of God is righteousness and peace and joy in the Holy Ghost.

It often happens that circumstances arise which demand prompt action. And sometimes precious opportunities have been lost because of delay. The one who should have acted promptly felt that he must first consult with someone who was far away and who was unacquainted with the true conditions. Much time has thus been lost in asking advice and counsel from men who were not in a position to give wise counsel. Let all God's workers be guided by the word of truth which points out their duty, following implicitly the directions Christ has given.

In 1883, I said to our brethren assembled in General Conference:

"Satan exults when men look to and trust in man. The one who is the object of this undue confidence is exposed to strong temptations. Satan will, if possible, lead him to self-confidence, in order that human defects may mar the work. He will be in danger of encouraging his brethren in their dependence upon him, and feeling that all things that pertain to the movements of the cause must be brought to his notice. Thus the work will bear the impress of man instead of the impress of God. But if all will learn to depend upon God for themselves, many dangers that assail the one who stands at the head of the work will be averted. If he errs, if he permits human influence to sway his judgment, or yields to temptation, he can be corrected and helped by his brethren. And those who learn to go to God for themselves for help and counsel are learning lessons that will be of the highest value to them.

"But if the officers of a conference bear successfully the burdens laid upon them, they must pray, they must believe, they must trust God to use them as His agents in keeping the churches of the conference in good working order. This is their part of the vineyard to cultivate. There must be far more personal responsibility, far more thinking and planning, far more mental power brought into the labor put forth for the Master. This would enlarge the capacity of the mind, and give keener perceptions as to what to do and how. Brethren, you will have to wrestle with difficulties, carry burdens, give advice, plan and execute, constantly looking to God for help. Pray and labor, labor and pray; as pupils in the school of Christ, learn of Jesus.

"The Lord has given us the promise, 'If any of you lack wisdom, let him ask of God, that giveth to all men liberally, and upbraideth not; and it shall be given him.' It is in the order of God that those who bear responsibilities should often meet together to counsel with one another, and to pray earnestly for that wisdom which He alone can impart. Unitedly make known your troubles to God. Talk less; much precious time is lost in talk that brings no light. Let brethren unite in fasting and prayer for the wisdom that God has promised to supply liberally.

"Go to God and tell Him as did Moses, 'I cannot lead this people unless Thy presence shall go with me.' And then ask still more; pray with Moses, 'Show me Thy glory.' What is this glory?—the character of God. That is what He proclaimed to Moses. Let the soul, in living faith, fasten upon God. Let the tongue speak His praise. When you associate together, let the mind be reverently turned to the contemplation of eternal realities. Thus you will be helping one another to be spiritually minded. When your will is in harmony with the divine will, you will be in harmony with one another; you will have Christ by your side as a counselor."—*Gospel Workers,* old edition, pages 235-237.

UNSANCTIFIED INDEPENDENCE

The Lord has not qualified any one of us to bear the burden of the work alone. He has associated together men of different minds, that they may counsel with and assist one another. In this way the deficiency in the experience and abilities of one is supplied by the experience and abilities of another. We should all study carefully the instruction given in Corinthians and Ephesians regarding our relation to one another as members of the body of Christ.

In our work we must consider the relation that each worker sustains to the other workers connected with the cause of God. We must remember that others as well as ourselves have a work to do in connection with this cause. We must not bar the mind against counsel. In our plans for the carrying forward of the work, our mind must blend with other minds.

Let us cherish a spirit of confidence in the wisdom of our brethren. We must be willing to take advice and caution from our fellow laborers. Connected with the service of God, we must individually realize that we are parts of a great whole. We must seek wisdom from God, learning what it means to have a waiting, watching spirit, and to go to our Saviour when tired and depressed.

It is a mistake to withdraw from those who do not agree with our ideas. This will not inspire our brethren with confidence in our judgment. It is our duty to counsel with our brethren, and to heed their advice. We are to seek their counsel, and when they give it, we are not to cast it away, as if they were our enemies. Unless we humble our hearts before God, we shall not know His will.

Let us be determined to be in unity with our brethren. This duty God has placed upon us. We shall make their hearts glad by following their counsel, and make ourselves strong through the influence that this will give us. Moreover, if we feel that we do not need the counsel of our brethren, we close the door of our usefulness as counselors to them.

To every church I would bear the message that man is not to exalt his own judgment. Meekness and lowliness of heart will lead men to desire counsel at every step. And the Lord will say, "Take My yoke upon you, and learn of Me." It is our privilege to learn of Jesus. But when men, full of self-confidence, think that it is their place to give counsel instead of desiring to be counseled by their experienced brethren, they will listen to voices that will lead them in strange paths.

The angels of God are in our world, and satanic agencies are here also. I am permitted to see the inclination of certain ones to follow their own strong traits of character. If they refuse to yoke up with others who have had a long experience in the work, they will become blinded by self-confidence, not discerning between the false and the true. It is not safe that such ones should stand in the position of leaders, to follow their own judgment and plans.

It is those who accept the warnings and cautions given them who will walk in safe paths. Let not men yield to the burning desire to become great leaders, or to the desire independently to devise and lay plans for themselves and for the work of God. It is easy for the enemy to work through some who, having themselves need of counsel at every step, undertake the guardianship of souls without having learned the lowliness of Christ. These need counsel from the One who says, "Come unto Me, all ye that labor and are heavy-laden."

Our ministers and leaders need to realize the necessity of counseling with their brethren who have been long in the work, and who have gained deep experience in the ways of the Lord. The disposition of some to shut themselves up to themselves, and to feel competent to plan and execute according to their own judgment and preferences, brings them into strait places. Such an independent way of working is not right, and should not be followed. The ministers and teachers in our conferences are to work unitedly with their brethren of experience, asking them for their counsel, and paying heed to their advice.

I am free to say to our brethren who with humility of heart are following the counsel of the Lord: If you know that God would have you engage in any work, go forward. Those who have the light and consciousness that God is leading need not depend upon any human agent to define their work. They are to receive the counsel of the highest Authority. Safety and peace and calm assurance are to be found only by following the counsel of the greatest Teacher that ever lived in our world. Let us not turn away from His unerring counsel.

But our impressions are not always a safe guide to duty. Human impulse will try to make us believe that it is God who is guiding us when we are following our own way. But if we watch carefully, and counsel with our brethren, we shall understand; for the promise is, "The meek will He guide in judgment: and the meek will He teach His way." We must not allow human ideas and natural inclinations to gain the supremacy.

AN APPEAL FOR UNITY

Workers for Christ are to strive for unity. We are the children of the same family, and have one heavenly Father. Let us not put on garments of heaviness, and cherish doubts and a lack of confidence in our brethren. We should not hurt our souls by gathering the thistles and the thorns, but instead we should gather the roses and the lilies and the pinks, and express their fragrance in our words and acts.

The following is part of a talk given to the ministers assembled at the General Conference in 1883:

"'Finally, brethren, whatsoever things are true, whatsoever things are honest, whatsoever things are just, whatsoever things are pure, whatsoever things are lovely, whatsoever things are of good report; if there be any virtue, and if there be any praise, think on these things.'

"The dealings of God with His people often appear mysterious. His ways are not our ways, nor His thoughts our thoughts. Many times His way of dealing is so contrary to our plans and expectations that we are amazed and confounded. We do not understand our perverse natures; and often when we are gratifying self, following our own inclinations, we flatter ourselves that we are carrying out the mind of God. And so we need to search the Scriptures, and be much in prayer, that, according to His promise, the Lord may give us wisdom.

"Though we have an individual work and an individual responsibility before God, we are not to follow our own judgment, regardless of the opinions and feelings of our brethren; for this course would lead to disorder in the church. It is the duty of ministers to respect the judgment of their brethren; but their relations to one another, as well as the doctrines they teach, should be brought to the test of the law and the testimony; then, if hearts are teachable, there will be no divisions among us. Some are inclined to be disorderly, and are drifting away from the great landmarks of the faith; but God is moving upon His ministers to be one in doctrine and in spirit.

"Brethren sometimes associate together for years, and think they can trust those they know so well, just as they would trust members of their own family. There is a freedom and confidence in this association which could not exist among those not of the same faith. This is very pleasant while brotherly love continues; but let the 'accuser' of the brethren gain admittance to the heart of one of these men, controlling the mind and the imagination, and jealousies are created, suspicion and envy are harbored; and he who supposed himself secure in the love and friendship of his brother finds himself mistrusted, and his motives misjudged. The false brother forgets his own human frailties, forgets his obligation to think and speak no evil lest he dishonor God and wound Christ in the person of His saints; and every defect that can be thought of or imagined is commented upon unmercifully, and the character of a brother is represented as dark and questionable.

"There is a betrayal of sacred trust. The things spoken in brotherly confidence are repeated and misrepresented; and every word, every action, however innocent and well-meaning, is scrutinized by the cold, jealous criticism of those who were thought too noble, too honorable, to take the least advantage of friendly association or brotherly trust. Hearts are closed to mercy, judgment, and the love of God; and the cold, sneering, contemptuous spirit which Satan manifests toward his victim is revealed.

"If Satan can employ professed believers to act as accusers of the brethren, he is justly pleased; for those who do this are just as truly serving him as was Judas when he betrayed Christ, although they may be doing it ignorantly. Satan is no less active now than in Christ's day, and those who lend themselves to do his work will manifest his spirit.

"Floating rumors are often the destroyers of unity among brethren. There are some who watch with open mind and ears to catch flying scandal. They gather up little incidents which may be trifling in themselves, but which are repeated and exaggerated until a man is made an offender for a word. Their motto seems to be, 'Report, and we will report it.' These talebearers are doing Satan's work with surprising fidelity, little knowing how offensive their course is to God. . . . The door of the mind should be closed against 'They say,' or 'I have heard.' Why should we not, instead of allowing jealousy or evil surmising to come into our hearts, go to our brethren, and after frankly but kindly setting before them the things we have heard detrimental to their character and influence, pray with and for them? While we cannot fellowship with those who are the bitter enemies of Christ, we should cultivate that spirit of meekness and love that characterized our Master—a love that thinketh no evil, and is not easily provoked. . . .

"Let us diligently cultivate the pure principles of the gospel of Christ—the religion, not of self-esteem, but of love, meekness, and lowliness of heart. Then we shall love our brethren, and esteem them better than ourselves. Our minds will not dwell on scandal and flying reports. But 'whatsoever things are true, whatsoever things are honest, whatsoever things are just, whatsoever things are pure, whatsoever things are lovely, whatsoever things are of good report; if there be any virtue, and if there be any praise,' we shall 'think on these things.'"

As a people, we have been reproved by God for doing so little. How important, then, that we guard carefully against everything that might dishearten or weaken the influence of one soul who is doing a work that God would have done. There are victories to be gained if we present a united front and individually seek the Lord for strength and guidance.

Pray for the Latter Rain

"Ask ye of the Lord rain in the time of the latter rain; so the Lord shall make bright clouds, and give them showers of rain." "He will cause to come down for you the rain, the former rain, and the latter rain." In the East the former rain falls at the sowing time. It is necessary in order that the seed may germinate. Under the influence of the fertilizing showers, the tender shoot springs up. The latter rain, falling near the close of the season, ripens the grain and prepares it for the sickle. The Lord employs these operations of nature to represent the work of the Holy Spirit. As the dew and the rain are given first to cause the seed to germinate, and then to ripen the harvest, so the Holy Spirit is given to carry forward, from one stage to another, the process of spiritual growth. The ripening of the grain represents the completion of the work of God's grace in the soul. By the power of the Holy Spirit the moral image of God is to be perfected in the character. We are to be wholly transformed into the likeness of Christ.

The latter rain, ripening earth's harvest, represents the spiritual grace that prepares the church for the coming of the Son of man. But unless the former rain has fallen, there will be no life; the green blade will not spring up. Unless the early showers have done their work, the latter rain can bring no seed to perfection.

There is to be "first the blade, then the ear, after that the full corn in the ear." There must be a constant development of Christian virtue, a constant advancement in Christian experience. This we should seek with intensity of desire, that we may adorn the doctrine of Christ our Saviour.

Review and Herald, March 2, 1897.

Many have in a great measure failed to receive the former rain. They have not obtained all the benefits that God has thus provided for them. They expect that the lack will be supplied by the latter rain. When the richest abundance of grace shall be bestowed, they intend to open their hearts to receive it. They are making a terrible mistake. The work that God has begun in the human heart in giving His light and knowledge must be continually going forward. Every individual must realize his own necessity. The heart must be emptied of every defilement and cleansed for the indwelling of the Spirit. It was by the confession and forsaking of sin, by earnest prayer and consecration of themselves to God, that the early disciples prepared for the outpouring of the Holy Spirit on the Day of Pentecost. The same work, only in greater degree, must be done now. Then the human agent had only to ask for the blessing, and wait for the Lord to perfect the work concerning him. It is God who began the work, and He will finish His work, making man complete in Jesus Christ. But there must be no neglect of the grace represented by the former rain. Only those who are living up to the light they have will receive greater light. Unless we are daily advancing in the exemplification of the active Christian virtues, we shall not recognize the manifestations of the Holy Spirit in the latter rain. It may be falling on hearts all around us, but we shall not discern or receive it.

At no point in our experience can we dispense with the assistance of that which enables us to make the first start. The blessings received under the former rain are needful to us to the end. Yet these alone will not suffice. While we cherish the blessing of the early rain, we must not, on the other hand, lose sight of the fact that without the latter rain, to fill out the ears and ripen the grain, the harvest will not be ready for the sickle, and the labor of the sower will have been in vain. Divine grace is needed at the beginning, divine grace at every step of advance, and divine grace alone can complete the work. There is no place for us to rest in a careless attitude. We must never forget the warnings of Christ, "Watch unto prayer," "Watch, . . . and pray always." A connection with the divine agency every moment is essential to our progress. We may have had a measure of the Spirit of God, but by prayer and faith we are continually to seek more of the Spirit. It will never do to cease our efforts. If we do not progress, if we do not place ourselves in an attitude to receive both the former and the latter rain, we shall lose our souls, and the responsibility will lie at our own door.

"Ask ye of the Lord rain in the time of the latter rain." Do not rest satisfied that in the ordinary course of the season, rain will fall. Ask for it. The growth and perfection of the seed rests not with the husbandman. God alone can ripen the harvest. But man's co-operation is required. God's work for us demands the action of our mind, the exercise of our faith. We must seek His favors with the whole heart if the showers of grace are to come to us. We should improve every opportunity of placing ourselves in the channel of blessing. Christ has said, "Where two or three are gathered together in My name, there am I in the midst." The convocations of the church, as in camp meetings, the assemblies of the home church, and all occasions where there is personal labor for souls, are God's appointed opportunities for giving the early and the latter rain.

But let none think that in attending these gatherings, their duty is done. A mere attendance upon all the meetings that are held will not in itself bring a blessing to the soul. It is not an immutable law that all who attend general gatherings or local meetings shall receive large supplies from heaven. The circumstances may seem to be favorable for a rich outpouring of the showers of grace. But God Himself must command the rain to fall. Therefore we should not be remiss in supplication. We are not to trust to the ordinary working of providence. We must pray that God will unseal the fountain of the water of life. And we must ourselves receive of the living water. Let us, with contrite hearts, pray most earnestly that now, in the time of the latter rain, the showers of grace may fall upon us. At every meeting we attend our prayers should ascend, that at this very time God will impart warmth and moisture to our souls. As we seek God for the Holy Spirit, it will work in us meekness, humbleness of mind, a conscious dependence upon God for the perfecting latter rain. If we pray for the blessing in faith, we shall receive it as God has promised.

The continued communication of the Holy Spirit to the church is represented by the prophet Zechariah under another figure, which contains a wonderful lesson of encouragement for us. The prophet says: "The angel that talked with me came again, and waked me, as a man that is wakened out of his sleep, and said unto me, What seest thou? And I said, I have looked, and behold a candlestick all of gold, with a bowl upon the top of it, and his seven lamps thereon, and seven pipes to the seven lamps, which are upon the top thereof: and two olive trees by it, one upon the right side of the bowl, and the other upon the left side thereof. So I answered and spake to the angel that talked with me, saying, What are these, my lord? . . . Then he answered and spake unto me, saying, This is the word of the Lord unto Zerubbabel, saying, Not by might, nor by power, but by My Spirit, saith the Lord of hosts. . . . And I answered again, and said unto him, What be these two olive branches which through the two golden pipes empty the golden oil out of themselves? . . . Then said he, These are the two anointed ones, that stand by the Lord of the whole earth."

From the two olive trees, the golden oil was emptied through golden pipes into the bowl of the candlestick and thence into the golden lamps that gave light to the sanctuary. So from the holy ones that stand in God's presence, His Spirit is imparted to human instrumentalities that are consecrated to His service. The mission of the two anointed ones is to communicate light and power to God's people. It is to receive blessing for us that they stand in God's presence. As the olive trees empty themselves into the golden pipes, so the heavenly messengers seek to communicate all that they receive from God. The whole heavenly treasure awaits our demand and reception; and as we receive the blessing, we in our turn are to impart it. Thus it is that the holy lamps are fed, and the church becomes a light bearer in the world.

This is the work that the Lord would have every soul prepared to do at this time, when the four angels are holding the four winds, that they shall not blow until the servants of God are sealed in their foreheads. There is no time now for self-pleasing. The lamps of the soul must be trimmed. They must be supplied with the oil of grace. Every precaution must be taken to prevent spiritual declension, lest the great day of the Lord overtake us as a thief in the night. Every witness for God is now to work intelligently in the lines which

God has appointed. We should daily obtain a deep and living experience in the work of perfecting Christian character. We should daily receive the holy oil, that we may impart to others. All may be light bearers to the world if they will. We are to sink self out of sight in Jesus. We are to receive the word of the Lord in counsel and instruction, and gladly communicate it. There is now need of much prayer. Christ commands, "Pray without ceasing;" that is, keep the mind uplifted to God, the source of all power and efficiency.

We may have long followed the narrow path, but it is not safe to take this as proof that we shall follow it to the end. If we have walked with God in fellowship of the Spirit, it is because we have sought Him daily by faith. From the two olive trees the golden oil flowing through the golden pipes has been communicated to us. But those who do not cultivate the spirit and habit of prayer cannot expect to receive the golden oil of goodness, patience, long-suffering, gentleness, love.

Everyone is to keep himself separate from the world, which is full of iniquity. We are not to walk with God for a time, and then part from His company and walk in the sparks of our own kindling. There must be a firm continuance, a perseverance in acts of faith. We are to praise God; to show forth His glory in a righteous character. No one of us will gain the victory without persevering, untiring effort, proportionate to the value of the object which we seek, even eternal life.

The dispensation in which we are now living is to be, to those that ask, the dispensation of the Holy Spirit. Ask for His blessing. It is time we were more intense in our devotion. To us is committed the arduous, but happy, glorious work of revealing Christ to those who are in darkness. We are called to proclaim the special truths for this time. For all this the outpouring of the Spirit is essential. We should pray for it. The Lord expects us to ask Him. We have not been wholehearted in this work.

What can I say to my brethren in the name of the Lord? What proportion of our efforts has been made in accordance with the light the Lord has been pleased to give? We cannot depend upon form or external machinery. What we need is the quickening influence of the Holy Spirit of God. "Not by might, nor by power, but by My Spirit, saith the Lord of hosts." Pray without ceasing, and watch by working in accordance with your prayers. As you pray, believe, trust in God. It is the time of the latter rain, when the Lord will give largely of His Spirit. Be fervent in prayer, and watch in the Spirit.

For further study: *Early Writings,* pages 36-38, 269-273.

How shall we follow Him to learn of Him who is our Teacher? We can search His word, and become acquainted with His life and works. His words we are to receive as bread for our souls. In every sphere where man shall be placed, the Lord Jesus has left us His footprints. We do well to follow Him. The Spirit by which He spake, we must cherish; we are to present the truth as it is in Jesus. We are to follow Him especially in heart purity, in love. Self must be hid with Christ in God; then when Christ, who is our life, shall appear, we also shall appear with Him in glory.—*Special Testimonies to Ministers and Workers* (Series A, No. 9, 1897), page 58.

Words of Greeting

TO THOSE ASSEMBLED IN GENERAL CONFERENCE OF NINETEEN HUNDRED THIRTEEN

My dear Brethren:

It is the privilege of our representative men in attendance at the General Conference to cherish a spirit of hopefulness and courage. My brethren, the Saviour has revealed Himself to you in manifold ways; He has filled your heart with the sunlight of His presence while you have labored in distant lands and in the homeland; He has kept you through dangers seen and unseen; and now, as you meet once more with your brethren in council, it is your privilege to be glad in the Lord and to rejoice in the knowledge of His sustaining grace.

Let His love take possession of mind and heart. Guard against becoming overwearied, careworn, depressed. Bear an uplifting testimony. Turn your eyes away from that which is dark and discouraging, and behold Jesus, our great Leader, under whose watchful supervision the cause of present truth, to which we are giving our lives and our all, is destined to triumph gloriously.

The attitude that our representative men maintain during the conference will have a telling influence upon all throughout the field, as well as upon the delegates themselves. Oh, let it be seen, my brethren, that Jesus is abiding in the heart, sustaining, strengthening, comforting. It is your privilege to be endowed, from day to day, with a rich measure of His Holy Spirit, and to have broadened views of the importance and scope of the message we are proclaiming to the world. The Lord

---

General Conference Bulletin, 1913, pages 33, 34.

is willing to reveal to you wondrous things out of His law. Wait before Him with humility of heart. Pray most earnestly for an understanding of the times in which we live, for a fuller conception of His purpose, and for increased efficiency in soul saving.

Often in the night season I am bidden to urge our brethren in responsible positions to make earnest effort to follow on to know the Lord more perfectly. When our workers realize as they should the importance of the times in which we live, there will be seen a determined purpose to be on the Lord's side, and they will become in truth laborers together with God. When they consecrate heart and soul to the service of God, they will find that an experience deeper than any they have yet obtained is essential if they would triumph over all sin.

It will be well for us to consider what is soon to come upon the earth. This is no time for trifling or self-seeking. If the times in which we are living fail to impress our minds seriously, what can reach us? Do not the Scriptures call for a more pure and holy work than we have yet seen?

Men of clear understanding are needed now. God calls upon those who are willing to be controlled by the Holy Spirit to lead out in a work of thorough reformation. I see a crisis before us, and the Lord calls for His laborers to come into line. Every soul should now stand in a position of deeper, truer consecration to God than during the years that have passed. . . .

"I rejoice," my brethren, "that I have confidence in you in all things." And while I still feel the deepest anxiety over the attitude that some are taking toward important measures connected with the development of the cause of God in the earth, yet I have strong faith in the workers throughout the field, and believe that as they meet together and humble themselves before the Lord and consecrate themselves anew to His service, they will be enabled to do His will. There are some who do not even now view matters in the right light; but these may learn to see eye to eye with their co-workers, and may avoid making serious mistakes by earnestly seeking the Lord at this time and by submitting their will wholly to the will of God.

I have been deeply impressed by scenes that have recently passed before me in the night season. There seemed to be a great movement—a work of revival—going forward in many places. Our people were moving into line, responding to God's call. My brethren, the Lord is speaking to us. Shall we not heed His voice? Shall we not trim our lamps, and act like men who look for their Lord to come? The time is one that calls for light bearing, for action.

Let those in every far-off country work unselfishly in the fear and love of God to advance the work; as missionaries for God, they can do much for it if they are connected with Him. They should draw nigh to God with full assurance of faith, lifting up holy hands, without wrath or doubting. God will make known unto them His pleasure; but all who do not work with an eye single to the glory of God, making Him their dependence and trust, who lean rather upon human wisdom, will make blunders. It is in doing the work of God that the richest experience is to be gained. Here is where you get wisdom, and find the promises of God verified.—*Special Testimonies to Ministers and Workers* (Series A, No. 9, 1897), page 35.

The Victorious Life

Sanitarium, California, June 14, 1914.

Dear Friend:

The Lord has given me a message for you, and not for you only, but also for other faithful souls who are troubled by doubts and fears regarding their acceptance by the Lord Jesus Christ. His word to you is, "Fear not: for I have redeemed thee, I have called thee by thy name; thou art Mine." You desire to please the Lord, and you can do this by believing His promises. He is waiting to take you into a harbor of gracious experience, and He bids you, "Be still, and know that I am God." You have had a time of unrest; but Jesus says to you, "Come unto Me, . . . and I will give you rest." The joy of Christ in the soul is worth everything. "Then are they glad," because they are privileged to rest in the arms of everlasting love.

Put away your distrust of our heavenly Father. Instead of talking of your doubts, break away from them in the strength of Jesus, and let light shine into your soul by letting your voice express confidence and trust in God. I know that the Lord is very nigh to give you victory, and I say to you, Be helped, be strengthened, be lifted out of and away from the dark dungeon of unbelief. Doubts will rush into your mind, because Satan is trying to hold you in captivity to his cruel power; but face him in the strength that Jesus is willing to give you, and conquer the inclination to express unbelief in your Saviour.

Do not talk of your inefficiency and your defects. When despair would seem to be sweeping over your

---

Reprint of a little tract, the last of Mrs. White's writing before her death.

soul, look to Jesus, saying, He lives to make intercession for me. Forget the things that are behind, and believe the promise, "I will come to you," and "abide with you."

God is waiting to bestow the blessing of forgiveness, of pardon for iniquity, of the gifts of righteousness, upon all who will believe in His love and accept the salvation He offers. Christ is ready to say to the repenting sinner, "Behold, I have caused thine iniquity to pass from thee, and I will clothe thee with change of raiment." The blood of Jesus Christ is the eloquent plea that speaks in behalf of sinners. This blood "cleanseth us from all sin."

It is your privilege to trust in the love of Jesus for salvation, in the fullest, surest, noblest manner; to say, He loves me, He receives me; I will trust Him, for He gave His life for me. Nothing so dispels doubt as coming in contact with the character of Christ. He declares, "Him that cometh to Me I will in no wise cast out;" that is, there is no possibility of My casting him out, for I have pledged My word to receive him. Take Christ at His word, and let your lips declare that you have gained the victory.

Is Jesus true? Does He mean what He says? Answer decidedly, Yes, every word. Then if you have settled this, by faith claim every promise that He has made, and receive the blessing; for this acceptance by faith gives life to the soul. You may believe that Jesus is true to you, even though you feel yourself to be the weakest and most unworthy of His children. And as you believe, all your dark, brooding doubts are thrown back upon the archdeceiver who originated them. You can be a great blessing if you will take God at His word. By living faith you are to trust Him, even though the impulse is strong within you to speak words of distrust.

Peace comes with dependence on divine power. As fast as the soul resolves to act in accordance with the light given, the Holy Spirit gives more light and strength. The grace of the Spirit is supplied to cooperate with the soul's resolve, but it is not a substitute for the individual exercise of faith. Success in the Christian life depends upon the appropriation of the light that God has given. It is not an abundance of light and evidence that makes the soul free in Christ; it is the rising of the powers and the will and the energies of the soul to cry out sincerely, "Lord, I believe; help Thou mine unbelief."

I rejoice in the bright prospects of the future, and so may you. Be cheerful, and praise the Lord for His loving-kindness. That which you cannot understand, commit to Him. He loves you and pities your every weakness. He "hath blessed us with all spiritual blessings in heavenly places in Christ." It would not satisfy the heart of the Infinite One to give those who love His Son a lesser blessing than He gives His Son.

Satan seeks to draw our minds away from the mighty Helper, to lead us to ponder over our degeneration of soul. But though Jesus sees the guilt of the past, He speaks pardon; and we should not dishonor Him by doubting His love. The feeling of guiltiness must be laid at the foot of the cross, or it will poison the springs of life. When Satan thrusts his threatenings upon you, turn from them, and comfort your soul with the promises of God. The cloud may be dark in itself, but when filled with the light of heaven, it turns to the brightness of gold; for the glory of God rests upon it.

God's children are not to be subject to feelings and emotions. When they fluctuate between hope and fear, the heart of Christ is hurt; for He has given them unmistakable evidence of His love. He wants them to be established, strengthened, and settled in the most holy faith. He wants them to do the work He has given them; then their hearts will become in His hands as sacred harps, every chord of which will send forth praise and thanksgiving to the One sent by God to take away the sins of the world.

Christ's love for His children is as tender as it is strong. And it is stronger than death; for He died to purchase our salvation, and to make us one with Him, mystically and eternally one. So strong is His love that it controls all His powers, and employs the vast resources of heaven in doing His people good. It is without variableness or shadow of turning—the same yesterday, today, and forever. Although sin has existed for ages, trying to counteract this love and obstruct its flowing earthward, it still flows in rich currents to those for whom Christ died.

God loves the sinless angels, who do His service and are obedient to all His commands; but He does not give them grace; they have never needed it, for they have never sinned. Grace is an attribute shown to undeserving human beings. We did not seek after it; it was sent in search of us. God rejoices to bestow grace upon all who hunger and thirst for it, not because we are worthy, but because we are unworthy. Our need is the qualification which gives us the assurance that we shall receive the gift.

It should not be difficult to remember that the Lord desires you to lay your troubles and perplexities at His feet, and leave them there. Go to Him, saying: "Lord, my burdens are too heavy for me to carry. Wilt Thou bear them for me?" And He will answer: "I will take them. 'With everlasting kindness will I have mercy on thee.' I will take your sins, and will give you peace. Banish no longer your self-respect; for I have bought you with the price of My own blood. You are Mine. Your weakened will I will strengthen. Your remorse for sin I will remove."

"I, even I, am He," the Lord declares, "that blotteth out thy transgressions for Mine own sake, and will not remember thy sins. Put Me in remembrance: let us plead together: declare thou, that thou mayest be justified." "I have not spoken in secret, in a dark place of the earth: I said not unto the seed of Jacob, Seek ye Me in vain: I the Lord speak righteousness, I declare things that are right." "Look unto Me, and be ye saved, all the ends of the earth: for I am God, and there is none else." Respond to the calls of God's mercy, and say: "I will trust in the Lord and be comforted. I will praise the Lord; for His anger is turned away. I will rejoice in God, who gives the victory."

Appendix Notes

Page 23. *Pamphlets denouncing the S.D.A. Church as Babylon:* Reference is made to a pamphlet entitled, "The Loud Cry of the Third Angel's Message," published by a Seventh-day Adventist lay member, Mr. Stanton, in the year 1893. This man, in his study of the Bible and the testimonies, focused his attention primarily on the messages of reproof and rebuke, forgetting that God had said that "as many as I love, I rebuke and chasten." Revelation 3:19. He concluded that the testimonies of reproof constituted a message of rejection, and that those who would join in sounding the loud cry must withdraw from the Seventh-day Adventist Church. The church, he asserted, had become Babylon, and those who would finish God's work in the earth and meet their Lord in peace must separate from the body.

An ardent disciple, Mr. W. F. Caldwell, was dispatched to Australia to carry the message to that land and to visit Mrs. White, who, it was supposed, would join their forces of "reform." Arriving in Australia, he discovered that while he had been crossing the Pacific to Australia, a testimony was on its way from New Zealand to America specifying the message of the "Loud Cry" tract as "one of the delusions designed to create confusion among the churches," and stating in the clearest language that "if you are teaching that the Seventh-day Adventist Church is Babylon, you are wrong." See the full letter on pages 58-62. Mrs. White met this misleading teaching in a series of articles in the *Review and Herald* entitled "The Remnant Church Not Babylon," now comprising pages 32-62 of this volume. This offshoot movement had but a very short life.

Page 26. *First-day Adventists:* Those who united in sounding the first and second angels' messages in the great advent awakening of the 1840's, but who rejected the third angel's message with its Sabbath truth, yet nonetheless continued to espouse the advent hope, are referred to by Mrs. White and by other early Sabbath-keeping Adventists as "nominal Adventists" or "First-day Adventists." Following the disappointment in the autumn of 1844, when Christ did not come as was expected, the Adventists divided into several groups. The principal survivors today are the Advent Christian Church, a small body, and Seventh-day Adventists. Relatively few among the Adventists immediately following the disappointment, maintained their confidence in the fulfillment of prophecy in 1844. But those who did stepped forward into the third angel's message with its seventh-day Sabbath.

Page 27. *Systematic benevolence:* In 1859 the leading brethren among the Sabbath-keeping Adventists came to see the necessity of a systematic plan of supporting the work of God, and from a conference at which this matter was studied, there came recommendations:

"1. Let each brother from eighteen to sixty years of age lay by him in store on the first day of each week from five to twenty-five cents.

"2. Each sister from eighteen to sixty years of age lay by her in store on the first day of each week from two to ten cents.

"3. Also, let each brother and sister lay by him or her in store on the first day of each week from one to five cents on each and every $100 of property they possess."—*Review and Herald,* Feb. 3, 1859, p. 84. Adopted by the General Conference, June 4, 1859.

As further clarification of involvements of point 3, James White, in the *Good Samaritan* of January, 1861, explained:

"We propose that the friends give a tithe, or tenth of their income, estimating their income at 10 percent on what they possess."

In the *Review and Herald* of April 9, 1861, James White explained how the brethren in Michigan applied this.

"They regard the use of their property worth the same as money at 10 percent. This 10 percent they regard as the increase of their property. A tithe of this would be 1 percent, and would be nearly 2 cents per week on each $100, which our brethren, for convenience sake, are unanimous in putting down."

Thus systematic benevolence embodied freewill offerings and a tithe reckoned on what would be considered a fair income from property held. The method of reckoning the tithe was, in the year 1876, discerned to be actually one tenth of the income to the individual from whatever source it might come, and this led to a concept which would reach out to a much larger number than those who were property holders. A pamphlet entitled "Systematic Benevolence, or the Bible Plan of Supporting the Ministry," published in 1878 by the Seventh-day Adventist Publishing Association, states the matter concisely in a question and an answer:

" 'How much ought I to give for the support of the gospel?'

" 'After carefully viewing the subject from all points, we answer, a tithe of all our income.' "

Page 32. *Pamphlet issued by Brother S:* See Appendix Note for page 23.

Page 41. *The one object on earth dear to the heart of God* (see also page 49): This assuring message from the pen of Ellen White was repeated by her on several later occasions:

"We should remember that the church, enfeebled and defective though it be, is the only object on earth on which Christ bestows His supreme regard. He is constantly watching it with solicitude, and is strengthening it by His Holy Spirit."—*Manuscript* 155, 1902 (Nov. 22, 1902). Published in *Selected Messages,* b. 2, p. 396.

"Trust to God's guardianship. His church is to be taught. Enfeebled and defective though it is, it is the object of His supreme regard."—Letter 279, 1904 (Aug. 1, 1904). Published in *Selected Messages,* b. 2, p. 396.

"Nothing in this world is so dear to God as His church. With jealous care He guards those who seek Him. Nothing so offends God as for the servants of Satan to strive to rob His people of their rights. The Lord has not forsaken His people."—Letter 136, 1910 (Nov. 26, 1910). Published in *Selected Messages,* b. 2, p. 397.

Page 57. *Eli Curtis:* On April 21, 1847, Ellen G. White addressed a letter to Eli Curtis, answering a number of questions which he asked concerning certain of his theological views. The body of her letter was published by James White in May, 1847, in *A Word to the Little Flock,* pages 11, 12 (currently available). Mr. Curtis is also referred to in *Selected Messages,* book 1, pages 60, 61.

Page 58. *Letter to Brother S:* Another letter dealing with this subject, addressed to Mr. Caldwell, an ardent disciple of Mr. Stanton and one who journeyed to Australia to carry the new message of "the loud cry" of the third angel to Ellen White and to solicit her support in the movement, is published in *Selected Messages,* book 2, pages 63-71.

Page 64. *Manifestation of the Holy Spirit condemned as fanaticism*: In 1893 the Spirit of God was poured out in a marked manner at the General Conference session in Battle Creek, and at the college. Unfortunately there were some who felt that this was an indication of fanaticism. See *Selected Messages,* book 1, pages 130, 131, for another reference to this experience.

Page 76. *The spirit which ran riot at Minneapolis:* The background of the 1888 General Conference held at Minneapolis, and its aftermath, is traced briefly in the Historical Foreword. This forms the basis for a better understanding of this and other statements in *Testimonies to Ministers* touching on the experience at Minneapolis.

Page 76. *Publishing institution at Battle Creek and unrighteous practices:* This and other statements relating to the publishing house at Battle Creek should be read in the light of situations which existed there in the 1890's, as described in the Historical Foreword.

Page 78. *One institution seeking to control other institutions:* The reader is directed to the Historial Foreword for the background of institutional relationships as they existed in the early and middle 1890's, and to steps which were undertaken at that time to consolidate various Seventh-day Adventist institutions into one working organization.

Page 79. *Minneapolis meeting:* See explanation in Historical Foreword.

Page 83. *Bicycle race:* See also page 398. In 1895, Ellen White was given a view of happenings in Battle Creek. Among other scenes which passed before her was one involving bicycles used in racing, and a strife for the mastery. See *Testimonies for the Church,* vol. 8, pp. 51, 52. At the time this scene was presented, the bicycle was not known as an economical means of transportation, but was rather a rich man's toy. Bicycles were being purchased by our young people in Battle Creek, not to provide needed transportation to work or school, but rather as a demonstration of superiority, for show, and in the seeking of supremacy. The young people were mortgaging their incomes for months in advance to buy what was then an expensive piece of equipment to be so used. Within a few years' time, the bicycle became a useful and inexpensive means of transportation.

Page 89. *Light despised by some:* See statement regarding the message of righteousness by faith in Historical Foreword.

Page 91. *Message sent through Elders Waggoner and Jones:* See statement regarding the message of righteousness by faith in Historical Foreword.

Page 96. *Those who have stood for years resisting light:* See statement regarding Minneapolis experience in Historical Foreword.

Page 117. *Book published by Elder Haskell:* The reference here is to a book entitled *The Story of Daniel the Prophet,* published in 1901 by Elder S. N. Haskell. It is a volume of 340 pages presenting a brief comment on the prophecies of Daniel. This statement by Mrs. White was penned in the year 1902. Three years later Elder Haskell published a companion volume entitled, *The Story of the Seer of Patmos,* commenting on the book of Revelation.

Page 146. *Sensuality, licentiousness, and adultery:* The minister is not free from subtle temptation. In fact, the minister often becomes the special point of Satan's attack. Sensuality, licentiousness, and adultery are presented as among the sins committed by those who bear the message. But on page 153, Ellen White indicates that it was "some" who were not true. These references are grossly misused if it is assumed that the rebuke applies to the ministry generally. It must be remembered that there was a Judas among the Twelve. The warnings stand forth that each may guard his own personal experience and that this condition shall not exist.

Page 160. *Ministerial institutes:* The institutes referred to here were held quite frequently in the late 1880's and early 1890's, sometimes extending over quite a period of time. Reference on page 401 indicates that such institutes were quite necessary following the General Conference of 1888, that our workers might be properly instructed and indoctrinated in those truths which they were presenting to the people.

Page 197. *Receiving gifts from Gentiles or heathen:* See also pages 202, 203. In the latter part of 1893, Elder A. T. Robinson, leading out in the work of the church in South Africa and wishing to secure land for the establishment of a mission among the natives, arranged for an interview with Cecil Rhodes, premier of Cape Colony and head of the British South African Company operating in Mashonaland. Rhodes was especially pleased with the plan outlined for operating a mission among the natives of that country, and handed to Elder Robinson a sealed letter addressed to Dr. Jemison, secretary of the company, to be given to him in Bulawayo. The brethren went to Bulawayo expecting to purchase land, and did not know until Jemison told them that Rhodes had ordered him to give them all the land they wanted. A tract of twelve thousand acres was selected, and this became the site of the Solusi Mission, the first one operated by the denomination among non-Christian peoples. A knowledge of this gift created considerable concern among certain leading brethren at Battle Creek, who feared that to accept it would be a violation of the principles of the separation of church and state. As the matter was discussed at the General Conference session of 1895, action was taken:

"That we ought not as a denomination either to seek or to accept from any civil government, chief, ruler, or royal chartered company, supreme, local, or otherwise, any gift, or donation, concession, grant, either of land, money, credit, special privilege, or other thing of value, to which we are not in common with all others justly entitled as men without any reference to our religious profession or religious work."

This was followed by another action:

"That in harmony with this resolution, that the General Conference Association be instructed to pay an appropriate amount for all government land that may be secured in Africa or elsewhere."—*General Conference Bulletin,* Feb. 21, 1895, p. 283.

The Foreign Mission Board ratified this action by recording that: "The lands secured from the government shall be purchased and not received as a grant." Before this action could be implemented, however, on January 30, 1895, Ellen G. White wrote a communication from

Australia in which she indicated: "With respect to the propriety of receiving gifts from Gentiles or the heathen," "what they would give, we should be privileged to receive." The next day she wrote the article appearing on pages 200-203, pointing out that certain "leading men" were "taking extreme positions." In the light of these two communications from Ellen White, the action of the General Conference session was never implemented.

Page 200. *Movements to pay taxes on the Sanitarium and Tabernacle:* At the General Conference session of 1893 the following action was taken:

"Whereas in view of the separation which we believe should exist between the church and the state, it is inconsistent for the church to receive from the state pecuniary gifts, favors, exemptions, on religious grounds; therefore resolved that we repudiate the doctrine that church or other ecclesiastical properties should be exempt from taxation and further, resolved, that we use our influence in securing the repeal of such legislation as grants and exemptions."—*General Conference Bulletin,* March 5, 1893, p. 475.

The E. G. White communication of January 31, 1895, giving counsel in this matter, was accepted by the leaders of the church as instruction which should guide in the matter of our relation to the paying of taxes on tax-free church property.

Page 212. *Everything not to center at Battle Creek:* See Historical Foreword.

Page 266. *Rural Health Retreat:* This institution, the second sanitarium established among Seventh-day Adventists, was located in northern California near Saint Helena. Later it was known as the Saint Helena Sanitarium, and today as the Saint Helena Sanitarium and Hospital.

Page 280. *Rule-or-ruin system:* See Historical Foreword.

Page 291. *Consolidation:* At the General Conference sessions of 1889 and 1891, actions were taken to consolidate the publishing interests of the denomination. The plan was not only to place the interests of the publishing work in one organization, with headquarters in Battle Creek, but also to consolidate the educational and medical work carried on by Seventh-day Adventists. See Historical Foreword for the background of the moves in this direction.

Page 331. *The present financial controversy:* This communication addressed to the General Conference session of 1897 and written in December, 1896, related to the issues of the Presidential campaign of William Jennings Bryan. Bryan was agitating certain monetary policies which he and his supporters felt held great promise. Some Seventh-day Adventists became involved in the issues. In her counsels Mrs. White repeatedly emphasized that our work was that of proclaiming the third angel's message, and that Seventh-day Adventists, as a separate and peculiar people, should not become involved in political questions.

Page 342. *Attitude toward the Testimonies:* The statement that some who stood as counselors had declared "that they would not receive the testimonies given" highlights the situation which existed in the mid-1890's as described in the Historical Foreword. However, at the General Conference session of 1901, more men who were firm in their confidence in the Spirit of Prophecy were drawn into positions of leadership.

In the opening session of that conference, after Ellen White had called for a reorganization of the work of the church, A. G. Daniells, who had been in Australia for many years, and who at this conference was to become the leading officer of the church, made his position clear when he stated, "We all feel that our only safety lies in obedience, following our great Leader. . . . If we walk in the light we have, go just as far as we can today, God will give us further light; He will bring us out of bondage into glorious liberty."—*General Conference Bulletin,* April 3, 1901, p. 27.

Certain leaders in the institutional work failed to respond to the messages of entreaty, warning, and counsel, and the changes which were called for were not made.

Page 342. *The president of the General Conference:* In 1896, the year of the writing of the message addressed to conference presidents and counselors in which Ellen White stated, "It is not wise to choose one man as president of the General Conference," the officers of the General Conference consisted of (1) a president, (2) a corresponding secretary, and (3) a recording secretary and treasurer. In this particular year, the foreign mission secretary and the educational secretary were also listed as officers of the General Conference, but in 1901, we find the officers listed only as president, secretary, and treasurer. The context of the statement made by Ellen White in 1896 makes it clear that she does not intend to teach that there should not be a president of the General Conference, but rather, as is stated on page 343, "counselors of the character that God chose for Moses are needed by the president of the General Conference." At no time in the writings of Ellen White, either prior to the year 1901, or subsequently, did she indicate that in the denominational plan of organization there should not be a president chosen by the delegates. In her writings, published and unpublished, there are many references to the president of the General Conference, to his responsibilities, and to the attitudes which he should manifest.

In the year 1902, the General Conference Committee, which at the session of 1901 had been empowered to organize itself and choose its own officers, created the office of vice-president of the General Conference, and selected a man to fill that office. From that time onward the burdens of leadership were shouldered by more than one man. The General Conference constitution provides for several general vice-presidents, and for a vice-president of each world division, of which there are thirteen.

Page 349. *The present order of things must change:*

See Historical Foreword relating to the situations in Battle Creek that are here referred to.

Page 359. *The General Conference is becoming corrupted*: See Historical Foreword for the setting of this and other strong statements appearing in this chapter penned in 1895.

Page 366. *Species of slavery:* See Historical Foreword concerning the situation at Battle Creek in the middle 1890's.

Page 373. *The Lord about to turn and overturn in institutions:* As explained in the Historical Foreword, certain of the institutions in Battle Creek were being managed by men who had lost their consecration of heart. Warning upon warning was sent, calling for a change in the policies which were being followed. Some attempts were made by some members of the boards to bring about changes, but these proved futile. Nor was there a favorable response to Mrs. White's appeal made at the time of the General Conference session of 1901. Near the close of the year, most solemn warnings appeared in a communication addressed to the managers of the *Review and Herald,* which were read to the Board in November, 1901. Ellen White wrote:

"I feel a terror of soul as I see to what a pass our publishing house has come."—*Testimonies,* vol. 8, p. 91.

On the same page she states: "I have been almost afraid to open the *Review,* fearing to see that God has cleansed the publishing house by fire."

Thirteen months later, December 30, 1902, the publishing house was destroyed by fire. The cause was never determined, but eyewitnesses report that the whole building seemed to burst into flames almost simultaneously. When informed of this disaster, Ellen White wrote: "I was not surprised by the sad news, for in the visions of the night I have seen an angel standing with a sword as of fire stretched over Battle Creek."—*Testimonies,* vol. 8, p. 97.

Page 374. *The counsel of men as the voice of God:* See Historical Foreword for the background of the situation in Battle Creek in the mid-1890's in which men were looking to men rather than to God.

Page 397. *The heart of the work enfeebled by mismanagement:* See Historical Foreword for background of the situation here described.

Page 398. *Bicycles and other needless things:* See Appendix Note for page 83.

Page 400. *Do not colonize:* The interests at Battle Creek had drawn many Seventh-day Adventists to that center. On a number of occasions Ellen White counseled that our people should scatter out and let their light shine. Consistently the counsel has come through the years, warning against Seventh-day Adventists' colonizing. At the same time she counseled those who would leave Battle Creek to guard against precipitous movements. See these counsels in *Selected Messages,* book 2, pages 361-364.

Page 401. *Ministerial institutes:* See Appendix Note for page 160.

Page 427. *Fornication is in our ranks:* Ellen White's words on page 404 are significant. "All should bear in mind that Satan's special efforts are directed against the ministry." Unfortunately some betrayed their trust. The solemn messages found in this section have served through the years as a warning. Stringent policies now in force, making it impossible for a minister once found guilty of a violation of the seventh commandment ever again to bear the sacred credentials, have been an effective means in meeting the situation here brought before the church leaders by Ellen White.

Page 460. *Vision at Salamanca:* See *Life Sketches,* pages 309-318, for the story of the vision given at Salamanca and of the presentation of the instruction given in this vision.

Page 462. *References to consolidation and confederation:* See Historical Foreword for the presentation of the steps which were taken, beginning in 1889, to consolidate the publishing and other interests of the denomination.

Page 467. *Prejudice and opinions that prevailed at Minneapolis*: See Historical Foreword for the backgrounds of the Minneapolis Conference of 1888.

Page 468. *Slighted, spoken against, ridiculed, and rejected:* Reference is here made to the attitude which some took in resistance to the emphasis given to the message of righteousness by faith at and following the General Conference session of 1888. See Historical Foreword for a fuller statement indicating that while some took the attitude here referred to there were many who received the message and gained a great blessing in their own personal experience.

Page 469. *"American Sentinel":* This journal published weekly by the Pacific Press was devoted to the interests of religious liberty. It was the forerunner of *Liberty* Magazine.

Page 472. *Snares of Satan:* As indicated in the credit, this chapter was published originally in the year 1884 in *The Spirit of Prophecy,* volume IV. This was a volume written for the church. As Ellen White planned for the presentation of the story that we now know as the "Conflict of the Ages" series, which could be circulated generally, she chose to leave out of the enlarged *Great Controversy,* published in 1888, some portions written particularly for the church. She recognized that there were some things which could be said appropriately to the church that were not as appropriate for those who were not church members.

Page 475. *Somebody is to come in the spirit and power of Elijah:* These words have been mistakenly applied by some to some individual who it was thought would appear with a prophetic message subsequent to Mrs. White's life and work. The three paragraphs comprising this article titled "Let Heaven Guide" are only a small portion of a talk given by Ellen White in Battle Creek, Michigan, the morning of January 29, 1890. As this was published in the *Review and Herald* of February 18, 1890, it carried the title of "How to Meet a Controverted Point of Doctrine." Other excerpts drawn from this article and used largely to fill out certain pages of this volume, may be found on pages 23, 104, 111, 119, 158, 278, and 386. The article has been reproduced in its entirety in *Selected Messages,* book 1, pages 406-416, with the portion comprising the excerpt entitled "Let Heaven Guide" appearing on pages 412 and 413. When the article is read in its entirety it becomes apparent that Ellen White, in this statement made just a little more than a year after the Minneapolis Conference to a group in Battle Creek, was speaking of her own ministry. Some had grown critical of her work. Note that in the paragraph preceding that which appears in this volume on page 475, Ellen White states:

"We should come into a position where every difference will be melted away. If I think I have light, I shall do my duty in presenting it. Suppose I consulted others concerning the message the Lord would have me give to the people, the door might be closed so that the light might not reach the ones to whom God had sent it. When Jesus rode into Jerusalem, 'the whole multitude of the disciples began to rejoice and praise God with a loud voice for all the mighty works that they had seen; saying, Blessed be the King that cometh in the name of the Lord: peace in heaven, and glory in the highest. And some of the Pharisees from among the multitude said unto Him, Master, rebuke Thy disciples. And He answered and said unto them, I tell you that, if these should hold their peace, the stones would immediately cry out' (Luke 19:37-40).

"The Jews tried to stop the proclamation of the message that had been predicted in the word of God."

Then she makes reference again to her own experience:

"Prophecy must be fulfilled. The Lord says, 'Behold, I will send you Elijah the prophet before the coming of the great and dreadful day of the Lord' (Mal. 4:5). Somebody is to come in the spirit and power of Elijah, and when he appears, men may say, 'You are too earnest, you do not interpret the Scriptures in the proper way."—*Selected Messages,* b. 1, p. 412.

That she was referring to her own experience is also made clear from the paragraph which follows, in which she declares:

"I shall tell the truth as God gives it to me. . . ."

Scriptural Index

Acts

Romans

1 Corinthians

2 Corinthians

Galatians

Ephesians

Philippians

Colossians

1 Thessalonians

1 Timothy

2 Timothy

Titus

Hebrews

James

1 Peter

2 Peter

1 John

Jude

Revelation

Index